Praise for *Three Felonies a Day*

"Now comes veteran defense lawyer and civil libertarian Harvey A. Silverglate with riveting case studies exposing in technicolor a pattern of serious abuses and convictions of innocent people in some of the most famous (as well as obscure) federal cases of recent decades. Abetted by compliant courts and easily gulled media, the feds brand as criminals good people who intended no crime."

> —Stuart Taylor, Jr., *National Journal* columnist and *Newsweek* contributing editor

"In *Three Felonies a Day*, Harvey A. Silverglate has written a work peerless in revelations about the mad expansion of federal statutes whose result is to define, as criminal, practices no rational citizen could have viewed as illegal. The book is chilling in its detail of the investigations and ruin that have befallen people ground up in this prosecution mill. Whether in the book's scathing chronicle of the destruction of Arthur Andersen, largest accounting firm in the nation, an obscure attorney, or the bizarre government case mounted against a Boston politician—to name a few—Harvey A. Silverglate brings home, unforgettably, the truth that everyone is vulnerable to the terrors wrought by out of control prosecutors.

No one reading this can fail to be gripped by these cases, by the hard bright light he shines on every step of these prosecutions, and the mindset that created them. It's a bombshell that was worth waiting for."

> —Dorothy Rabinowitz, *Wall Street Journal* editorialist and a winner of the Pulitzer Prize

(Continued)

"Gilbert & Sullivan wrote about how the punishment fits the crime. *Three Felonies a Day* shows how federal prosecutors have conceived of something truly frightening—punishment without crime. Harvey A. Silverglate, one of the truly hard-working and uncompromising defenders of our civil liberties, has written the ultimate horror-story of prosecutorial abuse. We, the public, should pay attention."

> —**Errol Morris**, documentary film-maker, winner of the Academy Award for *The Fog of War*, producer and director of the legendary documentary *The Thin Blue Line*

"This brilliant book lays out the terrifying threat to human rights posed by vindictive federal prosecutions, often sold as moralistic crusades to a gullible press and public. Anyone who cares about American democracy should read this gripping and vitally important expose."

> —**Steven Pinker**, Johnstone Family Professor, Harvard University, and author of *The Stuff of Thought*

"Harvey A. Silverglate masterfully chronicles federal prosecutors' vindictive enlistment of opaque criminal prohibitions to snare the unwary and to stunt civil society. A bloated criminal code that fails to warn before it strikes is tyranny's first cousin."

> —**Bruce Fein**, former associate deputy attorney general under President Reagan, and chairman of the American Freedom Agenda

---

"*Three Felonies a Day* is one of the most important books to be written about law in a generation. It should be read by anyone who cares about the rule of law.... Law-abiding citizens beware: Prosecutors wield Godlike power as they decide how to interpret vague and open-ended statutes that can turn the stuff of everyday life into a federal case. Individual freedom and the rule of law hang in the balance. *Three Felonies a Day* is more than a brilliant collection of great stories about law, although it is sure that: it is a manifesto from one of America's staunchest defenders of civil liberties demanding that all of us join in the fight for true freedom and the rule of law."

> —**Susan R. Estrich**, Robert Kingsley Professor of Law and Political Science, University of Southern California

---

"In *Three Felonies a Day*, Harvey A. Silverglate zeroes in on governmental misconduct—the brazen abuse by certain federal prosecutors of immense government power for purposes other than justice. The book is a clarion call—to prosecutors, reminding them what their true role is in a democracy—and to the public, reminding everyone of our collective responsibility firmly to oppose, discipline and prohibit such unacceptable abuses in order to protect the Constitution and the rights it guarantees. The book is a compelling read."

> —**Michael S. Greco**, former president of the American Bar Association

---

"To many readers, the book will read like a highlight reel of the most prominent and challenging cases to be brought in recent years.... Silverglate deftly combines the legal sophistication of a criminal defense expert with the plain speech and driving narrative of a journalist."

> —**Matthew W. Hutchins**, *The Harvard Law Record*

(Continued)

"[*Three Felonies a Day*] argues that federal criminal law is so comprehensive and vague that all Americans violate it every day, meaning prosecutors can indict anyone at all."

—**Adam Liptak**, *The New York Times*

"Technology exacerbates the problem of laws so open and vague that they are hard to abide by, to the point that we have all become potential criminals. Boston civil-liberties lawyer Harvey Silverglate calls his new book 'Three Felonies a Day,' referring to the number of crimes he estimates the average American now unwittingly commits because of vague laws."

—**L. Gordon Crovitz**, *The Wall Street Journal*

"After studying dozens of prosecutions dating back 25 years, among them cases he worked on and several that were tried in Massachusetts federal court, Silverglate concludes that federal criminal laws have run amok, enabling overzealous prosecutors to pin flimsy, headline-grabbing crimes on any one of us—even for well-intended behavior that does not appear to violate any law."

—**Tom Mashberg**, *The Boston Herald*

"In a work that is sure to stir sharp public debate, veteran defense-attorney-turned-author Harvey A. Silverglate examines the legally and politically charged issues surrounding recent federal criminal prosecutions."

—**Robert A. Cornetta**, presiding justice of the Salem
District Court

Three Felonies a Day

• • •

How the Feds Target the Innocent

HARVEY A. SILVERGLATE

ENCOUNTER BOOKS  NEW YORK · LONDON

First American edition published in 2009 by Encounter Books,
an activity of Encounter for Culture and Education, Inc.,
a nonprofit, tax exempt corporation.
Encounter Books website address: www.encounterbooks.com

Manufactured in the United States and printed on
acid-free paper. The paper used in this publication meets
the minimum requirements of ANSI/NISO Z39.48 1992
(R 1997) (*Permanence of Paper*).

PAPERBACK EDITION ISBN 978-1-59403-522-7

THE LIBRARY OF CONGRESS HAS CATALOGUED
THE HARDCOVER EDITION AS FOLLOWS:

Silverglate, Harvey A., 1942-
Three felonies a day : how the feds target the innocent / by Harvey Silverglate.
p. cm.
Includes bibliographical references and index.
ISBN-13: 978-1-59403-255-4 (hardcover : alk. paper)
ISBN-10: 1-59403-255-6 (hardcover : alk. paper)
1. Prosecution—United States. 2. Public prosecutors—United States. I. Title.

KF9640.S578 2009

345.73'05042—dc22

2009006511

CONTENTS

*To wife and partner Elsa Dorfman and son
Isaac Dorfman Silverglate, who have lived with
the often inconvenient consequences of my obsession
with liberty during decades of a tumultuous career
that continues unabated, and who have added
enormously to my insights;*

— and —

*Alan Dershowitz, who first nurtured my interest in
the criminal law and civil liberties when we arrived at
Harvard Law School in 1964 (he as professor and
I as student), and who has continued to nurture and
support that interest over the decades;*

— and —

*Dorothy Rabinowitz, who has insisted that I have an
obligation to write, in non-legalese English, about the
lessons learned and still being learned from that career,
and who pushed me relentlessly to complete this book.*

PREFACE TO THE PAPERBACK EDITION

Three Felonies a Day is the story of how citizens from all walks of life—doctors, accountants, businessmen, political activists, and others—have found themselves the targets of federal prosecutions, despite sensibly believing that they did nothing wrong, broke no laws, and harmed not a single person. In these wheels of injustice, vague laws are the lynchpin, functioning in very much the opposite way than originally intended: they obscure, rather than clarify, the law's demands.

Since the hardcover version of this book was published, there has been considerable tumult in the arena of vague federal legislation used as a tyrannical trap for the unwary innocent. While some raised consciousness has become visible on civil society's horizon, grave damage continues to be inflicted by out-of-control federal prosecutors.

Siobhan Reynolds knows firsthand how this phenomenon affects the medical profession. Her late husband, Sean Greenwood, suffered from a connective tissue disorder that caused chronic, debilitating pain. In 2002, after a decade-long search for a doctor willing to provide adequate relief, he finally found Dr. William Hurwitz, a nationally recognized pain specialist. Within months, however, Hurwitz was indicted under the Controlled Substances Act.[1] Unable to find another specialist, Greenwood died in 2006—a result hastened, Reynolds believes, by the federal government's crackdown.

Drawing on this personal experience, Reynolds founded the Pain Relief Network (PRN), a non-profit aimed at raising awareness of and pushing back against the ill-defined laws that restrict physicians from administering adequate pain medicine. The fact that her advocacy was met with resistance from federal drug warriors is perhaps no surprise. But what's shocking is the lengths to which one prosecutor went to silence this activist.

The case of Dr. Stephen Schneider and his wife, Linda, was much like others that attracted the PRN's support. The Kansas-based doctor and nurse were accused of over-prescribing pain medication—or, in the prosecutorial parlance, running a "pill mill." Reynolds assisted the Schneiders by helping them find legal counsel and expert witnesses for their defense, as well as publicly advocating for their innocence. Even though she had no formal role in the case, the government sought in April 2008 to gag Reynolds from making "extrajudicial statements" about the Schneider prosecution, a plainly unconstitutional request, which the district court wisely denied.

But the prosecutor was undeterred. In March 2009, Tanya J. Treadway, assistant U.S. attorney, issued a grand jury subpoena to Reynolds demanding a wide array of documents, financial records, and communications, including information about a billboard supporting the Schneiders, and a PRN-produced documentary film, aptly titled *The Chilling Effect*. The document demand was suggestive of a fishing expedition for evidence that Reynolds somehow attempted to obstruct the prosecution of the Schneiders.

Because much of this is clearly protected First Amendment activity, Reynolds was confident that the subpoena would be quashed. But the district court did not abide. When Reynolds refused to comply with the court order, she was fined $200 each day. Almost $40,000 later, she had no choice but to turn over to the government the thousands of documents it demanded.[2]

Still, Reynolds continued to fight, and with the assistance of Robert Corn-Revere, a renowned First Amendment lawyer, she appealed to the Supreme Court. Her petition seeking high court review emphasized the misuse of grand jury secrecy rules. Intended to protect the reputations of innocent persons appearing before the grand jury, the rules were here being turned on their head to effectively silence an activist and then hide those repressive actions.[3] Even Reynolds's publicly available petition for a Supreme Court hearing was ominously pocked with blacked-out passages.[4]

Much to Reynolds's and Corn-Revere's dismay, the high court refused to intervene. As a result of the lower court's imposition of Draconian fines, and the continuing threats to prosecute her and the PRN, Reynolds decided in late December 2010 to disband the organization. "Pressure from the US Department of Justice has made it impossible for us to function," she told PRN supporters.[5]

The intense pressure exerted by federal prosecutors was tragically illustrated in the case of Dr. Peter Gleason. When the first edition of this book went to press, Dr. Gleason, a psychiatrist who specialized in pain and sleep-related disorders, found his resources exhausted by an indictment for recommending the drug Xyrem to other physicians for uses not officially approved by the Food and Drug Administration, a practice which the law seemingly allowed.[6] Through a bizarre application of federal conspiracy law, Gleason was nonetheless charged and mercilessly hounded. When he persisted in defending himself, the government agreed to reduce the charge to a misdemeanor, thereby conceding that Gleason had not intended to defraud or deceive anyone. Gleason pleaded guilty, and in January 2010 he was sentenced to a $25 fine and one year of probation. In the civil arena, however, the government continued to pursue him. Effectively unable to practice medicine, and deprived of the total vindication for which he yearned and which he deserved, Gleason buckled under the accumulating burden. On February 7, 2011, he hanged himself. His sister, Sally Goodson, succinctly and accurately summed up his "crime" in a remembrance of her beloved brother: "Truthful speech to fellow physicians about the off-label use of an FDA-approved drug."

Just as federal prosecutors managed to disrupt the activism of Siobhan Reynolds and derail the medical practice of Dr. Peter Gleason, so the feds in late 2010 took up the task of finding some basis in federal law for putting Julian Assange, founder of the whistleblowing platform WikiLeaks, out of business. The international organization had made 2010 a landmark year for the exposure of government secrets. Among the groundbreaking releases: a video depicting U.S. military forces killing two Reuters journalists and nine Iraqis in 2007; Pentagon files detailing abuse of Iraqi prisoners as well as 15,000 previously unreported civilian deaths; and a steady stream of U.S. diplomatic cables dealing with subjects like Iran's nuclear program and alleged CIA torture.

Unnerved by this unwanted sunlight, American authorities took to combing the federal statute books, searching for a criminal law arguably violated by Assange. Legal commentators were reporting that the Department of Justice homed in on the 1917 Espionage Act, under which media organizations have only narrowly escaped prosecution in past leak cases.[7] But the underappreciated reality remained that a number of other statutes could potentially have been applied to Assange's unique breed of muckraking. These included trafficking in stolen property (which applies to both tangible and intangible property),[8] conspiracy (if the U.S. government could prove that Assange collaborated from the start with the original source of the military leaks), and the ever malleable wire fraud (which, by the statute's language, tells more about the *means* of the crime than its actual substance).

The still unfolding WikiLeaks saga also provided instruction as to how the feds, in trying to pin a crime on their ultimate target, intimidate that target's supporters. *Salon*'s Glenn Greenwald noted that his readers, even while believing strongly in WikiLeaks's cause, were apprehensive about offering their financial support. They worried about being put on a government blacklist, Greenwald wrote, "or, worse, incur[ring] criminal liability for materially supporting a Terrorist organization."[9] While Greenwald pointed out that it would be a stretch to apply this statute to WikiLeaks's supporters, a Supreme Court ruling in June 2010 nonetheless gave well-informed, rational citizens grounds to fear punishment.

The criminal ban against providing "material support" to organizations listed by the government as "terrorist" groups is an often-used tool in the post-9/11 "war on terror."[10] Fearful that even its peace-promoting activities might be deemed criminal, the Humanitarian Law Project, a human rights group, challenged the government's extraordinarily broad and vague definition of the phrase "material support."

After wending its way through lower courts for more than a decade— during which time the "material support" statutes were amended twice—the case finally reached the Supreme Court in its 2009–10 term. At issue in particular was whether and where *pure speech* might qualify as "material support." The solicitor general (later Supreme Court justice), Elena Kagan, asserted in oral argument that it would be a crime for a lawyer to file a friend-of-the-court brief supporting a group designated "terrorist" by the government, or to assist such groups in filing petitions with international bodies.[11]

The Court's decision offered the Humanitarian Law Project little comfort and even less clarity. Explaining how the law would effectively criminalize human rights advocacy,[12] a six-justice majority wrote:

> A person of ordinary intelligence would understand that instruction on resolving disputes through international law falls within the statute's definition of "training" because it imparts a "specific skill," not "general knowledge." ...Plaintiff's activities also fall comfortably within the scope of "expert advice or assistance": A reasonable person would recognize that teaching the PKK [Kurdistan Workers' Party] how to petition for humanitarian relief before the United Nations involves advice derived from, as the statute puts it, "specialized knowledge."[13]

Even the three dissenters—Justices Stephen Breyer, Ruth Bader Ginsburg, and Sonia Sotomayor—did not deem the statute vague, but instead would have invalidated certain portions because they conflict with the First Amendment's guarantees of free speech and association. Hence, not a single justice was prepared to declare any part of this exceptionally obtuse statute void on account of vagueness. One gets the disturbing impression that the Supreme Court fails to grasp the fundamental problem that even intelligent citizens with skilled legal counsel face when trying to deal with indecipherable prohibitions of this kind.

If proof were needed that the Supreme Court's asserted clarification of the statute provided no clarity at all, a dramatic example arose in December 2010. As Professor David Cole of Georgetown University Law Center, who unsuccessfully argued the *Humanitarian Law Project* case, pointed out in a *New York Times* op-ed, the wide-sweeping statute could be inadvertently violated, even by those who laid the groundwork for the current "war on terror." Former Attorney General Michael

Mukasey, former New York Mayor Rudolph Giuliani, former Homeland Security Secretary Tom Ridge, and former National Security Advisor Frances Townsend almost certainly committed "a federal crime...in Paris when they spoke in support of the Mujahedeen Khalq at a conference organized by the Iranian opposition group's advocates." The Mujahedeen Khalq had been dubbed a "foreign terrorist organization," and so providing it with direct or indirect "material support" was a felony, Cole wrote. He continued:

> Chief Justice Roberts reasoned [in his majority opinion] that a terrorist group might use human rights advocacy training to file harassing claims, that it might use peacemaking assistance as a cover while re-arming itself, and that such speech could contribute to the group's "legitimacy," and thus increase its ability to obtain support elsewhere that could be turned to terrorist ends. Under the court's decision, former President Jimmy Carter's election monitoring team could be prosecuted for meeting with and advising Hezbollah during the 2009 Lebanese elections.[14]

Yet the true depth and persistence of the vagueness problem in federal criminal law was not fully demonstrated until three days after the release of the *Humanitarian Law Project* opinion, when the Court decided another highly contentious case, this one dealing with so-called "honest services" fraud. The 28-word statute had enabled federal prosecutors to go after all kinds of public officials and private businessmen for depriving those who elected or hired them of their "honest services."[15] Remarkably, all nine justices agreed that the statute was unconstitutional as it was being enforced, because it failed to define the central term "honest services," and what conduct the statute required or prohibited was hardly intuitive. The only difference among the justices, which caused them to divide into majority (agreeing on the reasoning and result) and concurring (agreeing only on the outcome) camps, was that the majority was prepared to effectively rewrite the statute by limiting prosecutions to cases involving bribery and kickbacks. In contrast, concurring Justice Antonin Scalia, joined by Justices Anthony

Kennedy and Clarence Thomas, pronounced the judicial rewriting of the statute an improper foray into the legislative business of writing statutes, changing "a prohibition of 'honest services fraud' into a prohibition of 'bribery and kickbacks.'"[16]

And so the very justices who claimed three days earlier that the average citizen could and should be able to understand what constituted the rendering of "material support" to a foreign terrorist organization now concluded that those same citizens could *not* be expected to fathom the meaning of "honest services" fraud.

Notwithstanding this disparity, the "honest services" ruling was a step in the right direction. It represented a recognition by the justices that, without violating a specific state or federal law, public officials and perhaps sharp-elbowed businessmen should not face federal prosecution merely because their performance subjectively offends someone in the U.S. attorney's office. Time will tell, however, whether this recognition spreads beyond "honest services" fraud to the myriad other statutes that serve as traps for the unwary public official or private citizen who ends up in a prosecutor's sights.[17]

While it's true that politicians under indictment aren't likely to garner much public sympathy, a healthy skepticism is due when federal authority is imposed on matters primarily of state and local concern. Nothing short of the proper functioning of democratic governance is at stake. A recent series of prosecutions of much-maligned state and local politicians in Massachusetts provides a case in point.

Dianne Wilkerson quite clearly broke the law when, as a Massachusetts state senator, she accepted a cash payment from a businessman turned FBI informant. U.S. District Judge Douglas Woodlock, in handing down a three-and-a-half-year sentence in January 2011, excoriated Wilkerson for being part of a seemingly intractable "Gordian knot" of corruption by a long line of state political figures.

Upon first glance, Judge Woodlock had a point. At the time of Wilkerson's sentencing, Salvatore F. DiMasi, who was arguably more powerful than the governor during his four-year stint as Speaker of the Massachusetts House of Representatives, was under indictment for honest services fraud, conspiracy, and extortion. DiMasi's predecessor, Thomas M. Finneran, had also been federally indicted, for perjury and obstruction of justice. Likewise, Charles F. Flaherty, who served as House Speaker from 1985 until 1990, pleaded guilty in 1996 to tax evasion growing out of his alleged unlawful acceptance of gratuities. The day before Wilkerson's sentence, all three former Speakers appeared at the podium to greet and be cheered by the House members ringing in the new legislative session.

Timing was not on Wilkerson's side, as Judge Woodlock's incredulous tone made clear. Despite a decades-long series of federal political corruption prosecutions in the Bay State, "people go back to do it again," Woodlock lamented. "It's clear the sentencing imposed for criminal conduct here and, frankly, in other industrial states, hasn't been sufficient."[18]

Missing from the discussion was the possibility that recent Massachusetts House Speakers were not, in fact, so stupid, reckless, or obdurate that they committed serial felonies while unaware that the local U.S. attorney was still watching. As this book points out in Chapter One, Thomas Finneran was accused of perjury but ended up pleading guilty to the related crime of obstruction of justice, in no small part because he was promised probation, rather than prison time, if he admitted guilt. A close analysis of his testimony under oath demonstrated that he had not, in fact, perjured himself. Charles Flaherty's plea to tax fraud was likewise controversial, with even the prosecuting U.S. attorney conceding that "he had no proof that the speaker's extracurricular activities had affected any legislation."[19] And Salvatore DiMasi was indicted in part under the "honest services" section of the federal mail fraud statute that the Supreme Court later narrowed considerably.[20] Only a meticulous examination of the evidence in these cases could determine whether these former House Speakers in fact committed crimes, or whether Finneran and Flaherty pleaded guilty to violating amorphous statutes simply because of the threat of lengthy prison sentences in the event of conviction. Astute observers of the federal criminal justice system have long since given up believing that the guilty plea reveals *true* culpability. It's all too common for such pleas to be the product of risk avoidance at the expense of truth. In this sense, the scripted plea colloquy has become a big part of the corruption afflicting the entire system.

The behavior of such legislators has been dragged into the ambit of federal statutes vague enough to arguably encompass all manner of lawful, if self-benefitting, financial dealings. What may appear to federal prosecutors and judges to be felonious conduct, however, is often in accord with state law and longstanding political culture. If such culture is to change, it is a matter to be left to the voters—who in Massachusetts have chosen, for reasons of their own, to establish longtime one-party rule in the legislature. The result is a self-perpetuating political culture that has become ugly and dysfunctional, but not necessarily felonious. Where disfavored practices appear to carry the day, citizens would do well to express their outrage at voting booths, rather than allow unelected federal prosecutors to dictate their political choices.

Much like indicted pols, those in the financial realm accused of crimes aren't likely to engender public support. It's far more likely that the media will act as cheering section, rather than watchdog, regarding government assertions of power over such individuals.

Consider the trajectory of the Justice Department's high-profile campaign to put practitioners of "options backdating" in the dock. It all started when Erik Lie, a University of Iowa finance professor, published a paper demonstrating a glaring coincidence: It was extraordinarily common for public companies to grant stock options to their executives very shortly before marked increases in the stock price.[21] This, of course, made the options valuable—in the money—right away. Some news reporters, and then the Securities and Exchange Commission, began to delve into some of the examples. It turned out that, in fact, the options had been issued in many instances *after* the stock price increase, but were backdated to a period *before* the rise.

The news media, embodying the old adage that "dog bites man" is not news but "man bites dog" is, concluded that there must have been some species of fraud involved.[22] Later, the author of the study that started it all admitted that "at the time we published the paper, it wasn't clear that regulators would view the activity as illegal."[23] But view it as illegal they did, and with a vengeance—all without a statute or regulation clearly designating the widespread practice as fraudulent.

The campaign against options backdating reached its apex when Judge Jed S. Rakoff of the Southern District of New York sentenced James J. Treacy, the former chief operating officer of Monster Worldwide, to two years in prison for improperly accounting for backdated options on his company's books. (Because prosecutors could not articulate a theory for why and how backdated options somehow cheated anyone—stockholders, tax authorities, nor anyone else—they focused on the notion that because the options were accounted for erroneously in corporate income statements, they were somehow fraudulent. Some journalists concurred.)[24] Judge Rakoff blasted the defendant, saying, "It is disgusting that this practice went on."

But other judges, as well as some journalists, took a step back. They realized that this method for compensating executives over and above their salaries—the purpose, after all, of stock options—could not be said to have cheated anyone, since those executives were going to be paid bonuses by one means or another for improving the company's profitability (and thus lifting the stock price).[25] Indeed, in some cases prosecutors relied on the fact that defendants, when questioned about the practice and given the impression that backdating was a fraud, were less than forthcoming. They were thus indicted for the ever convenient crime of lying to a federal agent.[26]

Judge Cormac J. Carney of the Central District of California, who presided over the high-profile criminal backdating case against former executives of Broadcom Corporation, can probably be credited with turning the tide in this Wall Street scandal *du jour*. Days after setting aside a guilty plea from one defendant,[27] Judge Carney dismissed charges against two others in December 2009, finding that the case was built upon false or distorted testimony pried out of frightened (because threatened) cooperating Broadcom employees.[28] During the course of reciting the litany of the Justice Department's dirty-pool tactics to force witnesses to make the options practice sound secret and sinister, Judge Carney commented on the heart of the manufactured backdating scandal:

> The accounting standards and guidelines were not clear, and there was considerable debate in the high-tech industry as to the proper accounting treatment for stock option grants. Indeed, Apple and Microsoft were engaging in the exact same practices as those of Broadcom.[29]

Needless to say, neither Steve Jobs nor Bill Gates had been called on the carpet for his company's use of the same device that landed other executives in the hot seat.

Nearly a year later, in November 2010, Judge Otis D. Wright II sentenced Bruce Karatz, former CEO of KB Home, to probation, although the U.S. attorney's office had recommended a six-year prison term. Judge Wright explained that he would not imprison a man who simply did not harm either his company or its shareholders.[30] Thus even judges who could not get themselves to toss out such charges entirely were beginning to question why backdating was even a crime. The atmosphere, at least with regard to the backdating scandal, seemed to have begun to clear.

With an increased focus on financial fraud, vague prosecutions in this arena continued apace.[31] Yet like Judge Carney, some on the federal bench refused to play ball. One of the most trenchant counterattacks came in December 2010 from Alex Kozinski, the libertarian-inclined chief judge of the Ninth Circuit Court of Appeals. The court was hearing an appeal of one Prabhat Goyal, former chief financial officer of Network Associates, Inc.[32] The prosecution was based on a complicated government theory as to how Goyal supplied the firm's auditor with misleading and false information that caused the audited statements to overstate income. The charges ranged from securities fraud to lying to the auditor. After an exhaustive analysis, the panel not only reversed the convictions on all fifteen counts, but declared Goyal innocent, thus prohibiting the government from trying again.

Not fully satisfied with this relief, Kozinski added a concurrence in rather blunt language:

> This case has consumed an inordinate amount of taxpayer resources, and has no doubt devastated the defendant's personal and professional life....And, in the end, the government couldn't prove that the defendant engaged in *any* criminal conduct. This is just one of a string of recent cases in which courts have found that federal prosecutors overreached by trying to stretch criminal law beyond its proper bounds.[33]

Kozinski's opinion cited, among other cases, the infamous prosecution of Arthur Andersen LLP, discussed in Chapter Five of this book. There, a prosecution that destroyed the firm was found by the Supreme Court to have been based on behavior not criminal by any stretch of the law or the imagination. Kozinski continued:

> This is not the way criminal law is supposed to work. Civil law often covers conduct that falls in a gray area of arguable legality. But criminal law should clearly separate conduct that is criminal from conduct that is legal.

One wonders why such straightforward language is not more common among federal judges, even when courts reverse convictions on the ground that vague statutes have been stretched far beyond reason. The spirited protestations of Judges Kozinski and Carney are the exception rather than the rule.

But groups within civil society, not waiting for the federal bench, have launched an avowedly nonpartisan effort to rein in this species of prosecutorial abuse. In May 2010 an "odd couple" alliance of the conservative Heritage Foundation and the liberal National Association of Criminal Defense Lawyers (NACDL) published "Without Intent," a co-authored report detailing a major shortcoming of Congress's drafting of criminal laws.[34] The report found that of the 446 nonviolent, non-drug-related criminal laws presented in the 109th Congress, more than half lacked a requirement that a defendant act with criminal intent.

Whether by design or by mere consequence, Congress has been making it easier for average citizens who did not intend to break the law to be convicted in federal criminal courts.

Endeavors like that of Heritage and the NACDL—involving not only lawyers but also associations of businessmen, and latched onto from all points on the political spectrum—hold out hope for real reform of a system run amok.

The dangers in allowing the current trends to continue are illustrated vividly by a criminal justice system halfway around the world, where vagueness reigns supreme as a tool of social and political control. It was in late December 2010 that Moscow's Khamovnichesky Court convicted and sentenced Mikhail Khodorkovsky to a prison term of six years, to be served after the expiration of an earlier eight-year sentence. Khodorkovsky had amassed a wildly profitable oil company during the immediate post-Soviet years, when entrepreneurs engaged in a "Wild West" type rush to accumulate corporate assets under the lax administration of Russia's first president, Boris Yeltsin. But Khodorkovsky ran into legal troubles when he challenged President Vladimir Putin, a former Soviet secret police operative.

The arcane politics of the Russian state are debatable; the fact that Khodorkovsky was railroaded is not. His first case involved a charge that he and his partner, Platon Lebedev (also convicted twice), embezzled all of the oil—some 350 million metric tons—produced by their company, Yukos Oil, over a six-year period (1998–2003). This conviction was obtained despite the fact that no oil was found to be missing. In a separate case, Khodorkovsky was charged with failing to pay taxes on Yukos's profits from selling the oil—the very oil that Khodorkovsky was convicted of *embezzling*. As a result of the tax conviction, Yukos's assets were seized by the state, and then sold cheap to the state-controlled oil company Rosneft. Khodorkovsky was close to completing his eight-year sentence when the new conviction and additional sentence were handed down.

What was deemed most remarkable by observers of Khodorkovsky's legal travails, as well as by his Russian lawyer, Yuri Schmidt,[35] was that no observer of the proceedings could figure out what crimes, if any, were committed.[36] The prosecutors went about piling up reams of "evidence," the judge accepted the "evidence," and defense counsel argued futilely that none of the proceedings made the slightest bit of sense since nothing alleged against the defendants could by any stretch be deemed criminal.

The Khodorkovsky experience demonstrated to the world that all the Russians need in order to put a target of the regime in prison and seize his assets is a statute into which any and all conduct can be squeezed, in a trial fit for a Kafka novel. There is, to be sure, a vast difference between the Russian and American systems: the organizations within American civil society have been able to operate here without fear of imprisonment, and occasionally American courts or presiding judges point out that the Justice Department emperor too often wears no clothes. But Russia's difficulties constructing a criminal justice system in which clear statutes guide civil society, and fair trials decide whether a crime truly has been committed, furnish a warning to our society as to where we could be heading.

The U.S. criminal justice system would appear to be at a crossroads. Some skepticism has emerged even within courts and among judges, and some sectors of civil society have sounded the alarm and formed coalitions to fight the trend. Lawyers and scholars have taken to writing about the problem.[37] But the Department of Justice continues to press forward, and many media supporters of such efforts value the excitement of "perp walks" more than the importance of due process for people they are inclined to distrust, oppose, or even despise.

It is too early in the history of the practice of prosecuting and convicting citizens and organizations under vague federal statutes, and much too early in our society's effort to fight back, to predict whether the federal criminal justice system will be returned to its roots or continue along the path begun in the mid-1980s. But recent signs offer reasons for optimism.

FOREWORD

The very possibility that citizens who believe they are law-abiding may, in the eyes of federal prosecutors, be committing three federal felonies each day—which is the central thesis of this provocative and timely book—threatens the very foundation of our democracy. Our system of checks and balances depends on a vigorous judiciary and legislature serving as a brake on excessive prosecutorial zeal. It also depends on an alert private citizenry willing to exercise its constitutional right, indeed obligation, to petition the government for a redress of grievances. But when the executive branch, through its politically appointed prosecutors, has the power to criminalize ordinary conduct through accordion-like criminal statutes, the system of checks and balances breaks down.

Harvey Silverglate, an experienced and astute criminal lawyer, makes a compelling case that federal prosecutors are abusing their power by using the criminal law to prosecute law-abiding citizens whose conduct is arguably covered by extremely vague criminal statutes that are capable of reaching acts which are believed to be lawful by those who commit them. These prosecutors threaten to indict underlings for conduct that is even further away from the core of criminality unless they cooperate against the real targets. Because federal criminal law carries outrageously high sentences—often with mandatory minimums—these prosecutorial threats are anything but illusory. They turn friends into enemies, family members into government witnesses and employees into stool pigeons. Silverglate believes that we are in danger of becoming a society in which prosecutors alone become judges, juries and executioners because the threat of high sentences makes it too costly for even innocent people to resist the prosecutorial pressure. That is why nearly all criminal defendants today plead guilty to "reduced" charges rather than risk a trial with draconian sentences in the event of a conviction.

I litigated dozens of cases in a country that employed this tactic with a vengeance. That country was the Soviet Union in the 1970s and '80s. Every Soviet citizen committed at least three felonies a day, because the criminal statutes were written so broadly as to cover ordinary day-to-day activities. The Communist Party decided whom to prosecute from among the millions of possible criminals. They picked dissidents, refuseniks, and others who posed political dangers to the system. This began under Stalin when his KGB head, Lavrenti Beria, infamously said, "Show me the man and I'll find you the crime." Even after Stalin's death, the gulag was filled with ordinary citizens who had committed no crimes other than disagreeing with the powers that be. They were not prosecuted for dissenting. Instead they were prosecuted for violating the myriad laws regulating commerce and other day-to-day economic activities.

Several of my Soviet clients repeated the following gulag story: A new prisoner who has been sentenced to 10 years of confinement is introduced to the old prisoners who ask him what he is in for. He responds, "Nothing." The leader of the old prisoners responds cynically, "You're a liar. For nothing they only give you 5 years."

The Soviet legal system was evaluated by the Communist Party not by its ability to dispense justice but rather by its efficiency. As Aleksandr Solzhenitsyn put it in his masterful work on the Gulag Archipelago, a garbage disposal system is not judged by its fairness but rather by its ability to dispose of the garbage quickly and inexpensively. We are not the Soviet system and there is little danger that we will ever reach that nadir of injustice. But if Silverglate is correct, and the evidence he provides certainly supports his thesis, then we are moving in the direction of that abominable system of justice. The difference is that the Soviets were motivated by evil intentions—the desire to suppress legitimate dissent. The prosecutors in our country are often motivated by good intentions—the desire to suppress predatory crime. But the road to injustice, like the road to hell, is often paved with good intentions. As Justice Louis Brandeis once put it:

Experience should teach us to be most on our guard to protect liberty when the Government's purposes are beneficent. Men born to freedom are naturally alert to repel invasion of their liberty by evil-minded rulers. The greatest dangers to liberty lurk in insidious encroachment by men of zeal, well-meaning but without understanding.

Many current federal prosecutors honestly believe that they are doing God's work by creatively employing vague federal statutes to remain a step ahead of creative criminals. They think, and with some justification, that clear and specific criminal statutes can always be evaded by clever and conniving criminals who can achieve their nefarious goals without violating the precise terms of often anachronistic criminal statutes. New technologies present new opportunities for crime, and the criminal law has difficulty keeping pace with innovative criminals.

This problem of criminal law keeping pace with new developments was exemplified by a 1931 decision written by Justice Oliver Wendell Holmes. A man had stolen an airplane and transported it across state lines. He was charged under a statute that had been enacted in the early days of the automobile and that criminalized the transportation of "motor vehicles" in interstate commerce. Because it would require guesswork to decide whether Congress intended to include planes as motor vehicles, the Supreme Court reversed the conviction, requiring Congress to be clear about what it meant. Congress then amended the statute to include airplanes.

This story is often repeated when new technologies or financial instruments have given rise to new opportunities for deception, overreaching or sharp practices. It is up to Congress, not the courts, to decide which borderline conduct is to be criminally prosecuted and punished, and Congress should do so with unambiguous language capable of being understood by all citizens. Under the Constitution, there is no room for creativity by prosecutors who are understandably eager to send messages to miscreants who are themselves using creativity in circumventing anachronistic criminal statutes. An expression common when our Constitution was ratified was that a criminal statute had to be so clear that it could be understood when read by a person "while running." Today's federal statutes do not come close to satisfying that criterion.

The very real current threat of terrorism provides another context in which federal prosecutors are employing vaguely written statutes, some of them relating to the financing of terrorist activities. The financing of terrorism is a serious problem, deserving of federal concern. The statutes criminalizing such activities, however, are poorly drafted and open ended. In this area, as contrasted with some others, the federal government has suffered significant defeats at the hands of recalcitrant jurors. This would seem ironic at first blush, since the public is deeply concerned about terrorism and jurors are likely to reflect that concern. Yet, in several high-profile cases, juries have either acquitted or hung. I offer one possible explanation, though it is necessarily tentative and somewhat speculative. In terrorism cases, the political agenda of the government is apparent, and American juries are particularly sensitive to abuses of civil rights in the political context. That was true during the Vietnam War, and it apparently continues to be true in the war against terrorism. In purely financial cases that do not involve terrorism or any other obvious political issue, jurors are less likely to express skepticism about government overreaching. The Soviets learned this lesson early and disguised their political cases as purely financial ones. They were not concerned about jury reaction, but rather about public opinion, both domestic and international. Some American prosecutors have tried to disguise political prosecutions as terrorist-related financial cases, but some jurors have seen through the disguise.

The men and women of zeal who use elastic criminal statutes to prosecute citizens who they believe are exploiting or endangering other citizens may in fact be doing God's work, but they are not doing Jefferson's work or Hamilton's work or Madison's work or the work of the other founders of our secular nation and Constitution. They should leave to God (or public opinion) the punishment of immoral people who do not violate the explicit terms of criminal statutes. They should not take it upon themselves to right all the wrongs of an imperfect world but rather to prosecute only those defendants who, to paraphrase Shakespeare, have answered Hamlet's question "to be or not to be" a criminal, by deliberately and consciously crossing the line from immorality to felony. There should be vehicles other than criminal prosecutions for interpreting and testing the reach and meaning of vague statutes; civil and administrative proceedings are fairer vehicles than prosecutions for the creative common law expansion of a citizen's legal duties. Prosecutors should be empowered, as they are in some contexts, to seek declaratory judgments, injunctions or other civil remedies that carry monetary sanctions but not criminal punishment. Only after the law has been definitively clarified should prosecutors be permitted to seek criminal punishments.

The criminal law should always be retrospective. The constitutional provision against *ex post facto* laws should be read broadly to cover after the fact interpretations of vague criminal statutes. It is no accident that this important prohibition was included in the body of the Constitution even before the Bill of Rights was ratified. It is fundamental to a free society that its citizens be able to read the law and conform their conduct to it. As Justice Holmes said in the airplane case referred to above: "Although it is not likely that a criminal will carefully consider the text of the law before he murders or steals, it is reasonable that a fair warning should be given to the world in language that the common world will understand, of what the law intends to do if a certain line is passed. To make the warning fair, so far as possible the line should be clear." This approach to criminal justice will make it harder for the federal government to prosecute some innovative criminals, but that is the price a democracy must be willing to pay for the important principle that no person should ever be prosecuted unless he has made a conscious decision to violate the criminal law. It is said of one particular Roman tyrant that he placed the text of his law so high above the heads of the citizens that they could not read it. That is the way of tyranny, not democracy.

Silverglate brilliantly documents how the principle of fair warning is being violated on a daily basis by current federal prosecutors. He also shows that this is not a Republican problem alone nor one that has been limited to any particular recent administration. The Clinton Justice Department violated this principle as zealously as did the Bush Justice Department. Unless the culture of federal prosecution changes, it seems likely that this problem will persist regardless of who is elected president or who is appointed attorney general. This is a systemic problem that requires a systemic answer. I believe that at the heart of this problem is the structure of the Justice Department itself.

Our attorney general is a presidential appointee, generally from the president's party, often a trusted friend and political adviser. Recall Robert Kennedy, President Kennedy's brother and campaign manager; John Mitchell, President Nixon's law partner and campaign manager; and William French-Smith, President Reagan's personal lawyer, as perhaps the most striking examples of the closeness between presidents and their attorneys general. Although Janet Reno was not a friend of Bill Clinton, she came from his party and was recommended for the job by Hillary Rodham Clinton's brother. President George W. Bush's first two attorneys general were political cronies. The attorney general is supposed to be a trusted loyalist, a member of the president's Cabinet, a person in whom the president can confide on matters of policy and politics. That same attorney general is also supposed to be the nation's highest law enforcement officer—the person who ultimately decides whom to investigate and to prosecute.

Because our attorney general—unlike any official in other governments—plays these dual roles of political adviser and chief prosecutor, no one holding that job can be trusted to investigate and, if necessary, prosecute the president or other high-ranking members of his or her and the attorney general's administration. He or she would be in a clear conflict of interest, and the perception of unfairness would cloud any decision.

The same is true, though perhaps to a lesser degree, with any high-profile prosecution, especially any that has political or partisan implications. It is also true to some degree of all prosecutions, since winning and losing criminal cases reflects on the administration.

In other democracies, the two jobs that our attorney general performs are divided. There is a political officer generally called the "Minister of Justice" whose job it is to advise the president or prime minister and to be loyal to the party and person in power. There is also a non-political official, generally called the "Attorney General" or the "Director of Public Prosecutions," who has no loyalty to the incumbent head of state or his party and whose sole responsibility is to investigate and prosecute in a nonpartisan manner. Prime ministers and presidents have been brought down (and upheld) by such prosecutors, without any appearance of impropriety. Prosecutions in general have a less partisan feel and smell.

Our system of investigation and prosecution is unique in the world. We have politicized the role of prosecutor, not only at the federal level but in all of our states and counties as well. Nowhere else are prosecutors (or judges) elected. Indeed, it is unthinkable in most parts of the world to have prosecutors run for office, make campaign promises and solicit contributions. Prosecutors in other countries are civil servants who do not pander to the people's understandable wish to be safe from crime, or campaign on the promise to "be tough on crime." (Our penchant for voting on everything has reached laughable proportions in Florida, where even "public defenders" must run for office. I can only imagine what the campaign must be like.) But in the United States, prosecutors are not only elected, or in the federal system appointed in a generally partisan manner, but the job is a stepping stone to a higher office, as evidenced by the fact that nearly every senator or congressman who ever practiced law once served as a prosecutor. Winning becomes more important than doing justice, because voters vote for "winners" not "justice doers."

There is much that needs to be done to make our criminal justice system more just and less political. Requiring crystal-clear criminal statutes is an important beginning and a crucial step. Silverglate's book shows the way.

Alan M. Dershowitz
August 2009

INTRODUCTION
TRAPS AND SNARES FOR THE UNWARY INNOCENT

A little over a half-century ago, an Army veteran named Joseph Edward Morissette settled in small-town Michigan to raise his family. To support his wife and young son, the 27-year-old worked as a fruit stand operator during the summer and as a trucker and scrap iron collector during the winter. His seemingly normal life came to a screeching halt, however, when he was charged with stealing from the United States government in 1952. His case would ultimately wend its way through the federal court system and end up at the Supreme Court.

One time when Morissette was out hunting for deer with his brother-in-law, he came across a heap of spent bomb casings on a tract of uninhabited land located about half a mile from a traveled road and about six miles from the main highway. To Morissette, the casings appeared abandoned. There were no signs posted to the contrary, and, having sat in a pile through several harsh Michigan winters, the casings were showing signs of rust and decomposition. When Morissette failed to bag a deer to pay for his hunting trip, he collected some of the casings, crushed them with his tractor, and sold them as scrap metal. The casings yielded him $84.

The land turned out to be Oscoda Air Base, which the military used, according to the later Supreme Court opinion, as "a practice bombing range over which the Air Force dropped simulated bombs at ground targets."[1] A police officer, likely concerned about the large amount of bomb-shaped scrap metal heaped in the bed of Morissette's truck, asked him about the casings and referred the matter to an FBI agent. That, in turn, led to Morissette's being indicted in federal court on the charge that he "did unlawfully, willfully and knowingly steal and convert" property of the United States in violation of a statute that provided that "whoever embezzles, steals, purloins, or knowingly converts" government property is punishable by fine and imprisonment. Morissette was convicted and sentenced to two months in prison or a fine of $200.

Morissette hadn't realized that the casings were the government's property; he had taken them on the assumption that they were abandoned. In fact, he told the police officer who first questioned him that he did not think they were of any use or that anybody would care if he took them. Yet Morissette's "innocent intention" couldn't save him at trial. Despite the facts, the trial judge forbade Morissette's lawyer to argue to the jury that his client acted with an "innocent intention," because the judge concluded that Morissette's guilt under the statute was obvious and legally irrefutable: the bomb casings were on government property, and Morissette took them without permission. It was irrelevant that Morissette might have reasonably believed the casings were abandoned property, or even that this belief was based upon the government's own failure to post a notice to the contrary. The question of whether Morissette *believed* he was not stealing, and of the government's complicity in giving him that impression, did not matter.

It's important to note that the judge's interpretation of the law departed from centuries of English common law tradition, an evolving body of judge-made interpretive law with ancient roots, based on human experience and common sense. The common law tradition, with rare and narrow exceptions, does not punish those, like Morissette, who act with innocent intent. This approach to criminal law contains a vital moral component—our society punishes only those who intentionally rather than inadvertently violate the law.[2]

When the United States Court of Appeals for the Sixth Circuit heard Morissette's appeal in 1951, it upheld his conviction by a 2-1 vote. By the judges' stated logic, it was a "technicality" that Morissette, who they acknowledged made "no effort at concealment," never intended to steal. When it comes to statutory crimes defined by Congress, the two-judge majority argued, intent or knowledge is irrelevant unless Congress appears to provide otherwise. Morissette wisely sought, and obtained, Supreme Court review.

In its unanimous opinion, the Supreme Court threw out the appellate court's decision and, with it, Morissette's conviction.[3] Justice Robert H. Jackson discussed the historical role of *intent* in criminal cases and "the ancient requirement of a culpable state of mind" that must accompany a culpable act. To convict one of a crime, there must be "an evil-meaning mind with an evil-doing hand" (for the technically minded, the traditional common law notion of the combination of the *actus reus* and the *mens rea*).

Based on these centuries-old requirements, Justice Jackson concluded that the courts could not presume from Congress's silence that it did away with the criminal intent requirement, as this "would conflict with the overriding presumption of innocence with which the law endows the accused." Jackson noted that, had the jurors been allowed to consider Morissette's state of mind, "[t]hey might have concluded that the heaps of spent casings left in the hinterland to rust away presented an appearance of unwanted and abandoned junk," and from that they might "have refused to brand Morissette as a thief."

Jackson and his fellow justices obviously recognized the importance of their having decided to review the Morissette case, an undertaking extended to a small minority of litigants who seek review by the high court. "This would have remained a profoundly insignificant case to all except its immediate parties," Jackson noted in the Court's opinion, "had it not been so tried and submitted to the jury as to raise questions both fundamental and far-reaching in federal criminal law." And so this seemingly insignificant case had the potential to ensure the continued presence of fundamental principles of fairness and moral content in the federal criminal law. But how long would those positive developments last?

• • ● • •

A few years before he wrote *Morissette v. United States,* Robert H. Jackson was serving as Franklin D. Roosevelt's new attorney general. On April 1, 1940, Jackson assembled his cadre of chief federal prosecutors in Washington.[4] He wanted to speak to them about a matter of grave concern—and it wasn't the evils of crime or the need to use every crime-fighting tool to the fullest. Jackson's subject, instead, was the untoward consequences of excessive prosecutorial zeal.

After explaining why a federal prosecutor must choose cases carefully and recognize that not every crime can be pursued, Jackson turned to the heart of his talk: "If the prosecutor is obliged to choose his cases, it follows that he can choose his defendants." Here one finds "the most dangerous power of the prosecutor: that he will pick people that he thinks he should get, rather than pick cases that need to be prosecuted."

Jackson was no soft touch. He knew real crimes when he saw them. After serving as attorney general for less than two years, he would become a Supreme Court justice and serve as well as chief American war crimes prosecutor at Nuremberg. But Jackson also understood the proper limits of power and the dangerous human impulse to exert power over others. The federal law books, explained Jackson, are "filled with a great assortment of crimes," and a prosecutor "stands a fair chance of finding at least a technical violation of some act on the part of almost anyone." Prosecutors can easily succumb to the temptation of first "picking the man and then searching the law books, or putting investigators to work, to pin some offense on him."

Today, in spite of Jackson's warning, it is only a slight exaggeration to say that the average busy professional in this country wakes up in the morning, goes to work, comes home, takes care of personal and family obligations, and then goes to sleep, unaware that he or she likely committed several federal crimes that day. Why? The answer lies in the very nature of modern federal criminal laws, which have become not only exceedingly numerous (Jackson's main fear at the time of his admonition to his prosecutors) and broad, but also, since Jackson's day, impossibly vague. As the Morissette scenario indicated, federal criminal laws have become dangerously disconnected from the English common law tradition and its insistence on fair notice, so prosecutors can find some arguable federal crime to apply to just about any one of us, even for the most seemingly innocuous conduct (and since the mid-1980s have done so increasingly).

A study by the Federalist Society reported that, by the year 2007, the U.S. Code (listing all statutes enacted by Congress) contained more than 4,450 criminal offenses,[5] up from 3,000 in 1980. Even this figure understates the challenge facing honest, law-abiding citizens. Since the New Deal era, Congress has delegated to various administrative agencies the task of writing the regulations that implement many congressional statutes. This has spawned thousands of additional pages of text that carry the same force as congressionally enacted statutes.[6] The volume of federal crimes in recent decades has exploded well beyond the statute books and into the morass of the Code of Federal Regulations, handing federal prosecutors an additional trove of often vague and exceedingly complex and technical prohibitions, one degree removed from congressional authority, on which to hang their hapless targets.

This development may sound esoteric to some—until they find themselves at the wrong end of an FBI investigation into, or indictment for, practices they deem perfectly acceptable. It is then that citizens begin to understand the danger posed to civil liberties when our normal daily activities expose us to potential prosecution at the whim of a government official.

How these prosecutions work and what we can do about this perilous state of affairs is the subject of this book. The dangers spelled out here do not apply only to "white collar criminals," state and local politicians, and myriad professionals, though their stories will predominate in the chapters that follow. No field of work nor social class is safe from this troubling form of executive branch overreaching and social control, and nothing less than the integrity of our constitutional democracy hangs in the balance. After all, when every citizen is vulnerable to prosecution and prison, then there is no effective counterweight to reign in government overreaching in every sphere. The hallowed notion of "a government of laws" becomes a cruel and cynical joke.

• • ● •

When I began practicing law in 1967, I hung out my shingle as a "criminal defense and civil liberties lawyer." I linked the two practice areas because, during the turbulent '60s, it seemed that defending people accused of crime often was an exercise in the defense of freedom of speech, freedom of religion, freedom of association, or procedural due process of law. Our firm's typical cases involved what we called "the three D's": drugs, draft, and demonstrations. A few years later, a large number of gender discrimination cases were added to the mix, but much of our work remained focused on the three D's.

I recognized that I made a good part of my living defending people who did very bad things (assault, robbery, murder, mayhem, larceny, and fraud, for example). Many committed the crimes charged while some did not. However, the charges against them entailed conduct that reasonable people, ordinary citizens and lawyers alike, would rightly regard as criminal, and the indictments were based on statutes that were readily understandable. One could argue that some actions should not be criminal, such as possession of marijuana, but the crimes charged were usually clearly defined.

Then, about fifteen years into my law practice, I noticed a shift in the federal courts. More and more of my clients (physicians, bankers, academics, scientists, investors, newspaper reporters, accountants, artists, and photographers [the "three D's" had by then given way to a more diverse clientele]) were being investigated and prosecuted for conduct that neither they nor I instinctively viewed as criminal. As I prepared to defend against the charges, I could not rid myself of the unsettling notion that the federal criminal laws were becoming vaguer and harder to understand with the passage of time.

This chasm between federal and state law had in theory been established long ago, in 1812, when the Supreme Court ruled in a bribery case that federal crimes were entirely creatures of congressional statute and not successors to English common law.[7] As a result, Congress in writing statutes, and the federal courts in interpreting them, do not have the full benefit of the common law's wisdom and experience—with increasingly alarming consequences. As the Supreme Court said in 1985, "[W]hen assessing the reach of a federal criminal statute, we must pay close heed to language, legislative history, and purpose in order strictly to determine the scope of the conduct the enactment forbids."[8] This judicial exercise, often akin to reading tea leaves, has proven disastrous.

The deceptively simple exercise of divining congressional purpose in enacting a statute involves, for one thing, a dubious assumption that Congress acts with a single, much less a simple, intent. In practice, it is rarely clear what that intent was, since much federal legislation is the result of compromises that often are meant to gloss over genuine and sharp differences. For this and perhaps other reasons as well, Congress has demonstrated a growing dysfunction in crafting legislation that can in fact be understood.

As the post-New Deal regulatory and national security state took deeper root during the mid-20th century, the gulf between the defendant-protective common law tradition practiced in the states and the more malleable and prosecution-friendly federal law grew. More and more, courts departed from Justice Jackson's insistence on requiring proof of criminal intent to commit a crime, and instead subscribed to the belief that, if the nation is to be kept safe in an increasingly dangerous world, law violators must not be allowed to slip from the government's net, even when the law's prohibitions could not be understood with precision.

The danger posed by vague federal statutes was obvious to me, in part because I came of age during the era of anti-Jim Crow racial struggles in the American South. In what I now see is a historical irony, the threat back then appeared to be the abusive use of vague state breach-of-the-peace laws to turn back the wave of civil rights demonstrations in the Deep South. The 1965 Supreme Court decision *Cox v. Louisiana,*[9] decided while I was a law student, opened my eyes to just how much mischief can be done with vague wording of the law.

In that case, Reverend B. Elton Cox, leader of a group of civil rights demonstrators, was arrested in December 1961 for violating a 1950 Louisiana criminal statute that barred picketing "in or near" courthouses. Louisiana's anti-picketing law was not a unique product of the segregated South. A similar federal statute to halt picketing of federal courthouses by Communist sympathizers went on the books during the Red Scare era, and even northern states—notably Massachusetts and Pennsylvania—enacted similar laws.

In *Cox*, what seemed outrageous was the manner in which Louisiana officials enforced the Louisiana anti-picketing statute. Reverend Cox had made a point of getting permission from city officials to lead the demonstration across the street from the courthouse. He then led a 2,000-strong demonstration objecting to the arrest of 23 civil rights protestors the previous day. The demonstrators sang and marched peacefully until a small group of white-only lunch counter segregationists gathered nearby. Tension between the two groups escalated. The police recklessly sprayed tear gas into Reverend Cox's camp. The next day, the police arrested Cox for violating the anti-picketing law. He was sentenced to the maximum penalty of one year in jail and a $5,000 fine.

The Supreme Court summarily overturned Reverend Cox's conviction, calling the conduct of city officials "an indefensible sort of entrapment." The Court argued that the anti-picketing statute suffered from a "lack of specificity" in its mandate that demonstrations not take place "near" courthouses. Cox had received permission to lead a protest across the street—approximately 125 feet away. By telling Cox that he could lead the protest at that location but then arresting him, Louisiana officials violated his right to adequate notice and hence "due process of law." Here, the vagueness of the statute had enabled the state to mislead the citizen into running afoul of the law. *Cox* dealt a serious blow to the government's ability to pick and choose *capriciously* which citizens it will or will not prosecute and under what circumstances.

In other cases, however, the problem lay not with officials intentionally misleading citizens, but with the inherent vagueness of the statute itself. In a 1963 case, *Edwards v. South Carolina*,[10] 187 black high school and college students were convicted for "breach of the peace" during a peaceful demonstration against mistreatment of blacks. While the Supreme Court ruled the demonstration itself was protected by the First Amendment, it went further and deemed the statute unconstitutional because it was "so vague and indefinite" that it practically invited punishment of protected speech and protest. The Court noted that the Supreme Court of South Carolina defined the word "peace" as used in the statute as "tranquility." "These petitioners," said the U.S. Supreme Court, "were convicted of an offense so generalized as to be, in the words of the South Carolina Supreme Court, 'not susceptible of exact definition.'"

Troublingly, the doctrines of misleading the citizen[11] and "void for vagueness,"[12] which federal courts have applied in numerous cases with regard to state statutes, especially where states have used vague statutes to violate the federal constitutional rights of political, religious and racial minorities, have not been applied consistently or with equal rigor in federal cases, despite the modern-era explosion of vague federal criminal statutes and mountains of turgid regulations. When the Supreme Court considered an Oklahoma law that made it a crime to pay laborers less than the prevailing wage in their locality, it decided that the law's references to "locality" and "current rate of wages" left too much open to interpretation. That state law was unconstitutional, the Court determined, because its language was "so vague that men of common intelligence must necessarily guess at its meaning and differ as to" how best to comply with it.[13] The dangers posed by vague laws, relatively rare in modern state criminal statutes, are greatly exacerbated in the current federal criminal code. Such federal statutes have been stretched by prosecutors, often with the connivance of the federal courts, to cover a vast array of activities neither clearly defined nor intuitively obvious as crimes, both in commerce and in daily life.

I also began to notice that, as these bodies of law expanded, federal prosecutors grew more inclined to bring criminal charges for deeds that, at most, constituted arguable (sometimes *barely* arguable) civil offenses. Thus, they raised reasonably contestable federal questions that a federal court, in a civil proceeding, should have been allowed to resolve. The citizen, if wrong, would have to pay a price measured in dollars; and once the clear meaning of the statute or regulation was established, the citizen would be expected to adhere to it, next time on penalty of criminal indictment and conviction. I naively assumed that the federal courts would, by and large, insist that citizens be charged with crimes only when there was adequate notice of what constituted the crime.

I had reason, at the start of this trend, to think that the federal courts would rein in prosecutors. Consider the plight of Dorothy Garber. She ran afoul of the federal tax code, widely viewed as a confusing mish-mash of arcane, complex, and often conflicting rules and interpretations. As such, tax prosecutions traditionally were to be brought only where the regulation had been sufficiently clarified so that the taxpayer could reasonably be said to have intentionally violated a known legal duty to pay taxes owed. The taxing authorities were supposed to exercise wise discretion in deciding whether to seek to collect a tax in a civil enforcement proceeding, or to seek to punish criminally a tax evader who should have known better.

Garber's case reached the Florida federal courts in the late-1970s. This taxpayer was blessed (or perhaps, under the circumstances, cursed) with a rare trait: her body manufactured an extraordinarily valuable antibody used to make blood-typing serum. She frequently sold her antibodies to a pharmaceutical company by the process of plasmapharesis, i.e., the removal, treatment, and return of blood plasma from and to her circulation, a procedure that was both uncomfortable and potentially dangerous. She underwent plasmapharesis sometimes as often as six times a month and was handsomely paid for her trouble. In 1972, she earned a weekly salary of $200. In addition, she was provided a leased automobile and a $25,000 bonus. She earned a total of $87,200 that year and nearly as much in each of the two previous years.

Garber failed to report as income any of this money except her weekly $200 salary. Consequently, she was charged with criminal tax evasion. Her defense was intriguing, more a reflection of the conundrum of the federal tax code perhaps than of her alleged dishonesty. Examples of non-taxable transactions, some of which produce monetary gains, are found scattered throughout the tax code in various contexts. For example, if one owns some physical item, a "capital asset," and sells that asset for one's cost, however calculated, there is no taxable gain. If one is injured in an accident, compensation for pain and suffering is not taxable, in contrast to compensation for lost wages. These special categories of assets and of revenue, many of which get quite technical, often confound even the most experienced tax lawyers and accountants.

Garber, a lay person, argued that her body was a "capital asset" under the Internal Revenue Code, and that when she sold a portion of that asset, the sale was a non-taxable exchange because the tax cost basis of the asset with which she parted, i.e., her blood plasma, was precisely equal to the funds she received. The funds merely replaced the plasma she gave to the laboratory and therefore were neither proceeds of a business nor payment for services, either of which would render the proceeds taxable as "earned income."

The United States Court of Appeals for the Fifth Circuit saw the issue as "a unique legal question,"[14] noting that Garber testified "that she thought, after speaking with other blood donors, that because she was selling a part of her body, the money received was not taxable." The trial judge had told the jury that monetary proceeds of such plasma donations were taxable and refused to allow Garber's defense counsel to present expert witnesses who would say otherwise.

In reversing her conviction, the Court of Appeals decided not only that she had a right to present her capital exchange theory supported by expert testimony, but that "no court has yet determined whether payments received by a donor of blood or blood components are taxable as income." If Garber performed a service, it was taxable; if, on the other hand, "blood plasma, like a chicken's eggs, a sheep's wool, or any salable part of the human body," is tangible property, then her revenues were not taxable. Most importantly, the court declared that, because the law was vague and unsettled, "a *criminal* proceeding…is an *inappropriate vehicle* for pioneering interpretations of tax law."[15] In other words, the government should have brought a civil action against Garber to seek collection of the tax owed, not a criminal one to punish her.

Today, the Justice Department encourages federal prosecutors to do exactly what the *Garber* court condemned. In particular, federal prosecutors' novel use of long-standing but utterly formless "anti-fraud" laws, which cover increasingly vast areas of American life, threaten honest (and apparently law-abiding) business executives and other professionals, as well as other ordinary citizens. In 2003, Michael Chertoff, then-second-in-command of the Justice Department's Criminal

Division, even went so far as to boldly declare that federal prosecutors should exploit anti-fraud provisions to indict business executives because "criminal prosecution is a spur for institutional reform."[16]

The federal government's preference for criminal prosecutions (over either civil prosecution or "institutional reform" via the legislative branch) to expand the reach of the law is not limited to vague "anti-fraud" statutes and regulations. The same can be said for other now commonly used statutes—conspiracy, bribery, and extortion, among others. Even the most intelligent and informed citizen (including lawyers and judges, for that matter) cannot predict with any reasonable assurance whether a wide range of seemingly ordinary activities might be regarded by federal prosecutors as felonies.

• • ● • •

The trend of ambitious prosecutors exploiting vague federal laws and pursuing criminal charges instead of oftentimes more appropriate civil actions, something that they could not readily get away with in many state courts, has been alarming enough, but it's not the whole story. Indeed, the threat posed by federal prosecutors has become a veritable perfect storm lately, due to the convergence of this trend with the commonplace legal tactics that these prosecutors wield in order to get convictions in the vast majority of cases. Prosecutors are able to structure plea bargains in ways that make it nearly impossible for normal, rational, self-interest calculating people to risk going to trial. The pressure on innocent defendants to plead guilty and "cooperate" by testifying against others in exchange for a reduced sentence is enormous—so enormous that such cooperating witnesses often fail to tell the truth, saying instead what prosecutors want to hear. As Harvard Law School Professor Alan Dershowitz has colorfully put it, such cooperating defendant-witnesses "are taught not only to sing, but also to compose."[17]

There has been precious little legislative and judicial analysis of the expanded use of destructive coercive practices for "turning" prosecution witnesses, which may involve immunity for loved ones, cash stipends, new identities not encumbered by a criminal record, and other powerful inducements in exchange for "composing" to nail former associates. Although in theory the law requires that the government disclose to defense counsel all inducements given to cooperating witnesses,[18] jurors typically accept prosecutors' claims that such inducements are essential to infiltrate hidden criminal conspiracies. Moreover, as any criminal defense practitioner knows, in practice, many types of inducements and threats often are implied, the subject of a knowing wink of the eye by the prosecutor to the prospective witness's lawyer.

The "cooperation" framework is insidious. Prosecutors long have had the ability to offer witnesses valuable benefits, including money, in exchange for testimony that incriminates associates. Today, federal sentencing guidelines (once mandatory; still strongly suggestive and widely followed by judges) reward defendants who plead guilty and then give the government the testimony it seeks to prosecute others. Vague statutes exacerbate this problem by making it quite easy for one associate to testify that a former collaborator is indeed a crook.

The myriad ways in which federal prosecutors can craft or compose important witness testimony makes the prospect of the reduced sentence affiliated with a plea bargain much more palatable to defendants than the risk of a much higher sentence should they be found guilty at trial. The risk-reward ratio that innocent defendants weigh when deciding whether to challenge an indictment by insisting on a trial has tilted decidedly toward risk reduction via a guilty plea and cooperation against others.

The push for more plea bargains also has an effect on how thoroughly—and indeed whether at all—the prosecutions are tested in federal appeals courts to determine whether prosecutors are relying on cockamamie interpretations of federal statutes. When you can scare enough defendants to plead guilty in exchange for less prison time, the government wins by default since there is no real chance that an appeals court will say that the prosecution was wholly phony.

Increases in the number of plea bargains also have the functional result of hiding these prosecutions from the public and avoiding scrutiny by the press, because cases in which defendants take plea bargains receive much less attention than those that go to trial. On the other hand, as the circle widens to ensnare ever more "conspirators," prosecutors trumpet their willingness to "go wherever the evidence leads," and the news media are, far more often than not, prepared to report such news without an ounce of insight or skepticism.

Thus, more and more innocent conduct gets swept into the category of crime—not by legislatures, and only secondarily by judges and juries, but primarily by these dangerous and altogether too common prosecutorial practices. The problem is exacerbated by a white collar criminal defense bar composed largely of former federal prosecutors turned defenders who, by virtue of their experience in the federal government, well understand the risks of going to trial and therefore stress to their clients the benefits of cooperation over confrontation and the increasingly less likely prospect of vindication. While some former prosecutors turn into vigorous and skeptical defense lawyers (a few are among the most talented and principled in the nation, some of whom even left their prosecutorial jobs out of revulsion at the modern practices of the Department of Justice), a culture of assumed guilt, plea-bargaining, and deal-making has developed in defense circles which, more and more, are populated by capitulation-prone former prosecutors, especially at the higher echelons of the profession. The name of the game is to confess and cooperate, thus pleasing prosecutors who, in the not-too-distant past, were the comrades-in-arms of the newly-minted defenders. Through this flawed process, ordinary conduct is increasingly deemed criminal without the benefit of critical examination, much less an adversarial testing of the DOJ's often pioneering interpretations of federal law.

In turn, this prosecutorial strategy affects news coverage of high-profile cases that resemble public hangings in the Old West, often with the press decrying the latest "crime wave" and cheering the double-digit sentences imposed, with little or no critical media analysis and understanding. The criminal justice system and the news media (which in theory is supposed to be a check on government excess) feed one another instead.

Since the late-1980s, the federal bench, too, has been undergoing a transformation that has seriously eroded the extent to which judges can be relied upon to rein in bogus federal prosecutions. Judges, many of whom are former prosecutors, not only buy into the amorphous definitions of federal crimes favored by prosecutors, but they knowingly enable the tactics that allow prosecutors to present witnesses who bolster dubious prosecutions, thereby giving such cases the patina of substance. In a 1998 case, which served as a roadsign in the degradation of the federal justice system, lawyers for a Kansas woman named Sonya Singleton challenged the practice of offering leniency and even monetary rewards to cooperating government witnesses in exchange for their testimony. Prosecutors alleged that Singleton assisted her drug-dealing husband by wiring money for him in her name to a kingpin in California. Ms. Singleton and other co-conspirators were charged with multiple counts of money laundering and conspiracy to distribute cocaine. Before trial, she moved to suppress the testimony of Napoleon Douglas, a co-conspirator who had entered into a plea agreement with the government. The basis for her motion was that the government had impermissibly promised Mr. Douglas something of value, in violation of both federal law and the Kansas Rule of Professional Conduct. Specifically, Douglas had been promised that 1) he would not be prosecuted for any violations of the Drug Abuse Prevention and Control Act, stemming from his activities, other than perjury or related offenses, and 2) prosecutors would advise the sentencing court and parole board of the nature and extent of the cooperation provided.

Singleton's challenge was a shot across the justice system's bow, aiming directly at its increasingly corrupt "business as usual" culture, and she lost.

Not surprisingly, a federal statute makes it a crime to bribe witnesses; it is a felony to give or promise a witness "anything of value" in exchange for testimony.[19] The defendant's theory in *Singleton* was, if it is a felony (and it is) for any *defense* lawyer to promise a benefit to a witness, should it not similarly be a crime for *prosecutors*, by threats, money or other inducements, to coerce or bribe the vulnerable to "cooperate"?

Shouldn't *all* untoward pressures and inducements be removed from witnesses, so that truth, and not just naked self-interest, governs their testimony? The statute, on its face, makes no exception whatsoever for government use of bribery.

A three-judge panel of the Tenth Circuit Court of Appeals[20] followed the seemingly (one might even say unusually) clear wording of the witness-bribery statute and found no exception for prosecutors who threaten and then reward government witnesses for their testimony. The court drew the obvious conclusion that doing so is bribery. A panicked Department of Justice promptly sought and obtained further review by the full membership of the court, insisting the statute not be interpreted to mean what it says, lest the whole edifice of bought and coerced prosecution testimony collapse.

The full court reversed the upstart panel that had temporarily rocked the prosecutorial boat.[21] It ruled that "in light of the longstanding practice of leniency for testimony," it must be "presumed" that, had Congress intended to "overturn this ingrained aspect of American legal culture, it would have done so in clear, unmistakable, and unarguable language." Of course, that is precisely what Singleton argued and the three-judge panel found that Congress had done—spoken clearly *against* bribery of witnesses. The full court, however, pretending to know, without any clear evidence, what was on Congress's mind when it enacted a seemingly all-inclusive prohibition against interfering with the testimony of a witness, found that Congress intended an exception for prosecutors—a double standard if ever there was one.

It was hard for the defense bar to avoid profound disillusionment. The *Singleton* experience demonstrated that, even where Congress seems to have spoken clearly on the definition of witness bribery, the institutional imperative to obtain convictions at any cost prevailed.

Cynicism about the unlevel playing field granted to prosecutors by *Singleton* was amplified by a 1970 Supreme Court decision, *North Carolina v. Alford*. In that case, the defendant was charged with first-degree murder (with a potential death sentence attached to it) but decided to take a plea bargain in which he would accept a sentence for second-degree murder instead. However, unlike most defendants who take these deals, "Alford took the stand and testified that he had not committed the murder, but that he was pleading guilty because he faced the threat of the death penalty if he did not do so."[22] After his trial, Alford appealed and claimed that his guilty plea was the product of force or coercion because he had been facing the death penalty. The Supreme Court decided that his plea was not coerced and that it was lawful for the judge to accept Alford's guilty plea even though he maintained his factual and legal innocence. Instead of risking execution, Alford decided to throw in the towel and take a thirty-year sentence. In today's world of federal criminal law, many defendants will find themselves weighing reasons similar to Alford's that might lead them to take a plea bargain, including the recognition that innocence is all too often not an adequate and effective defense to a federal prosecution.

The Court's decision in *Alford* is a double-edged sword for defendants. In the short run, defendants situated similarly to Alford might benefit by being able to plead guilty and exchange the certainty of a lower sentence for the risky uncertainty of a much more onerous sentence. In the long run, however, *Alford* is bad news for federal defendants and the federal criminal justice system in particular, because it means those prosecutions will never go to trial and that, in turn, those prosecutions will never be challenged in appeals courts. In the longest view, federal prosecutors who exploit vague statutes are the biggest beneficiaries of the Court's decision in *Alford* precisely because they can structure deals that 1) defendants cannot refuse and that 2) mean that the prosecutors' creative interpretations of the laws are unlikely to be challenged or overturned through judicial review. The combination of *Alford* and *Singleton*, in the context of a system of federal laws that so often simply cannot be understood, has paved the way to an inescapable conclusion that the federal criminal justice system has become a crude conviction machine instead of an engine of truth and justice.

• • ● • •

This phenomenon, the synergy between vague statutes and coercive prosecutorial tactics, explains the anecdote told by Tim Wu in a 2007 article titled "American Lawbreaking," published in the online magazine *Slate*:

> At the federal prosecutor's office in the Southern District of New York, the staff, over beer and pretzels, used to play a darkly humorous game. Junior and senior prosecutors would sit around, and someone would name a random celebrity—say, Mother Theresa or John Lennon. It would then be up to the junior prosecutors to figure out a plausible crime for which to indict him or her. The crimes were not usually rape, murder, or other crimes you'd see on Law & Order but rather the incredibly broad yet obscure crimes that populate the U.S. Code like a kind of jurisprudential minefield: Crimes like "false statements" (a felony, up to five years), "obstructing the mails" (five years), or "false pretenses on the high seas" (also five years). The trick and the skill lay in finding the more obscure offenses that fit the character of the celebrity and carried the toughest sentences. The result, however, was inevitable: "prison time," as one former prosecutor told me.[23]

This is precisely the expansion of the criminal code that Justice Jackson warned of more than half a century ago. But there is an added danger that Jackson did not foresee: as the criminal code became broader, it also became more and more vague, or at least it has been interpreted so by prosecutors and often by courts as well. Because of this vagueness, the federal criminal law has become too often a trap for the unwary honest citizen instead of a legitimate tool for protecting society. There are too many people behind bars today who honestly believed, for good and sufficient reasons, that they acted in conformity with the law. Justice Jackson perceived the very early stages of the transformation (some would say perversion) of federal criminal law into such a trap. He decried the failure to limit federal prosecutions and convictions to people who knowingly and intentionally violated reasonably knowable legal duties, as is the ancient common law tradition.

Let's be clear. All segments of civil society and a wide variety of seemingly innocuous behaviors are at risk of being criminalized by an overzealous Justice Department ("civil society" being defined roughly as the private sector, even if one's work is government-regulated to some degree). The increasing power the federal government exerts over every element of the private sector, as demonstrated by the power to investigate, prosecute, and even convict defendants who have not committed a clearly defined crime, is a threat to the nation as a whole. Quite simply, it undermines a critical tension, an essential balance of power, between the government and the governed.

Consider some of the cases that will be discussed in more detail further on in this book:

Philip Russell, a lawyer from Greenwich, Connecticut, was indicted in 2007 for obstruction of justice because he destroyed child pornography, despite the fact that child porn is illegal even to possess ("contraband") and therefore holding, rather than destroying it, arguably would be criminal.

Michael Milken, under threat that the Department of Justice would prosecute his younger brother if the older brother did not take a plea bargain, pled guilty in 1990 to a felony that a judge later ruled (in a trial against a Milken cohort) did not constitute a crime.

The Department of Justice in 2002 indicted, and then convicted Arthur Andersen & Company, at the time one of the nation's "Big Five" accounting firms, for obstruction of justice simply because the firm followed its normal document-retention-and-destruction policy *before* receiving a document-production subpoena in connection with the government's investigation of Enron Corporation. By the time the Supreme Court unanimously reversed the conviction (because the jury had been instructed that it could convict even in the absence of any type of dishonesty), the firm had gone out of business. Faced with the threat of a ruinous prosecution on the basis of similarly dubious claims of wrongdoing, KPMG (a member of the then-remaining "Big Four"), believing that discretion was the better part of valor, admitted to readily refutable guilt and betrayed its former partners and employees in order to survive.

Federal prosecutors indicted Steven Kurtz, a college professor and politically radical artist living in Buffalo, New York, on a mail fraud charge in 2004 for engaging in a transaction that professors around the country engage in routinely. In truth, the mail fraud charge was simply a way for the government to justify the countless man-hours the FBI poured into the case after falsely, indeed bizarrely, concluding that Kurtz's cutting-edge artwork amounted to bioterrorism.

The Department of Justice reportedly looked into indicting *The New York Times* (and its top editors and reporters) for espionage for running a front-page story that exposed the National Security Agency's arguably unlawful warrantless communications surveillance program.

These are just a few of the prosecutions in which well-meaning professionals from all walks of life have been charged (or nearly charged) criminally for engaging in activities that most of us—lawyers and laymen alike—would consider lawful, often quite ordinary, and frequently socially beneficial. How has this happened?

Three Felonies
a Day

•••

How the Feds Target
the Innocent

HARVEY A. SILVERGLATE

CHAPTER ONE

Reeling in the Great White, and Other Tales of Fishing for State and Local Pols

— ●●● —

In column after column during the 1990s, *Miami Herald* columnist Carl Hiaasen obsessed over the "culture of corruption" besetting South Florida. One focus of his ire was Raul Martinez, the popular mayor of Hialeah, a heavily Cuban-American city just outside of Miami. Hiaasen was hardly a lone wolf howling in the wilderness: over the years Martinez would survive three corruption trials brought by the Florida U.S. attorney's office. Yet even Hiaasen thought the feds should call it quits after the second trial, when jurors voted 11-1 for acquittal. "[N]ot because he's innocent," the crusading columnist assured his readers, but because "most Hialeah voters adore Raul," having consistently returned him to office in spite of his legal travails. Still, all was not lost, in Hiaasen's opinion. The unsuccessful trials against Martinez provided "valuable civics lessons, proving beyond any doubt that Hialeah is as relentlessly corrupt as everybody assumed."[1]

But was Raul Martinez "corrupt"? Or was he an ordinary local politician, even a pol of above-average skill and charisma, who fell prey to a fishing expedition by federal prosecutors hell-bent on using every legal tool in their arsenal to assert their authority over local political arrangements? The press, all too eager to parade its hard-boiled realism while mounting the pedestal of moral guardianship, rarely bothers to ask such questions about the motives of federal prosecutors and the real offenses of state and local political figures. And yet one day, the feds would come after the Fourth Estate too, armed with many of the same statutes and misplaced legal arguments it began applying in the 1980s to pols.

Martinez was and remains something of a rarity in South Florida: a Cuban-American Democrat who garners political support from a broad spectrum of the area's enormously diverse electorate.[2] He came to Hialeah as a child, then married and had two children. After founding a Spanish-language weekly newspaper with his father, Martinez, like many successful professionals in that fast-growing part of the state, dabbled in real estate development. Elected to the Hialeah City Council in 1977, the ambitious Martinez quickly challenged the Democratic machine, which was run by then-mayor Dale Bennett. Martinez won the mayoral election, and his political career took off as he gained the trust and support of many segments of the community. He attracted a wide array of political supporters who felt that they wanted to hitch a ride on his star. It was widely thought that he was being groomed to run for the seat of legendary long-time Democratic Congressman Claude Pepper, with whom Martinez had developed a friendship. Such was Martinez's popularity that in 1982 the Florida legislature established new district lines that placed Martinez's residence in Representative Pepper's district.

On the Republican side, leaders were grooming then-State Representative Ileana Ros-Lehtinen. She was the daughter of a Cuban immigrant, Enrique Ros, who was a leader of Miami's large, predominantly Republican, and vociferously anti-Castro Cuban community. It would be an uphill climb for any Democrat to beat Ros-Lehtinen for Claude Pepper's seat, but Martinez, an evident up-and-comer, seemed poised to do precisely that.

State and federal investigators had long looked into allegations of corruption among local political bodies in Hialeah. In early 1985, *The Miami Herald* published a series of articles claiming that members of the Hialeah Zoning Board and City Council were "selling" their votes to developers in exchange for receiving lots or shares in the projects. As bad as that sounds, it's important to put these allegations in context. Florida laws governing local political office-holders are similar to those in most states. Local politicians are allowed, if not encouraged, to maintain private careers and businesses to support themselves and their families. Salaries paid to such political figures typically are modest, necessitating that anyone other than those with inherited or earned wealth maintain an income-generating occupation while in public office. In the 1980s, members of the Hialeah Zoning Board were unsalaried volunteers, while city councilors were paid a mere $2,600 per year, and the mayor's salary hovered around $50,000. Since such officials are paid so little in their elected positions, it might well be seen as a perk of office that one is allowed to parlay one's importance and prestige into increased business success. At the very least, state and local laws and political culture tolerate local officials' engaging in private business dealings that almost certainly benefit from their holding municipal office, as long as they do not engage in official acts, such as voting on municipal bodies on matters that directly affect their own financial interests. In an area where real estate development was exploding and where local city councils and zoning boards maintained dockets crowded with petitions for enactment of or relief from laws, it was perhaps inevitable that Martinez's civic life would fuse to some degree with his professional work.

What's crucial to bear in mind here is that states and municipalities do prescribe limits to these relationships, and in fairly straightforward terms. Typically, state and municipal conflict-of-interest laws prohibit public officials from playing both ends of a project or business venture. Moving to more serious criminal infractions, bribery takes place when the businessman initiates the idea of a payment, and it is extortion when the public official demands payment to refrain from harming the citizen's interests.

In 1989, a state investigation of Martinez had just closed, finding nothing in the way of bribery or extortion to pin on the mayor. Still, the federal investigation continued and, after the death of Representative Pepper, the feds ramped it up. "The timing raises further questions about the motivation of the prosecution," wrote *The Miami Herald*.

The United States Attorney at the time was Dexter Lehtinen, whose wife expressed interest in replacing Pepper when he had fallen ill.[3] Sure enough, Martinez dropped out of the congressional race when the corruption investigation made its way into the press. And Ileana Ros-Lehtinen sought and won Pepper's seat after his death.

Lehtinen did not want for doubters and critics. A "high-level administration source" was quoted in the *Herald* as saying that "of all the U.S. attorneys around the country, he was by far the one we scratched our heads about the most."[4] There were reports that the seriously wounded Vietnam War vet motivated his assistant prosecutors to win cases "by waving a plastic model of a Kalashnikov AK-47 assault rifle at a full staff meeting and handing out printed slogans: 'No Guts, No Glory.'" Stories circulated about Lehtinen's frequent volcanic tirades at staff meetings and elsewhere.[5] Writer T. D. Allman described Lehtinen in *Vanity Fair* as a Captain Queeg-like character who, a former subordinate told the writer, "runs this office the way Noriega ran Panama, through terror, fear, and intimidation."[6]

To quiet his critics while his wife ran for one of the state's highest offices, Lehtinen claimed that he was stepping out of the Martinez investigation and prosecution, leaving the decisions to the rest of his staff. And decide they did: On April 3, 1990, Martinez was charged in a complex, 64-page indictment alleging, at its center, a "racketeering conspiracy" and the crime of extortion under the federal Hobbs Act.[7]

For the most part, the technique by which the alleged extortion was accomplished was that real estate developers cut Martinez in on deals by selling him parcels of property at below-market prices. A typical deal for which Martinez was indicted was the Marivi Gardens project. Silvio Cardoso, star government witness, was an unsuccessful candidate for City Council in 1977. In the next election, he won after allying himself with the then-mayor and political boss Dale Bennett, who had built up a formidable political machine. When Martinez challenged and beat the Bennett mayoral machine in 1981, Cardoso switched sides and moved into Martinez's camp. Cardoso testified that his change of allegiance occurred because "I saw he [Martinez] was doing a good job for the city, and I worked with him. We worked on a lot of things together, the mutual respect for each other broadened where we have developed a friendship."[8]

The following year, Cardoso began to take advantage of his relationship with the new mayor. He decided to purchase and develop a plot of land named "Marivi Gardens." He needed a zoning variance to build more extensively on the property. Not surprisingly, Cardoso approached Martinez to see if he would be his partner. Cardoso explained that if he and the mayor became business partners, it would cement their friendship. He also believed that if the popular mayor were a partner in the project, it would attract buyers for the completed units. Martinez indicated his interest. Cardoso signed the purchase contract for the undeveloped property in January 1983.

Cardoso's application for the zoning variance for Marivi Gardens needed a recommendation from the Zoning Board to the City Council. When the matter came up before the Council, Cardoso, a member, abstained because of his interest in the project. The variance was allowed. Cardoso followed through on his purchase of the property in December 1983. Earlier that year, Martinez told Cardoso that he wanted to purchase one of the lots, but Cardoso replied that he intended to give, not sell, the lot to his newfound friend and political ally.

Cardoso further testified that he and Martinez never discussed anything that Cardoso expected Martinez to do. And, it must be recalled, Cardoso by this time was an immunized cooperating witness for the government, under pressure to help the prosecution. Nonetheless, he never said that Martinez had ever threatened him in any way. Nor did Martinez threaten to veto Cardoso's zoning applications, even though a veto was within his power.

Cardoso denied that Martinez's official power to obstruct the project had any reason to do with his wanting to give the mayor the plot. Rather, his motive was more generalized: "I felt it would be to my benefit politically, and economically in the future." Cardoso also noted that, if he cemented his business and personal relationship with Martinez, the mayor would refer real estate deals in Hialeah to Cardoso, because Martinez "did not have the time" to do them himself. "I would basically broker the deal."

As a result, Cardoso transferred the gift lot to Martinez, who duly declared it as income on his 1984 tax return. Three years later, Martinez sold the lot for $45,000. As Cardoso had anticipated, when he ran for election to the City Council in 1983, Martinez not only contributed to his campaign and helped get others to do so, he also escorted the candidate around Hialeah's campaign trail. Martinez even advised on the preparation of campaign literature. Cardoso was right: A business and friendship relationship with a popular and successful public official was not bad for business or political life.

Another government witness, Renan Delgado, testified similarly in connection with another real estate deal, Steve's Estates. Delgado sold property to Martinez on favorable terms, explaining that Martinez provided useful advice and assistance in his business. Delgado elaborated:

> Everybody wanted to be friends with the [mayor]—in the city where you work. He's my friend, but you also want to be friends, you know, for a lot of reasons. If you're in business in a city, in any city, you want to be friend[s] with your people that run the city.

Delgado's last sentence summed up quite succinctly the reigning business ethos in most municipalities. He explained that while he would have wanted to receive more of the money on the deal and give Martinez a less favorable price for the lots the mayor purchased, his decision to accept less money was "voluntary."

At this point in the story, it's necessary to step back and take a look at the law the feds used to go after Martinez. The Hobbs Act was enacted in 1951 during a period of public outcry over organized crime, essentially to deter extortionate threats by both private thugs and public officials seeking payoffs. The situation of public officials is, of course, different from that of gangsters. The latter could threaten citizens with all manner and kinds of violence to extract payments or property.

Corrupt public officials have a different tool to induce citizens to fork over money: the power inherent in political office by which officials can enrich or ruin private parties seeking government approval, assistance, or forbearance on a project.

Public sector extortion is in another way very different from extortion involving the neighborhood leg-breaker. In our political system, citizens who run for public office often have to raise significant sums of money to finance their campaigns. Campaign contributors sometimes donate out of a sense of civic virtue. Often their motive has something to do with official or unofficial legislative or executive support, or simply "greasing the wheels" for a project.

Under federal law, *bribery* of state officials (typically payments initiated by the citizen) is not a distinct federal crime, although it might be punishable under circumstances in which the citizen uses the mails or other tools of interstate commerce to carry out a violation of state law. Only *extortion* engaged in by the official violates the Hobbs Act.[9] In theory, this law is meant to prevent and punish the disruption to interstate commerce, over which the constitution gives the federal government much control, when local officials impede economic and commercial activity by blocking projects unless paid off. A major purpose of such regulation of interstate commerce has been to remove untoward burdens on the free flow of commerce. A state cannot, for example, selectively impose a tax on products made in and exported from another state, as this would disadvantage and hence slow the flow of goods from one state to another. And so, in theory, it seems reasonable for the federal government to forbid state and local officials from superimposing a "corruption tax" on economic activity.

The trouble commenced because the Supreme Court interpreted the Hobbs Act in a way that eliminated any meaningful distinction between extortion and bribery. It regards payment to a state or local official as inherently a product of the official's position and power. This becomes a serious problem for local officials who choose to continue their businesses and professions while holding public office, as we shall see in the Martinez case. Indeed, the prosecution of Raul Martinez by

Dexter Lehtinen's office demonstrates the ways in which the lack of clarity inherent in the Hobbs Act can be a prescription not so much for keeping interstate commerce free of debilitating corruption, but rather for imposing federal tyranny over local political systems and, not so incidentally, evening political scores and affecting electoral outcomes.

At bottom, the prosecution's case at the trial was all over the place: The mayor had used, or taken advantage of, or merely benefited from his official position in order to coerce, or accept, financial tribute from those whom he had the power to hurt or to refrain from helping. A delicate dance was played out, the feds alleged, between a fawning, sycophantic, and generous citizen-businessman, and a powerful local pol who remained in private business during his term in elective office and did not wall himself off from projects requiring government approvals.

In their lunge at Martinez, the feds also employed a technique dubbed "ladder climbing," once engaged in sparingly but now in greater, indeed routine, use. The idea is simple and operates much like it sounds: The feds put pressure on those in the lower reaches of the system, here, the citizen businessmen, in order to get them to testify against those above them on the ladder. Those who do not readily cooperate are threatened with prosecution, and they then face a choice between serving a long prison term or giving testimony deemed helpful to the prosecution of higher-ups. Some are actually prosecuted and become cooperative witnesses just before their trials, or after conviction and before sentence. Sometimes it takes an actual heavy sentence to coerce the witness.

The technique used to pressure witnesses in the Martinez case was a variation on this theme. Each of the developer "victims" of Martinez's alleged abuse of his official powers was deemed not only a victim of Martinez's extortion, but a co-conspirator in the criminal enterprise. And each was given immunity by Lehtinen's office in exchange for testimony. Such immunity was necessary to get the cooperation and testimony of the "victim" of the extortionate activity of the mayor. Without it, the victim-witness could incriminate himself by testifying and admitting to his role in giving the mayor a cut of the projects in exchange for official favors—at the very least a possible state bribery offense.

Sometimes witnesses seek immunity in exchange for their coopera-tion, but at other times immunity is imposed on them by a prosecutor who obtains an "immunity order" from a judge. The bottom line of an immunity order is that nothing the witness says in his or her testi-mony can be used by a prosecutor or court in a criminal case against the witness.

The defense's case consisted largely of cross-examining the govern-ment's witnesses to demonstrate that none of them was ever threatened by Martinez, nor was anyone offered zoning help in exchange for any financial advantage conferred on the mayor. Importantly, the defense pointed out to the jury that in Hialeah, as in most of Florida at the time, local political officials were expected to maintain outside employment and business interests. Indeed, part of Martinez's defense was precisely that he was on the way up, and therefore local business people vied to associate themselves with him. The immunized witnesses who testified for the government were hardly alone in wanting to hitch themselves to the Martinez political star. As one Florida House of Representatives member testified in the defense case:

> Mr. Martinez was so highly regarded in all parts of Dade County. He was one of the few Hispanics because he was so fluent in English, [who] was accepted wherever he went, and was very courteous to everybody. He was accepted in the Black community and in the Hispanic community and, of course, in the Anglo community.

Martinez's defense thus sounded very much like the government's prosecution theory. Businessmen gave Martinez good deals to encour-age him to ally himself with them and their enterprises, because they believed that their association with Martinez would be of enormous benefit to them. To the U.S. attorney's office, this was an extortionate (threatening) use of Martinez's official power. To the defense, it was a natural result of the combination of Martinez's golden career pros-pects, his official position and myriad contacts, and the realities and normal expectations of local politics involving, in particular, public of-ficials who earn only token compensation. (In addition to traditionally low salaries for these offices, there is the matter of campaign expenses. Cardoso testified that in 1983 he spent some $100,000 on his own campaign, and won a position that paid $17,000 per year.)

If there are to be legal limitations to this cozy but quite logical symbiotic arrangement, it would have to be imposed by clear conflict-of-interest or other laws limiting the business activities of public officials. It would also have to be accompanied, presumably, by increasing their salaries, without which there would be a clear risk that the middle class would absent itself from running for local elective office. Were public officials not allowed to earn a living while serving in public positions that pay very little, government would become the fiefdom of the wealthy (or, of course, the thoroughly corrupt). Martinez's business activities were conducted in the open, with money passing by check, not cash, and with properties passing by legal title held in the name of the mayor, not of a straw man. And still, he was indicted for extortion.

As Martinez's first trial concluded, it appeared that the scales were tipping toward the prosecution. Just before trial, Judge James Kehoe instructed the jurors about the law that would govern their deliberations. The prosecutors argued to the judge that the Hobbs Act did not require them to demonstrate a so-called specific *quid pro quo*, that is, something of value given by the public official to the businessman in exchange for something of value from the businessman. To convict Martinez, they had to prove only that the mayor engaged in merely "passive acceptance" of the benefits that his business dealings could bring him, "so long as the defendant knew or believed that the benefits he was receiving [were] motivated by a hope of influence." Betraying their complete ignorance of—or perhaps contempt for—the workings of local politics and the economic realities facing middle class candidates, the prosecutors added: "[I]f a politician wants to make money in business transactions, then he can stay out of politics."

Judge Kehoe bought the prosecution's argument and explained to the jury that the "passive acceptance of a benefit" by a public official constituted extortion "if the official knows he had been offered the payment in exchange for the exercise of his official power" or—and here is the

rub that likely got Martinez convicted—"that such payment is motivated by hope of influence." As for the question of whether Martinez
was "entitled" to the property given to him, that's a pretty slippery concept. While Cardoso did not "owe" Martinez participation in the deal,
the developer did perceive a business benefit to himself by involving
the popular politician.

Given the testimony and the jury instructions, it was no surprise that
the jury, while acquitting on several of the projects, convicted Martinez
of extortion relating to four of the deals. On July 22, 1991, Judge Kehoe
sentenced Martinez to a ten-year prison term. Lehtinen emerged victorious. Yet it was a Pyrrhic victory, since Lehtinen was forced to re-
sign just months later, due to his own erratic behavior. Martinez, now a
convicted felon, won re-election while awaiting appeal; and in 1994 the
Court of Appeals for the 11th Circuit reversed Martinez's conviction,
ruling that Kehoe had erred in his instructions to the jury by blur-
ring the line between extortionate threats and other non-threatening
arrangements by which a citizen might do business with a politician.[10]
This paved the way for a retrial that commenced in March 1996.

At Martinez's second trial, the jury, instructed in accordance with
the Court of Appeals' decision in the reversal of the first Martinez conviction, deadlocked, voting 11-1 for acquittal. Despite the prosecutors'
obvious inability to convince all but one juror that Martinez was an
extortionist, the U.S. attorney's office, this time without Lehtinen (who
had stepped down under fire), decided to pursue *a third trial*. When
that ended in acquittals on some counts and deadlock on others, the
government finally gave up.

Raul Martinez remained mayor of Hialeah, as the voters wished.
Almost two decades after his first congressional campaign, Martinez ran
again for Florida's 18th District in 2008, this time with significant support from the Democratic higher-ups. Yet his bid failed after a series of
October attack ads devastated the campaign.[11] Punctuated by the sound
of a prison cell door slamming, one ad claimed: "We know Martinez
is corrupt enough for Washington. But that doesn't mean we should
send him there." Despite the DOJ's repeated failures to tag Martinez as

a felon (much less as a prisoner), the damage was done. Even when the
federal prosecutorial juggernaut fails to directly dispatch its prey, the
wreckage can still destroy the lives of the powerful and the popular.

• • ● • •

The vagueness of the Hobbs Act, combined with the expanded use of
aggressive ladder climbing, made local politicians increasingly vulnerable to politically or professionally ambitious U.S. attorneys. Nowhere
was this more evident than in Boston in the early-1980s. It was a turbulent time in the city's political history, as the fabled City on a Hill aggressively sought to shed its image as a dilapidated backwater. Having
survived the embarrassment of the school busing wars of the previous
decade, then-Mayor Kevin Hagan White, whose father and grandfather both served as Boston City Council presidents, earned high marks
for restructuring municipal government and leading a campaign to
revitalize the historic Faneuil Hall/Quincy Market merchant district—
one of the country's first urban malls. Democratic Senator George
McGovern seriously considered White as a potential running mate in
his 1972 presidential bid, and many political insiders believed White
would eventually parlay his local popularity into his own run for 1600
Pennsylvania Avenue.

But before White could contemplate higher office, he would have
to survive a massive attack launched by an emerging political adversary named William Floyd Weld, who was appointed U.S. attorney
for Massachusetts by President Ronald Reagan in 1981. A graduate of
Harvard College (*summa cum laude*, 1966) and Harvard Law School
(*cum laude*, 1970) and the scion of a wealthy and prominent blueblood
family, Weld cut a decidedly patrician figure. Some suspected that he
had his own aspirations for high elective office, both state and federal.
His Republican and Yankee heritage, however, required Weld first to
prove himself in the rough-and-tumble world of Bay State politics.

As Weld assumed the U.S. attorney's mantle in 1981, a spate of high-
profile state and local political corruption prosecutions, most resulting in convictions, splashed across the papers. And they continued to

splash throughout Weld's tenure. *The Boston Globe*, Boston's influential regional equivalent of *The Miami Herald*, cheered on Weld and decried the local corruption without paying adequate attention to the details and the deeper issues of the proper and reasonable line to be drawn between true corruption and accepted local culture. The paper gleefully played Weld's cleverly orchestrated tune in a titillating 1984 article headlined: "[O]fficial corruption reaches dizzying heights."[12]

It was not unusual to have sudden eruptions of political corruption (or suspicions of corrupt activities) appear on the urban scene. For the politically ambitious Weld, however, the timing of Boston's focus on corruption couldn't have been more fortuitous. An aggressive crusade against patronage, culminating in the indictment of the high-profile mayor himself, would open up for Weld all avenues to the governor's corner office in Massachusetts' iconic Bullfinch-designed State House, with the distant gleam of the White House slowly appearing on the horizon.

There was only one problem: either Kevin White was cleaner than Caesar's proverbial wife, or he was exceedingly careful about not leaving an incriminating trail. With no detectable scent, much less hard evidence, emanating from White's office, the Department of Justice and the FBI began snooping around the lower reaches of Boston's infamous bureaucracy, where some sort of petty corruption could almost always be found regardless of who was the mayor. Climb the ladder by convicting lower-echelon functionaries and make deals in exchange for their testimony against their immediate higher-ups, went the theory, and Weld would eventually reach the mayor. And, as became evident to close observers of the subsequent unfolding legal proceedings, the U.S. attorney had the benefit of a then-nascent trend in federal law that allowed Weld to craft some of his criminal charges on the basis of conduct that was not so obviously criminal.

While Weld himself had no significant investigatory or trial experience, he assembled a crackerjack prosecutorial team to nab the mayor. The prosecutors got their opportunity to pursue White when they hooked a petty bureaucrat in the city's Building Department, who was also a former senior administrative assistant in the Boston Redevelopment Authority (BRA). Caught in a tape-recorded sting holding up a contractor, George Collatos pleaded guilty to extortion and subsequent perjury, admitting his attempt to extort $45,000 (though he had managed to grab only $12,500 before he was caught) from a local concrete company seeking the department's approval to build a plant in Boston. In 1982, he was sentenced to three years in federal prison.

Weld cut Collatos a deal. He would have his sentence reduced if Collatos would testify as to who higher up in the administration was in on this and other corrupt deals. Collatos did not have a sufficiently close relationship with Mayor White to convincingly claim that White was using Collatos as his bag man. However, Collatos did peddle the story that Theodore Anzalone (soon to be my law firm's client), an informal long-time fundraiser and intimate of White, conspired with Collatos to extort an $8,000 cash payment from the C.E. Maguire Company of Providence, a company with contracts to provide engineering services to the massive rebuilding projects undertaken at the time by the BRA. According to the resulting indictment, Collatos contacted John Slocum, president of the firm, in 1979 and told Slocum that he would have to pay Anzalone, acting for the mayor, a cash bribe to retain the city's business. Slocum supposedly handed two $4,000 cash payments to Anzalone in sealed envelopes, all arranged by Collatos. Anzalone, Collatos maintained, both insisted on the cash solicitation and knew that the money constituted a bribe destined for White.

Weld's strategy was to get Anzalone convicted of extortion by way of Collatos's testimony, fleshed out with some supportive declarations from Slocum, who was given a complete pass for any wrongdoing on his part. Pressure would then be exerted on Anzalone to implicate White, since neither Slocum nor Collatos could believably testify to any personal dealing with the mayor that would indicate the money ultimately was going to—or did—make its way to the top. According to this theory, only Anzalone, the mayor's intimate, could credibly implicate White.

It is a very dangerous mind-set in federal prosecutors that induces them to "climb the ladder" from the lower echelons up to the offices of the top officials. All too often, it matters little if there is not *yet* any actual evidence that a mayor is corrupt. The possibility that corrupt lower-echelon extortionate officials might be "on a frolic of their own" is too often discounted, in the hope of landing someone at the top. Nor did federal officials in Boston have any solid reason to believe that Anzalone could deliver truthful testimony against the boss. They were all too prepared to believe someone like Collatos, who boasted of his higher connection with Anzalone. Prosecutors in this type of case manage to convince themselves that "the fish rots from the head down," and that if they continue "squeezing" the underlings, they will eventually get something on the mayor. This mentality was (and remains) so pervasive within the Department of Justice that one could sense it animating the conduct even of prosecutors like Mark L. Wolf and Robert J. Cordy who, then and since, have enjoyed reputations for unquestioned probity and went on to attain high judicial positions where they distinguished themselves.[13]

Weld's team had a shaky case even at the lowest rung of the ladder, and they knew it. Collatos, the prosecutors realized, would not be the most credible witness. And proving that Anzalone had violated the federal extortion statute would require a credible witness testifying to a specific set of actions. The extortion statute, in theory, is triggered if payments are made in response to threats of loss of benefits if payments are not made. If the payments were voluntary campaign contributions, even if in arguable violation of *state* campaign financing laws restricting cash contributions, they were not evidence of *federal* extortion.

The discovery by Weld's investigators of two other transactions involving White and Anzalone kept alive the hunt for White's scalp. Combining the Maguire Company payoff allegations with two additional instances in which Anzalone was engaging in large cash transactions on behalf of White would virtually assure Anzalone's conviction on the extortion charge, they figured. The cash, the jury would likely conclude, even in the absence of any direct evidence of a link, *must* have come from the pattern of extortion engaged in by White with Anzalone's assistance as middleman. Upon closer inspection, however, as Weld and his team would learn three years later—though not until a grueling and ultimately fruitless prosecution ruined more than one man's life—the devil was not in the details this time around.

The first transactions involved a birthday party planned for the mayor's wife, Kathryn, to be held in March 1981 at Boston's renowned Museum of Fine Arts. The fete was cancelled, reportedly because city workers planned to picket the site. The state Ethics Commission conducted an investigation and found that Anzalone was a key fundraiser for the event. The commission also found that cash (presumably raised for both the party and a planned birthday gift for Mrs. White) had moved through different bank accounts in what some surmised to be an effort to disguise its origins. Neither the commission nor federal investigators, however, ever learned precisely from whom the cash *originally* came. Nonetheless, the feds added a count to its indictment of Anzalone (who was being charged with conspiracy, predicated on Collatos's testimony, to extort the C.E. Maguire Company) alleging that he and his associates distributed packets of cash to various individuals who, in turn, contributed the money, in the form of their personal checks, to the birthday party fund. The Ethics Commission concluded that 64 persons, all of whom were tied to White or the city administration, managed to pass some $50,000 to the birthday party fund via this circuitous route. When the party was cancelled, Anzalone gave refund checks to the 64 individuals, who cashed them and then returned the cash to Anzalone. The trail stopped there, at Anzalone.

In adding the birthday party saga to the indictment, the feds put to use a tactically clever mechanism to increase their chances of convicting Anzalone of the C. E. Maguire Company extortion charge. Without Anzalone's testimony, prosecutors could not determine the source of the birthday party cash. Weld, with no hard evidence, suspected that the money belonged to White as the product of presumed illegal payoffs. What seemed clear was that the bulk of the birthday party fund did not contain money actually belonging to the 64 donors. Only Anzalone, went the theory, could tell the feds where the money originated. The feds obviously wanted to put pressure on Anzalone to sing, but first they had to get him convicted so that they could make a deal. If the extortion charge and the birthday party money-laundering charge were tied and tried together, the jury would be led to speculate and conclude that somehow the birthday party cash must have been connected to an extortion enterprise.

The second money-laundering charge was even more strained. The indictment alleged that Anzalone transferred $100,000 in cash—the origins of which, yet again, the feds could not pinpoint—into a New York brokerage account set up in the names of the mayor's wife (Kathryn) and mother (Patricia). The supposed laundering device this time was cash Anzalone took to various branches of the Haymarket Cooperative Bank in the Boston area in November 1980, for which he received bank checks in return. Each check was in an amount between $5,000 and $9,000. The checks were then deposited in the brokerage account and Anzalone instructed the broker to purchase tax-exempt bonds.

To a hammer, goes the saying, everything is a nail. And so it was for Weld that Anzalone's series of transactions *must* have been configured to launder money that was acquired illegally, rather than simply to hide from scrutiny the possession or source of lawfully-acquired funds. Under federal banking regulations in effect at the time, a bank was required to report to the United States Treasury any cash transaction involving more than $10,000. This reporting was to be accomplished by the bank's filing a so-called Cash Transaction Report ("CTR"). The law made clear—or at least appeared to do so—that this obligation rested with the bank and not with the depositor. However, by Anzalone's breaking up the cash into under-$10,000 installments, the bank supposedly was kept from realizing that a total of $100,000 was involved in the aggregate series of check purchases. Then-applicable law further dictated that if bank checks rather than cash were deposited with the brokerage firm, the firm did not have to report receipt of over $10,000 in cash in connection with the White brokerage account. Finally, since the money was invested in *tax-free* bonds, the mayor's wife and mother would not have to report on their respective tax returns the interest accruing in the brokerage account.

To the feds, it seemed a perfect scheme to hide illegally gotten gains, because all reporting to governmental authorities was circumvented. To nab the great White, however, Anzalone's cooperation would be needed to confirm the feds' suspicions, and that cooperation, the feds believed, could be gotten only under the pressure of Anzalone's conviction and imprisonment. Collatos was the key to unlock Anzalone's cooperation.

Adding the two money-laundering counts to the extortion charge was thus meant to further bolster Collatos's testimony by linking together additional (otherwise unlinked) cash and check transactions. The jury's common sense would conclude that the cash used to fund both the birthday party and the brokerage account, laundered ostensibly to hide its origins, came from an illegal source, in this case extortionate activities by Anzalone on behalf of White. Tied together at trial, all three transactions would support one another: the money laundering counts explaining what happened to the extortion proceeds, and the Maguire extortion count explaining the cash's origins—all without any direct evidence linking the three. If convicted, the feds believed, Anzalone would face tremendous pressure to testify, at what the feds dreamed could be Kevin White's criminal trial, to precisely such a link. Weld would have his trophy catch.

Soon, however, the fabric of the government's strategy to sew all of these events together was torn apart. The trial judge, the late A. David Mazzone, after some initial hesitation, granted Anzalone's motion to separate the trial of the extortion count from the money-laundering counts. My then-law partner Nancy Gertner and I argued that, because no proof linked these transactions, the jurors should not be allowed to speculate precisely as the feds wished them to speculate, making unproven assumptions about the origins of the cash in order to strengthen a weak extortion claim. All of a sudden, the prosecution of the extortion claim turned almost entirely on the testimony of a self-confessed small-time extortion artist-cum-perjurer, Collatos.

The money-laundering trial began on June 13, 1984. The government's witnesses testified pretty much as expected: that they had received cash from Anzalone in exchange for providing checks to the birthday party fund, after which the transactions were reversed when the party was cancelled. Haymarket Cooperative Bank officials testified that they were kept in the dark by Anzalone's breaking down the transaction into under-$10,000 increments, resulting in their failure to file CTR reports.

The surprise, if any, came in the defense's case. Robert Coviello, a Boston lawyer, testified that Anzalone, an acquaintance for 20 years, asked for advice in 1980 as to whether he could lawfully take $100,000 in cash and invest it for Anzalone's client, Patricia White, without having to report the investment. Coviello testified that he advised Anzalone it would be lawful for him to break up the cash into under-$10,000 segments and to purchase a series of bank checks. Because each transaction would involve less than the $10,000 reporting-trigger figure, the bank would not have to report the transaction to the Department of the Treasury. "In my opinion, it was legal to take a large cash transaction and reduce it into a series of checks of $10,000 and less," Coviello told the jury. "There was no problem with it."

The defense theory was simple. The bank, while obligated to report cash transactions in excess of $10,000, did not know that each transaction was part of a series totaling $100,000. It therefore did not have to report Anzalone's transactions. Conversely, Anzalone, who had no obligation either to report cash transactions at all (the statute imposed that obligation *only* on the bank) or to purchase his checks in amounts exceeding $10,000 in order to trigger the bank's reporting requirement, had broken no law by transacting his business in a way that kept the bank from having to file a report. Introducing Coviello's testimony further buttressed Anzalone's defense that he acted lawfully, in good faith, and on the advice of legal counsel.

Judge Mazzone's jury instructions, however, followed a different script. Even though the reporting requirement of cash transactions exceeding $10,000 was, on the face of the statute, the bank's, the judge said a customer like Anzalone committed a crime by breaking up a larger transaction into several smaller transactions, each non-reportable, to cause the bank to fail to file the cash transaction reports that were its legal duty. Indeed, the bank would not even realize that the series of small transactions were related. The judge's reading of the cash transaction statute and regulations effectively sealed Anzalone's fate, since the defense did not contest the prosecution's evidence, but simply its— and the judge's—reading of what the statute and regulations required. Anzalone's supposed obligation to facilitate the bank's filing a CTR, nowhere in the statute or regulations, was woven out of whole cloth.

Predictably, the jury convicted Anzalone of the cash-laundering charge. He was acquitted, however, of laundering the birthday party funds. Judge Mazzone sentenced him to a one-year prison term, six months of which were to be served with the balance suspended and accompanied by a period of probation. The judge stayed the sentence temporarily while Anzalone appealed to the U.S. Court of Appeals for the First Circuit.

As Anzalone pursued his appeal of the money-laundering conviction, Judge Mazzone went ahead with the extortion trial, which became pivotal to the government's plan to "turn" Anzalone. While unarticulated in the indictment, the charges' subtext was clear: White was in cahoots with Anzalone in the extortion racket. Yet thinking that the six-month sentence imposed by Judge Mazzone on the money-laundering conviction was insufficient to get Anzalone to cooperate, the government would need a guilty verdict in the extortion trial and hence a more daunting prison sentence looming over Anzalone's head to get him, as the prosecutors saw it, to betray an old friend and testify against White. It did not matter that the feds had no evidence that White had committed crimes, nor that Anzalone may not have known anything that could get the mayor indicted, much less convicted. There was an assumption that if only Anzalone would sing, the mayor could be indicted. The first step in this process would hinge on George Collatos's testimony against Anzalone.

The government's case imploded when Collatos took the stand. Unbeknownst to the judge or the prosecutors, a few months before the trial Anzalone reported to me an astonishing story. Collatos had invited Anzalone to meet him in a dilapidated coffee house in Boston's storied North End, home to the city's largest Italian-American population. At LaBella's Coffee Shop, reported Anzalone, Collatos threatened him:

Unless Collatos was paid $200,000, he would testify to Anzalone's guilt at the upcoming extortion trial, despite knowing Anzalone was in fact *not* guilty of extorting the C. E. Maguire Company. If paid, however, Collatos said he would tell the truth and Anzalone would be acquitted. In other words, Collatos was demanding a payoff from Anzalone in order to testify *truthfully*. When Anzalone pointed out that he did not have $200,000, Collatos told him to get it from Kevin White. Ever the entrepreneur, Collatos had even figured out a mechanism by which White could transfer the payoff to Collatos: for $200,000, Collatos would sell the mayor an old nag of a race horse. On the surface, it would look like a legitimate transaction, but in fact it would be a bribe to Collatos to get him to testify truthfully. Anzalone told Collatos that he needed time to think about it and left LaBella's. He rushed to my office, located on the edge of the North End, to report Collatos's threat.

After discussing this extraordinary turn of events with Gertner, I instructed Anzalone to contact Collatos to set up another meeting at LaBella's. In one of the more theatrical moments of my career, I arranged for three witnesses to be secreted in the basement of LaBella's, ensconced beneath a trap door located just under the table where Anzalone would sit with Collatos. Due to a Massachusetts law making it illegal to tape-record someone without his consent, the eyewitnesses to Collatos's threat had to be unimpeachable, and they were: John Wall, a respected, indeed legendary, former federal organized crime and political corruption prosecutor who left the Department of Justice in disgust during the Nixon administration, since then working in private law practice in Boston; and Thomas Viles, a recent Harvard College graduate working for my firm as a paralegal before heading off to law school. A legal stenographer had fled in terror after encountering a mouse when she entered the basement space, but the former prosecutor and the paralegal stayed underground and took diligent notes while Collatos proceeded, sure enough, to extort Anzalone and White for a $200,000 payoff in exchange for his testifying truthfully at Anzalone's upcoming extortion trial. Anzalone turned down the deal and both left.

What did Gertner and I do with our case-shattering evidence? We sat on it. By keeping mum until trial, we prevented the prosecutors from having the opportunity to reframe their case to get around their as yet unknown "Collatos problem"—and what a problem it was! Instead, we *wanted* the government to organize its case around Collatos and rely on his credibility. That way, we could upend both Collatos and the prosecution in one fell swoop.

Collatos took the witness stand and told the jury his well-rehearsed story, blithely unaware of the drama that would soon unfold. During the cross-examination, Gertner caught him off guard by inquiring about the LaBella's meeting. Collatos tried to play dumb, but toward the end of his testimony he became increasingly evasive and visibly nervous. At that point, due to a technical trial rule, Gertner and I were required by the judge to indicate to him, at a hushed conference held at the side-bar of the judge's bench outside the jurors' earshot, the factual and legal basis for Gertner's continuing line of cross-examination. We disclosed to the judge and the prosecution team the whole sordid tale— the dingy café, the ensconced witnesses, the extortionate threat—that we were about to parade before the jury.

The prosecutors erupted. They desperately tried to formulate a convincing argument why the judge should exclude from the jury's knowledge this shocking evidence. They argued surprise. In reality, they must have known it was a lost cause. Gertner and I had no legal and ethical obligation to report to *them* Collatos's attempted extortion of Anzalone as soon as it happened. We had given the feds a taste of their own medicine, and they knew it. We had kept our "undercover" operation under wraps until it was time to spring the trap.

In a blatant attempt to intimidate the key eyewitnesses to Collatos's threat, two FBI agents visited paralegal Viles in the middle of the night. Viles reported that the agents threatened him with prosecution for "misprision of a felony," a federal statutory crime for failure to report a witnessed felony to the authorities. Viles told them to leave, but was understandably shaken up the next day. Gertner and I assured Viles that, in our view, neither he nor we had committed misprision, since the Supreme Court had some time ago limited the scope of that statute. Wall likewise received a middle-of-the-night visit.

Despite the FBI's threats, Viles dutifully testified as to what he had witnessed in the North End, as did Wall, who was more experienced in the ways of the Department of Justice (and whom the FBI agents proved utterly incapable of shaking). The combination of the testimony of a recent college student, and a legendary former federal prosecutor who left the Department of Justice because he considered the then-Attorney General, John N. Mitchell, to be a liar (Mitchell indeed ended up serving a prison sentence in the Watergate scandal), had its predicted impact. With Collatos's credibility irreparably damaged, Gertner was able to deliver an argument to the jury that capitalized on the prosecution's case being covered by the stench of Collatos's extortion—the very crime the feds were trying to prove against Anzalone! The jury acquitted.

Gertner and I then focused on reversing on appeal the money-laundering conviction. We reasoned that a citizen does not have an obligation to conduct business in such a way as to *maximize* his or another's legal duties, unless there is a valid and clear law requiring him to do so. There was no such law here, and so, in the absence of requirements to the contrary, a citizen in a free society is entitled to conduct his business in as much privacy as the law allows. We were therefore fairly confident on appeal.

Ultimately, our confidence was well-placed. The Court of Appeals saw through Weld's gambit and Mazzone's misdirected jury instructions, issuing its unanimous decision on July 1, 1985.[14] Anzalone, in short, had no obligation to do other than what he did when structuring his transactions to avoid activating the bank's obligation. If the government wishes to impose such an obligation on the banking customer, admonished the Court of Appeals, "let it require so in plain language."

Perhaps the most pointed observation the Court made concerning the government's seeking effectively to transfer the bank's reporting obligation to the customer was to warn against criminal laws that fail to inform "ordinary people" as to "what conduct is prohibited." This was a crucial point. Then, in a footnote, the Court of Appeals panel discussed the infamous "principle of 'crimes by analogy'"—a hallmark of the Soviet Union, not of the United States. Indeed, under the Soviet Criminal Code, any citizen was in constant danger of being prosecuted for virtually any action if it could be analogized to or derived from *something* in the criminal code.[15] It was a sure formula for government oppression. Each citizen was perpetually susceptible to being prosecuted at the whim of the authorities for some act that the law did not clearly specify was criminal.

And so the government's hunt for Kevin White hit a wall. All the Department of Justice could do after it lost the Anzalone appeal was to persuade Congress to amend the CTR law to make structuring by the customer as much a crime as when done by the bank. [16]

But the human wreckage of the effort to indict White had been substantial, even though neither man ever saw the inside of a federal prison. The rigors of the investigation persuaded the mayor to forgo his planned run for a record fifth term in City Hall. He also shed his White House ambitions. At the end of his fourth term he left office to take a teaching position at Boston University. A relentless U. S. attorney's office, furious over its defeat, subpoenaed Boston University's then-President John R. Silber, seeking to learn if the teaching job was awarded to White in exchange for his granting the university a favorable price for a city-owned building committed, during White's tenure, to be sold to B.U. Silber, an imposing intellect and himself a famously haughty practitioner of hardball, proved invulnerable to Weld's pressure and categorically denied to the grand jury, under oath, any such payoff to White. Weld's last-ditch effort to snag the mayor faded into history. White lived quietly thereafter.

Anzalone, his law practice in tatters after nearly every one of his clients had been visited by hostile FBI agents and then hauled before the grand jury, gave up lawyering and undertook the job of maintaining buildings owned or managed by his wife, Joanne Prevost Anzalone. Anzalone was never subpoenaed to the grand jury and asked about White. The prosecutors seemingly were not confident that they would get testimony to support their suspicions unless they held over the witness's head the threat of a long prison sentence—a threat that evapo-rated with Anzalone's acquittals. Anzalone continued to insist that he could not truthfully implicate the mayor in any criminal conduct.

Despite his failure to get White, Weld parlayed his "crusading pros-ecutor" image into the Massachusetts governorship in 1990 and won a second term four years later.

• • ● • •

The prosecutions in Hialeah and Boston, based on the shifting pa-rameters of federal bribery and extortion law, signaled the early stages of an expanding trend that manifested itself in a wide variety of areas of civic, business, and cultural life in which federal criminal statutes could be stretched to cover myriad situations, some of them quite un-predictable. That trend has involved ever more vague, excessively broad federal statutes with which to ensnare and abuse fundamentally law-abiding public servants, acting in accordance with the dictates of local law and culture.

The American Bar Association (ABA) noticed the same trou-bling trend in 1993. The ABA complained, in a report issued by its Committee on Government Standards, about statutes that are inter-preted and enforced "in broad and uncertain sweep" in areas "outside the core of bribery, extortion and illegal gratuities." Such enforcement actions taken under these statutes, criticized the ABA report, "unfairly burden employees with the fear of unwittingly committing a federal crime."[17] "This is an area," concluded the ABA, "in which we should be especially wary of introducing the threat of criminal sanctions." When state and local statutes, ordinances, and traditions do not clearly outlaw a practice, bringing federal prosecutions under general "fraud" statutes surely unfairly catches municipal workers by surprise, and then endan-gers those higher on the ladder.

Are the feds actually serving the best interests of citizens, or do these indictments simply take issue with local political culture and control, and with the unremarkable reality that people with an "in" with city officials have an edge in getting municipal business and jobs? Shouldn't these issues be decided on the basis of state and local political and legal notions of the acceptable bounds of human nature and political culture, rather than by the feds on the basis of law enforcement's judgment as to where to draw the line defining a truly corrupt political and business environment? Shouldn't it be the job of state and local officials to enact conflict-of-interest and other such laws and regulations to determine the acceptable limits of influence in their particular region, and shouldn't federal prosecutors be required to accept these decisions? And if we as a society are willing to leave these decisions in federal law enforcers' hands, should we not at least have the right to know how and where they draw the lines? It is one thing, after all, to be under the thumb of misplaced power but quite another to be subject to *undefined* rules.

• • ● • •

As the Martinez and Anzalone prosecutions demonstrate, the pliability of federal law makes it all too easy for a self-serving U.S. attorney to take down his or her political adversaries. The situation has become more precarious, it seems, with every successive administration. The administration of George W. Bush was no exception. Staying on the good side of the nearest U.S. attorney's office is no longer enough; simply being a member of the opposition party makes one vulnerable to indictment. The preliminary results of a study by Professors Donald C. Shields and John F. Cragan found that between 2001 and 2007 the DOJ opened investigations into seven times more Democratic public officials than Republican. The professors concluded that the odds of this discrepancy being a random occurrence were one in ten thousand.[18] Indeed, a July 2008 report detailed how decision-making in the Bush administration's DOJ was wrought with political bias.[19]

Given this state of affairs, it is not surprising that many quickly expressed skepticism over the 44-page indictment of Alabama Governor Don Siegelman, the most popular and accomplished Democrat in the history of modern Alabama politics, and three others, including HealthSouth Corporation's then-Chairman and CEO Richard M. Scrushy, in 2005.

"It was a clear case of selective prosecution," opined Scott Horton in *Harper's*. "If the theory applied to the Siegelman prosecution were to be applied uniformly, many in the Bush administration would be in prison."[20]

Forty-four former state attorneys general, both Republicans and Democrats, petitioned the House and Senate Judiciary Committees in July 2007 to look into suspected "irregularities" that "call into question the basic fairness that is the linchpin of our system of justice."[21] The attorneys general voiced their collective suspicion that Siegelman might have been "the victim of a politically motivated double-standard" by the federal prosecutors who recommended a sentence of 30 years but got the judge to impose what the attorneys general deemed a "harsh" sentence of seven years and four months.

The criticisms became even more severe after Alabama lawyer and Republican activist Jill Simpson came clean and told congressional investigators that she was a player in a plot, orchestrated by U.S. attorneys in different districts in Alabama, to remove Siegelman from the political stage via indictment.[22] Siegelman himself described the case in terms of an "abuse of power" that he attributed to the influence of then-White House political operative Karl Rove and then-Attorney General Alberto Gonzales.[23]

But with all this focus on the politics behind the prosecution, critics lost sight of the real story: Siegelman was prosecuted based upon conduct that by no reasonable stretch could be considered a crime. Or, perhaps more to the point, the conduct involved would not likely be seen by most public officials, or even by lawyers, as illegal.

The heart of the indictment focused on $500,000 in donations made by Scrushy, an important figure in the Alabama health care industry, in 1999 to a cause Siegelman frequently championed: the creation of a state lottery, the proceeds of which would fund the public school system. The pro-lottery campaign was ultimately unsuccessful and amassed a debt of nearly one million dollars. Scrushy's first installment of $250,000 helped fund the lottery effort, while a second installment of $250,000 went toward retiring the lottery campaign's debt. Later that year, Siegelman appointed Scrushy to the State of Alabama Certificate of Need Review Board ("CON Board"), a panel that decides if state hospitals may add new services.

Prosecutors alleged that the donations constituted a bribe of a public official.[24] Out of this one act, they alleged a violation of the federal bribery statute,[25] a criminal conspiracy,[26] a violation of the honest services mail fraud statute,[27] and extortion.[28] To top it all off, because the indictment fashioned the conduct as a racketeering enterprise, the defendants were subject to the draconian penalties of the federal Racketeer Influenced Corrupt Organization ("RICO") law.[29]

There were numerous problems with the indictment. For one thing, as Horton points out in *Harper's*,[30] Scrushy gained nothing from the alleged bribe. He had already served in this uncompensated position on the CON Board under three former governors. He testified, without contradiction, that he did not even want the position, but considered it a public service. This claim is bolstered by the fact that, in their indictment, prosecutors were never able to point to a single instance in which appointment to this board benefited Scrushy or his company financially. As Julian McPhillips, one of Montgomery, Alabama's foremost trial lawyers put it, "the CON board did not, and does not, regulate HealthSouth, nor does it regulate any other health care company in Alabama."[31]

Siegelman and his supporters throughout the ordeal took the position that the Scrushy contribution to an issues-oriented campaign (none of the money went to Siegelman nor his election campaign fund), and his subsequent reappointment to a volunteer position on a state board was routine political activity. This stance seems entirely correct, or at least perfectly reasonable. "George W. Bush singled out 146 individuals who gave or gathered $100,000 (to his actual political campaign) for appointment to far more desirable postings as ambassadors, cabinet officers, or members of his transition team. Not a single one of these appointments triggered a Justice Department investigation," wrote Horton.[32]

The combination of the slipperiness of federal bribery law, a hostile judge, and some questionable prosecutorial tactics appears to have led to Siegelman's conviction.

The judge in the case, Mark Everett Fuller, a long-time Alabama GOP insider and former member of the Alabama Republican Party's Executive Committee, drew the wrath of the bipartisan former state attorneys general not only for denying Siegelman, who was not a flight-risk, the right to remain free on bail pending his appeal, but also because "the shackling of the Governor in handcuffs and leg irons as he was taken out of the courtroom was shocking."

When Siegelman's lawyers asked the Court of Appeals for the 11th Circuit to release their client during the appeal on the strength of the substantial legal questions that the case presented, the appellate court twice sent the bail-pending-appeal question back to Judge Fuller, who twice declined the appellate court's pointed invitation for him to reconsider his denials. Finally, the Court of Appeals on its own ordered Siegelman released while the court studied what it deemed the "substantial question" raised by Siegelman as to the propriety of his conviction.[33] Presumably, the question of whether Siegelman's conduct constituted any crime at all will eventually be decided by the courts.

• ● ● •

Even when the law seems relatively clear, local and state politicians can find themselves in a world of trouble if a U.S. attorney is determined to go after them. Although bribery and extortion charges are the most favored weapons, resourceful federal prosecutors have much more in their arsenal.

The indictment of former Massachusetts House of Representatives Speaker Thomas Finneran, in 2006, is illustrative. Finneran, who had just taken a high-profile private sector job running a high-technology consortium, was elegant, quick-witted, famously arrogant, highly controversial, but fastidiously incorruptible.

In announcing that he had secured Finneran's indictment by a federal grand jury, U.S. Attorney Michael J. Sullivan solemnly declared that "a severe breach of the public trust" had occurred when, in 2002, Finneran testified as a witness in a civil lawsuit challenging the legality of a Massachusetts legislative redistricting plan. Sullivan charged that Finneran, then the House Speaker, lied about the extent of his knowledge of and involvement in the plan before it was disclosed to all members of the state House of Representatives. The testimony, the indictment alleged, would have been "material" to the claim by the citizens' group—the Black Political Task Force (BPTF)—that sued the state, claiming that the plan discriminated against African-American citizens by concentrating black voters in too few voting districts. As a result, the BPTF had asserted (and the civil court had agreed) that the probable number of House seats that would be held by black reps was reduced.

Finneran, a white Irish-Catholic politician, lived in and was elected by a district classified by the 1990 census as consisting of roughly 70 percent racial minority voters. Yet the district consistently re-elected Finneran by huge margins. This was no small feat in Boston, a city still uneasy about decades of racial distrust. Finneran enjoyed a respectable level of support among black voters, in addition to support in nearby Dorchester's Irish-American community and upscale Milton's middle-class neighborhoods, because he was a good politician. Two African-American candidates ran against Finneran during his 26-year tenure in the House (he resigned from the state legislature in 2004) and both were beaten handily. And yet, in group-identity obsessed Boston circles, this phenomenon was viewed not as a triumph of good government over racial balkanization, but rather as a sign of the failure of group-identity electoral politics correctly practiced.[34]

Finneran had also earned a reputation for a close and effective alliance with Representative Byron Rushing, a respected African-American pillar of Boston's black and politically liberal communities. George Keverian, one of Finneran's predecessors in the House Speaker's chair, was known to joke that only in Boston would Byron Rushing represent a primarily white district, and Tom Finneran represent a black one.[35]

Massachusetts had earned more than its share of high-profile political corruption prosecutions in both state and federal courts. Indeed, Finneran's predecessor, Charles Flaherty, pled guilty in 1996 to federal tax evasion charges. The State Ethics Commission had also found him guilty of taking bribes while in office, including free use of a posh Cape Cod vacation home. "Corruption is a way of life in Massachusetts," concluded the Ward Commission, a special panel appointed to look into corruption in certain state projects, in a high-profile 1980 study of the problem. Finneran was widely viewed as a stark exception, a breath of fresh air.

So how did this former public servant who conducted his office with a high degree of personal probity, without even a whiff of scandal, end up indicted?

The story begins with the panel of appointed judges before whom the civil redistricting case, which fell under the federal Voting Rights Act (VRA), was tried. On the panel were two highly respected and cerebral district court judges, Douglas Woodlock and Michael Ponsor, and a member of the Court of Appeals, Bruce Selya. While the written opinion that decided the redistricting case was signed by all three judges, it was authored by Judge Selya, the highest-ranking member of the panel.

Very early in the panel's opinion, which found in favor of the Black Political Task Force, Judge Selya added one of the gratuitous footnotes for which he had become somewhat notorious.[36] Selya made a fact-finding that the House committee in charge of putting together the redistricting plan "was content to leave the heavy lifting to Finneran" along with the chair of the committee designated by Finneran, Representative Thomas M. Petrolati, as well as their aides and staffs. "Finneran and Petrolati kept the process on a short leash," concluded Selya. Then came a crucial and, unbeknownst at the time, fatal footnote:

> "Although Speaker Finneran denied any involvement in the redistricting process, the circumstantial evidence strongly suggests the opposite conclusion. For one thing, he handpicked the members of the Committee and placed

Petrolati at the helm. For another thing, he ensured that the Committee hired his boyhood friend and long-time political collaborator, Lawrence DiCara, as his principal functionary. Last—but far from least—Finneran's in-house counsel, John Stefanini, had the Maptitude [redistricting] software installed on his computer in the Speaker's office suite and was one of only four legislative staffers who received training in how to use the software."[37]

It was not unusual to see Judge Selya go beyond the immediate requirements of a case to criticize, often in sarcastic and sometimes grandiloquent fashion, a party or a witness. He had earned a reputation for tossing around both his power and his perceived command of language. The opinion was laced with his trademark use of hundred-dollar words where a half-dollar word would suffice. Consider some of his phrases. He noted "the parties' *plenitudinous* submissions," rather than simply numerous filings. We're told that in a major voting rights case "the Supreme Court *limned* three threshold conditions," instead of simply outlined. And who could forget the "three-step *pavane*" that the plaintiffs had to perform in order to win the case. (*Webster's* defines a *pavane* as a "stately court dance by couples that was introduced from southern Europe into England in the 16th century.")

Judge Selya's seeming personal hostility toward Finneran emerged in the court proceedings and opinion in various contexts. For example, at one point the plaintiffs' lawyer asked Finneran whether he'd read a particular article in *The Boston Globe*. Finneran responded that he had "some doubt" whether he had. Judge Selya suggested during the court hearing, at which Finneran testified, that the Speaker was being less than candid, not crediting Finneran's entirely plausible (if not entirely obvious) explanation that sometimes it's just "physically impossible" to read everything every day.

At another point, Selya interrogated Finneran over whether the Speaker in fact appointed committee chairs. Under Finneran's leadership, the House, as was commonly known in Massachusetts at the time, was something of a dictatorship—sometimes benevolent, but not always. Finneran insisted that he only "recommended" chairs, but that House members had the final say over their leader's recommendations. When Selya asked Finneran whether "since you've been Speaker" the House has even once failed to approve "your recommendation," Finneran admitted, with notable candor, that he'd never met with a rejection of his candidate. In general, Selya assumed that Finneran was lying when he played down the level of his involvement in and power over House affairs. Yet Finneran, like most powerful figures in his position, would have thought it impolitic to be too blunt about the extent to which he was more or less a king and the House members his vassals. Thus, while Finneran in the end admitted the result of his exercise of power—his wishes were obeyed—he tried to preserve at least the façade of the sovereignty of the House members. This careful dance, this *pavane*, performed by Finneran during his entire cross-examination was, in the end, grossly misunderstood by Judge Selya, and reflected the clashing worldview of a life-tenured cloistered federal appellate judge versus that of a popularly elected state pol.

Finneran's *modus operandi* might have been better understood by a jury of 12 ordinary citizens who might well have acquitted the former Speaker had the case gone to trial. U.S. Attorney Sullivan, who had previously served in the state legislature, may have understood the realities of political life and leadership invoked by Finneran even when Judge Selya did not. But it was in Sullivan's long-term political self-interest to ignore his own experience in the State House and to accede to Judge Selya's unrealistic and excessively antiseptic notions of state politics.

The Selya footnote caught the attention, according to later newspaper reports, of at least two people who did not have a high opinion of, nor kindly thoughts toward, Finneran. The first was Pamela H. Wilmot, executive director of Common Cause, the well-known liberal advocacy and good-government group. The second was Jeanne M. Kempthorne, a former federal prosecutor, by then in private practice, and a member of Common Cause's board of directors. Kempthorne worked with Common Cause to persuade U.S. Attorney Sullivan to bring a perjury charge against Finneran. Common Cause's Board of Directors lobbied Sullivan to go after Finneran.[38]

Common Cause and the plaintiffs in the redistricting case had a right to feel irked by what they must have viewed as, at best, Finneran's testimonial arrogance and legerdemain, and, at worst, the crime of perjury. Sullivan, however, had a different obligation. He had to determine whether a federal crime had been committed by the former Speaker, whether the crime was sufficiently clear as well as serious enough to seek an indictment, whether it was in the public interest to expend governmental resources to prosecute the case, and, just as importantly, whether it was likely that 12 jurors would credit the government's evidence and interpretation of events "beyond a reasonable doubt" and unanimously vote to convict. By indicting Finneran, Sullivan missed on all scores and stood a good chance of losing the perjury case had Finneran stuck to his announced intention to fight rather than seek a plea bargain.

Perjury is, in theory, one of the harder federal crimes to prosecute successfully and is thus rarely charged. For one thing, another federal crime, that of making a false statement to a federal governmental official, is considerably easier to prosecute since it criminalizes any "material" false statement to such an official *without* the Speaker being under oath.[39] Furthermore, it is relatively difficult to secure a perjury conviction because the lie has to be shown to be a *clear* and *direct* as well as a *knowing* one. Vague, misleading, or "cute" testimony—that is, intentionally narrow, relying on word games and on the failure of a questioner to pin down the witness with sufficient clarity and specificity—is not sufficient. And, as in any prosecution for telling a lie, the lie has to be shown to be "material," which is to say, clearly relevant to the proceeding in which the witness testifies. In the Finneran matter, the prosecutor would likely have had problems convincing jurors that the Speaker in fact materially misled, or even tried to mislead, the three judges.

Sullivan charged that Finneran lied when he denied his own level and extent of participation in the redistricting process. Finneran testified that he saw the proposed redistricting plan at the same time it was presented to other House members by the redistricting committee. In fact, the indictment claimed, Finneran had considerable knowledge of and involvement in the process of crafting a redistricting plan. Indeed, anyone who knew Finneran would have found it hard to believe that he actually allowed his handpicked committee chairman, Thomas Petrolati, to proceed in something as crucial as the redistricting process without *any* involvement from the powerful Speaker, whose own district, after all, would be affected by the outcome.

The indictment claimed that prior to the time Finneran admitted seeing the proposed plan—on the day it was disclosed to *all* the House members—Finneran actually "met with the House Chairman [Petrolati] and others for the purpose of reviewing a redistricting plan." The indictment alleged that Finneran "made comments" at the meeting and "provided direction as to how that redistricting plan should be altered." On another date, Finneran "participated in a conference call" about a redistricting plan and, on other occasions, Finneran was present when "a redistricting plan was reviewed."

One flaw in the indictment was that Finneran's answers, while they may have seemed clear and categorical on the surface, appear upon closer inspection to be exacting responses to questions that the witness interpreted narrowly, as was his right. What, for example, does it mean to "review" a plan? To one person it might mean merely being told a summary of the contents, or reading a portion of it. To another, it might mean reading it in its entirety.

It's important to understand that a perjury defendant will seek to create what lawyers call "wiggle room" to convince a jury that his or her answer, taken literally and narrowly, is not a direct and clear falsehood. Is it admirable for a witness, particularly an important public figure, to play such word games with the opposing lawyer? Probably not. One need only recall President Bill Clinton's caviling about the nature of the word "is" in his notorious 1998 deposition in the obstruction of justice case involving Monica Lewinsky. But modern life, and in particular political life, can be notoriously complicated, and if the law of perjury did not allow for such wiggle room, it would be frightfully easy for vengeful or power-hungry prosecutors to go after the vast number of sworn witnesses who respond essentially honestly, but intentionally narrowly or broadly or extremely precisely, to questions in order to avoid unnecessary embarrassment or offense. Perjury law would become a trap for the unwary rather than a policy aimed at eliciting essentially truthful testimony. And indeed this transformation has already proceeded in federal law, with the building of "perjury traps" into official inquiries where prosecutors almost routinely bring "perjury" or "false statement" or "obstruction"[40] prosecutions even where the underlying crime under investigation turns out not to have been committed.[41]

It was thus readily understandable why Finneran shuffled while under legal attack for having a hand in a redistricting plan that was claimed to be unfair to African-American voters. Similarly, it was understandable that Finneran might have wanted to minimize (while not denying entirely) the extent to which he was involved in the process: he did not want to offend House members by touting his iron grip. But to take the giant leap that Sullivan did, transforming the everyday operation of politics and its accompanying decorum into felony perjury, betrays a troubling misunderstanding of basic American politics, assuming, of course, that Sullivan's misunderstanding was genuine rather than driven by his own ambitions.

Finneran had a right to feel that he was being unfairly tormented by the plaintiffs in the lawsuit. While he had a reputation as somewhat of a tyrant as House Speaker, any claim that he was a racist was, by all accounts, way off the mark. It may well have been, as the federal court concluded, that the redistricting plan, which created a new overwhelmingly minority district but also diluted the minority populations of three districts, had the potential to produce fewer black House members. On the other hand, as political realists are quick to point out, and as even the court recognized, most redistricting plans are at least partly about protecting incumbents, not intentionally marginalizing the electorate or any group within the electorate. Nonetheless, the court concluded that race ended up being "used as a tool to ensure the protection of incumbents." In so doing, while they protected black as well as white incumbents, the plans made it more difficult for black voters to attain more black representation. This fact allowed the court to conclude that the plaintiffs had met their evidentiary burden (or, in Judge Selya's baroque turn of phrase, "the plaintiffs have carried the devoir of persuasion anent each of the three preconditions...").

But the issue at Finneran's perjury trial, were he to receive a fair trial, would not have been whether his position was favorable or unfavorable to black voters. Nor would it have been whether he went overboard to protect incumbents both black and white. The issue would have been whether Finneran told a *direct* lie under oath on an issue *material* to the outcome of the redistricting civil litigation. And it was on the issue of materiality where Sullivan was likely to meet his most serious obstacle in putting Finneran behind bars.

As the three-judge federal court recognized in Judge Selya's opinion, the plaintiffs did not have to prove "intentional discrimination" under the VRA, but only "discriminatory effect." What mattered in the civil redistricting trial was not what Finneran intended, but what resulted, namely an unlawful dilution of African-American citizens' voting power.

This approach would have made Finneran's knowledge and intent irrelevant to the outcome of the civil redistricting trial, and hence not material in the criminal perjury prosecution. In fact, what really decided the outcome of the redistricting case was the testimony of expert witnesses and statisticians who persuaded the judges that the outcome of the redistricting had a negative effect on black voters. It was the *result*, not the intention, that counted. The questions posed to Finneran, and his answers (whether true, false, or "cute") were therefore likely immaterial to the three-judge court's deliberations and conclusions.

Even if this legal analysis were to turn out to be a bit strained, one final aspect of this case made the materiality of Finneran's allegedly false testimony even more questionable. The trial transcript demonstrated that he did *not* in fact deny all knowledge of or participation in the redistricting process. Rather, he seemed to be trying diplomatically to avoid making it appear that he pulled puppet strings while a powerless and irrelevant House danced, even while he made it clear that he did, of course, play some role. At one point Finneran admitted that he got his friend and long-time confidant, Attorney Lawrence DiCara, involved in the process and that the Speaker exercised a role in the redistricting process through DiCara. Finneran denied that he discussed with Petrolati matters relating directly to the configuration of the Speaker's own district. Of course, this could very well have been true and Petrolati still would surely have understood that he would have been foolish to promulgate any redistricting plan that would have made it harder for his boss and mentor to get re-elected. Finneran admitted to discussions with Petrolati and others, including his childhood friend DiCara. He even testified that he learned *before* the redistricting plan was presented to the House that it created a new district with a majority of racial minority voters, that he learned this from DiCara, and that he conveyed to DiCara his approval. Would a jury really believe, and conclude, that Finneran's failure to admit to *other* conversations about redistricting could be viewed as "material" to the three-judge court's conclusions as to the role played by the Speaker in, and his influence over, the resulting plan? Or would the jury conclude that Sullivan's and Selya's shot at the Speaker was simply much ado about nothing?

In a properly functioning criminal justice system, such an indictment would not have been brought. My view at the time the indictment was announced[42] was that Sullivan would not win the case unless he forced the former Speaker into a plea bargain. Sullivan, like all federal prosecutors, had many weapons at his disposal for applying such pressure. Not the least was his power to recommend that if Finneran were to plead guilty, the judge should avoid sentencing him to a prison term. Judges' propensity for following prosecutors' sentencing recommendations gives the feds awesome powers of persuasion that account for a very large number of guilty pleas in the federal system, including some lodged by innocent defendants.

It has rightly been said that a federal prosecutor can get a grand jury to indict a ham sandwich.[43] But a criminal charge should be brought only if the public interest requires it and if a jury is likely to find guilt beyond a reasonable doubt. It was unlikely that Sullivan would prevail before a jury. It is hard to argue against the notion that Finneran was acting precisely as any political figure in his position would have acted. That his two-step around the question of how to characterize his role in the redistricting matter might constitute the federal crime of perjury would surely shock anyone in his position, especially any experienced observer of state politics in Massachusetts, where the legislature has long been supreme and the House Speaker the king of the hill.

Nonetheless, Finneran, who had vacated the Speaker's chair when he retired from politics in 2004 to assume the position of president of the Massachusetts Biotechnology Council, pleaded guilty to obstruction of justice, by means of perjury, on January 5, 2007. He explained, according to The Boston Globe, "why he lied under oath during a civil trial when he claimed he didn't see the 2001 redistricting plan until it was filed with the House." He then paid his obligatory obeisance to federal power in what the Globe termed "an emotional apology" and a "public act of contrition."[44]

The prosecutor, Assistant U. S. Attorney John T. McNeil, recommended unsupervised probation for Finneran, rather than a prison term, in part because there was no evidence of any "racial animus" by the defendant. (One can only begin to imagine what the prosecutors would have said on this subject if Finneran had decided to fight rather than plead guilty!) Judge Richard G. Stearns, a scholarly and deliberative judge with a reputation for probity and independence, nonetheless unsurprisingly accepted the prosecutors' recommendation and sentenced Finneran to 18 months of unsupervised probation and a $25,000 fine, noting the defendant's "lack of any evil motive," his career of public service, and his unblemished personal life. (When the prosecutor and the defense lawyer agree on a disposition, even the most independent judge will usually accede and play his role in the script.)

In a barely noticed addendum, Finneran promised, in an unusual (and likely unconstitutional) agreement with the U.S. attorney's office, not to run for any political office for five years. Judge Stearns, noting his lack of power to enforce this agreement, referred to the court's belief "that Mr. Finneran is an honorable man and he will keep his word." In other words, the U.S. attorney had actually sought to remove from the state's voters the right to put Finneran back into the legislature, and the judge, recognizing the lawlessness of such a usurpation of power by a prosecutor, nevertheless urged Finneran to comply with the promise as a matter, not of law, but of honor. (That this occurred in a prosecution against Finneran for allegedly lying about an unlawful attempt to manipulate the choice of candidates in an election was an unrecognized irony in the outcome of the scripted morality play that unfolded on the day of sentencing.)

During the change-of-plea and sentencing hearing, a few things emerged that help explain why Finneran decided to plead guilty rather than to fight. Were he convicted, Judge Stearns noted, "in the ordinary course, the court would be expected to impose a sentence in the 10-to 16-month range."[45] Finneran, it was disclosed, had been suffering from an intensely painful degenerative hip disorder for which he eventually had surgery. His wife Donna suffered a similar knee problem. Given the government's willingness to recommend a sentence without incarceration, Finneran was being made an offer he felt he couldn't refuse.

During the sentencing hearing, Finneran offered a somewhat different explanation for his failure to be fully forthcoming about the degree of his involvement in the redistricting process than a mere reluctance to insult House members by publicly acknowledging his control over them. He told Judge Stearns that he found the civil suit's accusations "very troubling" and offensive, because "for 26 years I had represented a district that was overwhelmingly African-American, and I took great pride in my service of this district." He said that he was offended by the implication that he engaged in a "deliberate racial manipulation in order to depress or suppress legitimate efforts at minority representation." And so he had underplayed, but had not entirely denied, his role. Even the prosecutor admitted to the judge that there was no evidence "that [Finneran] feared representing a district with a large percent of black minority voters [or] that he had a personal desire to 'whiten' his own district." Finneran's explanation was given in response to Judge Stearns' expressed confusion about why Finneran would want to underplay his role in a redistricting process that, as Speaker, "it would have seemed almost unnatural had you not been involved." The sentencing judge, much like Judge Selya who started it all, simply did not understand the internal House politics and protocols of the matter.

As for U.S. Attorney Sullivan, he defended ending the case not with a bang but a whimper this way: "I think Mr. Finneran has had a career of public service that many people would admire...in terms of his passion and his advocacy for a wide range of issues." Nonetheless, the prosecutor had extracted (coerced might be a more accurate description) an unlawful pledge that this exemplary public servant would not run for public office for five years.

Only time would tell if Sullivan, whose term as U.S. attorney was almost certainly going to end (and in fact did) when President George W. Bush left office some two years later, had in mind his own ambitions for higher elective office when he insisted upon the five-year disqualification provision. That Sullivan, but for Finneran's legal problems and subsequent five-year disqualification from elective office, figured he might have to tangle for votes with the popular, fellow Irish-Catholic Speaker (now ex-Speaker) is an intriguing but unprovable speculation. Some would argue that Finneran's conviction alone would, as a practical matter, make him unelectable and hence no realistic obstacle to Sullivan's electoral ambitions, with or without the five-year disqualification. (Think back to the attack ads that sank Raul Martinez's 2008 congressional bid almost *two decades* after his conviction.)

But this was Massachusetts. The Bay State has a history of a rather forgiving electorate, especially when dealing with very colorful or very talented politicians. (Consider James Michael Curley, the famed Massachusetts governor, who was elected to Boston's Board of Aldermen in 1904 while serving a prison sentence for taking the civil service exam for a friend.) Certainly Finneran's agreement with Sullivan that the former Speaker would exit the political stage during Sullivan's post-Bush window of opportunity for elective office would not hurt the U.S. attorney's career plans. In fact, shortly after the Finneran plea, Sullivan did move up the federal hierarchy, becoming acting director of the federal Bureau of Alcohol, Tobacco, Firearms and Explosives. He was, indeed, a man on the move.

As for Thomas Finneran, he also faced the forfeiture of his $30,909 annual public pension, and was fired from his $416,000 a year job with the Biotechnology Council. His aggressive intelligence and quick wit enabled him to land a gig as a local radio talk-show host for the morning "drive time" commute in the 6:00–10:00 a.m. slot. (He also did some lobbying work.) He thus did better than some local politicians in similar shoes. But given the fact that he did not commit perjury, some would view the sentence and other consequences of his plea as rather harsh, and the gentleman's agreement not to run for office a deplorable infringement of his and the voters' constitutional rights.

The conviction continued to exact its toll on Finneran's life. As the year 2007 drew to a close (and only days before he was scheduled to enter the Massachusetts General Hospital for prostate surgery), the former House Speaker of Massachusetts, arguably once the single most powerful state official in the commonwealth, was pictured in *The Boston Herald* with tears in his eyes, pleading with the state Board of Bar Overseers for the retention of his license to practice law, which had been temporarily suspended when he got indicted. Finneran tried to explain to the panel that he hadn't been "aware of specific details of the [redistricting plan],"[46] and his supporting witnesses (influential lawyers from prior gubernatorial administrations) complained of "a political witch hunt" by Sullivan, whom they deemed a less than "impartial" federal prosecutor, but it all seemed too little and too late. The time for Finneran to have defended himself, and to have retained his dignity, had passed.

CHAPTER TWO

Giving Doctors Orders

——— •●● ———

Just before Rosh Hashanah (the Jewish High Holy Days) in 2003, federal agents handcuffed Dr. William Hurwitz in full view of his family and threw him into the back of a squad car. Hurwitz, a prominent physician in the suburban Washington, D.C., area, soon found his assets frozen and his bail set at a staggering $2 million. The government described the doctor, a nationally renowned pain specialist, as "no better than a street corner crack dealer" who "dispense[s] misery and death."[1] Prosecutors boasted in florid war on terror language that Dr. Hurwitz's case would help the Drug Enforcement Agency "root out" a subculture of physicians-turned-criminals "like the Taliban." This dramatic, SWAT-team style arrest and the lurid smear tactics that followed were more appropriate for a serial killer than for a licensed physician.

These are indeed perilous times to practice medicine. There has been much debate about whether it is becoming too expensive for doctors to practice because of the increasingly onerous rates for malpractice insurance. That debate centers on the question of who should bear the risk of medical mistakes and how high medical malpractice insurance premiums can rise before doctors begin to abandon certain areas of specialization.

What is given much less attention, however, is another risk attendant to medical practice, namely federal indictment. That risk is particularly acute for certain medical practitioners, such as those who treat chronic pain. It also extends to those physicians, hospitals, and clinics which collect fees from federal government medical programs, as well as many others. The list of physicians subject to all-too-easy indictment for violations of federal laws is long because the governing statutes and regulations are deceptively easy to violate. These laws are not readily understood by medical practitioners operating in good faith because they are vague, complex, and often self-contradictory. If one adds up the number of physicians who are threatened by this state of affairs, it constitutes nearly every physician practicing medicine today.

So how did Dr. William Hurwitz's nightmarish encounter with the feds come about? Prosecutors contended that the physician had crossed the line from healer to criminal drug merchant. He had done so by dispensing massive quantities of pain-killers to patients who had criminal records or whom he knew, or should have known, to suffer from addiction. Hurwitz faced a 49-count indictment for drug trafficking, conspiracy, and even running a criminal enterprise, all stemming from his narcotics-dispensing activities. The fact that he operated with a prescription pad rather than on a dark street corner did not matter. A drug dealer was a drug dealer.

One cannot truly understand Dr. Hurwitz's indictment without first understanding "the war on drugs," a political and cultural initiative that has handed the Department of Justice a goody bag of dangerously pliable statutes and regulations with which to criminalize yet another profession with its own time-honored practices and ancient standards.

Federal criminal regulation of narcotics began with the Harrison Tax Act of 1914, targeting the non-therapeutic, addiction-related, and recreational uses of opium, morphine, and cocaine, used at the time for a variety of medical conditions and procedures. This legislation marked the beginning of a long-running federal assault on the medical profession and its patients, particularly those addicted to narcotic drugs, whether for recreational or therapeutic reasons.

The Comprehensive Drug Abuse Prevention and Control Act of 1970 replaced this antiquated statutory taxation scheme with a law more directly controlling the use of narcotic drugs. Bureaucratic maneuvering led the initial agency charged with enforcing the act, the Bureau of Narcotics and Dangerous Drugs, to be replaced by the U.S. Drug Enforcement Administration (DEA) in 1973 as an arm of the

Department of Justice. In addition to its drug interdiction and anti-trafficking activities, the DEA has long had an intimate role in regulating the ability of doctors to prescribe certain medications. For example, physicians, researchers, and others with access to controlled substances are required to register with the DEA and apply for a unique identification number that allows the DEA to track who is authorizing use of or research into those controlled substances.

Title II of the 1970 Act (dubbed the Controlled Substances Act) classified drugs by weighing their potential for harm against their therapeutic benefits. Drugs such as marijuana and heroin, with no officially recognized therapeutic use but with a perceived high potential for addiction or other abuse, were placed in Schedule I. Schedule II listed narcotic and non-narcotic drugs including cocaine, methadone, oxycodone and its time-release formulation known as OxyContin®, as well as a variety of amphetamines and barbiturates that carried what the government deemed a high risk of severe addiction. Analgesics and other drugs with lower risk of addiction filled out Schedules III, IV, and V.

The classification of these drugs into categories purportedly balancing therapeutic value against addictive and recreational potential signaled the new, supposedly modern, more scientific approach to federal drug regulation. Such, however, turned out not to be the case. Instead of achieving a medically-rooted balance, the feds drew an arbitrary line between what they believed to be the appropriate medical administration of pain-killing drugs versus "drug dealing" by physicians. Worse, the regulatory language made it virtually impossible for even the most responsible pain specialist to discern when he or she crossed the line into an area the DEA would consider akin to "street dealing."

At the center of much federal drug law enforcement is a line drawn between drugs taken for "recreational" or "addictive" purposes rather than for therapeutic benefit. When a pain physician either gives a patient too much of a controlled drug or dispenses such drugs when he or she arguably should have known that some of it might get diverted to narcotics addicts, the physician is considered to be no longer engaged in the legitimate practice of medicine. The trouble is, the same approach applies whether a patient in pain takes more drugs than needed, redistributes drugs for addictive or recreational use, or is in real pain and seeks to get more medication due to an inordinate fear of being under-medicated. In the latter circumstance, a patient will sometimes exaggerate pain, with no ill intent.

The fundamental problem faced by physicians who prescribe controlled pain-killers in their medical practices is that a doctor's therapeutic standards and judgment often differ considerably from a law enforcement agency's definition of "abuse." What would seem to be the good faith practice of medicine to a physician can readily be deemed abusive by a narcotics agent or bureaucrat. In fact, there is no single standard for the appropriate administration of narcotics since one deals here with a physician's therapeutic discretion, which varies from doctor to doctor and from specialty to specialty. It's true that abuse and malpractice are committed by some pain-treating physicians, but the federal scheme for controlling abuse second-guesses physicians in a manner that pressures them to act more like cops than docs.

The indictment against Dr. Hurwitz charged that he had not just stepped, but leapt across the line separating acceptable from unacceptable prescribing practices for the powerful, and effective, analgesic OxyContin®. OxyContin® is an enormously important medication. Placed on the market by the pharmaceutical company Purdue Pharma[2] in 1996, OxyContin® is a form of the narcotic drug oxycodone and is a therapeutic improvement over the original because it is released more slowly and steadily into the patient's system. This "time release" aspect of OxyContin® makes it particularly useful for relieving extreme pain for hours at a time. While other types of pain medication might last only a few hours, orally administered OxyContin® delivers pain relief over 12 hours with a single dose. A pain victim can go about a full day's work or other tasks without constant and debilitating agony. As an analgesic, OxyContin® also produces feelings of relaxation and euphoria by targeting the central nervous system's opioid receptors. Of course, if OxyContin® is taken contrary to the instructions provided by the physician and the label, that is, if pills are crushed and snorted or chewed rather than swallowed whole, the narcotic effect is delivered in one huge euphoric "hit." Thus, this particular drug can be readily abused by drug addicts looking for a high.

Here is where things get truly murky: *any* patient who ingests increasingly large doses of a narcotic to achieve relief from pain can readily, and likely will, become physically *dependent* on that drug for pain relief, much like a diabetic becomes dependent on insulin. Others are more susceptible psychologically to becoming *addicted*.[3] As one prominent medical pain practitioner has observed, "the confusion between addiction and physical dependence is probably the biggest single misunderstanding about opioids."[4]

Treating physicians, of course, must navigate these shoals to make proper judgments about when continued administration of narcotics is clinically appropriate and when to wean the patient who exhibits signs of addiction. Of course, it is sometimes true that a patient becomes addicted and tells all kinds of phony stories to convince his or her physician to continue prescribing narcotics long beyond the point when the patient's actual medical condition warrants it. Physicians practice as much art as science in making proper judgments about their patients and have historically subjected the delicacy of such professional calls to licensing and peer-review controls.

Federal narcotics officers wield less subtle judgments and weapons. They are not always likely to recognize the weaning stage and can too readily assume that the doctor is maintaining an addict. Putting it charitably, they are inclined to err on the side of strict caution in these matters. Their worldview calls to mind H.L. Mencken's definition of Puritanism: "the haunting fear that someone, somewhere, may be happy." If one has any doubt about the DEA's often black-versus-white moralistic and punitive agenda, one need look no further than the way the agency deals with marijuana.[5] The fight for its approved medical uses has a long and continuing, largely unhappy history.[6]

Dr. Hurwitz was described by *The Washington Post* as "a major figure in national pain management circles."[7] Given Dr. Hurwitz's fame, it should come as no surprise that the feds would make him a high-profile target, an object lesson for the entire profession. Bringing him down was an opportunity and a challenge, even a coup. And this was facilitated by the endlessly malleable statutes and regulations in the narcs' arsenal. Then-Attorney General John Ashcroft himself announced Hurwitz's indictment, noting that the doctor had been involved in "traffic in [a] very dangerous drug." True to form, the news media fanned the flames.[8] *Newsweek* published a story in 2002 on "Oxybabies," a term analogizing the children of pregnant women who consume OxyContin® to "crack babies." *The Boston Globe* ran a page one article in August 2004, trumpeting the inevitable local arrival of a federal program targeting OxyContin® abuse.[9] A local official declared that "OxyContin® use can lead to heroin use." Another local official said OxyContin® abuse was "the number one health crisis in cities and towns at this time."[10] It didn't help that the image of an epidemic was facilitated by the spate of drug thefts from pharmacies and hospitals at the time. The specter of a crime wave was created by the prosecution statistics generated because prosecutors consider every prescription a separate felony count, so the charging statistics reach phenomenal numbers for each patient in these cases. These numbers became the stuff of screaming headlines in Dr. Hurwitz's case, even though his attorneys estimated that no more than five to ten percent of his patients misused or resold the drugs.

In court, federal prosecutors never claimed that Dr. Hurwitz actually sold the drugs, or prescriptions for them. Instead, they charged that his income was increased from patients who came to him in the belief that they could get away with faking or exaggerating their pain. Prosecutors claimed a "conspiracy of silence" whereby the patients would mislead the doctor and the doctor would cooperate by being too readily misled—"a wink and a nod" arrangement.

In Dr. Hurwitz's case, it turned out that some 15 of his roster of over 500 patients whom he was treating for chronic pain had been lying to him in order to get prescriptions and then resell the drugs. When federal agents learned of this, instead of alerting the doctor, they allowed the prescribing to continue and then made deals with the patients who had been lying to their doctor. Call it the medical version of ladder climbing: if the patients would testify against Dr. Hurwitz, they themselves would get lenient sentencing deals. It was, of course, easy to get many of the patients to tell whatever tales the agents and prosecutors needed to put the doctor behind bars for decades. The patients merely had to convince the jury that they gave the doctor enough information to know that they were abusing or reselling drugs that he prescribed.

A principal problem for Hurwitz's defense was that it was not enough for him to demonstrate that he treated his pain patients in "good faith." He also had to demonstrate that his prescribing practices were "in accordance with established medical norms." Those norms, in the kind of trial Dr. Hurwitz was facing, had been increasingly determined by the DEA rather than by the medical profession.

So it came as a relief when, just before Hurwitz's 2004 trial, the DEA appeared to make an about-face in a rare and overdue gesture of cooperation with health care professionals. It joined the Last Acts Partnership and the Pain & Policy Studies Group at the University of Wisconsin to produce a pamphlet that went up on the DEA's and other Websites: *PRESCRIPTION PAIN MEDICATIONS: Frequently Asked Questions and Answers for Health Care Professionals, and Law Enforcement Personnel.*[11] This FAQ pamphlet discussed the nature of chronic pain and the importance of managing it properly. To that end, it sought "balance" between the need to treat pain and the prevention of the abuse and diversion of pain medications. It also conceded what pain doctors had long known: in cases of chronic pain, "the parameters of acceptable medical practice include patterns of drug prescription— such as long-term administration of an opioid drug at escalating doses and administration of more than one controlled prescription drug." This description of proper medical practice found its way into the guide even though drug warriors had long claimed that in some contexts such escalation could be seen as a "red flag." The pamphlet listed other "red flags" physicians should consider in determining whether a patient was seeking medical advice and treatment in good faith. And in an "important disclaimer," it proceeded to warn that "lack of strict adherence to these suggestions does not imply that a particular practice is outside the scope of legitimate medical practice."

Crucially, the guidelines distinguished between physical "dependence," characterized by changes to the body resulting in withdrawal symptoms after use is stopped, and "addiction," marked by continued use despite enduring drug-related problems.[12] "Confusion" concerning the nature of addiction, the pamphlet conceded in a remarkable admission, "can lead to the withholding of opioid medication because of a mistaken belief a patient is addicted when he or she is merely dependent." And such confusion "can lead to inappropriate targeting of practitioners and patients for investigation and prosecution."

The guidelines finally made room for individualized treatment by giving physicians some flexibility to use their professional judgment in deciding how to read, and therefore treat, a patient. They attempted to clear up some questions related to opioid therapy, while admitting that the scientific literature is "limited" and that there is "multifaceted controversy" among experts. The approach was nuanced and balanced, with continual warnings that no one factor or group of factors was necessarily indicative of abuse. In other words, the FAQ not only gave physicians reasonably clear guidelines as to how to assess a case calling for opioid therapy, but also lent them some degree of freedom to exercise medical judgment. Now doctors would not only get to practice medicine, but they would not have to look at every pain patient as a potential trap.

Yet out of the blue this highly welcome FAQ was suddenly withdrawn less than two months after it was first issued in August 2004. Why? Because Dr. Hurwitz's lawyers wanted to use the booklet to defend their client at trial, and this triggered the drug warriors' recognition that, by providing both clarity and flexibility to physicians as the FAQ had done, it was more difficult to win their overzealous prosecutions. Winning cases prevailed over facilitating sound medical practice. Some within the DEA clearly agreed with the medical community on all of the facts of medical life set forth in the FAQ, but overall, the DEA was not going to admit to such agreement when it could result in the acquittal of a prominent pain-management physician it had already targeted. A "win at virtually any cost" mentality afflicts segments of the Department of Justice's Criminal Division in general and the drug warriors in particular.

With the withdrawal of the FAQ, the DEA killed two birds with one stone. It both cemented the case against Dr. Hurwitz and reversed its first tentative step toward accommodating the medical profession's fear of getting ensnarled in a professional and legal nightmare whenever physicians treated patients in severe pain. After Dr. Hurwitz's conviction was announced by the jury, U.S. Attorney Paul J. McNulty told *The Washington Post* that Dr. Hurwitz "was convicted of multiple drug-trafficking violations because he knew that many of his patients were abusing or selling prescription drugs."[13] Yet the patients who testified, in exchange for deals from prosecutors that protected them from getting slammed for their own drug abuse, gave the jurors details of precisely how they went about fooling the doctor— how they won the trust they later betrayed. As *Reason* magazine's Jacob Sullum characterized the trial and the jury's verdict, Dr. Hurwitz was convicted essentially of "trusting his patients too much."[14]

The Hurwitz conviction was later overturned by the Court of Appeals for the Fourth Circuit, an intermediate appellate court known for its tough law-and-order, pro-government rulings in criminal cases.[15] But even the reversal added to the fear that must beset every pain physician. The appellate court faulted trial judge Leonard D. Wexler for failing to instruct the jury that it must acquit Dr. Hurwitz if it found that he was operating in "good faith" and within "accepted medical practice." Said the appellate court: "As an initial premise, we agree with Hurwitz that a doctor's good faith generally is relevant to a jury's determination of whether the doctor acted outside the bounds of medical practice or with a legitimate medical purpose when prescribing narcotics." It continued: "Some latitude must be given to doctors trying to determine the current boundaries of acceptable medical practice." Thus, the physician could defend by proffering to the jury evidence of his "good faith." Yet the court went on to emphasize that the standard of good faith had to be an "objective" rather than a "subjective" one.

Judge Wexler's formulation at the trial meant that a physician, regardless of his expertise, could be convicted of a serious felony on the basis of what government expert guns-for-hire were willing to testify is the *objective* standard for "accepted medical practice." Although the Court of Appeals found this wanting, its own formulation was no clearer than was Judge Wexler's. The appellate court seemed to want to have its cake and eat it too. An objective standard for "accepted medical practice" governed such cases, but a doctor's subjective good faith also somehow mattered. As one of the judges on the Fourth Circuit panel noted, in agreeing with the reversal of the conviction but dissenting from the disarmingly "objective" standard that the appellate court sought to substitute for that of the trial judge: "I do not believe good faith should be objective; the two terms are contradictory, it seems to me." In other words, neither Judge Wexler's nor the Fourth Circuit's formulation took into account that physicians sometimes attempt patient cures by techniques that they, in their experience, have found effective, even if more establishment members of the profession, or narcotics officers, or lay jurors for that matter, have different ideas. The fundamental problem—and risk—facing pain physicians remained even after Dr. Hurwitz's appellate reversal. The bottom line is that while judges might understand the realities and exigencies of medical practice better than do the narcotics agents, they have thus far been unable to come up with an interpretation of the law that gives medical practitioners clear advice as to how to avoid personal and professional catastrophe.

The Department of Justice retried Dr. Hurwitz after the appellate reversal. It was a fascinating trial, for it provided a window on precisely what is wrong with seeking to control and second-guess pain physicians based on the amorphous criminal standards wielded by federal drug bureaucrats and prosecutors.

At his retrial, Dr. Hurwitz presented the testimony of two of the nation's leading pain experts from top-notch research hospitals and medical schools, Dr. Russell K. Portenoy of Beth Israel Medical Center in New York and Dr. James N. Campbell of Johns Hopkins University, both of whom testified without fee.[16] They explained to the jury the difficulty of finding pain physicians willing to prescribe sufficient quantities of opioids to give full pain relief to those patients needing it. The fact that such patients often use illegal drugs on the side complicates the physician's dilemma. Dr. Campbell testified that while he was initially not certain that Dr. Hurwitz's high-dose approach was reasonable, he was finally convinced by the results achieved. Dr. Hurwitz, he told the jury, was one of the few physicians left willing to deal with such "problem patients." Dr. Campbell thought such treatment to be within the "bounds of medical practice," contradicting the prosecutors' experts.[17]

In the end, the trial judge dismissed the most serious charges involving injury or death. The jury nonetheless convicted the physician on 16 counts of drug trafficking, acquitted him on 17 counts, and deadlocked on 12 remaining counts that the judge then dismissed. The 57-month sentence he received was a significantly more favorable result than the convictions on all counts that drew Dr. Hurwitz a 25-year sentence at the first trial, but it was far from ideal.[18] Of course, in the bigger picture, the fundamental problem still faced physicians in the business of trying to alleviate chronic pain: they treat patients at their own considerable risk. In the case of Dr. Hurwitz, he suffered personal and professional ruination.

John Tierney, a science columnist for *The New York Times* who reported on the trial, sought to find out why the jurors saw fit to convict Hurwitz on some counts despite the overwhelming testimony at trial that he made little or no money from his pain relief practice and that prestigious experts vouched for the professionalism of his approach to pain management in extreme cases. Tierney interviewed three of the 12 jurors, and they all said more or less the same thing. "The jurors were confused by the law," he wrote, noting that "the law is a ass (to quote Mr. Bumble from *Oliver Twist*)." The jurors agreed that the patients turned government witnesses "used the doctor shamelessly" and "exploited him," and that the doctor didn't get "anything financial out of it." But Dr. Hurwitz "fell down on the job," said one juror. "There were red flags," pointed out by the prosecutors, that Dr. Hurwitz "should have seen," said another.

Tierney then got to the heart of the matter:

> I asked the three jurors what they made of the distinc-
> tion made by Dr. Hurwitz's lawyers and by the judge: that
> this trial was not a malpractice case. In legalese, the jurors
> were to decide not whether Dr. Hurwitz had provided the
> proper "standard of care," but whether he had violated the
> Controlled Substances Act by prescribing drugs "outside
> the bounds of medical practice." The jurors said they were
> all aware of the distinction, but none of them claimed to
> understand it.
>
> > "I don't know that I know enough to be clear about
> > that gray area between malpractice and out of
> > bounds," Juror 1 said.
> >
> > "We just had to go with our gut," Juror 2 said.
> >
> > "That was definitely a struggle," Juror 3 said. "That
> > was a gray area."[19]

As Tierney put it, when a physician makes a medical judgment in this area, he or she can readily be reduced to a drug dealer. "All it takes is a second opinion from a jury."[20] Numerous physicians have been prosecuted for dispensing pain-relieving drugs, with personally and professionally crippling results. Some, after exhausting their financial resources, are ultimately found not guilty. Still others have their charges reduced through a plea agreement that nonetheless debilitates their practice. Most doctors charged with such violations have their assets immediately frozen, making it nearly impossible to assemble the resources to present an adequate legal defense. Doctors charged with criminal violations often have their reputations irreversibly tarnished in the press; this, too, makes it impossible for such a physician to work. And since most state medical boards will suspend an indicted physician until the outcome of his or her trial, physicians usually cannot work to finance their legal defense.

The case of Dr. Frank Fisher, though it did not result in conviction, illustrates the point.[21] Dr. Fisher had developed a practice comprised of approximately 3,000 patients in California. He treated about five to ten percent for pain. In 1999, Dr. Fisher was arrested and charged with several counts of murder (a "mass murderer," said prosecutors), fraud, and drug diversion. What had Dr. Fisher done to elicit such grave charges? Prosecutors claimed, among other things, that by over-prescribing narcotics he was criminally culpable for the death of a patient who died because her prescription lapsed *after* Dr. Fisher had been jailed.

The emptiness of the prosecutors' dramatic allegations was later hinted at when a judge dismissed the murder charges and lowered bail after a 21-day preliminary hearing. Four more years passed before the remaining felony charges were dismissed, and it was not until May 2004 that a jury acquitted Dr. Fisher of the remaining misdemeanor charges. By then, the damage had been done. Besides spending five months in jail, the financial burden of fighting for his reputation drained the 50-year-old Harvard alum's assets. After the acquittal, he had no choice but to live with his elderly parents.

Not only are doctors vulnerable to the threat of such prosecutions, but, just as important, chronic pain sufferers cannot obtain relief. A 2005 survey conducted by ABC, *USA Today*, and Stanford University Medical Center reported that "[just] 48 percent of frequent pain sufferers, and 50 percent of those with chronic pain, say they got at least a good amount of relief after seeing a medical professional."[22] According to Tina Rosenberg's 2007 cover story for *The New York Times Magazine*, the American Pain Society estimates that less than half of cancer patients are getting adequate relief for their pain.[23] Most of the estimated 50 million chronic pain sufferers in the United States are forced to rely on over-the-counter anti-inflammatory medicines, like Aleve® or Motrin®. These drugs are considered by drug warriors to be safer than prescription painkillers, but this reasoning is flawed. Because over-the-counter alternatives often don't sufficiently alleviate chronic pain, patients frequently overmedicate themselves, potentially leading to stomach bleeding and ulcers. According to some estimates by the American Gastroenterological Association, as many as 16,500 Americans bleed to death annually as a result of the over-prescription of anti-inflammatory medications such as ibuprofen and naproxyn, the active ingredients found in Motrin® and Aleve®.[24]

Perhaps the punchiest summary of the harrowing situation faced by patients in severe pain and the doctors who treat them came from Siobhan Reynolds, head of the Pain Relief Network. Pondering the Hurwitz trial juror's contention that Dr. William Hurwitz "fell down on the job," she asked, "What's the job? Hurwitz didn't fail as a doctor; he failed as a law enforcement officer."[25]

The kinds of tactics, and persistence, shown by federal agents and prosecutors in their war against Dr. Hurwitz are repeated time and time again.

Dr. Cecil Knox, a pain management specialist who ran a clinic in Roanoke, Virginia, was subjected to the indignities of a storm-trooper raid on his office, in full view of his patients, in February 2002. The federal agents, according to Maia Szalavitz's article in *Reason* magazine, were "helmeted, shielded, and wearing bullet-proof vests," and even threatened one of Dr. Knox's employees by putting a gun to his head and demanding that he "Get off the phone! Now!"[26] After being handcuffed and shackled with leg irons, Dr. Knox and several employees were handed a 313-count indictment. Despite the storm-trooper tactics and the scroll of charges, a jury later acquitted Dr. Knox of some 30 of the 69 charges he faced. The jury hung, however, on the rest of the counts because of a single juror who voted guilty. The government subsequently refiled 95 charges against the pain-relief specialist. Almost predictably, instead of risking a substantial sentence, Dr. Knox entered into a plea bargain, voluntarily surrendering his license to practice medicine. In January 2006, he was sentenced to five years of probation as part of the deal.[27]

The tyranny of anti-opioid prescription prosecutions also extends to Arizona, where highly respected pain physician Dr. Jeri Hassman was charged with over 350 counts of "drug dealing with a pen;"[28] to Florida, where Dr. James Graves was convicted in 2002 and sentenced to 63 years in prison for causing the deaths of four patients; and to South Carolina, where Dr. Deborah Bordeaux was convicted of drug-related offenses and sentenced to eight years in prison for working for just two months at a pain-management center.[29] There is little reason to believe that this pattern will change anytime soon without a major reaction by physicians and their professional associations, their patients, and citizens who understand how unrealistic it is to assume that young physicians will choose to go into such a dangerous specialty.

• • ● • •

By early 2006, two physicians were able to report in the authoritative *New England Journal of Medicine* that patients in severe pain continue to live in a realistic "fear of undertreatment of distressing symptoms... despite the efficacy of opioids...to treat pain." This fear on the part of physicians remains so great that pain doctors at times err so far on the side of personal caution that they commit legally actionable malpractice by failing to prescribe adequate pain-killers.[30] Just a couple of months later, George J. Annas, a nationally recognized medical-legal expert at Boston University, stated that "the DEA lately has seemed much more menacing to physicians than it had been, especially since the agency withdrew its support for pain-prescribing [FAQ] guidelines that had been adopted by the Federation of State Medical Boards."[31] Even so, Annas speculated with obvious horror at how much worse the situation would have become had the Supreme Court not delivered the drug warriors a rare setback in the DOJ's attack on Oregon's trailblazing attempt to legalize physician-assisted suicide.

Under the Oregon Death With Dignity Act (ODWDA), passed by that state's voters in a 1994 ballot referendum, state licensed physicians, acting within safeguards contained in the pioneering legislation, could prescribe lethal doses of a drug in response to a knowing request by a terminally ill patient in excruciating pain. These drugs, however, are regulated under the federal Controlled Substances Act (CSA) and therefore require a prescription written by a physician registered with the DEA. These drugs are typically prescribed in smaller doses for the relief of pain, but in more massive doses to hasten the inevitable process of dying.

Attorney General John Ashcroft, who possessed a law degree but not a medical one, decided in 2001 that prescribing lethal doses of such medications should not be deemed, by federal law enforcement, as "legitimate medical practice." He reasoned that since the art and science of medicine is to heal the sick, it was counter to that end to intentionally *kill* the patient. Therefore, ruled Ashcroft, such prescriptions would thenceforth be deemed violations of federal law. Transgressions could result in revocation of a physician's license to prescribe controlled drugs as well as criminal prosecution because, in the words of the applicable regulation, the prescription of the controlled substance was not "issued for a legitimate medical purpose." Ashcroft so decreed, even though the Oregon statute set out carefully nuanced guidelines that sought, for example, to distinguish patients in a terminal and unbearable state of physical pain from those acting in a state of depression. The statute reflected the best medical and political judgments in the state of Oregon, and yet the attorney general (a mere lawyer, operating from far-away Washington, D.C.) saw fit to wield effective veto power.

The tension between federal drug-dispensing regulations and the medical profession's need for flexibility and balance in treating patients has been around since the beginning of the 20th century. Congress made things worse, and considerably more vague, when it amended the CSA in 1984 to allow the attorney general to revoke a physician's license to prescribe regulated drugs if he or she thought that granting a doctor such powers would be "inconsistent with the public interest." However, Attorney General Ashcroft's "Interpretive Rule" broke new ground and went even further. He announced that assisting the death of a terminally ill patient by dispensing controlled substances was not a "legitimate medical purpose" and constituted a federal crime. This presented medical practitioners with a somewhat different situation than the typical vagueness problem that besets practitioners of more routine pain medicine who are suddenly charged with being drug dealers. Now, physicians who specialize in the relief of suffering at the end of a patient's life, and who are specifically authorized by state law to hasten death, would be faced with federal indictment for misuse of controlled drugs.

In a rare rebuke to federal drug warriors, the Supreme Court in January 2006 ruled 6-3 against Ashcroft and his Interpretive Rule.[32] The high court's language was unusually acerbic, especially given that the case was decided on an otherwise routine point of statutory interpretation. The Court's opinion pivoted on the technical question of whether Congress, in the CSA, gave the attorney general authority to define a physician's prescription of lethal doses of controlled drugs, under tightly regulated terms set by the state, to be a violation of acceptable medical standards and hence a federal crime.

The attorney general argued that all his Interpretive Rule did was elaborate his own regulations that require all prescriptions of federally regulated drugs be issued "for a legitimate medical purpose by an individual practitioner acting in the usual course of his professional practice." Such a determination, argued Ashcroft, was entitled to substantial "deference" by the federal courts. To a large extent, the Supreme Court's decision in the case turned on the degree of deference to which the attorney general was entitled.

Normally, Ashcroft would have been accorded enormous authority, since the federal courts have been extremely hesitant to do anything that would weaken the government's power to conduct its nearly century-old "war on drugs." But the high court posed a question that federal drug warriors were not accustomed to being asked: "Who decides whether a particular activity is in 'the course of professional practice' or done for a 'legitimate medical purpose'?" The Court noted that this latter phrase was "susceptible to more precise definition and open to varying constructions." Nonetheless, it was clear that the CSA did not authorize Ashcroft to declare illegal a "medical standard for care" that under state law was legal. The Court went on to observe that, while the attorney general can make decisions under the CSA that are *law enforcement* decisions, *medical* decisions would have to be made, under the terms of the statute itself, by the Secretary of Health, Education and Welfare. The secretary, in turn, has an obligation to consult with the "American medical and scientific community" on such judgments because "Congress sought to change the fact that criminal prosecutions in the past had turned on the opinions of federal prosecutors."

Previously, the federal courts could reliably be counted on to give the drug warriors virtually free reign. Now, the Supreme Court was pulling back some, limiting the attorney general's powers to combating the diversion of drugs to addicts and preventing "illicit drug trafficking." The attorney general, ruled the Court, could not define the prescription of narcotic drugs under Oregon's assisted suicide statute as illicit trafficking.

While the Supreme Court's decision provided no direct comfort to physicians engaged in the practice of pain relief, it did take the unusual step of expressing judicial skepticism about the ability and authority of the drug warriors to trump the judgment of the medical profession in another arena—the end of life. The Court concluded by urging Congress to regulate medical practice, in clear language, so as to prevent doctors from abusing their prescription-writing powers, but emphasized that the CSA had "no intent to regulate the practice of medicine generally."

Let us take a step back. The drug warriors were turned back when they sought, *by regulations*, to establish a national standard defining good faith and proper medical practice in end-of-life situations. But they continue to establish *de facto* national standards in the pain relief arena, not by administrative regulation, but rather by case-by-case prosecution. In this manner, the drug warriors have, in fact, achieved their aim of regulating pain medicine by an *in terrorem* series of prosecutorial strikes, most of which appear to have succeeded in frightening pain doctors and deterring them from following the best medical judgments of the profession and of state medical regulators. In this manner, a national standard for pain relief has been established, and it is a vague standard dictated by cops, not doctors.[33]

We have yet to see if and how Congress will react to these and future court opinions. Congress might decide to use the power acknowledged by the Supreme Court to make clear its intention to give the drug warriors the power to determine the parameters of good-faith medical treatment. The most potent danger is that Congress will allow the current vague statutory and regulatory framework to persist and, as a result, drug warriors will retain the *de facto* ability to regulate the practice of pain medication.

• • ● • •

As we have seen, federal law is sufficiently malleable so that a physician can be indicted, even convicted, for engaging in activity that he or she has good reason to believe is lawful. This vulnerability extends not only to physicians dispensing pain-management medicine and hastening death under a duly enacted statute (as in Oregon), but also to those complying with the enormously complex federal regulatory scheme, the Federal Food, Drug and Cosmetic Act (FDCA).[34] Just ask Dr. Peter Gleason.

When Dr. Gleason was picked up and arrested on a Long Island train platform, the Maryland doctor thought, "Well, this is a gag."[35] It was no joke. The U.S. attorney for the Eastern District of New York in 2006 indicted Dr. Gleason, a licensed psychiatrist who treated patients for, among other things, sleep-related disorders. The crux of the charge was that he illegally prescribed and promoted the drug Xyrem®, manufactured by Orphan Medical, Inc. Dr. Gleason touted the effectiveness of Xyrem® in the treatment of narcolepsy (a sleep-cycle disorder) and cataplexy (a condition associated with weak or paralyzed muscles). The Department of Justice was particularly concerned by this drug because it contained an active ingredient—gamma-hydroxybutyrate (GHB)—that prosecutors believed doubled as a "date-rape" drug, according to the indictment. The government also linked the drug to serious adverse side effects. The drug had earlier been prohibited by the FDA, but was then approved for medical use as Xyrem® in 2002. Like Oxycontin®, Xyrem® draws a wary eye from prosecutors and hence is prescribed hesitantly by physicians despite its important therapeutic uses. By bucking this trend, Dr. Gleason made himself a target.

When a drug is approved by the FDA for marketing, the manufacturer is required to include a label that tells the prescribing physician and the user what medical conditions the drug has been shown to be safe and effective in treating, as well as the recommended doses and other instructions for use. It is unlawful for a drug manufacturer to tell physicians or patients that a drug has been found useful in treating conditions other than those listed on the label or that a drug may be administered other than as prescribed on the label. However, it often happens that treating physicians learn, from experience, a colleague, a medical journal, or other such reliable source, that a drug is effective for certain so-called off-label uses.

The indictment charged Dr. Gleason with touting the drug for off-label uses, including "fatigue, chronic pain, weight loss...depression, bipolar disorders, fibromyalgia, insomnia and movement disorders such as Parkinson's disease." Physicians, however, are clearly allowed by law to prescribe drugs for off-label uses. The FDA prohibits only the drug *manufacturer* from promoting the product for such unapproved purposes. This accommodation was made so as not to unduly interfere with the practice of medicine and the hands-on experience of physicians. But because of the drug warriors' concern about a drug they viewed as having potential for "recreational" use and therefore abuse, a physician touting Xyrem® to his fellow physicians for off-label uses would be well advised to proceed with extreme caution bordering on paranoia, since, despite being legal, it could land him in prison.[36]

In fact, because obtaining FDA approval to market a drug for a particular use is so complex, expensive, and time-consuming, many manufacturers don't bother to obtain permission to market a drug for more than a single medical condition. For a long time, the drug Lyrica® (pregabalin) had been governmentally approved to treat only neuropathic pain, but pain physicians prescribed it usefully, but "off-label," for another pain condition, fibromyalgia. (It was later approved by the FDA to treat fibromyalgia.) Neurontin®, a drug approved for seizure disorders, has enjoyed wide off-label use to treat neuropathic pain. An ultra short acting form of the drug fentanyl, named Actiq® or Fentora®, FDA-approved only for treatment of cancer pain, has been found by physicians to be very effective for off-label use on non-cancer pain. Physicians routinely notify their colleagues, at professional conferences and elsewhere, of these uses based on experience. When I told a prominent physician about Dr. Gleason's case, she expressed considerable dismay because sharing off-label treatment successes among colleagues is ubiquitous within the medical profession and of great therapeutic value. The Gleason arrest and prosecution would "certainly put the fear of God into physicians," she predicted.[37]

So how did the Department of Justice manage to arrest Dr. Gleason for touting and using Xyrem®, despite his right to do so? It charged him, first, with working with the manufacturer in a joint scheme to promote the drug for off-label uses. Orphan, according to the indictment, paid for Dr. Gleason to attend events at which the drug was discussed among physicians. It was at such conferences and dinners that Dr. Gleason allegedly promoted the off-label uses, and he also advised physicians how to get various medical insurance plans and programs to pay for such uses. As a result, he was indicted for two crimes. First, he was involved, said prosecutors, in a "conspiracy" with the manufacturer to promote the off-label use of the drug. By alleging that the company paid for Dr. Gleason to attend the conferences at which he touted the drug, the indictment managed to tag the physician with prohibitions against such touting that, in theory, bind only the company. The indictment further charged Dr. Gleason with a conspiracy to commit health care fraud by advising physicians how to get public and private health insurance plans to pay for such off-label uses. Seemingly lost in this morass of conspiracy law, alleging a joint undertaking by a physician and drug manufacturer to do what the drug manufacturer could not do on its own, was the question of whether Dr. Gleason's medical practice in fact demonstrated the efficacy, for his patients, of Xyrem's® off-label uses.

The indictment was what a lawyer would call creative. By the macabre magic of the nearly formless conspiracy laws, the DOJ was able to turn an innovative and law-abiding physician into a criminal.[38] It was in effect able to write a statute—prohibiting physicians from touting and engaging in off-label uses—that Congress has resolutely refused to enact.

A physician in Dr. Gleason's position would want, for the sake of his reputation, to fight such a charge rather than to make a deal. Yet a deal might very well have been what prosecutors had in mind when they indicted Dr. Gleason, hoping perhaps that they could persuade him to testify against Orphan. But first, they had to dissuade the doctor from challenging the tenuous indictment in court, where the charges could unravel under scrutiny.

How did they do so? The indictment contained a "criminal forfeiture allegation" that sought to force Dr. Gleason to turn over to the government "any property, real and personal, that constitutes or is derived, directly or indirectly, from gross proceeds traceable to the commission of offenses." In other words, he would be forced to turn over a rather substantial amount of money and property. Often the net effect of such a forfeiture is to bankrupt the defendant. Frequently, when there is a forfeiture count in such an indictment, prosecutors seek a *pre-trial* freeze on the defendant's assets, depriving him of the ability to pay for top-flight criminal defense counsel. By depriving the physician of the ability to defend himself vigorously and therefore of the right to a fair trial, the government makes a guilty plea with an agreement of cooperation far more likely, indeed almost inevitable. It's a good bet that a federal criminal defendant is in for a hard, and usually losing, fight when his assets are frozen at the same time high bail is set. This is one reason the government tries so few of these criminal cases. In 2004, for instance, 90 percent of all criminal defendants brought before U.S. district courts were convicted, with 96 percent of those convictions resulting from guilty pleas.[39] In other words, federal prosecutors operate in a justice system where even a *trial* is a rare luxury for most defendants.

Despite early indications that Dr. Gleason would contest the charges, he eventually struck a deal. In August 2008, he pleaded guilty to a misdemeanor count of introducing a misbranded drug into interstate commerce. Because prosecutors agreed that Dr. Gleason had no intent to defraud or mislead, the felony charges were dropped. Nonetheless, Dr. Gleason faces up to a year in prison.[40]

Of course, it is a well-recognized problem within the medical profession that physicians occasionally fall prey to the temptation of too aggressively touting pharmaceuticals for both on-label and off-label uses in exchange for lucrative lecture fees and all-expense paid trips to medical conferences held in exotic locales. Some hospitals and medical schools consider such arrangements to be a conflict of interest and control or even ban them. Other institutions approach the problem by insisting that physicians disclose all payments received from pharmaceutical companies for research or for educational and promotional activities. Some physicians voluntarily refrain from taking such fees. Dr. Daniel J. Carlat, for example, a psychiatrist and medical author who was trained at Boston's renowned Massachusetts General Hospital, withdrew from the company-sponsored lecture circuit, from which he had previously earned some $30,000 a year to supplement his $120,000 salary. He feared, he said, that he was being paid "to say good things about drugs, regardless of what my actual opinions were."[41] Dr. Jerome P. Kassirer, of Tufts University, has written a book, *On the Take*,[42] about how medical people have become too cozy with large pharmaceutical companies.

All this is to say that abusive practices can be controlled with clear conflict-of-interest or mandatory disclosure rules developed within the profession and the industry or within medical schools. Failing that, state and even federal regulatory agencies might play a role. Indeed, in egregious cases, they might be dealt with by the criminal law, although this has proven to be a destructive tool thus far. Whatever legal regime is adopted to curb abuse surely should have the advantage of clarity, especially when the penalties are as draconian as they currently are under the federal criminal code.

• • ● • •

The feds' efforts to assert control over such controversial areas of medical practice as pain relief, end-of-life issues, and off-label prescriptions hardly exhaust the possibilities. Another area of federal involvement in medical practice is guaranteed to keep virtually all practicing physicians on tenterhooks, namely the complex and turgid framework covering government payment for a huge variety of medical procedures and services. Physicians, as well as group medical practice and hospital administrators, can be driven to distraction by these regulations, and bills for medical treatments later declined for payment can have serious financial consequences for a physician or hospital left empty-handed. However, a far more threatening situation develops when the Department of Justice decides to resolve billing disputes by invoking the criminal justice system.

Consider the plight of two obstetricians/gynecologists, Drs. Bert M. Avery and John G. Migliaccio, practicing together as A & M Surgical, Inc., in Lawton, Oklahoma. They were indicted and tried in the early 1990s for filing false claims for payment with the Civilian Health and Medical Program of the Uniformed Services (CHAMPUS), one of numerous government-funded medical coverage programs for federal (in this case, military) employees. (There are other federal health programs as well, including the vast Medicare insurance plan, that most physicians and hospitals come into contact with at some point.)

The charge seemed deceptively simple: the physicians were charged with engaging in a conspiracy to defraud the United States by billing the government for surgical services not covered by the program. Tacked onto the indictment for good measure was the ubiquitous mail fraud count.

The physicians had submitted to CHAMPUS claims for surgical procedures that included fallopian tube repair, a procedure not covered by the program. The female patients involved had earlier been operated on for tubal ligations, a female sterilization procedure more commonly known among laymen as having one's "tubes tied," a form of birth control. They wanted to have the procedure reversed in order to become pregnant. Reversal of tubal ligations, as noted, was not covered by the CHAMPUS program.

The indictment alleged that the two doctors concealed from CHAMPUS administrators the true nature of the surgeries performed to induce the program to pay for the non-covered ligation reversal surgeries. How did the doctors accomplish this fraud on the federal treasury? First, they failed to document adequately in the medical records these patients' previous tubal ligations. Second, in their claims for payment they labeled the fallopian tube repair surgery as "salpingoplasty" rather than the more common term "tubal reanastomosis." According to the prosecutors, the doctors did this to hide from the bureaucrats who reviewed the bills the fact that they'd performed a non-covered procedure. The surgeons further carried out their false billing scheme, according to the indictment, by taking advantage of a rather complex section of the regulations dealing with surgeries in which more than one procedure is performed at the same time.[43]

The question of guilt boiled down, in essence, to a contest over whether the surgeons' primary purpose in performing the surgery was to accomplish the tubal ligation reversal or to repair some other condition covered by the regulations and then incidentally to perform the reversal while the patient was already on the operating table. The government's expert witness testified that the primary purpose of the multiple surgeries appeared to have been to accomplish the ligation reversal in each case, even though the expert admitted that many of the patients had disease, and the expert did not identify a *single* patient who was *free* of disease. The defendant surgeons were adamant that each patient required surgery for a medical condition and that they performed the ligation reversals incidental to the major surgery rather than close up the patients and then re-schedule each for a follow-up, non-covered elective procedure. They were convicted, and they appealed.

It became obvious as the appellate panel examined the regulations and the facts of the case that there was some problem figuring out precisely what the surgeons could have done, consonant with medical ethics and patient safety, to eliminate questions about the legal propriety of their actions. Conducting two separate surgeries so as to eliminate any possible suspicion that the surgeons tried to get paid for the ligation reversals would, quite obviously, have exposed the patients to a serious health risk and would likely have been deemed malpractice. No competent and ethical surgeon would readily place his or her own interest in satisfying skeptical government bureaucrats and prosecutors above the interests of the patient to avoid multiple operations. To do otherwise would be a clear case of the tail wagging the dog.

The jury had convicted despite being instructed by the trial judge that "good faith" by a defendant would be a complete defense. However, the Court of Appeals noted that the real problem was that the regulations on this point were ambiguous. The court made the astonishing admission that "we have not previously addressed proper jury instructions in a false statement case such as this where the issue of ambiguity is inextricably intertwined with the defendant's intent and good faith," despite the fact that the false statement statute has been around since 1863. Well, better late than never. The court said that the jury should have been instructed "concerning reasonable interpretations of ambiguous requirements."

Proper jury instructions, the court realized, would likely have made a real difference in the outcome of the trial. In relation to two of the patients in particular, the court argued, the evidence showed "that the patients sought treatment for legitimate pelvic problems, regardless of the medical merits of [tubal ligation] reversals." In other words, the patients needed surgery for medical reasons, and the ligation reversals were done secondarily, while the patients were already on the operating table.

The doctors provided all of the necessary documentation to the CHAMPUS benefits office. The problem lay in the turgidity of the regulations concerning the coverage, or exclusion, of various surgical procedures. "Defendants did not plead honest mistake," wrote the appellate court. "Rather, they contended that the CHAMPUS universe contains ambiguous matter, and that their interpretation was reasonable." This contention should have been presented to the jury as a possible defense, along with the physicians' contention that the CHAMPUS office should have understood that "salpingoplasty" accurately described the surgical procedure that the regulations dubbed "tubal reanastomosis." The fault lay in the CHAMPUS clerical bureaucrats who had "the duty to evaluate claims and determine amounts of coverage and exclusions," concluded the appellate court. In other words, they should have known what "salpingoplasty" meant.[44]

Perhaps the most telling aspect of the case involved the conspiracy charge. A conspiracy is an agreement between two or more people to commit an illegal act. It is a separate crime from the illegal act itself, since such an agreement is a crime even if the conspirators never get sufficiently close to their goal to actually commit the substantive crime. If two people plan to rob a bank, and take steps to plan and then work toward the robbery itself, they are guilty of conspiracy even if they get caught before they actually leave for or arrive at the bank, much less pull off the robbery.

Conspiracy counts are frequently added to charges for the underlying "substantive" offense, just in case the jury concludes that the crime was never in fact accomplished despite the best intentions of the defendants. The appellate court here, however, was not disturbed by the mere piling on of a conspiracy count against the surgeons; courts have long tolerated that practice despite its being much criticized by legal scholars. But the judges did express astonishment at the government's evidence, presented to the jury, in support of the conspiracy charge. Put simply, the prosecutors tried to prove that the two physicians, who were, after all, partners in a medical-surgical practice, plotted ("conspired") together to commit the crime of submitting false invoices simply by virtue of the fact that they practiced medicine together. It was the astonishing circularity of this reasoning that struck the court as not only odd, but unacceptable as a basis for criminal liability, even for a crime as amorphous as conspiracy. Such a legal theory could turn quite ordinary daily activities of two partners into a criminal conspiratorial enterprise.

However, the ending of the case was not entirely a happy one. Dr. Avery was acquitted on all counts, but one of the counts against Dr. Migliaccio survived. The conviction on this lone count was reversed, but the government was given an opportunity to retry Dr. Migliaccio if it wished. Every other charge in the case was thrown out with no opportunity for retrial.

This one count against Dr. Migliaccio demonstrates another danger in these kinds of cases—the ability of the government to convince its witnesses to testify against a defendant even where that testimony, and the reasons for which it is offered, are very suspect. Here, the government presented one witness, a patient, who testified at trial, in contrast to all of the other patient-witnesses, that Dr. Migliaccio "told her to lie to the hospital staff about the nature of her surgeries."[45] The court expressed its skepticism concerning the truthfulness of this patient's testimony. The judges questioned how and why Dr. Migliaccio would advise the patient to "keep secret the nature of procedures to which other hospital staff were necessarily witnesses." This "remains a mystery," the judges wrote with evident sarcasm. The judges further noted that the witness testified to some conversations with the doctor, and then denied those very conversations took place.

In what was obviously a painful move by the appeals panel, the judges noted that their job was not to re-make nor second-guess the "credibility judgments" made by the jury, but rather to rule only on legal mistakes made by the trial judge. Since this witness made the claim—even if she later contradicted herself, and even if her testimony seemed wildly unlikely—that Dr. Migliaccio told her that he would lie and asked her to go along with the lie, it was a sufficient basis on which to retry the doctor for fraud, notwithstanding the ambiguity of the underlying regulations. And so, on this slim reed, Dr. Migliaccio could be subjected to another trial on this one charge, although next time around the trial judge would have to instruct the jury on the issue of good faith in the context of vague regulations. That would likely lead to acquittal, but only after an enormous waste of time and resources, not to mention aggravation for Dr. Migliaccio.

One of the greatest ironies of the outcome of this case was the fact that, prior to trial, the prosecutors tried to make a deal with Dr. Migliaccio to testify against co-defendant Dr. Avery in exchange for immunity. Dr. Migliaccio refused to betray his partner and instead joined him in the defendants' dock at the trial. It turned out that the defendant to whom the government offered immunity in exchange for singing (presumably finding him the less culpable of the two) was the one whose conviction, rather than being tossed out entirely, got reversed but remanded for a new trial. Such are the messy outcomes when the feds prosecute on the basis of such vague statutes. In order to obtain convictions, they have to convince patients to betray their physicians and physicians to betray their partners—even in a case where an objective review strongly suggests that no crime was committed at all.

In the end, however, the government decided not to retry Dr. Migliaccio. Perhaps the prosecutors read the Court of Appeals' opinion with sufficient care and discerned the judges' unhappiness with the prosecution in general, and in particular with the dubious testimony of the one patient who accused the surgeon of urging her to join him in lying to the government. The government finally called it quits and both physicians returned to the practice of medicine.[46] Tragically for the medical profession, and for the patients who depend on the sound judgment of good doctors, the ending was *unusually* satisfactory.

CHAPTER THREE

The Unhealthy Pursuit
of Medical Device
and Drug Companies

—— ●●● ——

For many Americans, the Internal Revenue Code is the most in-comprehensible federal thicket they will ever have to wade through. However, as anyone in the business of manufacturing, testing, and marketing pharmaceuticals and medical devices can attest, divining the dictates of the Food, Drug, and Cosmetics Act[1] (FDCA) and its at-tendant regulations runs a close second. Within that world, the saga of Lee Leichter stands out for its absurdity, pain, and duration.

Based on a chain of events involving the testing and sale of medi-cal devices for clearing clogged arteries, the government managed to charge 392 separate federal felony counts, including conspiracy to de-fraud the federal government, racketeering, mail fraud, and false state-ments made to the U.S. Food and Drug Administration (FDA). The experience proved devastating to Leichter's personal and professional life, along with those of his co-defendants. Only a steel will, fortified by Leichter's deeply held (and legally correct) belief that he had commit-ted no crime, enabled him to survive and eventually rebuild his life.

The legal team defending Leichter (on which I served along with my then-law partner Andrew Good and associate Philip Cormier) never had any doubt that his conduct conformed to a reasonable interpre-tation of the 1976 amendments to the FDCA, known as the Medical Device Amendments[2] (MDA). Nor did we seriously doubt that he acted entirely in good faith, which made the slow speed at which the wheels of justice churned in his case all the more frustrating. A Boston grand jury investigation commenced in 1990. An indictment followed in 1993. A 27-day jury trial concluded with a conviction on August 24, 1995. Then reversal on appeal came in March 2001. So it was that ultimate resolution of the case, on remarkably favorable terms, occurred after eight years of life-twisting turmoil for Leichter.

Leichter, who was indicted along with several other executives,[3] was head of regulatory affairs for United States Catheter and Instrument, Inc. (USCI), a division of New York Stock Exchange-listed C. R. Bard, Inc. He was not a lawyer, but he invested considerable time and energy in acquiring reasonable mastery of the enormously complex FDA regulations. The regulations govern the terms and conditions under which medical devices could be manufactured and sold to the medical profession for ultimate use on patients. In his final year of employment, before he was fired as a result of the federal investigation, he earned some $72,000 per year (not the princely sum paid to high-level executives) plus a modest bonus. The bonus was an indication that, until the investigation, the company was pleased with Leichter's work. He had a sense of deep devotion to his craft as well as competent knowledge of the letter of the law. Cohorts in his division often joked about how he would walk around with a set of the all but impenetrable regulations in hand, consulting the well-thumbed volume whenever a question arose about the FDA's reporting and testing requirements.

After Leichter was fired in 1990, he lived off his savings to support his wife and two school-aged children. He found it impossible to find alternative employment in the Boston area, where he and his family resided and local press coverage of the regionally based case was intense. He eventually moved to Florida where he found a job that paid significantly less. When the long investigation finally resulted in the October 1993 indictment, he was fired once again, but this time he was unable to find a job anywhere. (Indictments of New York Stock Exchange-listed corporations are, after all, national and not merely local news.) He started to travel around the country as a commission salesman of medical products, which proved so unsuccessful that the family had to sell their home. In the end, the extraordinary pressures of the case destroyed his marriage, which ended in divorce. Before it was over, Leichter had lived under strict bail conditions for a period of nearly eight years, five of those as a felon before that conviction was finally vacated by an appellate court. In a triumph of human resilience, he later remarried and assisted in putting the children from his first marriage through school.

What crime, sin, or both caused such enormous upset to this man's life and family?

The Medical Device Amendments (MDA) were aimed at providing reasonable assurance that medical devices, before being distributed and sold, were "safe and effective." The heart catheter devices manufactured by USCI, which provided the basis for the indictment of Leichter and the others (both higher and lower than he in the corporate pecking order), were "Class III" medical devices, meaning that they were the most inherently risky and hence the most heavily regulated.[4]

Heart catheters, which come in a wide variety of models, are devices for clearing clogged coronary arteries of plaque deposits that cause them to stiffen. When the stiffening process is sufficiently advanced, the arterial deposits block the flow of blood, resulting in potentially fatal heart attacks. This clearing procedure, known as "angioplasty," is often used as a less-invasive alternative to coronary bypass surgery. To perform an angioplasty, the interventional cardiologist inserts the catheter into the artery, "fishes" it inside the blood vessel to the site of the blockage, and inflates a "balloon" with liquid pumped through the catheter to push the plaque against the artery walls, thereby easing the flow of blood through the artery. The balloon is then deflated and the catheter withdrawn.

USCI's catheters were on the cutting edge of technology, but angioplasty nonetheless came with some risks to the patient. One misstep could lead to serious injury or death, either during or after the procedure. These risks, however, were viewed by cardiologists as less severe than invasive coronary bypass surgery. In many instances, doing nothing for such patients was by far the most dangerous alternative.

Before marketing Class III medical devices such as USCI's catheters, a device manufacturer has to submit to the FDA a "pre-market approval" (PMA) application. The information in the PMA application must assure the FDA that the device is both "safe" and "effective."[5] Along the way, as the product is perfected with an eye toward eventual marketing, or even after marketing, if there are any substantial changes that affect the safety and effectiveness of the device, the manufacturer is required to obtain approval for such modifications by filing a PMA Supplement. In this way, the FDA is kept abreast of the product's progress through development and then during use in the market. The FDA has the power at any time to insist on changes to the product or to pull the product off the market for reasons of public safety.

These twinned concepts—safety and effectiveness—are central to the medical device regulatory scheme (as well as to pharmaceutical regs). By law, the FDA must recognize that no drug or medical device can be 100 percent safe or always effective. Rather, the agency's decision whether to authorize a manufacturer to sell a regulated device is to be made after weighing several factors. Those factors include 1) an assessment of the category of patients for whom the device is intended (for example, will the patients deteriorate or die without intervention?); 2) the conditions under which the device will be used and the instructions for use recommended by the manufacturer in the label contained in the packaging; and 3) a weighing of the probable *benefits* to health from use of the device, against any probable *risk* of injury or illness from such use. The FDA's regulations summarize these factors in rather inelegant prose:

> There is reasonable assurance that a device is safe when it can be determined, based upon valid scientific evidence, that the probable benefits to health from use of the device for its intended uses and conditions of use, when accompanied by adequate directions and warnings against unsafe use, outweigh any probable risks.[6]

Thus, central to the FDCA regulations is the realization that no medical device can be 100 percent safe or effective. The goal of the manufacturers and the regulators is to balance "safety" and "effectiveness" in such a way that risks taken by physicians for their patients are judicious ones. In the end, after FDA review and approval of a PMA or a PMA Supplement, a device may be released to the market, where, hopefully, prudent physician judgment would dictate when it should be used. As we saw with pain specialists in the previous chapter, this balancing act often entails as much art as science, weighing risk and predicting success.

There are also conditions under which a medical device can be pulled from the market after it's been released. It is not unheard of for manufacturers voluntarily to recall a device, when experience in actual use demonstrates unforeseen problems that throw into question the balance of risk-versus-reward that allowed the initial release of the product. Nor is it highly unusual for the FDA to order the recall of a device that proves more troublesome than predicted, when the manufacturer will not issue a voluntary recall.[7]

Given the difficult judgments that have to be made at every stage of the manufacture, testing, and release of a sophisticated medical device, the FDA (in conjunction with the Department of Justice, which prosecutes violations of the FDCA) is supposed to reserve criminal prosecution for the clearest, most egregious and intentional evasions. That is, criminal prosecutions should become an option only when it truly can be said that the manufacturer deliberately fooled the FDA into authorizing the release of a device that the company knew, from undisclosed test results, posed a substantial risk to the public without an adequate counter-balancing chance of improving the health of the patient.

Lesser violations are supposed to be dealt with by admonitions, civil fines, retraction of approvals, and other sanctions that can be devastating to a manufacturer but which stop short of criminal prosecution of the company, its executives, and its employees. Errors of judgment or of supervisory duty, not accompanied by culpable criminal intent, might even justify a so-called "absolute liability misdemeanor" charge, but not a felony one. This, in any event, is the theory, but it is not always the practice.

When USCI released various models of heart catheters in the late-1980s, the company encountered an assortment of product defects and other physical problems with its catheters. In some cases, the wire tip of the catheter broke off during surgery. In others, balloons that had been inflated inside the artery during angioplasty failed to deflate, making it difficult to remove the device from the patient's artery. The FDA lodged a series of complaints against USCI and its executives and employees, claiming that they promoted uses of the product beyond the approved use set forth on the labeling; that they conducted field testing without FDA approval; that they made design and other modifications to the devices without obtaining FDA approval by the submission of a PMA Supplement; that they failed to do adequate testing when required; and that they moved the manufacturing site for one product without FDA notification or approval. The company offered a list of responses and defenses as lengthy as the list of FDA complaints, but in the end, when facing a potentially ruinous indictment, the company made a plea deal and agreed to pay a very substantial fine.[8] By refusing to defend itself, USCI also averted a penalty that is the equivalent of capital punishment for a company in the health care industry—a "debarment" order disqualifying the company from selling its products to government-funded health programs and institutions. Because virtually all health programs and institutions involve some federal funds, either through the Medicare and Medicaid programs or others, no medical device manufacturer can survive if debarred. Meanwhile, the individuals involved, who faced prison sentences and not mere fines, proceeded to trial.

The prosecution charged that the defendants had failed to seek PMA Supplement approval for modifications to the design and manufacture of certain catheters, in response to problems experienced by doctors, before distributing the modified catheters to the market. The criminal charges boiled down to claiming that the company had deceived the FDA to avoid the agency's taking the catheters off the market.

The FDA requires the manufacturer to include a sheet outlining "instructions for use" (frequently referred to as the "label") with each unit sold. In deciding what language to approve for the label, the FDA relies in large measure on test data supplied by the manufacturer. That data, in turn, derives from the laboratory and field testing conducted by the manufacturer and reported to the FDA. Physicians are supposed to read the label with care, so that they understand such matters as a device's demonstrated efficacy for certain conditions for which the device has been tested and approved, side effects, and method of use.

The individual USCI defendants had various explanations for why the devices experienced failures out in the field both during the testing period and after the release of the product. For example, some surgeons who used the catheter model where the wire tip broke off had failed to follow the instructions for use, which prescribed that the device be rotated a maximum of 360 degrees as the surgeon steered it through the patient's artery to the area of the blockage. Similarly, the balloon deflation problems stemmed from doctors' failure to properly prepare the device before angioplasty procedures, as required by the instructions.

It was reasonable, argued the defendants, to inquire of physicians whether a mishap had occurred while the product was being used properly or improperly, before deciding whether to report the mishap and corrective actions to the FDA. In other words, they believed they did not have to report failures to the FDA when those failures were caused by doctors' misuse of the products, rather than by design or manufacturing flaws in the products. The government disagreed and took the position that adverse consequences in the field, as well as the company's efforts to correct the problem, needed to be reported even if the problems occurred only when the device was misused.

One could argue for the reasonableness of either position. But this was a criminal trial, and so the defendants contended that the question was not which side had the more prudent or socially beneficial view, but whether the defendants' view of their legal obligations was sufficiently close to being correct, or at least reasonable and held in good faith in light of the lack of precision in the regulations, so that their conduct could not be deemed felonious.

As the trial unfolded, it became fairly obvious that the outcome would depend in part on how the trial judge would instruct the jury as to the meaning of the critical terms "safe" and "effective." The defendants asked that the jurors be instructed in the language of the statute and regulations, which, after all, discussed the concepts of "safety" and "effectiveness" in the context of the "intended...conditions of use." Since both the original and modified devices performed equally when used properly, they reasoned, this should end the case with a quick jury verdict of acquittal. It is important to note that the usage instructions, contained on the product's FDA-approved label, are written in administrative legalese, and so the meanings of "safe" and "effective" would, naturally, be judged in the context of the risk-reward calculus for all medical devices, rather than in absolute terms. The jurors, once made to understand that no device is entirely safe, but that a certain degree of effectiveness justified a commensurate degree of risk, surely would conclude that the defendants acted not only in good faith, but almost certainly in conformity to the regulations' terms, intentions, and spirit. The fact that there were some mishaps and some injuries from use of the product would not, reasoned the defendants, automatically produce a guilty verdict, since *some* mishaps are envisioned by the regulatory scheme. This was one of those rare FDA cases, thought the defendants, where the language of the regulations seemed clear enough to exonerate them of criminal liability.

In view of the feds' general tendency to charge targets with highly technical violations of laughably vague regulations, there was a certain irony in what the prosecutors did next. In the Leichter case, where the defendants actually had made painstaking efforts to comply with the law's technicalities, prosecutors suddenly reversed course: they asked the trial judge to instruct the jury that it should interpret the terms "safety" and "effectiveness" not in the context of whether the product had been used as technically instructed in the labeling, but rather in accordance with the "plain, ordinary meaning" found in the English language dictionary. According to the dictionary, observed the government, "safety" meant "freedom from danger or risks," and "effectiveness" meant "having a definite or desired effect."

The defendants and their lawyers were shocked by this shift. Such definitions might indeed derive from ordinary, everyday concepts, they argued, but dictionary definitions were hardly adequate to convey the particular meaning of the terms as used in the regs, which recognized that medical devices are inherently risky and that their effectiveness cannot be measured in absolute terms.

Judge Joseph Tauro, faced with the daunting task of getting the jury to understand the case well enough to render a verdict, decided to instruct the jury as neither the defendants nor the government requested. He instructed, instead, that the jury had to decide whether the defendants were guilty of "concealing or failing to report material facts" that should have been reported to the FDA, and had "knowingly and willfully, and with an intent to defraud, [failed] to submit" required information to the FDA. In other words, the judge did not weigh in on either side in the definitions war, and the jurors had to decide the case without benefit of the judge's instructions about how the regulations defined the crucial terms "safety" and "effectiveness." They were presented with the prosecutors' argument that they should consult "common sense" and the ordinary dictionary meaning of everyday words, versus the defense lawyers' more technical argument based upon an esoteric drug regulatory scheme.

The jurors sided with the government and convicted Lee Leichter and two of his co-defendants after six days of deliberations following a 27-day jury trial.[9] Judge Tauro, who had been on the federal trial bench since 1972, sentenced each to 18 months in prison, to be followed by two years of supervised release. This was considered a relatively light sentence, suggesting perhaps this experienced and thoughtful trial judge's discomfort with the question of whether a crime had actually been committed.

When it reviewed the convictions, the federal Court of Appeals for the First Circuit, based in Boston, recognized the reason for the trial judge's general inclination to let the jurors find their way through the tangle of FDA regulations. "Indeed, we have recognized that, in some instances, attempts to clarify inherently nebulous concepts can do more harm than good," wrote the three-judge panel in a remarkably candid admission of the existence of "nebulous" laws that could send citizens to prison for long stretches.[10] But the mess that the jury had to untangle here was too much even for a court that, on recent occasions, had allowed and would continue to allow prosecutions to proceed under circumstances where no defendant could reasonably have been expected to understand the applicable law.[11] This was "the relatively rare case," wrote the appeals court, where it was necessary to actually explain all of this to the jury by defining terms of a highly technical regulatory scheme. That was something Judge Tauro had failed to do.

Nonetheless, the Court of Appeals seemed almost to apologize for reversing these convictions. "In our view, the evidence of guilt in this case is quite substantial," the court wrote in an act of transparent contrition, perhaps with an eye to warding off the public and media storm that would inevitably erupt over the judges' perceived softness on white collar crime. "We do not believe, however, that the evidence is so one-sided as to render harmless" the trial judge's inadequate jury instructions, the court had to confess in order to legally justify reversing the jury's verdict.

Interestingly, Judge Tauro himself was far more skeptical about whether the defendants had committed a crime. He had considered, on the record, not sending the case to the jury but instead entering on his own accord a verdict of "not guilty," something a trial judge has the power to do when the case for innocence is overwhelming or the evidence of guilt inadequate. The Court of Appeals noted this in its opinion, perhaps in a further attempt to avert a feared public and media backlash for letting the defendants off the hook.[12] Still, the Court of Appeals felt obliged to call the evidence for serious crimes "substantial" if not "one-sided" in favor of the government.

The problem was that no one could say with any reasonable degree of certainty what those crimes were. Such is the confusing rhetoric of many federal courts: even in those relatively rare cases when they recognize the impossible burden imposed on ordinary citizens forced to figure out statutes and regulations that puzzle even experienced trial judges like Tauro.

One would have thought that in a situation so racked by ambiguity and the wreckage of a family, where the trial judge himself had indicated that he came close to throwing the case out, and where proper jury instructions would most likely have led to acquittal, the government would drop the case. Such was not to be.

The prosecutors, led by Assistant U.S. Attorney Michael Loucks, were at the time on the ascent. Created and organized by Loucks in 1985, the Health Care Fraud Unit of the United States Attorney's office in Boston was emerging as a national model for turning FDA enforcement into a prosecutorial industry and a money machine for filling government coffers.[13] Through the efforts of this unit, Boston became the high-profile national epicenter of the Department of Justice's "war" against pharmaceutical and medical-device manufacturers.[14] The DOJ targeted companies it saw as "ripping off" taxpayers and, in the process, endangering the public by selling devices and drugs either deleterious to health or promoted for off-label medical conditions. The unit did not like to compromise its reputation by appearing in the law reports and, particularly, in the press, as losing a case. With Leichter's case, Loucks and his cohorts were in a mood for compromise in order to avoid a retrial that might well have ended, this time, in acquittal. But they also wanted to save face.

Lee Leichter, too, had had enough. Given Judge Tauro's doubts about the case and bolstered by the Court of Appeals' reversal, but also wanting to end the matter while he was still young and healthy enough to start over, Leichter agreed to plead guilty to a "strict liability misdemeanor," an offense carrying relatively mild personal consequences (a maximum of one year in prison) and to which one may plead without an admission of an intent to break the law.[15] The chances of incarceration are also significantly lower than in the case of a felony, in part because some judges remain queasy with the notion of imprisoning a defendant who has not been found to have acted knowingly in violation of his or her legal obligations. Even though the DOJ increasingly seeks strict liability misdemeanors to convict and even incarcerate people who have shown no evidence of intent to violate the law, it remains a device that, happily, still makes some judges uncomfortable. Of course, it would be even better if there were more judicial unease about the felony convictions of defendants who supposedly violate statutes that are virtually impossible to understand.

Judge Tauro imposed a sentence on Leichter of one year probation, which would include eight months' home confinement. One could hardly ask for a louder statement of the trial judge's assessment of the case after more than a decade of investigation, prosecution, and legal trench warfare. Of course, Leichter's victory would not have been possible but for the corporation's adherence to its contractual obligation to advance funds for payment of its executives' legal fees, a lesson that was not lost on the DOJ when it later sought to pressure companies to renege on that obligation.[16] Leichter was able to get on with the rest of his life, and the medical fraud unit of the Boston U.S. attorney's office could use its resources to scout out its next victim.

• • ● • •

With Boston leading the way, prosecutions under the food and drug laws have been increasingly used to harass drug and medical device manufacturers. The prosecution of TAP Pharmaceuticals and several of its employees, following on the heels of the Leichter fiasco, helps fill out the picture. First, however, some background on the regulation of pharmaceutical sales practices is in order.

The complexity and uncertainty of the FDA regulations extend to the rules governing sales and promotional practices. Pharmaceutical companies and their officers and employees are legally obligated to avoid "fraudulent" promotional practices when their products are to any extent paid for with federal funds. Since no pharmaceutical product likely can survive without sales to or through federally funded health care programs, federal fraud charges can be brought against the purveyors of nearly every pharmaceutical brought to market.

The most common form of illegal promotion of approved pharmaceuticals is making secret, disguised, or otherwise improper payments by the manufacturer to induce a physician, group practice, or hospital to use that manufacturer's product in lieu of a competitor's. The practice is seen as particularly pernicious if a superior drug loses out to an inferior product because of what is effectively a salesman's bribe.

Federal drug regulators and prosecutors are also on the lookout for financial inducements given by manufacturers and salespeople to get physicians to prescribe a particular product that is neither more nor less effective than a competing drug, but that is significantly more expensive. For example, pharmaceuticals still protected by patents tend to sell for substantially more than similar products whose patents have expired. When a drug patent expires, competitors quickly produce copycat versions known as "generics." It would be unlawful, and surely most people would intuitively realize this, for a salesperson to bribe a customer's purchasing agent to buy, or a physician to prescribe, a more expensive brand name product instead of the equivalent generic (if in fact both products are equivalent). On the other hand, some physicians might want to stick with a known formulation by a known and trusted manufacturer, rather than take a chance with an unknown generic. Such decisions are supposed to be made by medical professionals who have evaluated the comparative merits of the products and who know their patients, not because they have been offered bribes by a pharmaceutical salesman.

Another sales practice federal enforcers track arises from the fact that a doctor is allowed, in theory at least, to use his or her professional discretion to prescribe a particular drug for a particular condition, whether or not the regulatory agency has approved the drug for that condition—that is, for "off-label" uses. Indeed, a physician may prescribe whatever drug he or she wishes, for whatever medical condition, his education and experience teach him is ameliorated by that drug. (The notable exception is the prescription of controlled narcotics, where federal drug laws limit a physician's discretion—the situation faced by the pain doctors discussed in Chapter Two.) The doctor might be in danger of a civil malpractice lawsuit should his or her judgment wander too far from accepted medical practice or scientific evidence, but the physician commits no crime for ignoring the limitations set forth on the FDA-approved label.

It is, however, a federal felony for a drug manufacturer or its sales representatives to seek to *induce* physicians to prescribe a pharmaceutical for off-label uses. Likewise it is a felony to bribe a physician or hospital to prescribe that drug rather than a competitor's product that might be cheaper, superior, or more appropriate. In such a scenario, both the manufacturer/salesperson and the physician or hospital administrator are vulnerable to federal indictment. There is a reasonable legal theory for this. If physicians, group practices, clinics, and hospitals that are dependent on federal reimbursement prescribe an expensive drug, not on its merits but rather because of personal under-the-table remuneration, the patient is endangered and the public treasury is robbed.

The Boston Globe, the major regional daily to which the Boston-based Health Care Fraud Unit cannily played in its early years, reported in 2003 that between May 1996 and May 2001 the Loucks prosecution team had "recovered $1.54 billion for federal taxpayers, more than 30% of all health care fraud settlements by the nation's 94 U.S. attorneys' offices."[17] These dollar figures continued to escalate, especially in Boston, but also elsewhere in the country as these prosecutions became priorities. By September 2007, the *Globe* was able to update its report by trumpeting, after a $515 million settlement with Bristol-Myers Squib in an off-label use case, that the Massachusetts U.S. attorney's office had "obtained more than $4 billion in health care fraud settlements since 2000." Lower down in the story, the article noted that U.S. attorney Michael J. Sullivan had conceded that his office had no evidence that the administration of the company's drug for off-label uses had in fact harmed anyone.[18]

As is often the case, in Boston and elsewhere, the federal "whistleblower" statute played a role in commencing the TAP investigation and prosecution. Under the so-called *qui tam* law, a person who has knowledge of a government rip-off may seek to attract the U.S. attorney's interest in pursuing the company.[19] The whistleblower is entitled to a substantial percentage of whatever the government collects. Such governmental interest in a civil lawsuit often triggers a parallel criminal investigation by the Health Care Fraud Unit. The whistleblower becomes a government witness, one with a strong financial incentive to see the corporation held liable for fraud. By combining a civil fraud lawsuit and a criminal prosecution, the Department of Justice gives the corporate defendant a potent incentive to settle. While a civil fraud suit might be expensive, a criminal conviction can put the manufacturer out of business. Since a guilty verdict in a criminal case makes it virtually impossible for the company to win an accompanying civil suit[20] (the finding of criminal guilt legally precludes a contrary finding in the civil suit), the two cases are almost invariably settled at the same time.

Corporations rarely fight such charges, even when they have the evidence to prove their innocence or are at least able to demonstrate that their interpretations of the arcane regulations were reasonable and hence not criminal. It is often cheaper to make a deal than it is to risk the enormous legal fees, publicity, and distraction that fighting entails. The government also holds a trump card. It may follow a criminal conviction with a "debarment" proceeding that would disqualify a company from doing business with any government-funded program or agency. This is typically seen, and for good reason, as a death knell for any company in the health care field. The threat of debarment is the main reason so few pharmaceutical companies fight a criminal charge. It is also why the accompanying civil case, whether initiated by the government or by a whistleblower, produces huge amounts of money for the coffers of government agencies (not to mention whistleblowers' bank accounts). The merits of the charges are decidedly secondary to the financial imperatives that, more often than not, determine the outcomes of corporate criminal cases.

Individuals, on the other hand, often have a far greater incentive to go to trial than do their corporate employers. Corporations that fight may lose large amounts of money or even go out of business. Individuals often are sentenced to ruinously long prison terms. Unless an individual defendant can negotiate a guilty plea in exchange for non-incarceration or a modest prison sentence, he has an incentive to go to trial, especially when he has a strong defense and is willing to risk a heavier sentence. Moreover, many corporate executives have clauses in their employment contracts obligating the company to pay their legal fees until and unless they are found guilty.

It was therefore only a slight surprise when, in July 2004, ten former employees of TAP Pharmaceuticals decided to go to trial on the charges to which the corporation three years earlier decided to plead guilty and pay a then-record $885 million fine and settlement. The real surprise came when federal prosecutors *lost* on their claim that the company's discounting sales and promotional practices constituted illegal kickbacks and bribes to induce physicians and hospitals to use TAP products.

When the employees first announced their intention to fight, it was widely seen in the legal community as a quixotic, doomed effort. The company, after all, had not only pled guilty and agreed to pay $885 million, it had also agreed to cooperate with prosecutors. TAP, to curry favor with the prosecutors, even waived the attorney-client privilege and allowed prosecutors to rummage through its files, which included memos of discussions and interviews between the corporation's lawyers and the individual defendants during an internal corporate investigation begun after the feds announced their criminal investigation.

The government's two star witnesses were an unnamed former TAP employee and one Joseph Gerstein, medical director of the Tufts Associated Health Maintenance Organization, which purchased TAP drugs. The former TAP employee had received a whistleblower bonanza of $77 million and, from TAP's civil settlement, split $17 million with the HMO. The former TAP employee was particularly enterprising. He banked $47.5 million more for whistleblowing in a related federal prosecution of drug manufacturer AstraZeneca in 2003. Critics and cynics might think that the government had effectively bought its testimony from both the whistleblowers and the corporation.

So what practices did the feds view as felonious? The indictment charged, among other things, that TAP salesmen sought to induce prescribing physicians to order free samples of the prostate cancer drug Lupron® instead of its "essentially identical," cheaper competitor, Zoladex®, by giving doctors free samples of the drug. The salesmen allegedly did so in the "expectation…that doctors receiving the free drug would prescribe that free drug, and would thereafter bill it to their patients and their insurers, including the Medicare program, and thus receive money from Medicare and others for the prescription of that free product." It is in fact a common practice to provide free samples to physicians. Samples are provided on the assumption doctors will become familiar with the drug's efficacy in their own medical practices. Later, once convinced of the drug's efficacy, many physicians give the samples to their indigent patients. These practices, it should be stressed, are commonly found in the pharmaceutical industry and medical profession.

The indictment claimed that, since physicians could use other means to obtain medication for their indigent patients, the free samples provided by the TAP salesmen were really a disguised bribe. Worse, some physicians gave the samples to their patients but billed Medicare for them anyway, a practice that the indictment claimed the salesmen must have suspected but to which they were "willfully blind." What's more, these sales inducements, aimed at causing physicians to prescribe the more expensive TAP product, were a form of fraud. Prosecutors rounded out the indictment by labeling as "fraud" still other sales-incentive practices common in the industry.

One of the more bizarre charges concerned financial grants given by the drug company and the salesmen, so-called "educational grants." Such grants could be used for a variety of purposes ostensibly related to medical education, such as "to pay for attendance at seminars and conferences of professional organizations, to purchase medical equipment, to pay for education for the physician's office staff," as well as for less clear-cut development activities, such as "to support marketing efforts, to finance parties, to pay for bar tabs at country club functions, to pay for golf outings." Such social events are an integral part of what the industry calls "professional development," but the indictment made it sound like the social aspects of these conferences were wholly separate from their educational functions and hence were clearly fraudulent bribes unrelated to medical practice.[21]

The indictment further alleged that the TAP salesmen, to hide the fact that they were providing "things of value" to hospital and HMO employees to influence their decisions about which drugs to buy, would also offer educational grants to the employer, with the expectation that it would directly benefit specific employees.

Normally, when a sales rep gives a real bribe to a corporate purchasing chief to induce the purchaser to buy that sales rep's products (a classic "kickback" arrangement), the bribe is kept secret from the employer. The employer is, after all, the victim when his purchasing agent is bribed to buy particular products over other cheaper or superior products. But in the TAP case, the salesmen not only informed the corporate customers that they were providing educational grants for the benefit of certain purchasing agents, but went so far as to give the grants directly to the employing organization rather than to the purchasing agents. The government viewed such openness as further proof of how sneaky the TAP salesmen were![22]

The government's case against one of the defendants seemed so lacking that the trial judge acquitted her before her case got to the jury.[23] As for the other nine, the jurors gave the 66-page, 156-paragraph indictment due scrutiny, deliberating for 23 hours after a three-month trial. Its verdict couldn't have been clearer: acquittals on all counts.[24] The jury, in its wisdom, cleaned up the mess made by prosecutors, regulators, and the judges who allow such cases to proceed to trial.

• • ● • •

In a case remarkably similar to that of the TAP salesmen (and less than a year after their acquittals), Loucks's fraud unit in April 2005 criminally charged the Swiss drug maker Serono SA and later indicted four of its former company executives. The indictment alleged bribery and conspiracy, among other crimes, charging that the defendants offered doctors free trips to a medical conference in France to promote the prescription of Serono's drug Serostim®.

The Serono case added one element absent from the TAP case, namely that the company and its sales reps not only offered inducements to prescribe Serostim®, but also that they sought to promote off-label uses of the drug. According to the off-label use charge, Serostim®, described as "a very expensive drug," had been approved by the FDA to treat "AIDS wasting, also known as cachexia, a condition involving profound involuntary weight loss in AIDS patients, with a preferential loss of lean body mass over fat mass." Meanwhile, with the invention of so-called AIDS cocktails, the incidence of AIDS wasting had decreased markedly. As a result, charged the Boston Health Care Fraud Unit, Serono "launched a campaign to 'redefine AIDS wasting' in order to create a market for Serostim® by expanding the disease state for which Serostim® could be prescribed as a treatment."[25]

To promote this off-label use of Serostim®, the company's sales reps allegedly distributed literature indicating that "wasting was being 'masked' by weight gain" occasioned by the use of AIDS cocktails, and that the "wasting" phenomenon, the loss of lean body mass, was still occurring, unnoticed. Even though Serostim® had been approved by the FDA for the AIDS wasting syndrome, prosecutors deemed the promotion of the product for that very condition an "off-label" use because physicians were being told that there still was a need to prescribe the drug.

In other words, the government sought to creatively redefine the manufacturer's labeling obligation, and to do so not by changing the regulation in order to give advance notice of the enhanced obligation when medical progress presented new circumstances, but rather by prosecuting the company and individuals who would have had no way of knowing the risk they were taking by following the literal wording of the regulation. Ordinarily, a controversial technical point of science such as this would, or should, be resolved by administrative and civil rulemaking based upon the best scientific evidence available. Alternatively, it could be determined by civil proceedings for violations before the rules have become clear, with fines resulting in the event of an outcome adverse to the company. If the company or its employees then continue to make claims not supported by the scientific evidence, indictment would be appropriate. In that case, any violation would be a clear and intentional one committed by defendants who had been put on notice of their new, enhanced legal obligation. But in the Serono case, the government proceeded by indictment in a novel area of law and on a contested issue of science.

It would be relatively simple, not to mention eminently more fair, for the federal pharmaceutical bureaucrats at the FDA to issue regulations giving the industry desperately needed guidance as to where the lines are drawn. During the process of promulgating new regulations, the government would learn the views of the companies about the realities of the marketplace, and could hear the scientists as well. The regulators could make clear the public health and federal treasury implications of the practices being examined. The companies would then have a set of regulations to follow, hopefully written in clear English, after which transgressions could truly be said to be intentional violations of known legal duties. If a prosecution can be regarded as "novel" or "creative," one must question whether it should have been brought on the criminal rather than the civil side of the court.[26]

Serono followed the game plan established by TAP Pharmaceutical. Serono did its *mea culpa* and agreed to pay a $740 million fine to settle the charge that it paid kickbacks to physicians to induce them to prescribe Serostim®, and that it promoted the off-label use of its product. This left two former vice presidents and two regional sales directors to face an April 2005 indictment. The alleged bribe was an all-expenses-paid trip to attend a medical conference in Cannes, characterized by the prosecutors as a payoff rather than a legitimate medical educational program, presumably because of its posh location. (One wonders about the future implications for government-attended conferences in renowned ski resorts and the like. Assistant U.S. Attorney Loucks, for example, was a featured speaker at Ski Aspen, a continuing education retreat for lawyers, organized by the North Carolina Bar Association in January 2007.)[27] As in TAP, the Serono case was launched at the behest of whistleblowers. Five Serono employees filed suit, for which they collectively reaped a lucrative pot totaling at least $51 million.[28] As in TAP, the corporation quickly folded, in large measure to protect itself from a "debarment" order. And as in TAP, the individual defendants were all acquitted by a jury. Unlike the TAP case, however, where the jury deliberated for 23 hours, the Serono jury dispatched the prosecutors' theory in fewer than three.[29]

• • ● • •

The Department of Justice's nonchalant attitude toward "creative" prosecutions based on extensions and interpretations of vague statutes and regulations is nowhere better illustrated than in the prosecution of Dr. Peter Gleason, the Maryland psychiatrist (see Chapter Two) facing charges for promoting a pharmaceutical for a non-approved, so-called "off-label" purpose.[30]

Since the FDA regulations ostensibly do not prohibit a physician from prescribing off-label uses for a regulated drug (only the manufacturer is prohibited), how can a physician be indicted for doing so? The DOJ charged the pharmaceutical manufacturer, Jazz Pharmaceuticals,[31] with joining with Dr. Gleason and encouraging him to tout its product for off-label uses. Since Dr. Gleason joined in a "criminal conspiracy" (an unlawful agreement) with a manufacturer that itself is not allowed to promote off-label uses, he became, in the eyes of the prosecutors, a conspirator in a jointly committed crime. He was tainted, essentially, by the company's unlawful purpose.

Daniel E. Troy, a prominent lawyer and the former chief counsel of the FDA, was quoted as warning that "this is a very, very scary development."[32] Dr. Steven Nissen, the interim chairman of cardiovascular medicine at the famed Cleveland Clinic, predicted that the case could "have a chilling effect on physicians, because when we give lectures, we assume that giving an opinion about the use of a drug is not going to get us into legal difficulty." One reason that physicians, even those connected to prominent medical establishments, were shocked at the Gleason prosecution, was because physicians rely on their and their colleagues' judgments and experiences as to the uses, including off-label uses, of pharmaceuticals all the time. Virtually any physician would admit, perhaps even boast, that he relies to a great extent on his own judgment and experience, as well as that of others expressed in medical journals, in deciding what to prescribe for various conditions. The manufacturer's FDA-approved label is just one source of guidance; experience is another.

The purpose of the indictment, Dr. Gleason thought, was to pressure the doctor to cooperate against the manufacturer; his "account is at least partly supported by a letter" in which the assistant United States attorney reported on efforts to obtain the physician's cooperation, reported *The New York Times*'s Alex Berenson.[33]

As it turned out, Jazz hitched itself to the prosecution team and only then notified Dr. Gleason that he would be facing the charges without the company's assistance. Even though the statute on its face applied only to the company, it would be the physician, alone, who would suffer prosecution and conviction for activity quite common and widely deemed benign within the profession. "They're just cutting me loose," the doctor lamented. In the Department of Justice's world of "eat or be eaten," whoever makes it to the prosecutor's door first generally gets the deal. There and only there is the "truth" written, or perhaps composed.

CHAPTER FOUR

Following (or Harassing?) the Money

——— ●●● ———

I think often of the prosecution of Michael Milken, the financial genius and guiding star of the brokerage firm of Drexel, Burnham & Lambert. Milken and his firm flowered in the 1970s and '80s when Milken created a whole new capital market capable of financing daring new ventures that threatened to upset many an old order. But the firm and its visionary leader suddenly crashed and burned at the climax of the Department of Justice's assault on the "decade of greed" in the late-1980s and early-'90s.

The case has gnawed at me, and not because I instinctively have more sympathy for my billionaire clients than for the penniless political radicals I've represented *pro bono*. Rather, the techniques used to force Milken to plead guilty to non-crimes were so raw and dangerous that it became obvious to me, shortly after I joined his defense team following Milken's unexpectedly harsh sentencing, that the same techniques would soon be applied to a much wider sphere of civil society which cannot afford to fight. The pain unjustly suffered by Milken and his family was real and palpable, and it became clear that if they can do this to him, they can—and will—do it to anyone.

Had Milken *not* been famous and wealthy, critics might have taken a closer and more dispassionate look at the fabricated case against him and the methods used to force him to plead guilty. As is so often the case with federal criminal prosecutions, the fabrication consisted, in part, of dubious testimony given by rewarded witnesses, and felony charges for conduct (admitted to by Milken) that, to informed and objective observers, did not appear to constitute crimes.

Michael Milken's pioneering development of higher-risk, higher-yield corporate bonds (dubbed "junk bonds" by his detractors) gave birth to some of the most important start-up (and, in a real sense, upstart) companies of the decade. Among these were such now well-known challengers to America's corporate status quo as McCaw Cellular, Barnes & Noble, MCI, and Ted Turner's Cable News Network (CNN). Any ambitious entrepreneur with more ideas than cash could urge Milken to convince his wide network of wealthy risk-takers to invest in an innovative enterprise in exchange for a higher-than-normal interest rate on the company's bonds, often combined with some stock option component (dubbed an "equity kicker") to make the investment more attractive should the company succeed. A number of his clients were money managers with great sums at their disposal, and they found that investing in Milken deals provided unusually hefty profits in return for risks that were only slightly more daring than more traditional investment vehicles. Milken's secret, if it was a secret at all, was that ventures deemed too risky by traditional banks and investment houses were in fact not all that perilous and offered the chance of substantially above-average returns, particularly as they revolutionized certain industries. He filled a gap and made him and his firm very rich. This did not go unnoticed by the envious nor the ambitious. All this restructuring infuriated elements of the corporate and investment-banking establishments, and it made Milken a target of opportunity for federal prosecutors.

Milken's problem was not simply that, in the go-go days of the '80s, prosecutors were overly sensitive to cries of "foul" by a business establishment unaccustomed to such ungentlemanly competition, or that the news media were particularly hungry for a good big-business scandal. Milken's biggest problem was that some of his most ingenious but entirely lawful maneuvers were viewed, by those who initially did not understand them, as felonious, precisely because they were novel—and often extremely profitable.

Drexel and Milken had been under investigation since the mid-1980s, and Milken received a "target" letter from the DOJ in September 1988 informing him that he was likely to be indicted. When the firm was indicted and then pled guilty in December 1988, it was obvious that the shoe would drop on Milken, since the firm agreed, as part of its plea bargain, to "cooperate" in the government's investigation of the firm's erstwhile *wunderkind*. When Milken was finally indicted in March 1989, the DOJ told the nation, on the second page of its massive 110-page indictment, that the financier had earned $45,715,000 in 1983, escalating each year until his "direct compensation" from Drexel reached $550,054,000 in 1987. Many reporters, it seemed, barely had to read beyond this page to conclude that Milken *must* be guilty.

The indictment appeared to be the ordinary mishmash of counts under the usual statutes-of-choice. These included mail fraud, wire fraud, securities fraud, and, to make the parts appear to add up to more than the whole (and to enable the government to demand asset forfeiture), racketeering. There was, however, one aspect of the indictment that made it likely that this wealthy, headstrong, and self-confident titan would enter into a plea bargain rather than fight to the bitter end. Milken's younger brother, Lowell, also was accused of being a key participant in his brother's "fraudulent" schemes. Lowell had a decidedly secondary role in Drexel's trading operations in comparison to Michael, but as the indictment was careful to point out, Lowell's compensation, while not near that of his older brother, was hardly a pittance. His "direct compensation," the indictment blared, had escalated from $10,180,000 in 1984 to $48,059,000 in 1987.

To knowledgeable observers, adding Lowell to the mix seemed diabolically calculated to pressure Michael to cut a deal rather than challenge the government's claim that Milken's Drexel deals were in any way criminal. (As one Milken lawyer put it, "if Lowell's last name were Smith, he would not be in the case.")[1] The inclusion of Lowell as a defendant lent a sense of unease to those who knew Michael well, for his public reputation as a finance whiz was exceeded by his private reputation as a deeply devoted family man. Michael, thought insiders, would not easily risk letting his younger brother go down the tubes. Lowell, for his part, put no pressure on his older brother to throw in the towel just to protect him.

The matter of Lowell Milken's being included in Michael's indictment, however, was on the back burner as long as a successful defense seemed feasible. And when the indictment was announced, the betting was that Milken would give the DOJ the legal fight of the decade, if not of the century. Rudolph W. Giuliani, who in 1983 began a spectacular five-year stint as the U.S. attorney for the Southern District of New York, had put together a team of tough, eager, and exceedingly ambitious (for themselves and their boss) prosecutors.[2] Giuliani's political ambitions were suggested by the fact that his group of lawyers and investigators, known as the "Yes Rudys!," included one tasked with tending to the boss's political future. As we now know, they did their job well. Giuliani would serve as mayor of New York for two terms (from 1994 to 2002) and would for a brief time be deemed a serious contender for the Republican nomination for president in the 2008 election.

Milken, for his part, assembled a legal team headed by the highly regarded Arthur Liman, lead litigator and legal strategist of the renowned New York law firm of Paul, Weiss, Rifkind, Wharton & Garrison.[3] Milken's lifelong friend and personal attorney, Richard Sandler, was a stickler for detail and had command of an enormous body of facts.

Developments over the next few months made a vigorous defense to the palpably weak charges inadvisable, however. Milken's legal team learned that the DOJ was planning to bring a "superseding" indictment with expanded charges. When FBI agents interviewed Milken's 92-year-old grandfather, it was taken as a hint that the feds were trying to involve, or at least harass, other family members to put still more pressure on the family head to take a fall. And there was always the possibility that, as the investigations continued, the Milken brothers could be indicted yet again, even if they won this trial. More ominous still, there were noises about indictments in various states. The chances of winning against all (even unmerited) indictments naturally decreased as the number of jurisdictions expanded. The message to Michael was that unless he gave up the battle and delivered to the DOJ the victory it craved, both brothers could look forward to a long stretch of trials that, statistically, would make a conviction somewhere along the line more than likely, followed by very lengthy sentences.

Finally, after using a host of bare-knuckled tactics to discourage Milken from testing its dubious criminal indictment, the government made the older brother an offer he could not refuse: if Michael would plead guilty to six felony counts and agree to pay $600 million, the feds would drop all charges against Lowell. Further, while a routine obligation to "cooperate" with the investigations and prosecutions would ordinarily be included in the plea bargain, Milken would not be obligated to give the feds any information in advance or to compose a script for testimony in any particular case. The plea agreement was unusual for another reason as well: the government agreed not to recommend any particular sentence to the judge.

The proposed deal did not do violence to Milken's conscience. He would not have to "sing" (or, worse, to "compose") incriminating testimony against friends and colleagues, as so many "cooperators" find themselves pressured to do. And so, to save everyone, especially his younger brother, Michael agreed to the plea bargain.

The six counts involved what appeared at first glance to be a garden variety of securities and tax fraud transactions. Three of the counts involved dealings with the infamous Ivan Boesky, a fraud artist and former Drexel client who made a pact with the feds to avoid a substantially longer sentence. These counts involved a securities industry practice known as "stock parking," which was never defined in federal law or regulations as a crime, and which was quite common in the industry. Two other counts involved transactions that Milken engaged in with David Solomon, a funds manager who likewise had turned government witness. The sixth count was merely a conspiracy charge covering the events in the first five.

While the entire world seemed to assume that Milken had confessed to actual crimes, a few recognized that the DOJ emperor actually had no clothes. At the time, *The Wall Street Journal* opinion writer L. Gordon Crovitz penned column after column questioning how and why the transactions constituted crimes. After the case was over, former University of Chicago Law School Dean and economist Daniel Fischel analyzed the case in a highly regarded 1995 book called *Payback*.

Fischel concluded that the six counts, and indeed the entire original indictment, described perfectly lawful transactions that required a huge stretch to be even remotely considered criminal.[4]

Yet at the time of his plea, neither Milken nor his attorneys publicly questioned the felony charges. After he had agreed to plead guilty, it was suddenly in his interest to see his plea accepted by Judge Kimba Wood of the U.S. District Court in Manhattan. If Milken questioned the charges, the judge would not accept his plea on the six counts and he would be forced to go to trial on the entire indictment. Giuliani got precisely what he wanted.

Immediately after Milken's lawyers announced his plea agreement in open court, in April of 1990, SEC Chairman Richard Breeden held a press conference to put to rest suspicions bruited about by the likes of journalist Crovitz: "Mr. Milken has been portrayed as wrongly accused and as having simply devoted himself to the financing of small or emerging businesses," announced Breeden. "His admissions today demonstrate that he stood at the center of a network of manipulation, fraud, and deceit." The skeptics were consigned, for the moment, to retreat.

As Milken's sentencing approached, the case went a bit off track. Pre-sentencing maneuverings began when DOJ lead prosecutors John Carroll and Jess Fardella filed a memorandum with Judge Wood that seemed to violate the spirit, if not quite the letter, of the agreement that the government would not make a sentencing recommendation. It claimed to describe "Milken's Other Crimes" and went on to ask that "Milken be sentenced to a period of incarceration that reflects the enormity of his crimes."

Judge Wood decided to hold a hearing on sentencing. At the hearing the government would be given 20 hours to present its evidence and arguments on its three strongest "other crimes," and the defense would have an opportunity to contest those claims. Milken's lawyers could not really argue that he had pleaded guilty to non-crimes, even if they believed such to be true, for that would wreck the plea bargain. But they were entirely free to contest the government's claim that "other crimes" had been committed. The sentencing hearing was set to become the first public clash between prosecutors and Milken's lawyers over whether Milken was the white collar criminal of the century.

Knowledgeable observers recognized that the government's courtroom presentation, in the fall of 1990, was a total bust. The definitive proof came when Judge Wood made her sentencing decision, saying she would not rely on the "other crimes" allegations because "the evidence established neither the government's version of Milken's conduct nor Milken's own version." It was perhaps too much to expect that, at this tense and highly visible stage of the case, Judge Wood would do a 180-degree turn and begin questioning the basis for Milken's plea to the six felonies. And, after all, she was not yet sure that Milken's protestations of innocence of the "other crimes" were entirely correct. But surely the government had taken its best shot and missed. Nonetheless, Judge Wood imposed an unexpectedly harsh ten-year prison sentence, in part because she believed that Milken "engaged in the additional misconduct of attempting to obstruct justice." This impression seemed to be based on testimony offered by former Drexel employees, now cooperating witnesses, that Milken acted secretively in the run-up to the investigation. In one typical bit of testimony, a Drexel underling recounted a meeting during which Milken didn't speak and instead communicated by writing notes on a pad and then deleting them. It is crucial to note that none of these witnesses ever actually testified that Milken instructed them to destroy documents, and the government apparently did not have enough confidence in these accusations to actually list obstruction of justice as one of Milken's supposed other crimes. Judge Wood's focus on these accusations was a bizarre and unexpected development.

At this point, Milken decided to ask a new set of lawyers to examine his plea. He hired Harvard Law Professor Alan Dershowitz, who in turn brought my law firm into the case. We did a close analysis of all six counts to which Milken had pleaded guilty and concluded—somewhat to our surprise—that he had pleaded guilty to six non-crimes. The legal team suspected that Judge Wood imposed the overly harsh sentence in part due to inexperience (President Reagan had nominated her to the federal bench in 1988) and in part out of a sense that she should not be seen as "weak" in the face of what prosecutors and the news media had labeled the largest securities fraud of the century. Perhaps she simply didn't fully understand some of the complexities of the transactions involved. She was also known to be sensitive to the news media (at the time she was married to an editor at *Time* magazine) and did not want to endure the "soft on white collar crime" label. The defense aimed to have the judge reconsider in a more rational, less tense moment.

The plan worked. Milken, in an effort to get Judge Wood to lower the sentence, agreed to testify in a prosecution of former Drexel Burnham Lambert colleague Alan Rosenthal. What prosecutors perhaps had not counted on was that Milken would deliver truthful and unvarnished testimony that would help, rather than hurt, Rosenthal.

Rosenthal had been an employee of the Drexel firm who worked with Milken on various deals, including the deal resulting in one of the six counts to which Milken had pleaded guilty. The charge, which was tried before highly regarded federal District Judge Louis Stanton, claimed that Milken and Rosenthal had organized a scheme favoring a Milken client, David Solomon, involving certain tax trades that produced tax losses. The government claimed the trades were shams and the losses illusory because Milken promised he would find Solomon a profitable investment at some point in the future, in order to reimburse him for the losses. (For tax purposes, losses for which an investor is guaranteed reimbursement are not real losses.)[5] Solomon had been granted immunity from prosecution and then was enlisted as a government witness against Milken.

Losses for purposes of taking a tax deduction must be "real" rather than "sham" losses. The government deemed Solomon's losses to be a sham because Milken had promised to find Solomon a favorable investment to make up for the loss. But this is not the same as a *guarantee* against loss. Contrary to the government's contention, Solomon undertook a real risk of loss. Milken could not argue the point in his plea bargain, as he was desperate to have Judge Wood accept his plea and his contrition. But neither Rosenthal nor Judge Stanton were in a similarly compromised position. Judge Stanton concluded that the tax losses were real, not illusory, and that Milken's promise to make up the losses by putting Rosenthal into profitable investments was a contingent, indefinite promise that did not render the tax losses illusory. Solomon, ruled Judge Stanton, was exposed to real economic risk, and the transaction was neither a sham nor a fraud.

Judge Stanton acquitted Rosenthal of that count and did not allow it to go to the jury. As for the remaining counts, the jury convicted Rosenthal of only a single minor charge, on which Judge Stanton imposed a probationary sentence. In other words, Judge Stanton found that the transaction from which the major charge against Rosenthal arose, the same "fraudulent" transaction to which Milken had earlier pleaded guilty and been sentenced to prison by Judge Wood, was perfectly lawful. Judge Stanton said from the bench that he understood how odd it was that he was acquitting Rosenthal on a count to which Milken had pleaded guilty. "I make this ruling in the full understanding of the anomaly that those persons who participated in it and have testified thought it was unlawful," he noted. But the judge did his duty under the law.[6]

Because Milken appeared to have testified honestly rather than "cooperatively" and therefore failed to incriminate Rosenthal, there was a widely shared assumption that Judge Wood would not reduce Milken's sentence.[7] However, fooled once, Judge Wood was not about to be fooled again. On August 5, 1992, perhaps contrite from her involvement in perpetrating the myth that Milken was a criminal, Judge Wood reduced his sentence on the basis of his "substantial cooperation" with the government (which got no one convicted) to two years. He was released in March of the following year.

• • ● • •

The frothy boom-and-bust that characterized the '80s and produced scapegoats like Milken was followed by the "technology bubble" of the '90s. That decade saw its own series of questionable federal investigations and highly dubious prosecutions.

As the clatter over new stock offerings by high-tech start-up companies grew to a crescendo, complaints emerged about how brokers were doling out their newly issued shares. These shares, for which demand substantially exceeded supply, were allegedly handed out in a way that took advantage of their scarcity. When the bubble burst as the decade wound to a close, many institutional and individual shareholders found themselves with massive losses in high-tech start-ups and initial public offerings (IPOs) of unseasoned technology companies. It was fertile ground for federal investigators and prosecutors on the prowl for, in particular, potential conflicts of interest in connection with the preparation of company research reports and the allocations of IPO shares. With so many disappointed, even devastated, investors nursing their wounds across the land, surely the explanation could be found in an epidemic of federal securities, mail, and wire fraud, rather than in poor judgment or old-fashioned human greed and its attendant follies among investors.

Frank P. Quattrone was one of the most prominent investment bankers in Silicon Valley during this frenzied period. As the head of the technology unit of Credit Suisse First Boston ("CSFB") in Palo Alto, he was at the center of CSFB's booming high-tech underwriting and associated businesses. His job involved attracting new underwriting business, helping manage high-tech offerings, and cultivating old and new clients in order to increase demand for CSFB's services. He did not decide how to allocate the scarce IPO shares being underwritten by CSFB. That job belonged to the Equity Capital Markets department, which mediated between the Investment Banking Division (where Quattrone worked) that represented companies selling the stock, and the Equities Division, that included sales people and stockbrokers who worked cooperatively with the buyers of the IPO shares—mutual funds, insurance companies, hedge funds, individual investors, and others. Some blocks of shares were allocated generally to certain stockbrokers in the Equities Division who sub-allocated them among their various customers. Equity Capital Markets personnel had to discern how to satisfy their customers' overwhelming demand for the allocated IPO shares being underwritten by CSFB—and it was no easy task.

The National Association of Securities Dealers (NASD) and the Securities and Exchange Commission (SEC) launched investigations in the spring of 2000 into suspicions that CSFB stockbrokers had received "kickbacks." These suspicions were aimed not at Quattrone, nor at the Investment Banking Division in which he worked, but at the Equities Division and Equity Capital Markets department. But as the investigation continued and demands for documents became all-inclusive, CSFB's lawyers received government requests for documents in the possession of some people in Quattrone's high-profile unit, which had advised the corporate issuers about many of the IPOs involved.

By November 2001, a federal grand jury in New York joined the hunt for culprits. The investigations, including that by the grand jury, focused on the suspicion that stockbrokers in the Equities Division were allocating hot new IPO issues to customers who would then confer benefits on CSFB and on the individual stockbrokers by paying more commissions on other transactions, arguably a species of kickback.[8] But the U.S. attorney never brought criminal charges based on this alleged kickback scheme. In January 2002, CSFB settled NASD and SEC civil charges related to these kickback allegations by paying $100 million. Later that year, NASD sanctioned two senior members of CSFB's Equities Division in connection with the same kickback investigation. Neither Quattrone nor any other member of CSFB's Investment Banking Division was charged. None were even interviewed in connection with the kickback investigation, according to Quattrone's legal counsel.[9]

Later in 2002, the NASD, the SEC, and the New York Stock Exchange launched yet another investigation, this time of several major investment banks that were suspected of "spinning" IPO shares, that is, improperly allocating IPO shares to executives of investment banking clients in order to gain financing business. NASD was delegated lead responsibility for the CSFB investigation, which focused on reports issued by Equities Division research analysts and "spinning" by CSFB stockbrokers. Quattrone testified before the NASD for two days in October 2002 about these issues. The investigation culminated in a December 2002 global settlement, consummated in April 2003, between the NASD, the SEC, the NYSE (and other regulators), and ten major banks, including CSFB. CSFB paid $200 million in that settlement.

Meanwhile Quattrone, who was in the middle of a bewildering myriad of civil and administrative proceedings, suddenly found that a federal grand jury was casting its eyes in his direction. The combination of proceedings required Quattrone and his lawyers to engage in a massive juggling act. In January 2003, the NASD told Quattrone that it was considering bringing disciplinary charges against him relating to the exaggerated value of a new stock issue and to the supervision of research analysts. Then, the following month, the U.S. attorney indicated that it was criminally investigating Quattrone based on an email he had sent in December 2000 during the prior kickback investigation, and the NASD requested a third day of testimony from Quattrone, in part to follow up on prior questions concerning that email. NASD refused Quattrone's request to postpone that testimony until resolution of the new and unexpected criminal investigation. It also refused his offer to cooperate in other ways. Instead, in March 2003, NASD brought civil charges against him for failing to testify and eventually barred him from the industry for life as a sanction, even though by that time he had completed the required testimony before the NASD over a period of three more days. Also in March 2003, NASD brought separate civil charges against Quattrone relating to the allocation of IPO shares to executives of investment banking clients and the supervisory structure for research analysts, based on rules that had never been applied to these practices. NASD dropped these charges shortly before trial.

The biggest threat faced by Quattrone, however, was the criminal indictment returned by the grand jury in April 2003 based on his December 2000 email. Following a by-now familiar pattern, however, Quattrone, who refused to make a deal and announced that he was prepared to fight whatever the U.S. attorney threw at him, was charged not for taking commission kickbacks, not for unlawful hyping of new issues by Equities Division research analysts, and not for allocations to executives of investment banking clients. Rather, he was charged with that old standby, obstruction of justice, allegedly committed during the 2000 SEC and grand jury probes into brokerage commission kickbacks. In other words, having investigated Frank Quattrone head-to-toe, the Department of Justice, finding no violation (even arguable) to which Quattrone was likely to plead guilty rather than fight, resorted to the ever nebulous obstruction of justice statute.

The nub of the indictment involved Quattrone's response to a single email sent on December 4, 2000, by one of his underlings, one Richard Char (a lawyer), to a group of his fellow CSFB bankers, including Quattrone. The email reminded staffers of the firm's "document retention policy" requiring that certain documents generated in a deal become part of the permanent record and stored in the company's archives, while draft documents created during the course of the deal be discarded. It noted, too, the circumstances during which the destruction-of-documents portion of the policy had to be suspended, such as when "a lawsuit is instituted." [10]

The policy Char reminded employees about was, of course, a guide to both the retention of permanent documents and the corollary destruction of drafts, notes, and other such documents that company policy did not decree merited permanent retention. Bear in mind that the investment bankers, after all, were not the focus of the 2000 kickback investigation, and CSFB's general counsel's office had not notified the group that the firm had received subpoenas requiring them to save their documents.

Quattrone was indicted because of his December 5th response to the Char email (dubbed by the courts as Quattrone's "endorsement email") that was short, simple, and to the point, and that the government claimed was meant to result in the destruction of documents that were subject to federal subpoenas:

> having been a key witness in a securities litigation case in south texas (miniscribe), I strongly advise you to follow these procedures. [lower case spelling in the original.]

Quattrone's attorneys pointed out that although CSFB's general counsel's office had received, in October 2000, an SEC subpoena calling for the production of documents relating to over 300 CSFB IPOs, as well as a similar subpoena from the grand jury in November 2000, the general counsel's office did not promptly notify all affected bankers to preserve documents responsive to the subpoenas; such notice was not sent until December 7, 2000, *after* Quattrone had sent the email that was at the center of the indictment against him. Quattrone's big problem, however, was that it hardly mattered what he knew about the investigation and when he knew it. Innocent intent was not an adequate defense in the eyes of the prosecutors.

Nor was it sufficient for the trial judge. United States District Judge Richard Owen, appointed to the federal trial bench in 1973 by President Richard Nixon and widely reputed to be one of the most pro-prosecution judges in the entire federal court system, showed palpable bias against Quattrone. Judge Owen, many trial observers noted with varying degrees of frankness, exhibited a marked pro-prosecution bent during the trial. He clashed repeatedly with Quattrone's trial attorneys, especially noted litigator John Keker who made it a point to document, for the record, the judge's increasingly evident bias.

After a jury deadlocked at Quattrone's first trial, a second jury convicted him of all three counts: obstruction of justice, obstruction of an agency proceeding, and witness tampering. In September 2004, Judge Owen imposed an 18-month prison sentence.

The Second Circuit Court of Appeals, while ruling there was sufficient evidence that Quattrone's jury *could* have concluded that he was urging the destruction of documents relevant to the various government inquiries and hence that he might have acted with "corrupt intent," nonetheless reversed the conviction. The three-judge appellate panel unanimously held, in 2006, that Judge Owen's instructions to the jurors had allowed them to convict Quattrone without concluding that there was a "nexus," or relationship, between Quattrone's endorsement email and the impact it might have on the destruction of documents that, but for the destruction, would have had to be produced for the government. Only with the establishment of such a nexus could the defendant's conduct, ruled the court, be considered intentional obstruction of justice. Without such an intent, Quattrone's actions were merely a rather unremarkable, even routine, instruction to employees about the company's equally unremarkable, routine document-retention-and-destruction policy.

Judge Owen, it turned out, had instructed the jury that if it found that Quattrone had urged the destruction of documents that were covered by subpoenas (even if he did not know that they were covered by subpoenas), this was sufficient evidence on which to find an intentional obstruction that amounted to a felony. This instruction, held the Court of Appeals, entirely eliminated the crucial requirement that the defendant had to be proven to have acted with corrupt intent to disrupt the investigation. Without such proof of corrupt intent, said the Second Circuit, the case was "a bare-bones strict liability crime" (a serious felony pinned on a defendant even in the absence of a conclusion that he acted intentionally to violate the law). While the Court of Appeals did not indicate whether it believed Quattrone's explanation for his sending the confirmatory email was true (it was not, after all, the role of the appellate court to judge witness credibility, a task left to the jury), it did note that Quattrone's lawyers had placed into evidence "several innocent explanations for his conduct" and that "each has some basis in the record." In other words, Quattrone had produced evidence, including his own testimony, to bolster his claim of innocent intent, and Judge Owen had a duty to allow the jurors to decide whether a nexus existed between Quattrone's actions and a corrupt intent to violate a known legal duty.

Interestingly, the Court of Appeals took the extraordinary step of ordering that Quattrone's retrial take place before a different trial judge.

While the appellate panel went out of its way to avoid direct criticism of Judge Owen, it admitted gingerly that "portions of the transcript raised the concern that certain comments [of Judge Owen] could be viewed as rising beyond mere impatience or annoyance." And so, said the court, both "the interest and appearance of justice are better served by reassignment" of the case to a different judge. This is as close as polite appellate courts get to criticizing even the most outrageous actions of a trial judge. And while some courts of appeal routinely assign retrials to a new judge when a conviction has been overturned, in this case the mention of the controversy concerning Judge Owens's conduct obviously was not meant to be missed. The reassignment of the case was anything but routine.

Four days after the Court of Appeals released its March 20, 2006, opinion, the SEC overturned the NASD's decision that had barred Quattrone for life from working in the securities industry. The NASD, ruled the SEC, violated its own rules and should not have summarily dismissed Quattrone's claim that he was entitled to assert his Fifth Amendment privilege to postpone testimony before the agency while criminal proceedings were pending. Two months later, the NASD dropped all of its remaining charges against Quattrone.[11] The NASD sought to justify its retreat on the ground that witnesses had scattered to other occupations and were no longer subject to NASD jurisdiction as registered securities-industry employees.[12] Quattrone's lawyers pointed out the more likely cause: Neither the NASD nor any other government agency had rules outlawing the practice until 2002, long after the conduct charged. "Frank Quattrone played by the rules, and the practices at issue were legal, common in the industry, and approved by CSFB's senior management and legal counsel at the time," explained one of Quattrone's lawyers, Kenneth G. Hausman.[13]

The independent press by and large played the role of cheering section for federal prosecutors until it became obvious that the case was more witch-hunt than legitimate prosecution. During and after Quattrone's legal victories, there was very little objective assessment of the case in the press. The staunchly conservative, pro-business *Wall Street Journal* editorial page, which virtually alone had earlier championed Michael Milken, was likewise supportive of Quattrone and used his Second Circuit reversal to drive home the lesson: juries can fairly decide these corporate fraud cases, editorialized the *Journal*, only "if they are given appropriate guidance from the court about where to draw the line on criminal behavior. In the rush to judgment in the post-bubble...days that line was not always clearly drawn."[14]

What was more unexpected, and oddly predictive of the outcome of the case, was Roger Parloff's 2005 column in the more middle-of-the-road *Fortune* magazine, published months before the Second Circuit's reversal of Quattrone's conviction, headlined "Why Quattrone Deserves to Walk."[15] "There was no evidence," explained Parloff, "that the timing of the file-cleaning email was anything other than unfortunate coincidence."

But perhaps the most interesting comment came from an unanticipated source, namely Kathleen Ridolfi, director of the North California Innocence Project run out of Santa Clara University's Law School, to which Quattrone donated time and money while temporarily out of the banking business during his legal travails. Ridolfi said that her project would likely have had to close its door but for the assistance of Quattrone, who raised more than a half million dollars for the organization. "He has a lot of courage," Ridolfi said. "He stood up to the charges despite huge risks. I love the guy."[16]

So the story ended relatively well for Frank Quattrone. Of course, he lived under a harsh spotlight for many months and with the possibility that he could land in federal prison for many years. The cost of skilled legal counsel to handle such a case would have bankrupted many. But it's unlikely that the legal system, nor the news media that reports these cases, learned much about the dangers of vague statutes and regulations, overreaching prosecutors and enforcement agencies, and the toxic mix of ambitious prosecutors and pro-prosecution judges. The NASD in 2002 finally proposed[17] more specific rules delineating impermissible practices in the underwriting and distribution of IPOs.[18] With clearer rules, it would be unlikely that IPO underwriters would again get caught up in a securities fraud investigation for sales practices such as those allegedly broadly engaged in by Wall Street before that time.

But the same could not be said for the "obstruction of justice" area of the law, for the government took steps to make sure that this particular trap for the unwary would remain as useful to prosecutors post-Quattrone as it had been earlier. As *The National Law Journal* reported in the aftermath of the case, with the passage of the Sarbanes-Oxley Act of 2002, the government assured that changes in the law would "ease [the] way for prosecutors."[19] The Act, explained the *Journal*, "eliminates the need for prosecutors to show that a defendant knew of a specific investigation prior to the shredding of documents." And it cited as a source Patrick Robbins, former head of securities fraud prosecution in the San Francisco U.S. attorney's office, who had by that time gone to his professional reward as a partner in the San Francisco office of Shearman & Sterling, the high-prestige "white shoe" corporate defense law firm.

• • ● • •

If a "man on the street" survey were conducted asking what crime home décor maven Martha Stewart ended up spending five months in federal prison for,[20] the answer would likely be "insider trading." That, however, would be wrong. Insider trading was merely the crime for which she and her Merrill Lynch stockbroker were investigated, and for which the Securities and Exchange Commission sued her civilly. Because these days no lawyer, no judge, and surely no home décor maven can readily discern the boundaries of what qualifies as insider trading, prosecutors looking to pin a criminal rap on Stewart took advantage of her *fears* that her trading ImClone shares *might* indeed have been criminal. They focused on her answers to their questions when they interviewed her and ended up charging her with making false statements to federal authorities and a host of other "obstruction" crimes. The usual stuff. Only this time, the feds couldn't resist the temptation to add a cutting-edge charge of securities fraud (about which more later). This was, after all, *Martha Stewart*, founder and CEO of the publicly traded company Martha Stewart Living Omnimedia ("MSLO"), and at that time one of the most famous women in the world.

The federal false statement statute makes it a felony to lie to any federal officer on any matter deemed "material" to that agency's carrying out its mission or to commit a host of other "obstruction" crimes.[21] A mind-boggling array of federal employees is covered by this statute, and misstatements, declared to be lies, may emerge from an equally mind-boggling array of interactions between a citizen and his or her government.

Martha Stewart and a friend were flying to a Mexican vacation spa on Stewart's private jet on December 27, 2001. During a refueling stop, Stewart called her Merrill Lynch broker, Peter Bacanovic, and learned that a friend of hers and one of Bacanovic's other clients, Samuel Waksal, was attempting to sell all of his and his family members' shares in ImClone Systems, a company in which Stewart owned a modest stake.

Since Waksal was the CEO of ImClone, Stewart and her broker came to the logical conclusion that there must have been a compelling reason to sell. Of course, there are many reasons why insiders sell their stock, such as needing money to pay taxes or to buy another asset for diversification, but Waksal's seemingly frantic efforts to dump his entire family's holdings suggested something out of the ordinary about the company's prospects. Bacanovic's assistant, Douglas Faneuil (who ended up testifying against both Stewart and Bacanovic), speaking for his boss, told Stewart that ImClone had not yet issued a news release about the sale, but that Bacanovic thought Stewart would "like to act on the information" he had. Stewart consequently ordered the broker to sell all of her shares, producing approximately $230,000.

It turned out that Waksal sold his shares—illegally—because ImClone had just learned that the FDA had turned down the company's application for approval of its major product, an anti-cancer drug called Erbitux®. The public announcement, which came on December 31, caused an 18 percent drop in share price. When a Merrill Lynch internal review noticed the ImClone trades by Waksal and Stewart, in advance of the Erbitux® announcement, it conducted an internal investigation and reported the matter to the SEC. Within days, both the SEC and the U.S. attorney in Manhattan began civil and criminal insider trading investigations.

The prosecution of Waksal was a straightforward matter, even under the often uncertain rules governing insider trading. He was a clearly defined "insider" at ImClone, the adverse material information he possessed had not yet been publicly announced, and he dumped a large number of shares owned by him and his family.

Winning an insider trading case against Bacanovic and Stewart would be far more difficult. Although Bacanovic had violated his employer's rules against sharing information with one Merrill Lynch client about the investment activities of another, neither he nor Stewart owed a fiduciary duty to ImClone. Moreover, Bacanovic and Stewart knew only that Waksal was selling his shares. They did not know why.

But the government got lucky: once a federal investigation was launched, Stewart and her broker were less than candid in their responses to the government's questions. It is possible that they believed that Stewart's trading constituted insider trading and consequently decided to cover up the reasons for Stewart's sale of her ImClone shares, but it was also possible that Bacanovic was concerned simply with having violated Merrill Lynch's internal rules against sharing information about one client with another, and that Stewart thought her piggybacking on Waksal's selling would not look good to her adoring public.

Whatever his or her motive, each told a "story." The SEC brought legally dubious civil insider trading charges on the very same day that the DOJ brought criminal obstruction charges—June 4, 2003. The SEC agreed to a common arrangement: to wait until the criminal case ended before pursuing its civil case.

According to the government's version of the facts at Bacanovic and Stewart's joint criminal trial, the broker and his client agreed that they would tell a false cover-up story to investigators. The story centered on a supposed preexisting agreement between Bacanovic and Stewart that if ImClone's share price were to drop below $60, Bacanovic would sell all of Stewart's stock in the company. When Bacanovic was interviewed under oath by the feds, this is the story he told. Stewart told the same tale, but not under oath.

It was not an accident that Stewart stumbled into a false statement prosecution. One of the oddest features of federal criminal law is that, while it is the felony of perjury to lie when under oath, it is likewise a felony to lie even when not under oath. It is the counterintuitive nature of the federal false statement statute that makes it such an effective snare for the unwary citizen. Observers of the federal criminal justice system are often suspicious that investigators are all too ready to give their targets plenty of opportunity to lie, even when the underlying conduct being investigated is likely not criminal at all. (Nor is it entirely irrelevant to note that there are no similar restrictions on the ability of government officials to lie to citizens with impunity.)[22]

The feds' job was made much easier by an intentional policy, developed over decades among legislators, securities regulators, and prosecutors, to keep the securities laws vague. Fundamental to the insider trading laws is the notion that a person who holds an "insider's" position in a publicly traded company owes a duty of good faith to that company. This does not prohibit him or her from buying and selling securities in the company; indeed, insiders, normally far more than members of the general public, are more likely to invest in the companies they manage. What the insider trading laws make clear, and what the federal courts have affirmed over the years, is that an insider may not trade in the shares of his company while in the possession of material non-public information. While the definition of "material" is subject to considerable latitude, an insider understands that if he is about to buy or sell shares of the company and there is some important development afoot, positive or negative, that has not yet been released to the public, he would be foolish to trade without consulting with a legal specialist for advice or waiting for the public release of the information. The crux of the theory is that the insider has a duty to his company to refrain from taking advantage of such information. (While in effect the restrictions on insider trading might be seen as an effort to level the playing field between insider and other investors, in reality it is highly unlikely that most investors will ever possess the level of knowledge and sophistication that an insider has concerning the company.)

Insider trading became a crime, though not a clearly delineated one, when Congress enacted the Securities and Exchange Act of 1934 as part of an effort to clean up perceived corruption in the securities markets, thought to have played a role in the stock market crash of 1929. The statute is extraordinarily broad and vague, in part because the SEC, which the act created, is authorized to flesh out the regulatory language putting into effect the intent of the statute. That statutory provision prohibits "any person, directly or indirectly," to "use or employ, in connection with the purchase or sale of any security…any manipulative or deceptive device."[23] The act authorized the SEC to issue regulations to put into effect the intent of the statute. However, the commission's regulations often tend to mimic rather than expand significantly upon the statute's broad-stroke wording.[24] And historically, neither the SEC, which is in charge of administrative and civil enforcement of the anti-fraud provisions, nor the DOJ, which handles criminal prosecutions under the act, has been eager to spell out the nature and definition of such concepts as "securities fraud" or "insider trading."

Rather—and this is a crucial point—legal definitions of fraud have for the most part been developed in the course of the pursuit of actual cases by the SEC as it has brought enforcement actions, and by the DOJ as it has brought prosecutions, for alleged "fraudulent" conduct in the purchase or sale of securities. These enforcement actions and prosecutions have, of course, come after the fact. Only after an action or a prosecution is won by the government is the investment world thereby put on notice that the activity prosecuted should be added to the inventory of "fraudulent" activities.

In fact, in the 1980s, both Congress and the SEC had an opportunity to provide clarity to securities fraud law and decided not to. At that time, Congress enacted two statutes meant to bolster the SEC's and DOJ's "war against insider trading": The Insider Trading Sanctions

Act of 1984 substantially increased the penalties for insider trading. The Insider Trading and Securities Fraud Enforcement Act of 1988 (ITSFEA) further upped the ante for both civil and criminal insider trading violations, provided for sanctions against people who "recklessly…failed to take appropriate steps to prevent" violations by others, and provided bounty payments for whistleblowers. The ITSFEA passed Congress by a unanimous vote (410-0) in the House and by voice-vote in the Senate. Yet remarkably, neither statute does anything to define precisely what insider trading is.[25]

At the time, a few witnesses protested that it was inappropriate for Congress to increase penalties for insider trading without defining the practice once and for all. But the SEC opposed any such effort, telling the committee that it was not a good idea to be "freezing into law either a definition which is too broad, or too narrow to deal with newly emerging issues," and Congress went along. The same problem emerged when ITSFEA came before Congress four years later. This time the penalties were increased so drastically that clearer definitions became even more urgent. But Chairman John Dingell of the House Committee on Energy and Commerce claimed that any definition of criminal insider trading would provide criminals with a "roadmap for fraud." Dingell explained that his committee "did not believe that the lack of consensus over the proper delineation of an insider trading definition should impede progress on the needed enforcement reforms encompassed within this legislation."[26]

Now, given that the law of insider trading is basically made up as it is enforced, the first person accused of a particular innovation in the panoply of fraud becomes an instrument by which the law is extended. Often such people plead guilty and make a deal to avoid the risk of conviction and a higher sentence. Others who contest the charges have their cases resolved by court rulings that extend, or contract, the definition of "securities fraud." Published court opinions are deemed "notice" to the world that henceforth a particular practice will be considered fraudulent. Of course, the individual whose conviction produced that opinion had no such notice. Besides, not all court opinions are clear, and often they are sufficiently narrow so as to not provide much guidance for similar (but not precisely the same) conduct.

Most securities lawyers would agree that Martha Stewart's sale of ImClone shares did not fall within the recognized range of insider trading activity.[27] After all, she never had substantive inside information that she got directly or indirectly from Waksal. All she learned from her broker was that Waksal was selling. She did not know why. This is doubtless the reason why the DOJ chose the safer route of charging obstruction. Plus, there was the added advantage that the SEC had reason to believe that Stewart would settle a civil insider trading case, and in a manner favorable to the government's expansive definition of the term, if she were to first lose the *criminal* obstruction case. Had there been no obstruction to prosecute, it is anyone's guess whether the DOJ would have tried to use this case as a vehicle for expanding the judicially-accepted definition of insider trading. But the fact is that a potential obstruction or false statement charge can almost always be teased out of an agent's interview of an individual. Even if the feds cannot put their finger precisely on a statement that the interviewee made that is demonstrably false, they may always rely on the obverse side of the coin and allege that there is something that the target *omitted* that, in the context of the full investigation, was intended to mislead the authorities. Since the citizen is damned by what he or she says, or even fails to say, it is very hard to envision a citizen's encounter with a fed that cannot be the basis for such a prosecution.

While the DOJ did not include cutting-edge criminal insider trading charges in the Martha Stewart indictment, leaving that to the SEC in its companion civil action, which Stewart settled for $195,000 after her criminal conviction,[28] the feds could not resist the temptation to include a charge of securities fraud, albeit a quite novel one.[29] The count charged that Stewart engaged in fraud following press reports about her sale of ImClone stock that hinted at a coming scandal, as a result of which stock in her own company, MSLO, began to plummet. "In an effort to stop or at least slow the steady erosion of MSLO's stock price," alleged the indictment, and in order to calm investor concerns, Stewart "made or caused to be made a series of false and misleading public statements during June 2002 regarding her sale of ImClone stock." These public statements, released by MSLO, omitted, according to the indictment, the true reason why Stewart sold her ImClone shares—namely, her secret possession of information concerning Waksal's sales activity. "These false and misleading statements" were contained in Stewart's written public statements, statements she made "at a conference for securities analysts and investors," and statements made "on behalf of Stewart by Stewart's attorney to *The Wall Street Journal* published on June 7, 2002." The information conveyed to the *Journal* contained the same defense that Stewart and her co-defendant and their lawyers later offered to the jury at the criminal trial, that Stewart's sales were put into effect based upon a preexisting plan to sell if the share price dropped below a preset trigger point.

Stewart's efforts to defend herself publicly were, according to the indictment, "acts, practices and courses of business which operated and would operate as a fraud and deceit upon purchasers and sellers of MSLO common stock." In other words, the DOJ claimed that Stewart's public statements following the breaking of the scandal constituted a separate crime because it might have been intended to stem the precipitous drop in her own company's shares. Put more starkly, a press release suddenly was capable of constituting an act of securities fraud—a decidedly cutting-edge interpretation that would not readily have occurred to most corporate executives or even lawyers.

The idea of criminalizing a target's pre-indictment efforts to launch a public defense was ultimately too much for Judge Miriam Goldman Cedarbaum. She dismissed the count after the prosecution's case ended but before it reached the jury. But since the issue never made it to the Court of Appeals, there is no authoritative precedent preventing prosecutors from bringing such a charge against another person with the temerity to defend himself or herself in the press and before industry groups while facing a criminal investigation. The chilling effect this ploy will likely have on those under investigation in the future is incalculable. Meanwhile, brokers and investors still did not know authoritatively whether they were allowed to trade after learning that an insider is buying or selling.

•••••

It is hard for most people to have much sympathy for former Enron Corporation chairman Kenneth L. Lay, and perhaps rightly so. His energy company became the poster child for George W. Bush-era corporate excess and cronyism. His public image is that of a chief executive who made sure that the lowly worker bees in his employ lost their pensions, while those in the highest echelons reaped huge windfall profits from the corporate failure. When he died after his conviction but before his appeal, the government, which had to pick up the pieces of his employees' broken financial futures, got little from his once-astronomical fortune.[30]

In a *New York Times* article headlined "The Enron Case That Almost Wasn't," published after Lay's conviction, reporters Alexei Barrionuevo and Kurt Eichenwald laid out what they described as "the legal hurdles on the path to Mr. Lay's conviction."[31] These hurdles "were so daunting that some prosecutors privately worried that they would never even be able to charge Mr. Lay with any crimes." In the face of "millions of pages of documents, deconstructing complex accounting mechanisms, unwinding complex trading transactions," the prosecutors focused on a more basic gut-wrenching rather than mind-boggling theme: "Mr. Lay chose to lie—to his shareholders, his employees and his banks—and those lies were his crimes." The reporters characterized this new approach as resting on proof "that the company publicly portrayed itself as strong and vibrant, even though executives like Mr. Lay knew that it was rotting from the inside."

This strategy, concluded the reporters at the end of the trials, enabled the government to vastly simplify a case that otherwise would have to focus on the details of "a hodgepodge of often impenetrable activities." Based on the transactions involved, "the case against Mr. Lay was never clear-cut, prosecutors say." For a while it even seemed "that their quarry might remain permanently beyond their reach." The reporters made clear that they had direct access to members of the Department of Justice's Enron prosecution task force, including the lawyer who headed the force for its first two years, Leslie R. Caldwell. "We had to focus on the big picture, and not just the individual transactions," Ms. Caldwell told the *Times*. In short, the prosecution's case was built on a platform of supposedly fraudulent optimism not supported by the underlying facts and transactions, which were in turn supposedly too complex for jurors to understand and which were, in any event, not fully and accurately disclosed to the investing public.

The omnibus "lying" theory got a boost when in early 2004 Enron's former treasurer, Ben F. Glisan, Jr., told a grand jury that Mr. Lay "knew he was lying in 2001 when he provided upbeat statements about Enron's prospects even as the company was plummeting toward bankruptcy proceedings." Another task force former director, Andrew Weissmann, told the reporters that this testimony "was a real turning point" in putting together a prosecution of Lay. "I was relieved," Weissmann said.

Pursuing this new theory, prosecutors looked into a variety of Lay's contacts with the investing community and the public, as well as Enron's employees. There were Lay's statements made to Enron employees in an "online forum" in which Lay said that he was buying Enron shares, part of an effort to buck up their confidence in the company for which they worked. But, according to prosecutors, his failure to mention his sales of shares "amounted to securities fraud." (The claim that unduly optimistic or even misleading public statements made by corporate executives can constitute a form of "securities fraud" brings to mind the creative charge in the Martha Stewart trial, i.e., that Stewart issued false public denials of criminality when news of her ImClone trades reached the news media.)

The *Times* reporters described the conviction of both Kenneth Lay and his second-in-command Jeffrey Skilling, Enron's former CEO, as follows: They were "convicted of multiple fraud and conspiracy charges. The jury found that both men carried out their crimes by misleading investors and employees about Enron's performance." This was, and remains, the accepted view of what the trial was all about. Even more legally sophisticated and trained observers than Barrionuevo and Eichenwald have characterized the trial in this fashion. Professor Ellen S. Podgor of Stetson University School of Law, a long-time highly-regarded criminal defense practitioner and academic, blogged on June 1, 2006 that the trial "was not a technical accounting fraud case," but rather "a simple case of—did Lay lie to people—and did Lay & Skilling participate in illegal activities that caused harm to many." The prosecutors, she noted, "did an outstanding job of keeping the case simple."

However, Professor Podgor, unlike the *Times* reporters, went on to ask the crucial question of whether there was a problem in the case being kept so simple. "The government had an array of offenses available in its arsenal that were so broad that it is easy to fit just about any conduct," she pointed out. Podgor noted, for example, Lay's conviction "of one count of wire fraud." She highlighted former Chief Justice Warren Burger's description of the wire fraud statute: "A stopgap device to deal on a temporary basis with the new phenomenon, until particularized legislation can be developed and passed to deal directly with the evil."[32] Podgor stressed that to some people in the business world, "the criminality" of their conduct "is not apparent" without more specific guidance being available.

The commentary about the Lay prosecution dances around a fundamental issue not given sufficient attention in trials like Lay's. Where should corporate executives trying to deal with severe problems that have arisen draw the line between, on the one hand, being completely frank about the problems with employees, the media, and the investing public, and, on the other hand, seeking to avoid the kind of panic (and likely destruction of the company resulting from loss of confidence) that complete transparency is almost certain to cause? And does "spinning" rather than letting it all hang out constitute a federal fraud, especially where more than enough information is publicly available elsewhere from which a careful observer might conclude that the spin is overly optimistic?

In Enron's case the issue was particularly acute. A sudden loss of confidence in the company's fundamental soundness would almost certainly have pulled the plug on, for example, Enron's ability to obtain crucial financing, as well as on its stock price that was collateralizing a number of large loans. None of this is to say that corporate executives are wise to get their companies into a situation where full disclosure at industry forums, at press conferences, and in press releases likely would lead to a loss of confidence and resulting corporate collapse. Enron's executive overseers appear to have been exceptionally foolish, even reckless, in executing their precarious balancing act. But whether it is, without specific legislation spelling out the law's contours, criminal fraud to seek to save the company in a crisis by painting a rosier picture (to take a classic public relations approach) than would be painted with fuller disclosure, is a reasonable question to ask. In a context where the full facts are disclosed in the details (sometimes in the footnotes) to the financial statements, corporate executives' surface optimism might not so readily and fairly be seen as criminal fraud. This is a question on which reasonable people might disagree.

In *The New Yorker* magazine of January 8, 2007, the highly respected essayist Malcolm Gladwell published an article entitled, "Open Secrets: Enron, intelligence, and the perils of too much information."[33] Gladwell was writing about the case assembled against former Enron CEO Jeffrey Skilling, a companion case to Lay's that Barrionuevo and Eichenwald in the *Times* called "the parallel case assembled against" both. Trial Judge Simeon Lake addressed Skilling on October 23, 2006, immediately before imposing a 24-year (essentially a life) sentence. "The evidence established that the defendant repeatedly lied to investors, including Enron's own employees, about various aspects of Enron's business," the judge intoned. Gladwell quoted from the lead prosecutor's closing arguments to the jury at Skilling's trial: "This is a simple case," the prosecutor had argued. "It's black-and-white. Truth and lies."

Gladwell makes some disturbing observations about the "black-and-white" nature of the case. He notes that in July 2000, Jonathan Weil of *The Wall Street Journal*, having just had a conversation with an acquaintance in the investment-management business who urged Weil to examine the sources of Enron's income, wrote a column for the Texas regional edition of the paper. Weil focused on certain accounting practices of Enron, known as "mark-to-market" accounting, that results in the reporting of income as *current* income even though it is not expected in hard cash for some years in the future. It is an aggressive form of financial reporting, especially for certain industries, but it is well-known and generally accepted within the accounting profession.

Weil had bothered to obtain and examine Enron's annual reports and quarterly SEC filings, and he compared the figures on both income statements and cash-flow statements. While it took Weil some time to figure it all out, he came to the conclusion (he checked with an accounting professor at Michigan State University) that much of Enron's reported income was "unrealized;" it was anticipated rather than actually received. Looked at from a current cash-in-hand perspective, reported Weil, the company had a significant loss rather than a profit for the quarter studied.[34]

Weil invited Enron executives to comment on his reporting. Weil told Gladwell that a half-dozen executives flew to Dallas to meet with Weil and answer his questions. The officials readily acknowledged that the earnings of the company were almost entirely what the company anticipated realizing at some point in the future. The real issue subject to debate was how confident the company was, or should have been, that these earnings would materialize. These questions, the executives told the reporter, were answered by the company's enormously complex mathematical models.

When a Wall Street financier and short-seller named James Chanos read Weil's column, reported Gladwell, Chanos delved into the publicly filed and readily available Enron financial reports. Cash flow was negligible, he discovered. "They were basically liquidating themselves," Chanos told Gladwell. As a result, he proceeded to short-sell Enron shares, a financial maneuver that reaps profits if and when the price of the stock declines. Bethany McLean, tipped off by Chanos, wrote an article in *Fortune*, headlined "Is Enron Overpriced?," in March 2001.

As analysts and investors followed suit and began to look at Enron's financial statements, confidence plummeted. Enron, in the energy-trading business where confidence had to be maintained, experienced a disastrous loss of confidence and filed for bankruptcy in December 2001. The information contained in Enron's publicly available financial statements thus brought the company down when the financial press and the investment community finally bothered to read them.

An additional problem, above and beyond the accounting treatment of anticipated profits, made Enron's financial reporting extremely difficult to assess. A considerable number of the firm's non-earning assets were off-loaded into what were called "special-purpose entities" ("SPE"). SPEs, Gladwell noted, "have become commonplace in corporate America." The end result of the use of this particular vehicle by Enron had the effect of removing losses or dubious investments from the company's balance sheet and avoiding having the losses affect Enron's reported current income. Gladwell concluded that the use of this accounting strategy in Enron's case was "not only legally questionable but extraordinarily risky" and, in the end, helped trigger the crisis in confidence when its house-of-cards came to the attention of the financial press. "Legally questionable" accounting devices, in murky areas where experts will differ, are not usually thought to be a proper basis for a criminal prosecution that has to be proven to a jury "beyond a reasonable doubt." But the use of this device was disclosed in the footnotes to Enron's financial statements, approved by the company's auditor. Is it fraud when questionable accounting practices, approved by an auditor, are hidden in full view?

Gladwell draws attention to another aspect of the Enron scandal that bears consideration when one is trying to decide whether a fraud involving covering up the truth about the company's financial position was committed. He cites Professor Victor Fleischer of the University of Colorado Law School, who noted that Enron was not paying any taxes. The reason, Fleischer pointed out, was that the IRS recognized that Enron's earnings were illusory. Any investor seeing this in Enron's published financial statements should have wondered why he should believe in earnings that the IRS, always looking to maximize taxes and hence earnings, conceded were non-existent.

Gladwell concluded his *tour de force* by noting that in the spring of 1998, six Cornell business school students, as a class project, did an analysis of Enron. This was long before even a whiff of scandal arose. In six weeks, these students came to the conclusion that the stock of this darling of the investment community, one of the nation's most respected companies at the time, was significantly overpriced. The first page of their report had a boldfaced conclusion: "Sell."

New York Times business and financial columnist Joe Nocera, in his "Talking Business" column on January 6, 2007, sought to attack the accuracy of Gladwell's *New Yorker* essay. Nocera attacked Gladwell's implication that "the Enron scandal was as much the fault of investors as it was any Enron executive now in prison." Nocera argued that the notion that the feds tried to criminalize "flawed business decisions" is not "remotely true." Yet Nocera admits that Gladwell's "central point is largely correct." Nocera claimed nonetheless that "no matter how you slice it," the Enron executives "lied to the investing public about the true condition of the company" and "that's against the law." Nocera mocked the disclosures "usually in some buried footnote." He complained that the SPEs "were not always used for some legitimate purpose" but were "mostly…used to hide poorly performing assets." Nocera opined that not enough details were disclosed in some instances, and that, in any event, "the point is not the sheer volume of disclosure; it's whether disclosure illuminates or obfuscates. Enron usually did the latter." As for the Cornell business students, Nocera noted that they did not predict that Enron would go bankrupt, but only that its high-flying stock was in for a price decline. All in all, Nocera conceded much of what Gladwell posited about a plethora of information being "hidden in plain sight" but decried the misleading ways in which the company's financial results were reported. Gladwell likely would not disagree that the reporting was misleading, but would argue only that it was enormously (perhaps overly) inclusive.

The importance of the Gladwell/Nocera debate lies not in any notion that either of them can, or should, be considered a legal expert. Indeed, such is far from the case, and neither likely would claim such a mantle, but it is revealing that two writers who report on such matters have such diametrically opposing views on the importance, quality, format, and value of disclosure. In particular, their dispute in part focuses on the problems caused by *over*-disclosure, and how that might function, in effect, as *under*-disclosure. In the midst of such a dispute come federal prosecutors, after the fact and with rather little warning as to where the line is to be drawn, to announce that a particular form of corporate disclosure, which was sufficient to scare off some investors, constituted a felony sufficiently serious to land an executive in prison for life.

CHAPTER FIVE

Accounting for the Perils Facing Business Support Services: The Late Arthur Andersen & Co. and Its Repercussions

—— ●●● ——

In their zeal to appear to bring justice to the thousands of people who tragically lost their retirement money and pensions when Enron folded and who were now calling for blood, prosecutors sometimes went off in directions indicative of an out-of-control legal system. I refer, specifically, to the Department of Justice's pursuit of Enron's long-time auditor Arthur Andersen, LLP, then one of the five largest accounting firms in the country, now defunct.

The DOJ's scapegoating of Arthur Andersen is a horror story that, despite the accounting firm's eventual Pyrrhic victory in the Supreme Court, almost certainly will be repeated again and again in other corporate and professional sectors of civil society. Indeed, it was later nearly repeated in connection with other national accounting firms—KPMG,[1] for example, and Ernst & Young,[2] both of which had by then learned the lesson that it is futile to resist and best to "cooperate" for the sake of expediency, not to mention financial prudence and the firm's survival. With the Arthur Andersen experience fixed clearly in the rearview mirror, each of these firms chose to save itself by sacrificing individuals to criminal prosecution and by admitting error and even fraud where they likely had not existed.

Andersen, an internationally respected member of the "Big Five" group of accounting firms,[3] was a major obstacle to a successful conviction of

Enron's higher-ups. After all, the controversial transactions that "hid" Enron's losses had been reviewed and approved by Andersen auditors. Enron or any of its individual corporate executives charged with fraud could invoke, as a highly effective defense, the fact that they relied on professional advice from one of the nation's premier accounting firms.

As we've seen, under traditional notions of criminal law, someone may be convicted of certain classes of felonies only if there is evidence that he knew or had reason to know that his actions were in violation of the law. The defendant must convince the jury not necessarily that he acted correctly, but merely that he relied in good faith on expert advice and therefore intended to act properly and thought he was doing so. In order for this defense to succeed, Enron would have had to provide its auditors at Arthur Andersen with all relevant information and documentation; the relationship between the auditing firm and the corporate client would have had to be honest and above-board; and the advice given would have had to be reasonable enough that the client would not have had good reason to believe it was erroneous or given in bad faith simply in order to please or accommodate the client.

Two seemingly opposite paths emerged for the DOJ prosecution team: one, to ally with the Andersen firm and convince leading accountants to testify against their clients; or, two, to sweepingly discredit the firm and disable it from testifying for the Enron defendants. Either way, as one experienced white collar criminal defense lawyer succinctly put it, "for the prosecution, the road to Enron went through Arthur Andersen."[4]

Recognizing this, the DOJ at first resorted to its traditional playbook and sought to make a deal with Andersen to defer prosecution if the firm would agree to cooperate in the government's assault on Enron. Under such a deferred prosecution agreement, Andersen would have had to open all of its records and make all of its employees available to the prosecutors, including an agreement to give court testimony if requested. Only after Andersen proved its willingness to comply with the government's terms and assist fully in the prosecution of the firm's former client would Andersen be allowed to go on its way. Such a deal would have saved the accounting firm from the destruction that was ultimately visited upon it, but it would not necessarily have reflected the truth of Andersen's position at the time it actually performed Enron audits, or even later. One white collar criminal defense lawyer concluded that Andersen's refusal to buy the DOJ's offer of deferred prosecution amounted to an "inability of Andersen management to come together to save the firm."[5]

Whether Andersen was motivated by principle or by insufficient skill in cutting a cynical deal to save itself, an agreement with the DOJ was not to be. And so the prosecutors' path became clear. Arthur Andersen had to be dealt with—indeed, had to be eliminated—as a credible source of testimonial support for the defense of Enron or any of its indicted officers.

Since the firm's auditing practices were not readily cast as criminal, the feds creatively indicted Andersen on a completely different charge: obstruction of justice. As was the case with investment banker Frank Quattrone, described in Chapter Four, they alleged that Andersen's partners and employees intentionally and knowingly advised personnel to destroy relevant documents with the goal of obstructing the government's investigation. With the help of a pliable obstruction statute and with the cooperation of a federal trial judge in Texas, the DOJ succeeded in disabling Andersen from playing any useful role in the defense of the Enron defendants.

The indictment itself effectively destroyed the firm. No auditing firm can successfully operate once indicted, and Arthur Andersen rapidly, and predictably, disintegrated. Companies simply will not, and in nearly all jurisdictions may not, employ auditors under such a cloud. To the extent there was anything left of the firm after indictment, a 2005 jury conviction in the federal district court in southern Texas administered the *coup de grace*. By that time, this one-time auditing powerhouse had gone from 28,000 employees in the United States to a staff of some 200. The skeleton crew's sole task was to clean up loose ends, dealing mostly with remaining litigation and other fallout facing the firm and its former partners.

It came as a shock to court-watchers when the high court announced on January 7, 2005, that it would review the obstruction of justice conviction won by the Department of Justice against Andersen. Deeply embedded in Supreme Court law and lore is the notion that the high court will not review a case unless the question presented is of direct and practical importance to the party seeking review. Further, the Court normally will review a case only if it presents a question of some importance to the development of legal doctrine. Under the circumstances, the likelihood that the court would agree to review Andersen's conviction was seen as so remote that the office of the Solicitor General—the branch of the DOJ that specializes in arguing the government's cases before the Supreme Court—did not even bother to file an opposition to Andersen's petition seeking review.[6] While the firm and its scattered former partners doubtless had an emotional investment in getting the conviction reversed, as a practical matter the case hardly registered on anybody's radar screen. Nor was the Supreme Court faced with an issue of seemingly practical importance to the smooth future operation of the law, since the obstruction of justice statute under which Andersen had been convicted was superseded by the Sarbanes-Oxley Act of 2002, which sought to plug what were suddenly seen as "loopholes" in the federal regulatory scheme after the Enron debacle.

The obstruction of justice accusation arose out of a 2001 address by Michael Odom, an Andersen partner, to a general training meeting of 89 Andersen employees shortly before the Enron collapse. He urged all those present, including some members of the Enron audit team, to follow Andersen's document-retention policy. That policy, replicated in some form in virtually every large or middling business enterprise in the country, was meant to regularize the accounting firm's practices concerning not only retaining certain documents for specified periods of time, but also destroying documents when the retention period ended. Documents were destroyed, of course, not only for space conservation purposes, but also to assure the confidentiality of matters contained in those documents.

Odom's admonition at the Andersen staff meeting about the firm's document-retention policy focused on both aspects—its purpose to retain documents that might be called for in governmental or other investigations, and its purpose to routinely destroy documents after a specified period of time as long as no investigation was known to be in progress. According to the Supreme Court, he urged those assembled at the meeting that "[I]f it's destroyed in the course of [the] normal policy and litigation is filed the next day, that's great…. [W]e've followed our own policy, and whatever there was that might have been of interest to somebody is gone and irretrievable."

Six days after Odom met with the Andersen staff to discuss the firm's document-retention policy, Enron released its third-quarter financial results, including a $1.01 billion charge against earnings, which could be interpreted to reflect an earlier overstatement of the company's financial health.[7] Sure enough, the following day the SEC notified Enron by letter that it had opened an investigation back in August; it now requested information and documents. On October 19, 2001, Enron sent a copy of the SEC's letter to Andersen. The following day Andersen in-house lawyer Nancy Temple, on a conference call of Andersen's Enron crisis-response team, reiterated the earlier advice given by her colleague Odom. She instructed everyone to "[m]ake sure to follow the [document] policy."

Temple's advice, while it later played a substantial role in getting Andersen convicted of obstruction of justice, was "the kind of thing lawyers do all the time," observed Stephen Bokat, vice-president and general counsel of the U.S. Chamber of Commerce, which later filed a friend-of-the-court brief on behalf of Andersen with the Supreme Court. "There but for the grace of God go I," he added in an interview by Tony Mauro in *The National Law Journal*.[8]

On October 23, Andersen employee David B. Duncan, who had for years headed the firm's engagement with Enron, directed compliance with the document policy. All of these steps, by various Andersen personnel, seeking to assure compliance with the firm's document-retention policy, the Supreme Court noted, were followed by substantial destruction of paper and electronic documents. This, of course, was entirely predictable, since the policy, like all such policies that are ubiquitous across all organizations that generate paper documents, directed not only *retention*, but also *destruction* of documents after a certain period of time, in the absence of a likely, threatened, or actual proceeding to which they might be relevant.

It was not until October 30 that the SEC opened its formal investigation and sent Enron—not Andersen—a letter requesting accounting documents. Document destruction at Andersen continued, noted the Supreme Court, "despite reservations by some of [Andersen's] managers." It was not until November 8 that the SEC served Andersen itself with subpoenas for records. The next day, Duncan had his secretary send an email that stated: "Per Dave [Duncan]—No more shredding.... We have been officially served for our documents."

Andersen was indicted in March 2002. The charge was that the firm "did knowingly, intentionally and corruptly persuade...[its] employees" to withhold and alter documents for use in "official proceedings."

The two sides had argued vigorously at the trial over how the trial judge should instruct the jury on the meaning of the word "corruptly."[9] In the end, the jury was told by the judge that, "even if [Andersen] honestly and sincerely believed that its conduct was lawful, you may find [Andersen] guilty." The trial judge agreed with the DOJ's position, and instructed the jury that it could convict "if it found [Andersen] intended to 'subvert, undermine, or impede' governmental fact finding by suggesting to its employees that they enforce the document retention policy." The jury convicted, and Andersen was fined $500,000, though the fine was the least of its problems by that time, since the indictment, not to mention the conviction, had already sounded Andersen's death knell.

The Supreme Court noted that these instructions called for the conviction of Andersen merely because of the destruction of documents pursuant to the firm's document-retention policy. "No longer was any type of 'dishonest[y]'necessary to a finding of guilt," wrote the high court, "and it was enough for [Andersen] to have simply 'impede[d]' the Government's factfinding ability." In the end, the Court vindicated Andersen, and in May 2005 unanimously overturned the firm's conviction, owing to problems with the trial judge's jury instructions. The law was intended, said the Court, to punish the act of "knowingly... corruptly persuad[ing] another to impede an official investigation." At the crux of the dispute was the notion that there could have been perfectly lawful reasons for Andersen, or any other party in a similar situation, to follow its document-retention policy before receiving a formal notice from the government that an investigation was underway. Not every act that makes the government's work harder can be considered a criminal obstruction of justice. The high court noted that persuading a person to "withhold" testimony or documents from a government proceeding "is not inherently malign." It gave some readily comprehended examples, such as "a mother who suggests to her son that he invoke his right against compelled self-incrimination...or a wife who persuades her husband not to disclose marital confidences." Likewise, it is not corrupt for a lawyer to persuade or advise a client to "withhold" documents from the government in the course of an investigation where, for example, those documents might be covered by a legal privilege. If there is a legal basis for the client's refusing to turn over documents to the government, the lawyer who gives such advice is surely "obstructing" the investigation and even intending to do so, but is not doing so with corrupt intent.

The Court's criticism of the Department of Justice, of the trial judge who followed the department's lead in crafting instructions to the jury, and of the Congress that wrote such an obtuse statute, was even more stinging. "Indeed, it is striking how little culpability the instructions required," the justices wrote. The Supreme Court was particularly taken aback by the judge's instruction to the jury that "even if [Andersen] honestly and sincerely believed that its conduct was lawful, you may find [Andersen] guilty." "The instructions," concluded the high court, "also diluted the meaning of 'corruptly' so that it covered innocent conduct."[10]

What the Court was trying to explain to the government is that citizens, and those who advise them, have no obligation to make the government's job easy. There are certain statutes and regulations that govern when cooperation must be forthcoming and that define the nature of that cooperation. In the absence of a law clearly stating the citizen's obligation, the citizen is free to go about his or her business. It did not matter that the Andersen firm's document-retention (and destruction) policy made the government's job harder. Making the government's job harder simply was "not inherently malign," except when in violation of a specific law.

The underlying problem in the Andersen prosecution is in fact present in a very large (and growing) number of federal prosecutions, but it arose in this case in a form sufficiently stark that it caught the attention of the high court, which noted caustically that both Congress and the DOJ shared the blame for the destruction of a presumptively innocent firm. Justice Anthony Kennedy told the government's oralist, Deputy Solicitor General Michael Dreeben, that the DOJ's definition of crime in this case amounted to a "sweeping position that will cause problems for every corporation or small business in the country."[11]

• • ● • •

The executed, if exonerated, corpse of the Arthur Andersen firm—left unceremoniously rotting in the public square—caught the attention of another of the Big Five (now the Big Four) national accounting firms, KPMG. The firm came under investigation for its involvement, beginning around 1997, in the creation and promotion of particularly aggressive tax shelters, an effort that produced some $124 million in fees for the firm by 2001. The Internal Revenue Service (IRS), however, was not impressed and, when it got wind of the nature of these esoteric tax-avoidance mechanisms, declared them abusive and refused to allow tax deductions to filers who had used the schemes.

Typically, the IRS's playbook would have had the agency deny deductions taken by tax-filers who used the shelters, whereupon taxpayer-initiated civil litigation in the federal courts would commence over the disallowance, with substantial interest and penalties assessed if and when the taxpayer lost. But the government used a different playbook this time, one developed in its tussles with other sectors of civil society since the mid-1980s, the technique that put Andersen out of business.

The U.S. attorney in Manhattan opened a criminal investigation focusing on KPMG, several of its partners and employees who were involved in the tax-shelter program, and even one of the outside attorneys at the law firm of Sidley & Austin who had approved the shelters. By February 2004, the government told some 32 KPMG partners and employees, past and present, that they were subjects of a grand jury investigation. (A subject is a person or entity deemed by prosecutors within the orbit of the matter being investigated, but against whom there is not yet sufficient evidence to indict. It is somewhere between a mere witness, and a "target" against whom the prosecutors feel they already have sufficient evidence to indict.)

At first, KPMG fought to defend its handiwork and its profits. It resisted the investigation and sent three of its partners to testify and defend the firm and the shelters before a U.S. Senate Permanent Subcommittee on Investigations hearing in November 2003. Meanwhile, competitor national firms PricewaterhouseCoopers and Ernst & Young, which had likewise been caught up in the shelter investigation, quickly settled. KPMG persevered in defending not only the legality of the shelters, but also its several roles as creators and sellers of the shelters, auditors and tax preparers for the firm's clients, and authors of "opinion letters" on the validity of the devices (i.e., formal written advice regarding the legality of the anticipated tax benefits from a sheltered investment).[12]

KPMG's initial decision to fight the investigation was hardly irrational. The tax shelters it sold and helped create were of a genre characterized by complex schemes designed to help high-income taxpayers reduce their taxes by obtaining outsized deductible write-offs against income. The history of the Internal Revenue Code can be written, from one perspective, as a constant cat-and-mouse game between the IRS on the one hand, and wealthy taxpayers and their lawyers and accountants on the other. Congress could eliminate the textual basis for these devices by amending the Code in order to simplify it and remove the loopholes. It has instead made a veritable hobby out of writing loopholes into the tax code, often in response to lobbying efforts, campaign contributions, or other pressures—unseemly, perhaps, but common in our politics. For whatever reasons, the Code and the even more massive volume of regulations seeking to explicate the Code's provisions remain a tangle of sometimes impenetrable text that virtually invites tax avoidance. (Lawful "avoidance" should not be confused with illegal "evasion," which consists of steps to avoid a known legal duty by, for example, simply not reporting earned income such as wages, tips, or commissions.) No surprise, then, that lawyers and accountants have built a profitable industry around helping wealthy individuals reduce their tax burdens through these lawful (if constructed within the technical rules) means.

Some tax shelters are fairly common and widely used. Certain real estate investments, for example, where property is purchased largely with mortgages, on which interest payments are currently deductible and where improvement costs are amortized over a period of years, can yield substantial deductions against current income, with a large payoff at the end when the appreciated property is sold, with the profit taxed at a lower capital gains rate. These devices are seen by many as unfairly favoring the wealthy, but this is a political and not a legal criticism. Indeed, the very respectable American Bar Association publishes a manual on "asset protection strategies." Tax shelters are one such strategy to help the rich keep their money.

The shelters at the center of the KPMG investigation proved to be considerably more esoteric and controversial. For one thing, the IRS considers a tax shelter legitimate only if it is primarily a real investment, with the tax benefits secondary. A shelter, to be legal in the eyes of the IRS, must serve a "legitimate economic or business purpose," rather than serving merely as a device to avoid taxes.

The "business purpose" doctrine is a creature of the IRS's interpretation of the congressional statute that is the Internal Revenue Code. The Code itself is exceedingly difficult to understand, and this complexity has created a huge industry that produces a rather high standard of living for armies of accountants and lawyers. The IRS, according to two highly reputed white collar crime experts at Stanford, uses this "business purpose" doctrine, which has "no explicit statutory support," to "disallow tax results which are otherwise consistent with the technical provisions of the tax law." In other words, the IRS follows the spirit of the law, as it divines it, rather than the letter. The whole notion that the IRS somehow knows how much "real gain" (in contrast to tax savings) has to be produced before a shelter is deemed legitimate is, according to these experts, "the moral equivalent of that much-loved definition of pornography" articulated by the late Supreme Court Justice Potter Stewart: "I know it when I see it."[13] When it comes to a legitimate versus a bogus tax shelter, the Stanford experts tell us, "the IRS knows it when it sees it."[14]

Senator Carl Levin of Michigan, however, who was present at the subcommittee hearing attended by the three KPMG partners, took a different view of the matter. He told the Senate in the summer of 2005 that there was a fairly clear line between "abusive tax shelters" and the "legitimate" variety. "Interest paid on a home mortgage or Congressionally approved tax deductions for building affordable housing," said the Senator, were examples of the legitimate variety. The "abusive" shelters, said Senator Levin, "are complicated transactions promoted to provide large tax benefits unintended by the tax code."[15]

The litmus test offered by Senator Levin clarified nothing. Citizens obviously have a legal obligation to follow the *letter* of the law. But if the line between legal "tax avoidance" and criminal "tax evasion" is drawn according to someone's view of what Congress in its heart of hearts "intended," then the law indeed becomes a trap for the unwary (or even for the wary). As *The Wall Street Journal* editorialized in criticizing the government's pursuit of the KPMG accountants via a criminal proceeding, "the finger-waggers in Congress might acknowledge their role in creating the 6,000-page, 2.8 million-word, tax code Frankenstein that facilitates the tax-avoidance industry."[16]

Congress could, of course, enact into law the informal IRS test for the validity of a tax shelter—that it serve a legitimate economic or business purpose, not just that of creating tax deductions. But even this standard would prove elusive, leaving the creators of shelters very little guidance. The problem, as the *Journal* put it, is that the standard for tax shelters is that "it's OK to avoid taxes in any of the myriad ways Congress approves of," but "abusive if Congress didn't intend it—assuming anyone can ever figure out what Congress really intends."[17]

The shelters at the heart of the KPMG investigation and, later, of the indictment, were four creatures that were truly worthy adversaries of the "tax code Frankenstein." Even their names had an other-worldly quality: FLIP ("Foreign Leveraged Investment Program"), OPIS ("Offshore Portfolio Investment Strategy"), BLIPS ("Bond Linked Issue Premium Structure"), SOS ("Short Option Strategy"), and variants of these. Here is how the eventual indictment described the FLIP and OPIS shelters (in a case, it must be noted, that ultimately was supposed to be decided by a jury of ordinary citizens):

> In all material respects, FLIP and OPIS were the same. FLIP and OPIS were generally marketed only to people who had capital gains in excess of $10 million for FLIP and $20 million for OPIS. These shelters were designed to generate substantial phony capital losses (i.e., in excess of $10 million for FLIP and in excess of $20 million for OPIS) through the use of an entity created in the Cayman Islands (a tax haven), for purposes of the tax shelter transaction. The client purportedly entered into an "investment" transaction with the Cayman Islands entity by purchasing a purported warrant or entering into a purported swap. The Cayman Islands entity then made a pre-arranged series of purported investments, including the purchase from either Bank A (which at the time was a KPMG audit client) or Bank D of either Bank A or Bank D stock using money purportedly loaned by Bank A or Bank D, followed by redemptions of those stock purchases by the pertinent bank. The purported investments were devised to eliminate economic risk to the client beyond the all-in cost and minimize the amount of the all-in cost used for the investment component. The purported investments were also devised to last for only approximately 16 to approximately 60 days.

Because of the complexity of the regulations and the devices constructed to take advantage of the letter of the law, a system has evolved whereby taxpayers are able to test the correctness of their deductions only when the IRS balks and disallows them. The taxpayer may challenge the IRS's disallowance in the federal courts. If the taxpayer loses, it costs him or her not only the deduction but interest and, often, steep penalties. In an extreme case, the IRS can even tag the taxpayer with civil fraud penalties. To be on the losing end of tax shelter litigation can be extraordinarily expensive for the taxpayer, but at least it does not land him or her in prison for 20 years merely for guessing wrong or taking faulty advice.

As the DOJ increased the pressure on KPMG to switch sides rather than continue the fight to protect itself and its targeted partners (and its client), the firm's resistance weakened. It hardly matters, after all, if in the end KPMG could prove that its shelters were legitimate, or even sufficiently close to the line that their purveyors could not be said, beyond a reasonable doubt, to have violated a known legal duty. Saving the firm from Arthur Andersen's fate became paramount. Once the firm caved in, the plight of the individual DOJ targets would become enormously more dreary.

Why would KPMG's capitulation so severely weaken the individual partners who, in theory, would be left free to fight for their own vindication? The answer lies partly in corporate sentencing guidelines enacted by Congress in 1991 that apply to executives and employees in white collar cases. That law severely limited judicial discretion in imposing sentences,[18] while giving prosecutors enormous power to enhance sentences (by demonstrating certain aggravating factors) or reduce them (via mitigating factors). The most important mitigating provision, that effectively transferred sentencing authority from judges to the DOJ, allowed the prosecutor to inform the judge whether the defendant, after a guilty plea or conviction but before sentencing, had "cooperated" in aiding the government to prosecute and convict other miscreants. Since "cooperation" became one of the very few avenues to a lower sentence, corporate defendants faced enormous pressure to please prosecutors. The guidelines formalized and bolstered what previously had been an informal arrangement by which cooperation resulted in lower sentences.

Recognizing the enormous advantage that the sentencing guidelines had handed federal prosecutors, the DOJ sought to expand and institutionalize this advantage within the department's practice. Beginning with former Deputy Attorney General Eric H. Holder, Jr. (later the U.S. attorney general) in 1999, succeeding heads of the DOJ's Criminal Division issued memoranda that expanded the definition and scope of what could be deemed adequate corporate cooperation to qualify for mercy.[19] With regard to corporations, in contrast to somewhat different guidelines for individuals, former Deputy Attorney General Larry D. Thompson, then-head of the DOJ's Criminal Division, issued in January 2003 a memorandum titled "Principles of Federal Prosecution of Business Organizations."[20] It laid out various criteria for judging whether, and to what extent, a business entity was truly cooperative. Corporations were expected to open their books and records to investigators, including records otherwise protected by legal privilege, such as the theretofore sacrosanct attorney-client privilege. They had to encourage employees to open up to and cooperate with the government, and to fire those who refused. Companies that had a policy of advancing funds for legal fees for corporate employees were also encouraged to refuse such fees to non-cooperating employees.

Cooperation, in short, involved the company's doing virtually anything and everything asked of it by prosecutors. While some details of the so-called Thompson Memorandum were modified in subsequent years, largely as a result of criticism by judges, legal scholars, civil libertarians, and industry representatives, the heart of this approach remains.[21]

KPMG, if it could be persuaded to switch rather than fight, would be able to supply a crucially important legal element to the DOJ's intended prosecution of the individual targets. The weakest part of the government's case was the underlying issue of whether the shelters were so clearly fraudulent that the individuals must have believed, indeed known, that they were phony. For one thing, consider the requirement that certain tax shelters have to be registered with the IRS. The indictment alleged that the defendants had criminally failed to register the shelters. Yet there was documented evidence, later revealed, that there had been considerable disagreement within the IRS itself as to whether these tax shelters had to be registered. The non-registration was an important part of the government's criminal case, since its theory was that the tax partners failed to register the shelters for fear that the IRS would instantly declare them fraudulent and disallow the deductions for each affected tax filer. If in fact there was no registration requirement for these particular shelters, or the defendants genuinely believed such, this theory of demonstrable criminal intent goes out the window.[22]

Furthermore, there was a real question as to whether the shelters themselves might have presented a legitimate, or at least a sufficient, question so that a jury could find "reasonable doubt" and acquit. This was demonstrated later when, on July 20, 2006, a federal judge in the Eastern District of Texas ruled preliminarily in a civil tax case brought two years earlier that one of the shelters (the BLIPS) was valid because the government could not retroactively change the way it dealt with such issues. The lawsuit was brought by two Texas lawyers who had made a fortune in anti-tobacco litigation, used the shelter, were denied large deductions, and, in accordance with proper procedure, sued the IRS for a determination of the shelter's legitimacy. They won the preliminary round and were heading for a full trial. This was widely considered a serious setback for the government's assault on these shelters. After all, even if this finding were later reversed on appeal,[23] the case demonstrated that at least one federal judge thought the taxpayers' position on the shelter device was reasonable. Could this be the foundation upon which criminal tax conspiracies are fairly built?

Given the potential weakness at the heart of the DOJ's intended criminal case (the issue of the legality of the shelters), the government arrived at a strategy for strengthening this aspect of its case for presentation to the jury. Part of the deal it made with KPMG, once the partnership changed law firms and began to negotiate a cooperation agreement, was that the firm would admit that the tax shelters it had so eagerly and profitably promoted over several years were in fact a fraud. This and other obligations by both the government and its new ally KPMG were spelled out in great detail in a remarkable "deferred prosecution agreement" negotiated between the DOJ and KPMG's new lawyer, Robert S. Bennett of the Washington office of the mega-firm Skadden, Arps, Slate, Meagher & Flom.

Bennett had substantial, and lucrative, experience in negotiating such deals for other corporate clients. As Laurie P. Cohen reported in *The Wall Street Journal*,[24] Bennett a year earlier had negotiated a corporate rescue deal for HealthSouth with Birmingham, Alabama, U.S. Attorney Alice Martin.[25] A triumphant Bennett told Jonathan Weil of the *WSJ* that he was now "confident under the new leadership that KPMG will not only survive but will flourish."[26]

The deferred prosecution agreement between the government and KPMG, dated August 26, 2005, provided that KPMG would admit to the facts and conclusions set out in a comprehensive government memorandum detailing how and why the shelters were fraudulent, and that the tax partners and others knew it. KPMG agreed to cooperate with the government "fully and actively." The firm agreed to do its best "to make available its recent and former partners and employees to provide information and/or testimony as requested by" the government. It would waive all privileges, including the attorney-client privilege, thus giving the government full access to all records and memoranda, including interviews between its employees and the company's lawyers. The firm even agreed to take on a government-approved monitor to make sure it complied with the settlement agreement and followed recommended business practices.

KPMG also agreed, in a breathtaking stipulation, that it, its employees, and even its lawyers would not "make any statement, in litigation or otherwise, contradicting the Statement of Facts or its representations in this Agreement." In other words, the partnership making the agreement had to warrant that a host of individuals financially dependent on it would not stray off the reservation. These witnesses had agreed to sing, and even to the extent some might already have "composed," they were not to deviate from the agreed storyline. Indeed, the agreement, recognizing that some individual employees of the partnership might at some point go off-script, included an Orwellian provision that if the DOJ decided that some statement contradicted the official version in the Statement of Facts and the settlement agreement, the DOJ would give the company notice and it would have 48 hours to issue a "repudiation" of any such "contradictory statement."

If KPMG complied with all terms of the settlement agreement, the criminal charges would be dismissed rather than brought forward. The DOJ retained sole discretion to determine whether KPMG had at any point violated its cooperation agreement. The agreement contained within it KPMG's "deferred" guilty plea to the criminal charge, and if at any point through the end of 2006 the company violated (in the government's eyes) the agreement, its guilty plea would move from "deferred" to active status. The company would then stand indicted, subject instantly to the unraveling that destroyed Arthur Andersen.

Rather than having to prove to the jury that the shelters were in fact illegal, the DOJ took this short cut. KPMG's agreement to help the government in this fashion would enable the DOJ to turn a very shaky prosecution into a truly dangerous one for the individual defendants. And it was all made possible not primarily by the truth, not by the facts, and not by the law governing tax shelters, but rather by the enormous leverage that the DOJ held in determining whether the firm would live or die.

The deferred prosecution agreement was signed August 26, 2005. The indictment of eight former partners of KPMG as well as one of the lawyers who advised the company on the propriety of the shelters was made public a mere three days later. In reporting on the indictment of the individuals as well as the terms of the company's deferred prosecution agreement, Floyd Norris, in a "news analysis" in *The New York Times*, noted that a once "proud and confident" accounting behemoth that had a reputation for being "certain of its own righteousness" had been unceremoniously "brought to heel." Early in the investigation, Norris explained, KPMG had taken the position that neither the SEC, IRS, nor DOJ could control how it conducted its business. "It viewed accounting as a self-regulated profession that should not face government control." Under "new leadership" and with new legal counsel, the firm had "been forced to grovel, as it realized that its continued existence might be in question if the Justice Department chose to file criminal charges against it." [27]

Norris's analysis in the *Times* was rather typical of the approach taken by much of the news media in reporting the KPMG struggle. It did not seriously question the danger to liberty when the government could get a party to "grovel" under these circumstances. Furthermore, the analysis nowhere questioned the veracity of the firm's sudden admission of fraud in the face of the potent weapon wielded by the DOJ. It failed to take into account the charges made by the defendants' lawyers, reported in the accompanying news article:

> KPMG's statements in court were the product of extreme duress and are not worth the paper they are printed on,' said Robert H. Hotz, Jr., of the firm Akin Gump Strauss Hauer & Feld, representing one of the indictees. Robert S. Fink, one of the leading tax litigators in the country, representing another former KPMG partner, told the press that 'the government is attempting to criminalize the type of tax planning that tax professionals engage in on a daily basis.' He suggested that 'if the government wants to put an end to these types of transactions, the proper response is for Congress to change the law, not to scare professionals away with indictments.

Perhaps these statements were viewed by a skeptical press corps as standard for lawyers trying to defend their indicted clients in the court of public opinion. However, another way of viewing the matter is that the lawyers were trying, probably in vain, to touch upon issues fundamental to the fairness and accuracy of the prosecution.

The indictment charged a single over-arching conspiracy to design and market, and conceal from the IRS, phony tax shelters. The conspiracy charge was broad enough to include, as well, acts to obstruct the operations of the IRS. This was an obvious attempt to try to insulate the indictment from a defense that the shelters themselves were legitimate. Yet notwithstanding the breadth of the indictment and the fact that the government had the newly contrite accounting firm on its side, claiming that everyone knew that the tax shelters were unlawful all along, the ongoing legitimate dispute over this central question obviously continued to gnaw at the prosecutors' confidence, especially in view of the feisty resolve shown by some of the defendants and their lawyers to fight the charges.

Almost predictably, the DOJ issued a "superseding indictment" on October 17, 2005, adding not only ten additional defendants (for a total of 19), but also 45 new counts (for a total of 46), including charges for obstruction and making false statements to the IRS. These obstruction counts were separate from the conspiracy charge, an apparent further step to rescue at least part of the indictment just in case the defendants were able to demonstrate to a jury that the shelters were sufficiently legitimate to defeat the standard for criminal IRS fraud. The government was taking no chances that the truth might wreck its ability to get a conviction.

The government thus put together a case which, even if wrong on the merits of its fraud claims concerning the tax shelters themselves, would cause the defendants to begin to tumble like dominoes. "It's a lot like the scene in 'The Godfather' where Marlon Brando explains how he's going to make an offer they can't refuse," Joseph Grundfest, a Stanford University professor of business and ethics and former SEC commissioner, told *The Wall Street Journal*.[28] *The New York Times* quoted E. Lawrence Barcella Jr., a lawyer representing one of the new defendants, as reminding the world that no court had yet determined that the shelters were illegal.[29] However, this inconvenient, stubborn fact appeared to matter less and less as the government's successful, though dubious, strategy unfolded.

In time, various individuals involved in the shelters and named in this or related indictments began to fold, plead guilty, and agree to testify. On March 27, 2006, David Rivkin, a former KPMG partner in San Diego named in the indictment, pleaded guilty and agreed to cooperate. Rivkin stated, in open court during his plea, that he knew the tax returns to be false at the time for some of the firm's wealthy clients.

Judge Lewis A. Kaplan of the United States District Court for the Southern District of New York (Manhattan), playing out the same dubious scenario enacted in federal courts countless times each day all over the country, solemnly informed Rivkin that his eventual sentence would depend upon the extent of his "cooperation" with prosecutors.[30] By December of 2006 there were two additional such guilty pleas by persons not actually charged in the main KPMG indictment—Domenick DeGiorgio who pleaded guilty in August 2005, and Chandler Stuart Moisen in December 2006.[31] On September 10, 2007, David Amir Makov pleaded guilty to a single count of conspiracy to engage in tax fraud, and, as part of the morality play, he announced that three of the remaining defendants were likewise involved in committing fraud. Unsurprisingly, Makov agreed that the "sole purpose" of the BLIPS shelter was to generate "paper losses" rather than real economic activity.[32]

Yet one additional weapon wielded by the government did not sit as well with Judge Kaplan. Based on the terms of the Thompson Memorandum, the prosecutors put pressure on KPMG to withdraw from its earlier agreement to pay the attorneys' fees for its indicted former partners. One factor prosecutors should take into account when deciding whether a company should be indicted, according to the memo, "is whether the corporation appears to be protecting its culpable employees."[33] (Of course, the process that determines whether an employee is or is not culpable—the trial—requires substantial fees to pay for competent defense attorneys to assist in fairly and correctly making this determination.)

When the defendants complained to Judge Kaplan that their lawyers' fees were being cut off by KPMG under pressure from the prosecutors to appear to be cooperative, the judge reacted sharply, questioning aloud whether the DOJ violated the defendants' rights to the effective assistance of legal counsel, a right guaranteed by the Sixth Amendment to all criminal defendants and an essential element in assuring them a fair trial. This was no small gesture. After holding a highly contentious and heavily publicized hearing, Judge Kaplan ruled on June 27, 2006, that the government's pressure on KPMG was improper and unconstitutional. "KPMG refused to pay because the government held the proverbial gun to its head," wrote the judge. He postponed the trial in order to allow for litigation between the defendants and KPMG over

the payment of fees. The government took an appeal, further postpon-
ing the trial. How the issue would eventually be resolved by the higher
courts was less telling, perhaps, than Judge Kaplan's finding that the
prosecutors were using their power to try to disable the defendants
from defending themselves.[34]

As the tax shelter criminal conspiracy case unfolded, it became clearer that the government was doing all it could to avoid a fair showdown
on the merits of the central issue that started the case—were the tax
shelters sufficiently and transparently phony so that those who devised
and sold them could be said to have acted criminally, in violation of a
clear and known legal obligation? Did the government sufficiently lack
faith in its own legal theories so that it wanted to avoid a fair test of
those theories, relying instead on pressure tactics to produce pleas of
guilty, and coerced witnesses, up and down the line?

Interestingly, while all of this was going on, Congress, in reaction to
the Enron and other corporate "scandals," enacted legislation imposing
significant new audit and other obligations on accounting firms. The
so-called Sarbanes-Oxley law created the Public Company Accounting
Oversight Board (PCAOB) to exercise new and strict supervisory powers over public auditing firms. One duty of the PCAOB was to establish
standards for when an accounting firm that performs auditing services for a company could also provide other services and products that
might constitute a conflict of interest, such as the sale of tax shelters.
Such regulations, of course, if they can be honed with sufficient clarity, would eliminate any question as to whether in the future a firm
like KPMG could have acted as it did. However, this attempt at clarifying the law and the obligations of accounting firms going forward did
nothing to dim the resolve of the DOJ to punish the former KPMG
partners and others for engaging in arguably dubious but not clearly
illegal conduct in the past. Meanwhile, a substantial number of careers
and lives ended up as wreckage on the shoals of a pioneering prosecution where nobody could reliably draw the line separating criminal
from, at worst, questionable and, at best, perfectly lawful (even if aggressive) conduct.

One further provision of the deferred prosecution agreement might under ordinary circumstances raise the eyebrow of a disinterested observer. It turns out that KPMG, in the words of the agreement, "has been involved in an engagement to audit the Department of Justice's financial statements." Because KPMG had entered into the deferred prosecution agreement, the DOJ agreed that it would allow the firm to continue as its auditor. Such was the high degree of confidence now placed by the government in its erstwhile prey—an auditing firm that the government at one time saw as a veritable house of fraud but which had since seen the light of redemption. The partnership between the DOJ and the accounting firm would continue, both in and out of the prosecutorial arena—profitably for both.

• • ● • •

At times, state attorneys general have gone out of their way to act as lone heroes and emulate their federal counterparts, especially if the state law enforcement officers were looking to the prize of higher office. Such an attorney general was New York's Eliot Spitzer, who, in 2005, very publicly went after "Wall Street" in what turned out to be something of a dog-and-pony show played out on one stage, with the feds operating next door.

There is, perhaps, no better example of the difference between state criminal jurisprudence, bound by state legislation and common law principles, and the out-of-control federal system as it has evolved, than the titanic battle between Spitzer and insurance magnate Maurice R. "Hank" Greenberg, whose business vehicle, the American International Group, Inc. ("AIG"), was at the time the world's largest business insurance company. Attorney General Spitzer, widely thought to have his eye on higher elective office (he later won the New York governorship), went after AIG and Greenberg starting in 2005 for a number of accounting practices alleged by Spitzer to have improperly inflated AIG's earnings and net worth.

At the center of the Spitzer-Greenberg controversy was a transaction between Greenberg's AIG and the General Re insurance unit of

mega-investor Warren Buffett's Berkshire Hathaway investment company. As was the case with the KPMG tax shelters, the question was
whether the transaction had real economic purpose or was instead an
artificial transaction meant only to bolster the appearance of AIG's financial strength on its books. There was talk of indicting AIG and its
feisty chairman. Greenberg vehemently denied the impropriety of the
accounting treatment AIG employed and lodged a bold public challenge to Spitzer to, essentially, put up or shut up. Tagging along in
the investigation were, more ominously, the Securities and Exchange
Commission and the Department of Justice.

Now, it's important to understand that the federal McCarran-
Ferguson Act of 1945 gives primary responsibility to the states for regulating and taxing insurers. Under its terms, "even the SEC can go only
so far with its accounting cudgel," observed *The Wall Street Journal's*
Deborah Solomon at the time of AIG's troubles with the law. While
there were increasing calls for "greater federal oversight of the industry," including proposals to repeal the act altogether, she reported, it
was still in effect in 2005.[35] But that didn't stop the federal criminal
justice system from swooping in on AIG.

As a result of the enormous pressure placed upon AIG by simultane-
ous state and federal investigations, its board finally forced out its long-
time leader. Greenberg did not leave quietly. Instead, he threw down a
gauntlet in his letter of resignation submitted March 28, 2005.[36] A mere
two days later, the company admitted, according to a page one *Wall
Street Journal* report, "to a broad range of improper accounting that
could slash its net worth by $1.77 billion." In what the *Journal* dubbed
the company's "extraordinary confession," the new leadership suddenly
(but, to sophisticated observers, not surprisingly) agreed with state and
federal investigators that the questioned transactions "appear to have
been structured for the sole or primary purpose of accomplishing a
desired accounting result."[37] In other words, they were fraudulent.

Predictably, this sudden confession of error, a complete turnabout
from the position stoutly and consistently advanced by the company under Greenberg's chairmanship, as well as by its auditors and

its lawyers, made criminal prosecution of the company unlikely. *The Wall Street Journal*, noting that "no major financial-services company has survived indictment in recent history," with specific reference to Arthur Andersen, reported that AIG's more benign fate was a result of the fact that AIG's board, without Greenberg, "has been cooperative" and was "earning praise from New York Attorney General Eliot Spitzer." Obviously, it was earning points with the feds as well.

Now that AIG's new leadership admitted to fraud supposedly committed by Greenberg and other former company employees, prosecutors were free to focus on those individuals. But in the end, Spitzer's office did *not* indict either the company or any of its former employees, including the recalcitrant Greenberg. Instead, on May 26, 2005, the state filed a *civil* complaint against AIG, Greenberg, and one other former executive, alleging the impropriety of a number of Greenberg's accounting practices, a variety of state fraudulent business practices, state securities fraud, common law fraud, and violations of New York State's insurance laws.

When AIG issued its 2004 annual report, repeating the company's abject confession of error, which had been filed with the SEC in May of 2005, a still unrepentant Greenberg had his law firm release a "white paper" to the news media, contesting the characterization of the transactions as erroneous, much less fraudulent.[38] Spitzer, eyeing the New York governorship, shot back, telling the press that the lawsuit might be enlarged "to include additional civil fraud charges against Mr. Greenberg." State insurance law, however, simply did not render the AIG/General Re transaction criminal, and even Eliot Spitzer could not make it otherwise. On the same day, his office announced that it would not bring criminal charges against Greenberg.[39]

That didn't stop Spitzer from boasting to the press that he "had enough evidence to pursue a criminal case against Mr. Greenberg." Sounding more and more like the gubernatorial candidate that he was, Spitzer went on television and announced on *This Week With George Stephanopoulos* (ABC News) that "the evidence is overwhelming that these were transactions created for the purpose of deceiving the market. We call that fraud. It is deceptive. It is wrong. It is illegal."[40] Still, while "we" might dub the transactions "illegal," New York State's criminal law apparently did not, and Spitzer knew it. Spitzer could huff and puff, and the media could be taken in for a while, but in the end New York's criminal fraud law was not Silly Putty®. It had real form, substantive meaning, and actual limits, and it put the brakes on the Spitzer juggernaut.

The same could not be said for the feds, however. At that very same time, federal prosecutors were trying to determine whether Greenberg committed the crime of masking AIG's true financial condition by engaging in a sham transaction with General Re.[41] The case against Greenberg, who the feds by now recognized was going to fight rather than make a deal, obviously was not strong enough without the "cooperation" of other former AIG, as well as General Re, executives who could be pressured to adopt a revisionist view of what they and others did.

And so it could not have come as a surprise to Greenberg and his lawyers that, in early February 2006, federal prosecutors announced the indictments of four former General Re executives and a former executive of AIG, charging them with the old standbys, namely conspiracy, securities and mail fraud, and making false statements. The feds were also "possibly ratcheting up the pressure on other senior executives," according to *The New York Times*. In June of the prior year, two other General Re executives had pleaded guilty to charges that they'd engaged in a sham transaction to assist AIG's effort to artificially bolster its financial position. And in February 2008, when the five AIG and General Re executives who went to trial were convicted, federal prosecutors sought the equivalent of life sentences. Clearly, the DOJ was seeking to climb the ladder on the rungs of plea-bargaining executives who suddenly came up with new versions of history. Later, the DOJ would pressure the convicted defendants in hopes they could be persuaded to sing and compose, heading toward Greenberg at the apex. "It moves prosecutors that much closer to the possibility of criminal charges against executives above the level of people who have already been charged," observed former federal prosecutor turned white collar criminal defense lawyer Robert A. Mintz to *The New York Times.* "Certainly prosecutors will pressure these defendants to assist them in their investigation in exchange for a more lenient sentence."[42] In what had become a matter of course among the media when covering so-called white collar crime, the *Times* report did not question the ethics or social benefit, much less the truth-seeking capacity, of such a prosecutorial game plan.

A few days after the AIG and General Re executives' indictments, AIG issued a ritual public apology for its illegal conduct and announced a $1.64 billion settlement—in effect, a large cash tribute paid in exchange for staying in business.[43] Greenberg, for his part, was thrown into fighting trim. He announced the following month that he was itching to go to war with Spitzer in the civil fraud suit *before* Spitzer left office in November of 2006 to enter the gubernatorial primary.[44] Spitzer's office, however, was in no hurry to get the case tried. "We're handling this like any other case," said Spitzer's deputy, Michele Hirshman, at the same time denying a claim by "at least one AIG board member" who told *Business Week* that Greenberg's ouster by the AIG board was necessitated by Spitzer's threat to indict the company unless Greenberg were kicked out.[45]

It had turned out to be an empty threat, however. Even New York State's legendarily tough, creative and ambitious attorney general finally had to admit he could not indict under state law. Spitzer and his staff understood, in the end, that while state prosecutors in New York could indict Maurice Greenberg and any other ham sandwich, they could not convict where the law did not specifically cover the questioned activities and where the target was not inclined to roll over and play dead.

The feds, on the other hand, not only can indict a ham sandwich, they can convict, and all too often they can make the conviction stick on appeal. As University of Southern California Gould School of Law Professor Susan Estrich told me, "Federal law makes life a law school hypothetical in which there are always crimes to be found by a 'good student.'"[46] Eliot Spitzer was a good student, but he was unable to charge a crime under state law. The feds suffered no such limitation.

So far, because of AIG's ritual apology, it has been able to avoid federal criminal indictment. Though Greenberg hasn't yet been charged in any federal indictment, it seems almost inevitable, given the patterns seen elsewhere in this book, that the feds will seek to use the convictions of the five other AIG and General Re executives in order to "climb the ladder" and get an indictment against AIG's big kahuna. Until that happens, though, Greenberg still potentially faces civil charges brought by the Securities and Exchange Commission for the transactions that brought down the other executives. In May 2008, federal District Judge Christopher Droney tentatively allowed the process to move forward since, as *Fortune* reported, "[he] said there was 'sufficient evidence' for a civil jury to conclude that Greenberg had initiated the problematic transaction."[47]

Almost completely missed in the widespread news coverage of the whole sorry affair was the question of how and why the feds had entered the fray with criminal indictments and continuing investigations in the first place. The Department of Justice did not have to await the repeal of the federal McCarran-Ferguson Act of 1945, nor the enactment of new congressional legislation giving the federal government additional oversight jurisdiction in the insurance industry. Department of Justice prosecutors, without the adoption of any such federal laws, were able to indict and convict former executives of General Re and AIG, thus beginning their climb up the ladder for Hank Greenberg.

CHAPTER SIX

Lawyers: Government Offense Against the Best Defense

—— ••• ——

Christ Church in Greenwich, Connecticut, could not be more genteel. As a child, former president George H.W. Bush attended this Episcopal church, and many years later he held his parents' funerals in its august sanctuary. Now it was on the brink of a scandal.[1] In October 2006, a church employee discovered that church organist Robert Tate had been storing illicit pictures of children, child pornography, on his church-issued laptop computer. Soon thereafter, the church sought legal advice from respected local attorney Philip Russell, who recommended that Tate be immediately terminated from his employment by the church. On October 9, Russell took possession of the laptop and destroyed the hard drive, which contained images of naked young boys.

Many lawyers would have done precisely the same thing, on the theory that the law allows, perhaps even requires, the destruction of "contraband," or material considered harmful and illegal for anyone except those in law enforcement to possess under any and all circumstances. Dealing with contraband can be very tricky, even for a sophisticated lawyer with criminal law experience. The very act of possession is criminal. It is illegal to possess heroin, for example, which federal narcotics laws regard as having no approved medical uses. No prescription nor any medical condition justifies its possession by anyone, at any time, for any reason. Child pornography is in the same category.

Had the hard drive containing the pornographic images been found in the possession of either the Church or its lawyer for "safe-keeping," he would have had to do a lot of explaining to avert criminal charges.

Likewise, turning the computer over to the police would likely have subjected both the church and its lawyers to questioning, if not suspicion and an investigation. So what was Attorney Russell to do? Should he take possession of the pornography-laden hard drive and hold on to it, thereby arguably committing a serious felony every moment it was in his possession? Should he turn in the hard drive, thereby arguably incriminating (and betraying) his client, the church, which, after all, owned the laptop? Or should he keep the hard drive in the laptop and simply leave it in the church office, where anyone entering the office, including impressionable young children, could access it? Faced with such difficult choices, he decided to destroy what the law considered contraband. It was a defensible, even honorable, decision.

But, unbeknownst to Russell, three days earlier the feds had begun to investigate Tate, having been tipped off to his involvement in child pornography. The U.S. attorney's office considered the computer hard drive to be evidence in its investigation. And so, to the shock and dismay of members of the bar, the feds charged Russell with obstruction of justice and destruction of evidence, a felony that carries a 20-year maximum prison sentence. The February 2007 indictment did not claim that Russell knew, at the time he destroyed the images, that the feds had already begun an investigation. Prosecutors even acknowledged that Russell destroyed material that it was illegal to possess. But they indicted him nonetheless.

Lawyers across the country had that sinking feeling: "There but for the grace of God go I." The Russell prosecution was only the latest in a long line of dubious legal assaults against members of the bar. Lawyers, as a group, are not particularly popular, and those who take on criminal matters often sink to the bottom of an already rather low pile. Still, the independent bar has been a bulwark against government overreaching and official repression since before the founding of the republic. (Virtually every American schoolchild knows the story of John Adams's defense of the British redcoats in the Boston Massacre.) America's lawyers, as a profession, are more directly involved in opposing certain governmental goals than perhaps any other group. And when government overreaches in any arena controlled by law, it is frequently the lawyers who show up at the frontlines. The same may be said for opposition to governmental attempts to over-regulate an industry. So a prosecutorial assault on lawyers who are, essentially, just doing their jobs, is a matter that should be of particular concern in a free society.

Shock turned to anger when the trial judge in Russell's case, Alan H. Nevas of the U.S. District Court for Connecticut, let the indictment stand and ordered Russell to stand trial. He was able to do so because Russell was charged under two lesser known provisions of the Sarbanes-Oxley Act of 2002, which, as seen in the previous two chapters, was supposedly designed to restore investor confidence in the wake of the Arthur Andersen corporate accounting scandal—namely Section 802 ("Criminal Penalties for Altering Documents") and Section 1102 ("Tampering with a Record or Otherwise Impeding an Official Proceeding").[2] These new obstruction provisions broadened the obligation to retain documents so that a party could not destroy them in contemplation of a future investigation even if no formal investigation had begun (or the holder of the records did not know of any such investigation) and no subpoena had been received. The new statute made it a felony to "knowingly alter, destroy, [or] mutilate…any document or tangible object with the intent to impede, obstruct, or influence the investigation or proper administration of any matter." Since Judge Nevas concluded that, under the new obstruction statute, it was unnecessary for the government to have specified in the indictment that Russell had in mind any particular investigation, or that his intention was that of "obstructing or interfering with" any official proceeding or investigation, it would be up to a jury to decide, at trial, whether there could have been any such link in Russell's mind when he destroyed the hard drive in the church computer used by Robert Tate.[3]

Legal and business experts immediately objected to the vagueness of the obstruction provisions under which Russell was ordered to stand trial. "The revised language," noted one business writer, "implied that people could face criminal charges by tampering with documents before they become evidence in a federal investigation."[4] The intersection between ordinary document-retention-and-destruction policies, which are ubiquitous in industry, and the federal crime of obstruction of justice, was becoming impossible to navigate with any confidence. The application of this statute to a criminal defense lawyer handling contraband injected a new dimension to the apprehension, which bordered on terror. Even Mark A. DuBois, the Chief Disciplinary Counsel for the Connecticut Bar Association (surely an "establishment" figure and hardly a maverick from the criminal defense bar) told *Greenwich Time* that he was troubled by how attorneys like Russell are forced by the feds to act as soothsayers. "The operative issue for the criminal lawyer to decide is 'what's evidence and when does something become evidence,'" he said. "How prescient does a lawyer need to be? Now if you guess wrong you've got big problems, because it is a serious crime."[5]

Wholly aside from the issue of at what point in time Sarbanes-Oxley requires the preservation of potential evidence, Irwin Schwartz, a highly regarded Seattle criminal defense attorney and a former president of the National Association of Criminal Defense Lawyers, questioned how a lawyer could be indicted for destroying *contraband* materials. Schwartz was also puzzled about how and why a statute written to preserve corporate records was suddenly being used to criminalize the destruction of material that, unlike corporate records, it is a crime to possess under any circumstances.[6] Again, what was Attorney Russell to do?

Lawyers across the country expressed outrage and befuddlement to the press and on blogs and in email list-serve discussions. Stephen Gillers, New York University Law School professor and one of the nation's most respected and sought-after experts on legal ethics, explained the urgency of the situation to an Associated Press reporter: "Every criminal defense lawyer in the country has to be alarmed at the indictment," said Gillers. "It's going to upset a lot of assumptions about how lawyers can represent clients. I think this is a boundary-pushing case."[7] "This is indeed an upsetting case," observed another lawyer. "The government cannot argue both (1) simple possession of child pornography is itself victimization [of children]... and yet (2) criminalize the termination of the victimization by destroying the images." Added the lawyer: "It is as if the primary purpose of the criminal law is to create prosecutions, rather than encourage conforming behavior to the law." The lawyer then asked the question from the vantage point of a parent: "Does the parent who finds their child's 'stash' only have the choice of turning their child into the police or becoming an accomplice themselves?"[8]

The vagueness of the statute as it was used in the Russell prosecution raised yet another problem. This was highlighted by a remark made to the Associated Press reporter by Jon Schoenhorn, president of the Connecticut Criminal Defense Lawyers Association. Schoenhorn focused on the perversion of the attorney's historically understood role as trusted legal adviser to his or her client. "The most troubling aspect," Schoenhorn told the reporter, "is it tried to make lawyers shills or hand maidens for police and government investigators." In other words, anything that the lawyer does that makes the prosecutor's job harder is seen as a crime. Local criminal lawyer Lindy Urso put it best when he told a reporter: "I don't like to consider my own interests when I am defending a client." He questioned whether the statute "encourages attorneys to weigh protecting their clients or themselves."

The problems with the prosecutor's interpretation of the statute can be spun endlessly. Meanwhile, Philip Russell stood accused of a career-wrecking felony. Russell's lawyers, Robert M. Casale and Thomas Williams, had advanced these arguments when they asked the court to dismiss the indictment. At bottom, they argued, the prosecution's oblique interpretation of the statute would force attorneys (who, unlike ordinary citizens, have a constitutionally mandated duty to represent clients zealously) to become lapdogs to prosecutors.

To the prosecutor, however, there was no lack of clarity in the statute and no perversion of the lawyer's historic role. "Those who possess child pornography or hinder the prosecution of those who do by destroying evidence and impeding investigations will be prosecuted, particularly when the obstructionists are attorneys and officers of the court," Connecticut U.S. Attorney Kevin O'Connor, who spearheaded the investigation, told *Greenwich Time*. In the brief[9] he filed opposing Russell's request that the judge dismiss the indictment, O'Connor claimed that "this statute is specifically meant not to include any technical requirement...to tie the obstructive conduct to a pending or imminent proceeding or matter."[10] The statute, explained O'Connor (with no apparent sense of the absurd or the outrageous), "does not require corrupt intent."

The defense team pointed out that Russell had good reason to destroy the hard drive. They cited several recent cases in which lawyers and experts were threatened with prosecution for the mere possession of child pornography, even for entirely proper purposes. In one brief, Russell's lawyers referred to a 2003 case in which a defense expert was given permission, by a state trial judge in a state child pornography prosecution, to copy the computer hard drive in order to do an analysis of the images.[11] A federal prosecutor threatened defense counsel that such possession exposed the defense team to federal prosecution, since federal law does not make an exception for such possession by defense lawyers and experts. In another example cited by Russell's lawyers, "a prosecutor in Nevada threatened to arrest a defense attorney for possession of child pornography even though the judge in the case had previously authorized counsel to possess the disputed images in order to assist in the preparation of his client's defense."[12] Under circumstances such as these, it is hard to fault Attorney Russell for destroying the computer drive.

None of these arguments held sway. After the judge denied Russell's motion to dismiss the indictment, the beleaguered lawyer hedged his bets and entered into a plea bargain: the Sarbanes-Oxley indictment was dismissed and Russell instead pleaded guilty to a less serious charge of misprision of a felony. The damage to Russell's life was thus minimized, although his career likely would never fully recover. But, from society's vantage point, a very troublesome legal precedent was set.

The misprision statute, which forbids concealment of "knowledge of the actual commission of a felony,"[13] is potentially as troublesome for attorneys as the obstruction provisions of Sarbanes-Oxley. It has been judicially interpreted to require some active element of misleading investigative authorities rather than simply failing to report a crime.[14] But when the lawyer is representing a client with whom he has a relationship characterized by long-standing legal principles of confidentiality and loyalty, drawing that line can be extremely difficult, if not impossible. And neither the Supreme Court nor Congress has lent much clarity to the matter.

Even though it would have signaled a revolutionary change in the definition of the "attorney-client privilege," the application of the misprision statute to Russell's situation went unquestioned because it was part of a plea bargain aimed at averting an even more serious charge. If anything, it is an essential part of a lawyer's job to lawfully withhold information from prosecutors, or from anyone who might use it to harm his or her client's interests. Our system of justice is an adversary system, where the lawyer must adhere to an attorney-client privilege of confidentiality. This privilege is a logical extension of the defendant's Sixth Amendment right in a criminal case to enjoy the effective assistance of counsel, and derives from an even older English common law doctrine protecting the attorney-client relationship in both criminal and civil matters. Thus, the application of the federal misprision statute to what a lawyer learns directly from a client or even elsewhere while representing that client is a legally delicate matter. To whom do lawyers have a primary duty and owe their loyalty—clients or prosecutors?

Until these questions are resolved either by the Supreme Court or by congressional action, lawyers for clients who possess contraband will have no way of knowing what to do. This will leave them to the tender mercies of federal prosecutors. Departing from the status quo in a case involving the client's possession of contraband, after all, carries its own risks; it encourages the client either to continue possessing the contraband, thus exacerbating his crime, or to destroy it, thus committing a second crime to compound the original possessory crime. There is simply no way for the lawyer to handle such a situation without jeopardy. No matter what he or she says or does, either the client or the lawyer must engage in arguably criminal conduct and thereby subject himself to legal jeopardy.

When the law becomes a trap for the unwary, it becomes an engine of oppression rather than a statement of the moral and ethical requirements of a society's citizens. At the very least, this prosecutorial behavior will discourage lawyers from taking child pornography (or, for that matter, heroin) cases, and will deprive citizens, under investigation or indictment, of legal counsel from an attorney who is concerned with the client's legitimate interests rather than with the lawyer's own reputation or liberty.

• • ● • •

Long before Sarbanes-Oxley was even a twinkle in legislators' eyes, obstruction of justice statutes had been slippery territory for lawyers and especially for criminal defense attorneys, who are entrusted with all manner of confidences in their line of work. Criminal defense lawyer William J. Cintolo's nightmare began long before he realized it. The FBI had installed an electronic listening device on the first floor apartment at 98 Prince Street, in Boston's North End. The neighborhood was home to a good part of the city's Italian-American population, as well as to the Massachusetts branch of the Mafia. With their bug firmly planted in the Prince Street apartment, the feds managed to record conversations at the headquarters of Boston's Angiulo crime family between January 19 and May 3, 1981.

On the first day of the feds' monitoring, Gennaro Angiulo, the head of the family and the organization, discussed an overdue loan-shark debt owed by one Louis Venios, proprietor of the Mousetrap Lounge. Over the next few days, Gennaro ("Jerry") Angiulo and his brothers Michele ("Mike"), Francesco ("Frank'), Nicolo ("Nick"), and Donato ("Danny") discussed finding Venios to learn what efforts he was making to repay the debt. Someone suggested contacting Venios's son-in-law, Walter LaFreniere, to see if he might be able to shed light on either the status of the debt or Venios's whereabouts. It was a useful contact. On February 5, LaFreniere delivered some of the overdue cash. He clearly was interested in protecting his father-in-law.

The Angiulos, it turned out, were not the only ones interested in talking to Venios. While the Angiulo mob's conversations about collecting Venios's past-due debt were going forward, secretly recorded by the FBI, a federal grand jury a few blocks away was hearing evidence in what would eventually lead to a massive racketeering indictment against the Angiulos and their associates in crime. Venios had been subpoenaed to appear before the grand jury and did so on February 26. As is common on the part of both loan sharks and their customers, Venios invoked his Fifth Amendment privilege against self-incrimination and refused to testify. His son-in-law, LaFreniere, while represented by a lawyer, did the same two weeks later. Father-in-law and son-in-law were obviously sticking together, trying not to incur the wrath of the Angiulo organization.

The Angiulo brothers knew about the grand jury, of course, and were getting nervous about it. Which of their organization's activities were under scrutiny, and who was being called to give evidence? The brothers were particularly concerned because grand jury proceedings are conducted in secret. Unless a witness is willing to report back what has happened inside the grand jury room, it's virtually impossible to get reliable intelligence about what has transpired or even which witnesses have shown up. Lawyers for witnesses are not allowed to accompany their clients inside the grand jury room and must depend on their clients to brief them. Witnesses and their lawyers are allowed to disclose what happened, although only the witness can speak from firsthand knowledge. Meanwhile, inside the grand jury, questions are posed to witnesses by federal prosecutors. On occasion, one or more of the 23 members of the grand jury (who are sworn to secrecy) ask questions. By majority vote a grand jury may bring an indictment, normally drafted by the prosecutors, against the target(s) of the investigation.

The Angiulos obtained whatever grand jury information they could from Venios and LaFreniere. But they naturally could not be confident they were getting the truthful or whole story, since the witnesses had gone inside the chamber alone. Gennaro was heard saying on the FBI tape that while he had great confidence that Venios, with whom he had a long relationship, could be counted on to keep his mouth shut, he was not so sure of the relative newcomer and suspected weakling LaFreniere. It was at that point that Gennaro came up with the idea of volunteering the Angiulo brothers' own lawyer, Cintolo, to advise LaFreniere. Having LaFreniere represented by an experienced and friendly lawyer like Cintolo would not only help prop up the witness but would also serve as a link between the Angiulos and LaFreniere.

Upon the suggestion of Donato Angiulo, LaFreniere contacted Cintolo seeking legal advice and representation for the grand jury proceedings. Of immediate concern was that the prosecutors would follow the typical pattern in such cases: when met by a witness's invocation of the Fifth Amendment privilege against self-incrimination, the prosecutors normally obtain a directive from a federal judge ordering the witness to testify and giving him legal assurances that nothing that he says would be used against him. Such an "immunity order" eliminates the witness's right to continue to invoke his privilege against self-incrimination. At that point the witness either agrees to testify or is jailed by the judge for the duration of the life of the grand jury or until he relents. Grand juries typically sit for 18 months at a stretch, and in a long and difficult investigation it is not unusual to renew a grand jury term for a second 18-month period. In this way, a recalcitrant immunized grand jury witness who refuses an order to testify could spend as long as 36 months in prison.[15] And if the witness testifies but he lies, he then is subject to even longer penalties for perjury.

There is not much that a defense lawyer normally can do, except to advise the immunized client-witness that, if he does not want to testify, he is better off serving a contempt sentence than committing perjury. Indeed, it is widely viewed, within the legal profession, as a lawyer's ethical obligation to advise a client against perjuring himself and then to leave up to the client the decision whether to testify or to risk a contempt citation.

When LaFreniere contacted Cintolo after his first appearance before the grand jury, the lawyer instructed his new client to write a complete description of what had occurred during the proceedings. He told LaFreniere to recount all questions asked (and which questions LaFreniere had refused to answer on Fifth Amendment privilege grounds while represented by his prior legal counsel). After that initial appearance, the prosecutors told LaFreniere that they were not satisfied with leaving the matter there. They advised the witness to have his lawyer contact them because the government was intent on forcing him to testify. A dreaded immunity order clearly was coming.

But there was a problem. Cintolo, in addition to representing the Angiulo brothers, represented Gennaro's son Jason Angiulo as well, and Jason had also been subpoenaed by the grand jury. Jason, unlike LaFreniere, was a "target" (that is, someone ultimately to be charged and not just a witness). Targets, unlike prospective witnesses, are almost never immunized. Prosecutors want their hides, not their testimony. (Often the coerced testimony follows as a result of a conviction and a very long prison sentence.) As Cintolo later testified at his own trial, he informed LaFreniere of his representation of Jason Angiulo and said that he could represent both of them only if LaFreniere maintained the same position he held at his first grand jury appearance and before he had contacted Cintolo—a refusal to testify. Were LaFreniere to decide to testify, Cintolo would be put into a conflict-of-interest position, he explained to LaFreniere, since he would be representing a member of the Angiulo family on the one hand, and a witness against the family member on the other. But crucially, Cintolo explained, as long as LaFreniere had made a firm decision to refuse to testify, Cintolo could undertake the representation of both. Their interests and intentions were in harmony rather than in conflict, since neither Jason Angiulo nor Walter LaFreniere was going to testify. Cintolo's decision to represent LaFreniere turned out to be, as we shall see, very much in LaFreniere's best interests. It might well have saved the client's life.

Cintolo's advice to LaFreniere was technically correct, although views within the legal system vary on the question of whether it is prudent for a lawyer to represent both a witness and a target, even if both clients are informed of the dual representation, and even if the witness initially decides, entirely on his own accord and while represented by other legal counsel, to refuse to testify against the target. In prosecutorial circles especially, it is widely assumed—and not without good reason—that by the witness's retaining the same lawyer who represents the target, the witness loses the benefit of the lawyer's unfettered and unconflicted legal advice as to whether the witness should *continue* to maintain his refusal to testify. However, as we shall see, special circumstances in this case arguably made it in LaFreniere's best interests to be represented by a lawyer who had a relationship to, and credibility with, the Angiulo family.

The situation heated up when FBI monitoring agents, listening covertly to the Prince Street conversations, overheard Gennaro Angiulo instruct two of his lieutenants, Richard Gambale and Peter Limone, to kill LaFreniere. Gennaro was getting increasingly uncomfortable with the idea that LaFreniere might decide to testify and incriminate Jason Angiulo. The monitoring agents promptly contacted LaFreniere by telephone and sought an immediate meeting. At the meeting, the agents informed LaFreniere that Gennaro had put out a contract on his life and that he would likely be murdered within a day or two, prior to his next scheduled grand jury appearance. The agents, not wanting to disclose that their source was an electronic bug, attributed their information to an informant. They offered LaFreniere FBI protection, a frequent prelude to obtaining a witness's cooperation. But LaFreniere, who had already received an invitation to meet with Gambale that evening, turned down the agents' offer.

LaFreniere reported all of this to Gambale on the phone, disclosing not only the FBI contact but also his own concern that perhaps Gambale wanted to murder him. Wisely, LaFreniere turned down the invitation to meet with Gennaro's henchman. Gambale dutifully reported back to Gennaro, who contacted Cintolo and suggested that the lawyer meet with his increasingly nervous client, LaFreniere. Gennaro disclosed to Cintolo that the FBI agents had told LaFreniere that there was a "hit" contract on him, although Gennaro did not actually confirm the existence of such a contract, much less his own role in ordering it. Nor, strikingly, did Gennaro *deny* to Cintolo that a contract on LaFreniere existed. Still, Cintolo could not be certain whether LaFreniere was really in mortal danger.

Cintolo, having undertaken to represent LaFreniere, tried to do what he could for a witness-client who had already indicated that he preferred to suffer the consequences (namely, a contempt sentence) of refusing to testify even if immunized. Very few options exist for a defense lawyer with a client who refuses to testify in the face of an immunity order, but Cintolo did what he could. He sought a continuance of the grand jury appearance to give him and his client more time to prepare. He fought against a government attempt to get him disqualified on conflict-of-interest grounds from representing *both* Jason Angiulo and LaFreniere. Even though both clients waived any such conflict, the judge agreed, predictably and properly, with the government that both a witness and a target of the grand jury should not have the same lawyer. Cintolo filed an appeal of that order, which he promptly lost. As a result, he was forced to drop his representation of Jason Angiulo. In the meantime, Cintolo was able to garner information about where the grand jury inquiry was heading, information he shared with the Angiulos.

The Angiulo mob was indicted on September 19, 1983, in a massive racketeering case built largely on the electronic bug the FBI had installed at the Prince Street headquarters. Eventually, the conviction of all major members of the group resulted in its dismantling. For a time, Boston was free of a ruling Mafia crime family while other criminal groups vied for the newly vacated top spot. The prosecution was considered one of the most successful in the annals of Department of Justice assaults on organized crime.

But taking down the Boston Mafia was not enough for the DOJ. In December 1984, the feds indicted Cintolo for obstruction of justice growing out of his representation of the Angiulos and LaFreniere. The DOJ claimed that even though he had technically been disqualified from representing Jason Angiulo before the grand jury, Cintolo continued representing the interests of the Angiulo family during the grand jury investigation. The prosecutors alleged that Cintolo had used his position as attorney for LaFreniere not to further LaFreniere's interests, but to gather information for his "true" client, the Angiulo mob, and to make sure that LaFreniere continued refusing to testify against the family.[16]

The surreptitious Prince Street recordings were played for the jury at Cintolo's trial. The tapes showed that the Angiulos were concerned that LaFreniere would weaken and testify once immunized, and that they consequently suggested to LaFreniere that he hire Cintolo; the Angiulos also suggested to Cintolo that he accept LaFreniere's request for representation. At a later meeting, the bugging tapes demonstrated, Cintolo shared with the Angiulos the questions that LaFreniere had been asked at the grand jury, questions that the client had duly reported to Cintolo, along with the fact that LaFreniere had refused to answer. (Earlier, the Angiulos had been told by Venios what questions were asked of him at the grand jury, and Gennaro duly reported that to Cintolo.)

There was some controversy at the trial about whether the lawyer actually knew or had reason to know that one of his clients, Gennaro Angiulo, had in mind to murder his other client—Walter LaFreniere. The plot to murder LaFreniere was caught on tape; Cintolo was not in the room when it was hatched. However, Cintolo was aware of the Angiulos's concern about whether LaFreniere could stand up to pressure and accept a contempt sentence rather than cave in and testify. Cintolo also had learned, well before he was indicted and while the bug was still recording the goings-on at Prince Street, from a federal prosecutor and from LaFreniere, that "an informant" had told the FBI that the Angiulos were determined to assassinate LaFreniere. Cintolo testified that he did not believe there was a "hit" contract on his client, but rather that it was concocted by the FBI to scare LaFreniere into becoming a cooperating (and protected) federal witness. But, of course, Cintolo could not be certain. (Such phony FBI scare tactics are hardly unknown, as any experienced criminal defense lawyer can recount.)

At the time that the "hit" contract was issued, Gennaro Angiulo had gotten information that LaFreniere, when the feds tipped him off to the murder plot, was trying to reach Cintolo. Angiulo promptly told Cintolo that the reason LaFreniere was trying to reach the lawyer was because the feds had just warned his client that a contract had been put out on his life. Remember, Angiulo never did tell Cintolo whether there was or was not a plot to murder his client, much less that Angiulo had ordered the hit. The prosecutors took the position that Cintolo had heard enough to put two and two together and recognized that one group of his clients was out to murder (and thus silence) the other client. It remained a contested point whether Cintolo knew that Angiulo was sufficiently nervous about whether LaFreniere was a stand-up guy to launch a plot to murder him.

The heart of Cintolo's obstruction prosecution was not that he played any role or had any knowledge of the plot to assassinate one of his clients to protect the others. Rather, the indictment charged that by representing both the targets of the grand jury and a witness whose testimony was sought, unsuccessfully, against the targets, and by encouraging LaFreniere to keep silent even in the face of a contempt-of-court prison sentence, Cintolo had abused his role as a lawyer and had thereby obstructed—indeed, polluted—the processes of justice.

The prosecutors sought to bolster their case by arguing that the tactics Cintolo employed while representing LaFreniere were frivolous legal maneuvers destined to (and in fact they did) lose in court. At bottom, the government's position was that there was nothing that Cintolo could, or should, have done for LaFreniere except assist him while he testified. While a witness, the government conceded, has every right to refuse to testify on the basis of the constitutional privilege against self-incrimination, a lawyer who advises a client to invoke the privilege, and who continues to represent the client who remains recalcitrant even in the face of an immunity order, is, in the government's eyes, guilty of obstruction of justice *if his true allegiance is to another client*, namely the target of the investigation or prosecution. And so the Cintolo prosecution proceeded on a theory that while each of the tactical moves engaged in by Cintolo on behalf of LaFreniere was lawful in itself, the whole of the representation, being a sham based on Cintolo's true allegiance toward the Angiulos, constituted the crime of obstruction of justice.

The judge at Cintolo's obstruction of justice trial didn't buy the theory in its entirety and told the jurors that the evidence did not demonstrate Cintolo's actual knowledge of a plot to kill LaFreniere. The jury nonetheless handed the Mafia-hunting DOJ another victory. Cintolo was convicted, sentenced to two years in prison, and automatically disbarred.

Members of the criminal defense bar recognized immediately the threat posed by such a prosecution and its underlying theory. It greatly hinders the ability of any perfectly honest and ethical criminal lawyer to render zealous representation to a client or clients. All lawyers are taught in law school that, as a matter of professional ethics within an adversarial system of justice, a lawyer must not merely represent a client, but must do so with "utmost zeal." The defense lawyer is tasked with doing anything and everything within the law to protect the client from prosecution or penalty. In Cintolo's case it was precisely his observance of that ethical requirement that the DOJ sought to punish. A special challenge is presented to both lawyer and client when the very path taken by the lawyer to protect the client is seen not as the fulfillment of the lawyer's constitutional role and duty, but rather as a criminal venture by a rogue shyster or Mafia foot soldier with some goal in mind other than proper and lawful vigorous representation.

Responding to the government's attempt to turn Cintolo's representation of LaFreniere into a crime, the criminal defense bar made its views known. When Cintolo's case went up to the U.S. Court of Appeals for the First Circuit, two groups filed an *amicus curiae* ("friend of the court") brief on his behalf. In their joint *amicus* brief, the Massachusetts Association of Criminal Defense Lawyers (which I co-founded and which I co-chaired at the time, with my then-partner Andrew Good) and the National Network for the Right to Counsel, chaired by Boston attorney Max D. Stern, registered a stark warning: to allow the conviction of Cintolo on the facts presented would send a chill down the spine of every ethical and effective criminal lawyer in the country and, in the process, deprive defendants of their constitutionally mandated right to counsel.

"Never before, to the knowledge of *amici*, has a jury been permitted to determine whether an attorney should be held criminally liable for actions taken by the attorney in the course of advising and representing his client, on the ground that the motive for the maneuvers was delay rather than a *bona fide* belief in their eventual success on the merits," the defense lawyers' brief warned. Equally startling was the notion that a jury would be allowed "to determine that a lawyer's advice to and representation of multiple clients was 'corrupt,' and hence unlawful, for the reason that the advice given to one client provided benefits to another client as well." The brief pointed out that every action taken by Cintolo on behalf of either or both clients was in itself lawful, but that somehow his course of conduct was being viewed as criminal because the subjective "motive" was in some way "corrupt." To allow this to happen, warned the defense lawyers, "changed the requirement that the lawyer act 'within the bounds of the law' from an objective limitation on what the lawyer may do in defense of the client, to an undefined proscription against any conduct which a prosecutor can convince a judge or jury was undertaken with a 'corrupt' motive."

The criminal defense bar's *amicus* brief did not seek to defend truly illegal, corrupt conduct by a lawyer. It did not adopt an "anything goes" approach, which would have been a legally frivolous and tactically disastrous argument. Rather, it cited such authorities as the American Bar Association for the proposition that it's the lawyer's job to advise the client on his or her alternatives, but the client makes the decision.[17] And in the case of LaFreniere, he was entitled to make the decision to refuse to testify, even after being granted immunity, and to suffer the legal consequences of a contempt sentence. The defense lawyers further cited a 1985 federal court decision warning that once a lawyer has undertaken to represent a defendant and has explained all conflicts of interest to him, he may not withdraw from the representation except under compelling circumstances.[18]

The defense lawyers' group urged the Court of Appeals to disallow prosecutions of lawyers under this general, amorphous obstruction of justice statute. Instead, the court should rely on "the more specific clauses and statutes which the government has available to punish illegal conduct of this sort." For example, a lawyer may clearly be prosecuted if he "knowingly filed false statements with the government, or threatens a witness to alter his testimony, or bribes a judge or juror." Such conduct, noted the *amicus* brief, is a crime no matter who commits it.

The defense lawyers then made an argument that should have made clear why the lawyer's conduct could not be viewed as criminal without destroying his ability to represent his clients. "Because the defendant's conduct was not itself criminal," the brief argued, "the government had to prove that defendant had, at least, encouraged, endorsed or stimulated the illegal conspiracy in order to prove his intent to join it." Yet Cintolo, whose voice had been secretly recorded by the FBI, had remained silent every time the Angiulos brought up their criminal schemes. "Not a single statement or action by [Cintolo] indicates that he was encouraging the Angiulos to undertake their criminal plans to obstruct justice."

This latter point becomes particularly important when discussing the contract against LaFreniere. It may or may not be that Cintolo suspected such a contract was out on his client's life, and even that his other client, the Angiulo family, was responsible for this threat. If so, any experienced criminal defense lawyer, who is privy to many dark secrets when representing real criminals, recognizes that a certain amount of discretion is essential in seeing that no further harm be done. In the case of LaFreniere, Cintolo did precisely what any ethical and effective lawyer should have done to protect the life of a client who had already decided that he would not testify against the mob: Cintolo told the head of the mob that LaFreniere had decided not to testify and instead to serve his sentence for contempt. Cintolo thereby very likely saved the life of his client LaFreniere, whether or not he knew or suspected it.[19]

The brief filed by the Department of Justice, signed primarily by then-United States Attorney (and later FBI Director) Robert S. Mueller III, took a more simplistic, Manichean view. Because Cintolo's representation of LaFreniere was seen as benefiting Cintolo's other client, the Angiulo family, his representation of LaFreniere was, said the brief, "a sham." The DOJ brief twisted the murder plot on LaFreniere's life, arguing that because Cintolo undertook the representation of LaFreniere after he had reason to suspect that his other client, the Angiulo family, planned to murder LaFreniere, the lawyer in effect joined in the conspiracy to murder his other client. (As stated above, it was more likely, particularly as events unfolded, that Cintolo *saved* LaFreniere's life by helping LaFreniere put into effect the decision he'd made, before Cintolo became his lawyer, to refuse to testify against the Angiulos.)

It was clear that the prosecutors were somewhat disturbed by the arguments made by the criminal defense bar *amici*, since the prosecution's brief repeatedly made direct reference to those arguments and sought to refute them. Normally, friend-of-the-court briefs play a decidedly backseat role compared to the party himself. But in this case it was clear that the battle was between the Justice Department and the criminal defense bar, not just one criminal defense practitioner who happened to be representing a very unappealing group of clients.

If the prosecutors were disturbed that the defense bar came to the aid of Cintolo, the Court of Appeals seemed doubly challenged when it concluded the proceedings by affirming Cintolo's conviction. Much of the three-judge panel's opinion responding to Cintolo's claims actually addressed those raised by the *amici*. The court began with a reference to what it termed "the fabric of federal law which Congress has woven to prevent obstruction of justice."[20] But the opinion hardly laid out the strands of this supposed "fabric." It instead repeated the government's mantra: Cintolo's "corrupt" intention transformed traditional criminal defense work into the sinister practice of obstruction of justice. Despite the fact that there was no evidence that LaFreniere ever entertained the notion of testifying against the Angiulo family, the appellate court referred to Cintolo's "efforts to inhibit LaFreniere, after the latter had been granted immunity, from testifying truthfully before the grand jury, or from cooperating in any way with the investigation."

An assumption (an entirely improper one that misconceives the role of the criminal defense lawyer in the adversary system) pervades the court's opinion: it was somehow Cintolo's job to encourage his client to cooperate with the FBI, even if such cooperation was against the client's own view of his best interests and security. In fact, it was Cintolo's obligation to protect his client from *both* the FBI and the mob as best he could. Both sides, after all, were trying to use LaFreniere for their own ends. For the system to work, criminal defense lawyers must look out for their clients' (not their own, and certainly not government prosecutors') best interests. The Court of Appeals therefore embarked on the dangerous path of equating a lawyer's assisting the FBI with the lawyer's duty and role in the adversarial system. This was a revolutionary idea that would seriously undermine the role of the independent bar in providing legal representation when a citizen is charged by the federal government with a crime. This revolution was effectuated by an appellate court too readily buying the DOJ's "obstruction" theory based upon an utterly vague statute that would not readily be so interpreted by most lawyers, nor by anyone concerned about maintaining an independent bar within civil society.

The Court of Appeals was particularly hard on Cintolo about the murder contract on LaFreniere's life. The FBI bug had picked up the conversation in which Gennaro Angiulo informed Cintolo that the FBI agents told LaFreniere that an "informant" reported the contract to the Bureau. The Court of Appeals contorted this part of the eavesdrop recording to make it sound as if Cintolo were utterly unconcerned about LaFreniere's well-being. "Cintolo's only response to this grisly piece of news," wrote the court, "was to mention calmly that he had instructed LaFreniere to talk with no one, and to refer all calls to him." Of course, Cintolo had no other option if, realistically, his goal was to protect LaFreniere's life. Were he to assume a holier-than-thou posture and advise or warn Angiulo to leave LaFreniere alone, he would have destroyed any trust that Angiulo had built up toward the lawyer. Indeed, he would have cut off whatever avenue remained available to get information from Angiulo that would have affected LaFreniere. Cintolo would have destroyed his ability to allay Angiulo's potentially murderous concerns. Instead, Cintolo did what was obviously in the best interests of his client LaFreniere. He sought to assure Angiulo that he had the confidence of LaFreniere and that LaFreniere had not changed his stance, consistent from before Cintolo began to represent him, that he would not testify. Without receiving such assurances, Angiulo might well have proceeded with the contract on LaFreniere's life.[21]

The most telling portion of the First Circuit's opinion was its view that, even if it were true that Cintolo acted to further LaFreniere's interests, it would not have been enough. The court, like the DOJ, saw Cintolo as obligated to convince LaFreniere to cooperate with the feds, even at the risk of the client's own life, and even if contrary to the consistent urging of his own father-in-law. (Recall that LaFreniere's father-in-law, too, risked contempt rather than testify.) "In any realistic light," the court wrote, "the most authentic victim of Cintolo's behavior was not his nominal client, but the due administration of justice." The Constitution, they argued, did not require them "to insulate lawyers from encroachments on the 'zealous representation' of clients accused of crime."[22]

The court concluded that the general obstruction of justice statute required that Cintolo's conduct be deemed a crime. This is precisely what the *amici* most feared: an equation between the traditional work of the criminal defense lawyer and the crime of obstruction of what the court saw as the interests of justice. All of a sudden, it was as if the defense lawyer was supposed to be working for the FBI rather than for his client.

Cintolo's efforts to protect his client from both the government and the Angiulos were seen, instead, as having "the corrupt aim of frustrating a federal grand jury." The lawyer's long-understood and entirely proper role in our constitutional system, as an advisor to his clients rather than a government handmaiden, made no difference. "As citizens of the Republic equal under law, all must comply with the statute in the same manner," wrote the court. But, of course, that plainly and simply cannot be true. Based on the structure of the criminal justice system and on the instrumental role they play in it, defense lawyers are charged with a highly specialized and very different task than prosecutors, police, judges, and laymen. Their vigorously representing the interests and rights of those fighting the government should not be seen as the crime of obstruction of justice.

The Court of Appeals concluded its analysis with one of the least helpful tautologies imaginable: "Since the omnibus clause of the [obstruction of justice] statute quite clearly proclaims that all obstructions of justice are prohibited, we conclude that section 1503 gives 'fair notice of the offending conduct'...which is all the constitution requires." In a somewhat ironic concession, however, the court acknowledged the need for clarity in criminal statutes. One of the precedent cases it invoked in this regard was the First Circuit Court's 1985 opinion, a mere two years earlier, in *United States v. Anzalone*. Recall how in that case the court praised the American criminal justice system as superior to the old Soviet Union's precisely because the Soviet legal system penalized, under its "crime by analogy" provision, "any socially dangerous act [that] has not been directly provided for by the present Code." With the Cintolo opinion, the *Anzalone* era had ended rather abruptly. The new era was announced without irony, much less shame.

William Cintolo served 18 months in federal prison. Upon release, he worked as a legal assistant and applied for readmission to the Massachusetts Bar. To the surprise of many observers, he was readmitted in 1996 on his first application, filed as soon as he was eligible. It is rare for the Supreme Judicial Court of Massachusetts to readmit a lawyer so quickly when the offense underlying his conviction is as serious as obstruction of justice, much less in an "organized crime" context. More revealing still is the fact that Bar Counsel, the chief legal disciplinarian that supervises lawyers' ethical problems, did not file an opposition to Cintolo's application for readmission. After being readmitted, Cintolo has resumed a successful criminal defense law practice.

Walter LaFreniere, the supposed victim of Cintolo's betrayal, it should be noted, did not testify at Cintolo's trial. Presumably the client's own view as to whether his lawyer had acted on his behalf was not important to either the Department of Justice or the federal court. And in no other context did LaFreniere say that Cintolo's representation worked against his best interests. Cintolo's sin, in the end, was that he provided truly effective assistance of counsel, as is required by the Sixth Amendment. This principle of our legal system is often derided by laymen, until they find themselves in trouble and suddenly need the advice of a lawyer upon whose loyalty they can count.

• • ● • •

The American Bar Association (ABA), with more than 413,000 members, is the largest membership organization of lawyers in the United States, and it enjoys worldwide respect. In the U.S. it has the status of arbiter over a number of areas of self-regulation within the legal profession, including suggested ethical codes, provision of legal counsel to criminal defendants and impoverished citizens in certain civil matters, and other pressing legal and social issues. For more than half a century, the ABA has also evaluated U.S. presidents' federal court nominees to help ensure excellence on the federal bench. In recent years, the ABA also has adopted more than a dozen policy positions critical of the federal government's failure to protect constitutional freedoms in the fight against terrorism. The ABA has even weighed in against the vagueness of federal prosecution standards in state and local corruption cases, as discussed in Chapter One.

Another important authority exercised by the ABA is that it supervises the law school accreditation process. In 1995, the Department of Justice filed a civil lawsuit against the ABA alleging that it had violated the nation's anti-trust laws in the way it accredited law schools. The anti-trust laws seek to prevent power centers of industry from obtaining a stranglehold over particular areas of commerce that allows them to maintain artificially high prices—the classic monopoly. The DOJ alleged that the ABA accredited law schools in a way that kept the costs of operating such schools artificially high. This, in turn, allegedly ended up costing consumers (law students and their tuition-paying families) more than would have been the case if legal education operated in a free market, unfettered by the monopolistic practices supposedly imposed by the ABA.

According to the DOJ's 1995 complaint, the ABA allegedly kept law school tuitions artificially high by requiring law schools to engage in certain expensive practices. For example, it was alleged that the ABA required that professorial salaries be kept at a certain national median level, and that teaching loads for professors be severely limited. The ABA allegedly required law schools to provide professors with paid leaves of absence to conduct scholarly research, as well as low ratios of teachers to students. All in all, alleged the DOJ, the high cost of legal education could in part be attributed to the choke-hold the ABA had on the accreditation process, law schools' need for accreditation to attract students, and the ABA's abuse of this process in order to make life easy for the professoriate, who themselves had a self-serving lock on the ABA's accrediting process.

The ABA's Section of Legal Education and Admission to the Bar vigorously disputed the DOJ's claims. The ABA had long defended its accreditation standards as necessary to keeping the quality of legal education high and to protect the public from poorly educated lawyers. The profession's internal efforts to maintain some kind of quality control over professional standards and competence was part of a long-term trend, commenced in the 19th century. The ABA's methods for establishing standards to assure the quality of legal education were doubtless controversial, and it was perhaps not surprising that the executive branch, long chafing under the power of the ABA to, for example, rank nominees to the federal bench, would strike out at the organization in some manner. An executive branch effort to break what it deemed the ABA's choke-hold over law school accreditation and standards was, therefore, no great surprise to knowledgeable observers. Reasonable people will agree or disagree about the validity of the DOJ's allegations and the social benefits of the ABA's legal accreditation practices. Rather than test their respective positions in court, the ABA, facing millions of dollars in defense costs, and the DOJ, employing a cutting-edge legal theory, agreed to settle. A "consent decree" with a ten-year term settling the case was filed by the parties at the same time the complaint itself was filed by the DOJ. The U.S. District Court for the District of Columbia approved the settlement in June 1996.

Ten years later, much had changed. It was a post-9/11 world, and the federal government and the organized legal profession were in a series of bitter clashes. The ABA was criticizing many of the federal government's initiatives that the ABA considered unnecessarily and unconstitutionally elevated perceived security over the historic rule of law. In particular, the ABA took issue with the Bush administration's frequent use of so-called "presidential signing statements." With unanimous approval of the ABA Board of Governors, a bipartisan task force investigated the issue in the spring of 2006. The task force unanimously concluded that the abuse of such signing statements violated the separation of powers.[23] These clashes ratcheted up the historic tension between federal administrations and the organized bar. That tension seemed to ooze out in the battle over the consent decree.

As the consent decree's ten-year termination date approached, the DOJ informed the ABA that it was not satisfied with ABA compliance with the settlement terms. In early 2006, the DOJ informed the bar association that it planned to file a petition asking the court to hold the ABA in civil and possibly *criminal* contempt for allegedly violating the settlement agreement. The DOJ claimed, among other technical violations, that while the 1996 settlement required that "no more than half of the members of the [accreditation] Standards Review Committee be law school deans or faculty," allegedly (and disputed by the ABA) one committee member was not a practicing lawyer but a faculty member whose presence on the committee in 2005-06 exceeded the 50 percent requirement.

The ABA, represented again by its 1996 outside defense counsel, and the DOJ in the spring of 2006 entered negotiations lasting several months in order to resolve the contempt imbroglio. Boston attorney and ABA President Michael S. Greco had served as chair of the ABA Standing Committee on Federal Judiciary, which evaluates presidential nominees to the federal bench, in 1988. When the negotiations became bogged down and difficult (and increasingly expensive), Greco instructed ABA's counsel to request an in-person meeting with the U.S. Attorney General, Alberto Gonzales, to discuss the matter. Accompanied by ABA defense counsel and ABA staff, Greco traveled to Washington to meet with Assistant Attorney General Thomas O. Barnett, of the Antitrust Division, who was accompanied at the meeting by numerous DOJ colleagues. During the lengthy and tense meeting, Barnett informed Greco that the DOJ was considering filing a petition with the court seeking a *criminal contempt* order against the ABA and its leaders.[24]

The specter of government officials threatening the leaders of the nation's premier professional association of lawyers with imprisonment, growing out of a dispute over technical compliance with some of the provisions of an anti-trust consent decree, was surprising to some, and caused outrage among others, at the ABA. Again facing millions of dollars in crippling defense costs, the ABA decided to settle the dispute, on the condition that the DOJ back off its insistence that the ABA admit to contemptuous conduct in connection with the 1996 consent decree. The DOJ agreed, and a settlement was reached.

The settlement agreement, however, did not stop the DOJ from issuing a news release on June 23, 2006, alleging that the ABA's conduct constituted civil contempt. In the news release announcing the agreement, the DOJ misleadingly stated that "the ABA acknowledges the violations" set forth in the DOJ's petition for a contempt order.[25] Before filing the final drafts of the settlement documents with the court, the DOJ had refused to show them, or the press release, to the ABA's defense counsel. To correct the public record as it saw it, the ABA countered with a short news release issued June 27, 2006, in Greco's name. The release noted that "contrary to the impression resulting from a press release issued last week by the Department of Justice, the stipulation executed by the parties and the order entered by the court make clear that there was no finding of civil contempt."[26]

The DOJ's news release seemed to be another gauntlet thrown down at the feet of the nation's premier bar association. "No one is above the law and those who do not comply with their obligations under court orders must be prepared to face consequences," said AAG Barnett. "The Antitrust Division has sued many professional trade associations, which, like the ABA, have violated the antitrust laws," observed Anne K. Bingaman, also an assistant attorney general in the Antitrust Division. "Lawyers must keep their own house in order as well."[27]

To the public, perhaps these dueling announcements sounded routine. There is, however, a deeper and more ominous meaning to the DOJ's aggressive behavior. What the public did not know was that the Antitrust Division, in an effort to intimidate the ABA, had flexed its muscle at the settlement meeting attended by Greco, by suggesting, in a face-to-face meeting, that it was seriously considering proceeding criminally if the organization and its leaders did not toe the line. That the Department of Justice, part of the government's executive branch, would threaten the leaders of a premier professional association in this manner, attempt to discredit the ABA, and by such a tactic seek to diminish the ABA's historical role of representing the legal profession, speaks volumes about the DOJ's attitude toward an independent bar. The federal contempt power is broad and amorphous, but there was considerable shock in ABA circles over this particular stretch of the law and the DOJ's tactics. It was a particularly disturbing development in view of the fact that the ABA, and Greco in particular, had in the years after the 2001 terrorist attacks been highly critical of DOJ policies on the detention of "enemy combatants," the use of physically coercive interrogation techniques thought by many to constitute torture, and other assertions of executive branch prerogative. In this context, the threat of criminal prosecution had to be taken very seriously indeed. If federal prosecutors had no compunction against threatening the leaders of the nation's leading organization of lawyers, then surely there could be few areas where they would be modest about their ability to indict, and convict, the proverbial ham sandwich.

• • ● • •

Amorphous powers granted to, or simply assumed by, the executive branch in fighting the war on terror have provided additional areas for prosecutors to seek to intimidate members of the bar. In the summer of 2005, the American Civil Liberties Union (ACLU) found itself embroiled in a lawsuit it brought against the federal government, seeking to have the federal court in Connecticut invalidate a strict gag provision contained in the so-called "National Security Letters" (NSL) section of the USA Patriot Act, enacted after the terrorist attacks of September 11, 2001. National Security Letters are documents delivered to some institution or repository of records or accounts—a bank or a library, for example—by federal law enforcement agencies, seeking access to information about customers, clients, book borrowers and such. They differ from traditional search warrants because they issue upon the authority of the Department of Justice, rather than a federal court. For this reason, they are highly controversial.

The ACLU and a state affiliate, the ACLU of Connecticut, represented a library in Connecticut that had received an NSL seeking information about what materials certain borrowers had taken out of the library. Despite the fact that the FBI was requiring such sensitive information (the right to read without government monitoring or interference, after all, is protected by the First Amendment) and notwithstanding that the NSL was issued by the FBI pursuant to the terms of the USA Patriot Act without any court authorization, the ACLU was not allowed to reveal the identity of its own client and the details surrounding the NSL or the lawsuit. The litigation was being conducted entirely in secret in accordance with a remarkable gag provision in the statute.

The ACLU's chief lawyer on the case sent an urgent message to all ACLU affiliates and state chapters, disclosing only the very limited amount of information that the DOJ agreed that the ACLU lawyers could issue, and they had to include the following startling warning:

> The statute under challenge includes a strict gag provision, 18 U.S.C. 2709(c). We initially filed the case under seal to avoid violating the gag provision. The ACLU is now able to

disclose certain redacted[28] documents in the case because, after negotiations, the government has agreed that we can disclose these facts.

Because of the gag, all ACLU staff must be extremely cautious when speaking publicly about the case. It is imperative that you review this memo closely and use ONLY the scripted answers below in responding to the questions (or similar questions on the same issues). Failure to abide by the script below could put you, as well as National staff, at risk of criminal prosecution for violating the gag. It is particularly important that you use ONLY the scripted answers in describing our client or the NSL demand itself. The gag puts all of us in an awkward position, because the press and other organizations can comment freely based on the publicly available information about the case, while we are quite limited in what we can say.[29]

Thus, one of the nation's premier civil liberties and free speech litigating organizations was in a position in which it was not clear what it could and could not disclose without subjecting itself, its lawyers and staff members to criminal liability. Lawyers had been tossed into a legal twilight zone where they performed the most routine functions of the job at great and unknown personal peril.

CHAPTER SEVEN

Doing Their Duty
(or Committing Espionage?)
and Other Media Twilight Zones

— ● ● ● —

The press is dubbed "the Fourth Estate" for good reason. The Constitution establishes three branches of the federal government—legislative, executive, and judicial—to divide power in the hope that each will check and balance the others. In turn, the First Amendment protects the press, which, it is hoped, will robustly monitor, and thereby check the power of, those who govern us. A free press is essential to the cultivation of an informed citizenry, and thus to Constitutional democracy itself. If you have any doubt about that, just remember that when modern tyrants seize power, they almost always shut down the press first.

For a free press to function, reporters and the news organizations they work for must have access to the sources whose confidentiality they promise, and are therefore bound, to protect. In a sense, news-gathering is an elaborate, delicate network of relationships based on organized trust. That is why 31 states and the District of Columbia have some form of "shield law" protecting reporters from the obligation to share their sources in a court of law. (Four additional states—Iowa, Nevada, New Mexico, and Texas—have other laws that provide journalists with some, though fewer, protections.)[1]

A federal shield law has been gaining support in Congress in recent years. (No state shield law can function to protect a reporter from a federal subpoena or court order.) In part, that's because federal muzzling and harassment of the Fourth Estate has been on the increase since the mid-1980s. Naturally, vague federal criminal statutes and legal doctrines have been at the heart of this development. The seeds of this movement can be traced to the Vietnam War era, when a highly contentious relationship developed between the executive branch and the national press. The federal government's modern campaign to rein in and intimidate the press took flower, however, at the same time that other sectors of civil society were being seriously targeted. The end of that movement is not yet in sight.

Just ask former gossip columnist Jared Paul Stern. Now, it's true that when one contemplates the grave importance of a free press, one usually has in mind the high purpose of national security reporting, say, or covering economic policy or legislative debates. We will get to the ways our access to that kind of information has been imperiled in short order, but Stern's very different story is instructive. If the feds can and will go after him in the way they did, imagine what they could do with more serious fare.[2]

The media-fed, media-implicated scandal that enveloped *The New York Post*'s Page Six gossip feature in late 2005 and early 2006 was broken in a big way by none other than *The New York Times*, and on its front page no less. The *Times* reported that a private investigative firm hired by supermarket magnate and high-level gadfly Ronald W. Burkle had captured Page Six contributing columnist Jared Paul Stern on surreptitiously recorded videotape in Burkle's Tri-Be-Ca apartment in Manhattan. On the tape, Stern appears to be asking for a $100,000 initial payment plus $10,000 a month, ominously described by the *Times* as a "monthly stipend...in return for keeping negative information about [Burkle] out of the [*Post*]." Burkle, who had earlier claimed in letters to the *Post* that embarrassing Page Six stories about him were false, had arranged to meet Stern at a Manhattan hotel "after a friend suggested Mr. Stern could give him some insight into Page Six." At that meeting, Burkle alleged, Stern asked Burkle to become a source for Stern's gossip pieces. Burkle reportedly declined, but agreed to buy 60 shirts from Stern's clothing line as a favor. (Stern had developed a line of designer men's clothing and was in the process of trying to promote the brand.) Burkle's lawyer, Martin D. Singer, then lodged a number of litigation threats against the paper, all to no avail. However, the *Times* story went on to report, "an employee of Mr. Burkle received an e-mail message from Mr. Stern, a contributor who worked two days a week for Page Six, suggesting that Mr. Burkle could change the column's treatment of him."

The text of the email is crucial to understanding what transpired between Stern and Burkle. "I understand Ron is upset about the press he's been getting," the email states. "If he's really concerned, he needs a strategy for dealing with it and regulating it rather than merely reacting. It's not easy to accomplish, but he certainly has the means to do so." It was at this point, the *Times* reports, that Burkle "suspected he was being extorted" and "reached out to his attorney, who then reached out to law enforcement." What followed was right out of the Justice Department/FBI playbook. Stern agreed to meet Burkle at least twice in late March at Burkle's loft, where Burkle's security team, including a private investigations firm, video-recorded the meetings. A federal agent and a prosecutor joined Burkle's security detail "to monitor the recording."

As told by the *Times*, the Stern story read like a fairly cut-and-dry case of blackmail (a run-of-the-mill state crime) but also the federal offense of "extortion" when facilities of interstate communications (mail, telephone, email, and the like) are used in an attempt to coerce someone into doing something he or she does not want to do. Lawyers for high-profile "victims" who report such attempts to the authorities frequently bring in the feds, in part because the federal definition of "extortion," like many federal crimes, is notoriously broad and loose. As a result (and in keeping with the trends we've seen throughout this book), a wide variety of conduct, much of it lawful though often not very pretty, can be spun as criminal.

Skepticism is naturally aroused by the fact that the *Times*' sources turned over to the paper only six heavily edited minutes of roughly three hours of recordings. What's more, it was Burkle, not Stern, who

asked, "How much do you want?" Throughout the snippets reported in
the *Times*, it is Burkle who tried to put into Stern's mouth the magic
words signifying extortion. But he never quite succeeded, since Stern
was not threatening Burkle, but rather trying to enlist him as an investor in Stern's clothing line and to convince the supermarket mogul to
hire him as his media adviser. Stern did not threaten to retaliate should
Burkle turn him down.

It's also important to note that Stern was only a twice-a-week contributor to Page Six, so it's almost certain he did not have the power
to deliver on any broad-ranging promises about Page Six coverage.
More importantly, in additional transcript excerpts published by *Post*
archrival *The New York Daily News*, Stern makes reasonably clear that
he is not seeking to extort Burkle: "It is not a stickup," Stern assures
the mogul at one point. Stern's attempt to become a media consultant
to Burkle is suggested when he offers to "help you when it is needed."
When Burkle, obviously at the suggestion of the feds monitoring the
conversation, tries to get Stern to adopt the description of "protection"
for the service Stern is offering, Stern demurs, saying that he is offering
"help," not protection. "Protection," Stern admonishes Burkle, "adds
overtones." When Burkle suggests that maybe he should pay the Page
Six editor $100,000, Stern again demurs: "Well, I don't think you want
to do that." Instead, he lectures the would-be media consultant, "you
need a strategy," not protection. Stern offers to show Burkle how to
become "a friend of the paper" rather than a subject of its gossip pages.
If Burkle can ingratiate himself with the Page Six editor, in particular,
he could become an insider rather than an outsider. And what if Burkle
refuses to pay Stern for these services, the mogul, obviously hoping to
entrap his prey, inquires. "We can still be friends, but we're not going to
be as good friends," Stern rejoins.

What one sees here is the kind of pitch PR men and women
make every day in the Big Apple and elsewhere. The only difference
is that Stern, by playing on both teams, arguably engaged in a nasty
conflict of interest that perhaps should have gotten him fired (it did),
but not indicted.

To anyone experienced in criminal law, it is all too obvious what was going on. Burkle likely was coached to try to put certain key "buzz" words into the target's mouth. Just as obviously, the sting failed to produce precisely what had been anticipated. Stern resisted the bait and stuck to his proposal rather than adopt Burkle's suggestion of a "protection" arrangement. The real story here is the collaboration of the businessman, his private legal and investigatory henchmen, and their federal prosecutor and FBI allies to try to set up an arguably sleazy— but, crucially, not criminal—gossip columnist for a federal bust. They failed to snare Stern, but that did not mean the columnist was in the clear. Whether the feds were going to bring criminal charges would likely depend on whether they felt they could spin the encounters to a jury much as Burkle's team spun the scenario to the *Times*.

Why the leaks from the investigative camp to the *Times*? One likely aim was to put sufficient pressure on a ruined Stern to force him into a plea bargain so that a court would never be asked to rule on whether the tapes show an extortion or simply a sleazy gossip columnist making a fool of himself. Common sense might dictate that it would be a huge stretch to make an extortion case out of the almost comic scenario, but the federal extortion statute governing threats to injure reputation or property is not quite a paragon of clarity or of discernable limits.[3]

Federal courts have held that not every threat to a person's reputation rises to the level of extortion and that "the objective of the party employing fear of economic loss or damage to reputation will have a bearing on the lawfulness of its use."[4] If Stern's objective was to get a consulting relationship with Burkle, any prosecution theory that he was seeking to extort $100,000 as a kind of protection racket weakens considerably. Since the extortion statute criminalizes speech, after all, care must be taken that the speech is in fact part of a criminal plan and not of ordinary daily commerce, even the tawdry commerce at the intersection of wealth, celebrity, gossip, and image building—in short, so much of modern American media. Besides, what could a two-days-a-week contributor to the *Post*'s gossip page deliver in terms of control of the paper's coverage of Burkle, other than advice on how Burkle could position himself to gain the paper's friendship? Could it reasonably be said that Stern possessed an intent to threaten Burkle with fear of property or reputational harm in order to extract a payoff? Is this the stuff of an extortion prosecution? Common sense might say no, but it was hardly obvious that the feds would write off the case without exploring avenues to indict Stern.

Of course, the feds did not have to rely solely on the federal reputational extortion statute. There was always the handy, infinitely malleable general wire fraud statute covering any seemingly off-color activity accomplished with the use of the phone or Internet.[5] Don't forget, too, wire fraud's equally elastic ally: mail fraud.

And in the event that not even mail or wire fraud charges could be brought against Stern, the feds could reach further into their virtually bottomless arsenal. Creative federal prosecutors in 1988 began to expand the definition of fraud to include "a scheme or artifice to deprive another of the intangible right of honest services." Under such a theory, Stern could be charged with wire fraud committed not against Burkle, but against his employer, *The New York Post*.[6] In other words, prosecutors had the option of claiming that Stern swindled his own newspaper out of his "honest services." In this way, a reporter's arguable ethical lapses, to the extent one can even say that tabloid gossip columnists are somehow bound by a commonly understood code of ethics, can readily be made into a federal felony that carries a lengthy prison term.

It was not until January 23, 2007, that Jared Paul Stern learned that he would not be indicted.[7] One may or may not be sympathetic to Stern, but it seems nearly indefensible that a gossip columnist should suffer the consequences (ranging from expense, humiliation, and aggravation to fear) of being a target in a sting simply because federal criminal laws against extortion and fraud can be interpreted to include such a wide and undefined variety of professional behaviors. Though Stern wasn't indicted in the end, there had been a real possibility that he would be. In his case, such an outcome could have led to jail time. Moreover, the simple fact that Stern became a target and the subject of a major investigation carried with it a potentially substantial chilling effect for his and other reporters' speech. If it can happen to Stern, it can happen to any reporter seeking to persuade a potential news source to cooperate with a story rather than become its subject, something reporters do regularly as part of their jobs.

The application of extortion and fraud statutes against reporters to combat the tactics they use in reporting their stories can readily go well beyond gossip columnists. Consider a hypothetical situation where a reporter tells a potential source that if he discloses information to the reporter, on a confidential basis, the reporter will not publish his name, but that if the reporter is forced to seek and then finds the information elsewhere, the resulting newspaper story will attack the source and seek to sully his reputation. Would that be grounds to seek an indictment against the reporter for extortion? In a word, maybe—depending, perhaps, on what the federal prosecutor ate for breakfast.

· · ● · ·

To be involved in the news media today—whether print or electronic, "new" media or old—is to find oneself in a precarious situation, operating at the whim of federal prosecutors and other bureaucrats. Possible sanctions, ranging from prison terms to crippling fines, constantly loom. The age-old tactic of sending a message *in terrorem* by randomly eliminating a few to instill fear in the many has been used with increasing and alarming regularity.

How on earth did we get here? To understand the mounting peril today's journalists face, a bit of legal history is in order. Central to part of that history is the doctrine of "prior restraint," which refers to the government's power to prevent publication of material *before* it is actually published, by means of a statute, ordinance, or a court-issued injunction. Prior restraint orders are especially repugnant to press freedoms because they stop a story from ever getting to the public in the first place. Since the Supreme Court's landmark 1931 opinion in *Near v. Minnesota*,[8] the federal courts have been loath to prevent contentious material from being published. But even when a court denies the government's request for prepublication restraint, it does not insulate the publisher from post-publication liability, either civil or criminal. In the hypothetical case of a defamatory book or article, even where the offended party could not convince a court to enjoin publication, that party still has the ability to sue the newspaper or book publisher civilly for post-publication money damages. Publication of government secrets, on the other hand, opens the publisher to potential indictment.

The prior restraint doctrine harkens back to colonial days, when British authorities licensed printers and publishers and could therefore cut off publication before the public learned what the author wished to convey—and what the British government didn't want them to hear. After the American Revolution the First Amendment sought to temper that power, of course, but that didn't stop early federal authorities from trying to punish writers and publishers *after* publication of damning material. On July 14, 1798, while the United States was engaged in an undeclared war with France, Congress passed the infamous Sedition Act, which criminalized the publication of "false, scandalous, and malicious writing" critical of the government or public officials. John Adams's Federalist Party created the statute to silence criticism from Thomas Jefferson's Democratic-Republicans. Remarkably, the statute criminalized speech critical of the government, the Congress, and the president—all notwithstanding the protections of the First Amendment. Twenty-five men, mostly prominent Republican newspaper editors, were arrested and their papers closed down. Vermont Congressman Matthew Lyon was arrested, along with Benjamin Franklin's grandson, Benjamin Franklin Bache, on charges that he had libeled President Adams. A public outcry against the statute ensued. Some historians assume that it was this development that sent Jefferson, a staunch free speech advocate, to the White House. Once he took office, President Jefferson pardoned all those convicted under the Sedition Act, which was allowed to expire in 1802.

Still, another post-publication criminal threat to the news media looms: the Espionage Act, which has been with us, with occasional amendments, since its initial passage in 1917 to quell dissent against U.S. entry into World War I. It is not exactly a model of clarity.[9] The typical image of someone engaged in espionage is the foreign agent seeking to learn classified national secrets for transmission to an un-friendly government (what might be dubbed "James Bond" activity). But the act is broader (and vaguer) than that, covering the transmis-sion of any classified information by any means, including by one who "publishes" in a manner that is prejudicial to American security. There is a tremendous amount of legal flexibility in open-ended terms like "publishes." Journalists, trying to discern the limits beyond which they cannot go without undue risk, need guidance to do their jobs without unknowable and unquantifiable, almost paralyzing, risk.

In the famous *Pentagon Papers* case, the U.S. Supreme Court raised the specter of just such a risk. In that suit, two dailies, *The New York Times* and *The Washington Post*, won a heralded victory over Richard Nixon's Department of Justice in 1971. The papers convinced the Supreme Court that the First Amendment prohibited prior restraint of the press's right to publish the *Pentagon Papers*, a classified govern-ment study of the events between 1945 and 1967 that led to America's deep involvement in the Vietnam War. (*The Boston Globe* also had a set of the *Papers* that it proceeded to publish, but its litigation lagged behind and was mooted when the Supreme Court ruled for the *Times* and *Post*.) It was leaked to the press by Daniel Ellsberg, who at the time worked for the Rand Corporation, a private think tank that conducted the highly classified project. Nixon and members of his administration were furious about the publication, which began its run one morning in what was described as a multi-part series, and was seen by admin-istration press critics as more a demonstration of media power and hubris than a public-spirited revelation meant to enlighten citizens and history. After all, the *Papers* cast prior presidencies in a far poorer light than the Nixon administration, which had inherited what was by then widely referred to as the Vietnam "quagmire."

The newspapers that published the *Pentagon Papers* and sought to avoid a prior restraint order kept in mind the example, laid out by the Supreme Court in *Near*, of the type of information that might appro-priately trigger a court injunction. In a footnote in *Near*, the Court suggested that prior restraint might be appropriate to prevent a newspaper from the "publication of the sailing dates of transports or the number and location of troops" during wartime. While the Court ultimately would not find that anything in the *Pentagon Papers* quite rose to the level of what has become known in the law as "the troop ship exception," it was telling that the *Near* court saw national security as a likely area in which prior restraint orders might sometimes be justified.

The Supreme Court's decision in the *Pentagon Papers* case[10] is widely viewed as a high-water mark in the history of press freedom. And in many ways it was. It set a high standard for the government to get a court to issue an injunction against publication on grounds that it would harm important governmental interests, including national security. Indeed, even some of the justices in the majority opined that publication was likely to be injurious to the nation's security interests, but they felt that the argument for such harm was neither sufficiently powerful to justify an injunction, nor clearly proven. In a number of daily installments, the newspapers resumed their publication of some of the nation's more closely guarded (and embarrassing) diplomatic and military history secrets.

Although this victory for the press was a resounding reaffirmation of the prior restraint doctrine, it nonetheless contained the seeds (little noticed in the widespread media euphoria at the time) of potential future harassment. If cultivated, those seeds could someday prove every bit as potent a weapon against a free press as the prior restraint power that the Justice Department had sought unsuccessfully. Buried in the media's historic victory were indications, supported by a majority of the court's justices, that publication of classified information arguably bearing on national security could be punished by post-publication criminal prosecution under some of the most draconian statutes in the federal criminal code—including the espionage laws.

A bit of nose-counting is required to see how and why a majority of the *Pentagon Papers* justices went out of their way to warn the newspapers of possible post-publication indictment. The phrase "went out of their way" applies because an analysis of situations in which newspapers would be exposed to criminal penalties was not necessary to re-solve the specific prepublication injunction question before the Court. Instead, this discussion occurred in that part of the Court's opinion called *obiter dicta*, or incidental remarks not essential to the justices' ruling, and therefore not binding as precedent. Three justices (Byron White, Potter Stewart, and Harry Blackmun) went so far as to suggest that the Justice Department consider indicting the newspapers *after* publication. The Nixon administration's failure to prevent publication, warned Justices White and Stewart (who would have approved a prior restraint order), "does not measure its constitutional entitlement to a conviction for criminal publication."

The White-Stewart opinion, approved by Blackmun, proceeded to list numerous statutes that arguably criminalized such publication, including the Espionage Act and a plethora of amendments over the years prohibiting communication of documents relating to the national defense. It also identified as proscribed the "willful publication" of any classified information concerning "communication intelligence activities" of the United States. Two justices (Burger and Harlan) did not specifically address the question of post-publication criminal prosecution of the newspapers, but their endorsement of the idea can be inferred from the fact that they approved of an injunction against publication in the first place. If the breach of national security represented by publication of the *Pentagon Papers* was sufficiently serious to justify the extraordinary remedy of an injunction, then it clearly would warrant post-publication prosecution.

Still, it was not as if the five Supreme Court justices who opined that the newspapers might have committed a crime in exercising their constitutional right to be free of prior restraints, had reached a verdict condemning the newspapers as felons. They gave the press a bit of wiggle room. Most of the justices never said that the papers would be guilty. They merely hinted, in often dark tones, at the possibility, and at the government's undoubted power to indict and seek convictions. Justice Stewart listed "provisions potentially relevant to these cases." He "would have no difficulty in sustaining convictions under these sections on facts that would not justify…a prior restraint." But later, in the same opinion, he stressed: "I am not, of course, saying that either of these newspapers has yet committed a crime or that either would commit a crime if it published all the material now in its possession. That matter must await resolution in the context of a criminal proceeding if one is instituted by the United States." It is reasonable to interpret Stewart's hedging as less an expression of doubt as to whether the espionage laws applied to the publication of the *Pentagon Papers*, and more as the typical reluctance of any jurist to be seen as pre-judging a potential case.

Equally foreboding was Sanford J. Ungar's highly regarded 1972 book, *The Papers & The Papers*. He concluded that the main reason why President Nixon and Attorney General John N. Mitchell did not prosecute media targets who had published the *Pentagon Papers* was that, by that time, the Watergate scandal had broken, Nixon was on his way to impeachment or resignation, and Mitchell was on his way to indictment and federal prison.[11] Later, Whitney North Seymour, the moderate Republican U.S. attorney for New York at the time of the *Pentagon Papers* imbroglio, wrote in his autobiography that the DOJ sent emissaries to enlist the cooperation of Seymour's office in securing an indictment of the newspapers, and of individual employees. Fortunately for the reporters, Seymour responded "[n]ot in this District."[12] Soon thereafter, Watergate came to the media's rescue.[13]

Nixon's Justice Department lost its attempt to get a court order barring publication of the *Pentagon Papers*, and it never brought criminal charges against the newspapers, publishers, editors, and reporters. However, Nixon's prosecutors did bring espionage charges against Daniel Ellsberg, the former Rand Corporation employee who had smuggled a copy of the study to the *Times* and other newspapers. This was hardly unexpected. Ellsberg had clearly violated the terms of his security clearance and had conveyed admittedly classified documents to the news media. He was the leaker from within who blew the whistle, even though he was clearly prohibited by law from doing so. Ellsberg's motives may have been admirable or considered patriotic among opponents of the Vietnam War and critics of the process by which America became involved in it, but his violation of the Espionage Act seemed more plausible than any supposed violation by the media. Ultimately, it was only the extraordinary campaign of unlawful activity undertaken by the administration—break-ins to obtain dirt on Ellsberg, a tawdry effort to buy the judge's favor by inquiring into his interest in the position of FBI director, and other unethical and unlawful tactics—that tainted the prosecution and gave the trial judge cause to dismiss the indictment against Ellsberg in the middle of the trial.[14]

Once before there had been a serious effort (or at least an urge accompanied by some degree of follow-through) to indict a newspaper for espionage. The *Chicago Tribune*, an isolationist newspaper that had opposed the Roosevelt administration's efforts to involve the United States in the Second World War on the side of the British, published a page one article on June 7, 1942, just after the American Navy's critical victory in the Battle of Midway. The report told the world (the American public, the Allied world, and anyone among the enemy who happened to keep up with the American press) that crucial information about the make-up and location of the Japanese naval fleet had been "well known in American naval circles several days before the battle began."

The *Tribune* story conveyed sufficient details (attributed to "reliable sources in…naval intelligence") such that a Japanese reader with top-ranking intelligence connections would have realized that the Americans had cracked the all-important Japanese naval codes. By sheer good fortune, no one in Japanese military circles appears to have learned of the *Tribune* report, and the Japanese military continued using the same codes for the duration of the war. Regardless, the Roosevelt administration was furious and chagrined.

Gabriel Schoenfeld, a writer on intelligence matters for *Commentary* magazine, reports that Roosevelt's prosecutors backed down at the stage where they began to present evidence to a federal grand jury.[15] To tell the tale to the 23 members of the grand jury to induce it to indict the newspaper would have entailed yet another security breach, for the Americans' breaking of the Japanese codes would have had to be disclosed to that many more civilians, not to mention the stenographer who was taking notes of the grand jury proceedings and other ancillary participants. The Department of Justice and the Roosevelt War Department concluded that pursuing a prosecution of the newspaper posed too high a risk of further compromising national security, and the newspaper was let off the hook.

It is widely believed in the legal community that one reason the Justice Department has been reluctant to indict the news media for espionage is the degree of risk that additional national security secrets would have to be disclosed at the public trial. This phenomenon has come to be known as "graymail," the subtle or sometimes overt threat by a potential criminal defendant that, if indicted, he or she would disclose, or demand the disclosure of, additional government secrets necessary for his defense. Beginning in 1980, however, remedial legislation has severely limited a defendant's ability to extract or disclose, publicly, classified information in the process of self-defense.[16] It marked the trajectory of things to come.

• • ● • •

The press, as well as the leaker, may have emerged victorious from the *Pentagon Papers* case, but the seeds were planted for much more difficult times in the future. Soon after the imbroglio came to an end, two leading academic authorities set out to study the intersection between laws protecting national defense secrets and the right of the news media to publish or otherwise disclose such secrets. "The longer we looked" into the matter, wrote Professors Harold Edgar and Benno C. Schmidt, Jr., "the less we saw." "Either advancing myopia had taken its toll, or the statutes implacably resist the effort to understand," they noted in a highly regarded article reporting their findings, published in the *Columbia Law Review* in 1973.[17] "We have lived throughout the present century with extraordinary confusion about the legal standards governing publication of defense information," they concluded.

Edgar and Schmidt's message to journalists was actually more dire than a simple concern about the vagueness and breadth of the Espionage

Act's provisions, which allowed the act to be applied to what, even by then, had become an almost routine and widely accepted set of practices. Government officials or bureaucrats leaked what they wanted the public to know, and eager reporters and newspapers were able to inform (or titillate, as the case may be) their readers with "inside scoops." With the *Pentagon Papers* clearly in mind, Edgar and Schmidt wrote:

> If these statutes mean what they seem to say and are constitutional, public speech in this country since World War II has been rife with criminality. The source who leaks defense information to the press commits an offense; the reporter who holds onto defense material commits an offense; and the retired official who uses defense material in his memoirs commits an offense.

They argued that this unhealthy situation had managed to exist for many decades before the *Pentagon Papers* litigation because the relationship between the press and government officials had not been terribly hostile and adversarial. To the contrary, there was a "naturally symbiotic relationship." Members of the legislative and executive branches did not pay much attention to the vagueness and breadth of these statutes as they related to the news media (in contrast to the statutes' coverage of clandestine foreign espionage that was punished far more severely). The authors concluded that "the ambiguity of the current law is tolerable" and the limits untested, largely because of "the general discretion with which secret information" had been used.

Something similar could have been said about the government's interest in newsgatherers working with other kinds of sources. But almost immediately after the Supreme Court's *Pentagon Papers* opinion, the government-press relationship began to fray. Around that time, three cases wended their way to the Supreme Court, each involving a journalist subpoenaed to give evidence in a criminal investigation. One of those cases involved a federal investigation of the Black Panther Party. *New York Times* reporter Earl Caldwell was ordered to appear before the federal grand jury with the notes and tape recordings of interviews he had conducted with party members. After gaining the

Panthers' confidence, Caldwell (whose access was probably facilitated by his being black) wrote feature-length articles detailing the highly controversial party's activities and attitudes. Caldwell and the *Times* fought the subpoena, arguing that placing a reporter in the position of acting essentially as an informant or investigator for the government would cripple the trust between journalist and source that is essential to good reporting. They argued that the First Amendment's press freedoms clause overcame the Department of Justice's interest in using the media to augment the grand jury's investigative powers.

The 1972 case, *Branzburg v. Hayes*,[18] proved divisive for the Supreme Court, which split 5-4 against the press. However, one member of the majority, Justice Lewis Powell, wrote a separate "concurring" opinion in which he qualified his support for the government. Referring to the majority's argument that "harassment" (left undefined) of the press through abuse of the subpoena power would not be tolerated, Justice Powell argued that a journalist's "asserted claim to privilege should be judged on its facts by the striking of a proper balance between freedom of the press and the obligation of all citizens to give relevant testimony with respect to criminal conduct." This balancing act should be undertaken, Justice Powell wrote, "on a case-by-case basis [that] accords with the tried and traditional way of adjudicating such questions." This would protect "legitimate First Amendment interests," he concluded. In other words, Powell believed that instead of setting out a broad and sweeping principle in favor of either the press or the government, courts should examine the specific facts of each case to see who has more compelling interests that need to be protected: the journalist's need to protect the source or the prosecutor's need to subpoena the evidence.

Earl Caldwell never had to turn over his Black Panther material to the government because the grand jury's term expired by the time the Supreme Court ruled. Nonetheless, his case became a precedent (law binding on lower courts). Congress has never enacted a so-called shield law to clarify the extent, if any, to which protection is accorded those whose news-gathering function would be impeded by a breach of the confidential relationship between journalist and source. As noted earlier in this chapter, "[in] addition to case law, 31 states and the District of Columbia have enacted statutes—shield laws—that give journalists some form of privilege against compelled production of confidential or unpublished information."[19] But because federal law trumps state law, a state-imposed newsgatherer's privilege provides absolutely no protection from a federal subpoena.

For years after *Branzburg*, an uneasy stasis developed in which the feds sought to subpoena reporters on occasion, but where the lower federal courts generally judged the validity of those subpoenas on the basis of Justice Powell's balancing test. Subpoenas were issued to journalists pursuant to DOJ guidelines that put some burden on the prosecutor to justify his resort to compulsion.[20] This uneasy but generally effective partial truce was for a time honored by both sides. The press provided information only on a last-resort basis and, even then, in limited fashion. The DOJ compelled such cooperation on a highly selective basis. A practical balance had emerged because it was far from clear whether, and to what extent, journalists or prosecutors would prevail in a legal contest to test the limits, or simply the practical meaning, of Justice Powell's oracular but seemingly controlling concurring opinion.

Still, since guidance is provided only on a case-by-case basis, with the decision as to whether to enforce a subpoena largely within the discretion of lower federal court judges who themselves have varying attitudes toward the press, the news media does not know where it stands in any given instance of reporting. The media therefore cannot intelligently weigh the risks it faces in doing what many reporters and editors consider to be their jobs. This is no more true anywhere than among journalists who work in the field of national security. This confusion was highlighted when the government sought in 1979 to muzzle a magazine for divulging national security secrets. In *United States of America v. Progressive, Inc., Erwin Knoll, Samuel Day, Jr., and Howard Moreland*,[21] the government obtained a temporary injunction against the leftist magazine *The Progressive* (the injunction being the type of prior restraint severely limited in the *Pentagon Papers* case) to prevent publication of an article by activist Howard Moreland entitled "The H-Bomb Secret: How We Got It, Why We are Telling It." Even though Moreland's information had been compiled from public domain sources, including a children's encyclopedia and the open-to-the-public government library at Los Alamos,[22] the Department of Energy claimed the information fell under the secrecy provisions of the Atomic Energy Act of 1954. That statute more or less carved out of the more general Espionage Act the protection of secrets dealing with atomic and hydrogen weaponry.

Two separate trials were conducted—one in public, the other in a closed courtroom known as an *in camera* proceeding. The defendants, Moreland and the editors of *The Progressive*, refused to accept security clearances and therefore were excluded from the closed hearings at their own trial. Their lawyers accepted such clearances but were placed in the absurd position of being forbidden from conveying information they learned to their clients.

Once the hearings concluded, a Wisconsin federal judge ruled that "a preliminary injunction would be warranted even in the absence of statutory authorization because of the existence of the likelihood of direct, immediate and irreparable injury to our nation and its people."[23]

After the magazine appealed the prior restraint, Charles Hansen, an activist and computer programmer, published an open letter in Wisconsin's local *Madison Press Connection* that served as a gloss to Moreland's article. It claimed that other government scientists had put as much information about the hydrogen bomb into the public sphere as Moreland's article had, and complained of the government's hypocrisy in charging Moreland for publishing the information. As more information came out about the hydrogen bomb, the government, for its part, decided to drop the case, as "[t]here was no further point in protecting a secret that is no longer a secret."[24]

There also may have been some fear among prosecutors that appellate judges would issue a strong opinion overturning the trial judge's prior restraint. The government now had a useful precedent, albeit decided by a lower court and hence resting on rather weak authority, on which it could rely. The case constituted the longest prior restraint in American constitutional legal history. Moreland's article was published in the November 1979 issue of *The Progressive*, but not before Moreland and the magazine were put through the wringer.

• • ● • •

The post-*Pentagon Papers* fraying of the relationship between the federal executive branch on one hand, and the press on the other, had produced a series of clashes in which the Department of Justice sought, in the absence of a federal shield law, to force reporters and news organizations to disclose sensitive information, including particularly the identities of their confidential sources. This process had been unfolding gradually over three decades. It has accelerated markedly since the so-called war on terror began after the attacks of September 11, 2001.

The first high-profile post-9/11 press freedom case was launched in 2004. Special Prosecutor Patrick Fitzgerald had been appointed (ironically, under pressure from several national daily newspapers) to get to the bottom of a suspected leak, from somewhere in the Bush administration, of the covert identity of Valerie Plame, wife of diplomat Joseph Wilson, who had been feuding publicly with the administration over the lead-up to the Iraq War. Columnist Robert Novak, the first reporter to disclose Ms. Plame's status as a covert CIA agent, attributed the information to "two senior administration officials." Other columnists followed. The suspected violation of the Intelligence Identities Protection Act threw all of Washington into an uproar. Fitzgerald issued grand jury subpoenas to a number of prominent reporters, including Matthew Cooper of *Time*, Tim Russert of NBC News, and Glenn Kessler and Walter Pincus of *The Washington Post*. Another, Judith Miller of *The New York Times*, served an 85-day prison term before she finally testified after obtaining a waiver of confidentiality from her source, Vice-Presidential Chief of Staff I. Lewis "Scooter" Libby. Libby's waiver to Miller was widely believed to have been coerced by Fitzgerald's insisting that all staffers sign, waiting to see who would refuse.

The Plame leak investigation proved particularly frustrating for the newspapers, their reporters, and their lawyers. In the first place, because of the considerable secrecy surrounding all investigations into leaks of classified information, it was difficult for the media's lawyers to argue that the judge should follow Justice Powell's *Branzburg* concurrence and conduct a balancing test, weighing the importance of the information for the government's prosecution against the damage that would be done to the reporter's ability to do her job if disclosure were coerced. Of course, there is never assurance that a given judge would adopt the Powell approach rather than conclude, simply, that the majority in *Branzburg* did not adopt a balancing test but, instead, rejected any journalist's privilege entirely. Chief U. S. District Judge Thomas Hogan ruled that Fitzgerald's need for Miller's testimony was sufficiently critical to override Justice Powell's notion of a qualified privilege. The *Times*'s lawyers, without access to the secret record, could hardly argue effectively to the contrary.

Yet there were other, equally disturbing problems with the Miller contempt citation that Chief Judge Hogan issued and the U.S. Court of Appeals for the District of Columbia Circuit affirmed. (The Supreme Court turned down further review.) As David B. Rivkin, Jr., an expert in national security law who served in the Reagan and first Bush administrations, and Bruce W. Sanford, a First Amendment practitioner, wrote in an op-ed column in *The Wall Street Journal*, it was hardly clear that there was any violation of the Intelligence Identities Protection Act in the first place.[25] "The law," they wrote, "requires a prosecutor to show that a person has disclosed information that identifies a 'covert agent' (not an 'operative') while actually knowing that the agent has been undercover within the last five years in a foreign country and that the disclosed information would expose the agent." They proceeded to demonstrate the high likelihood that these conditions did not exist in the "leak" in that case, and that therefore journalists were being coerced "for refusing to divulge their sources to a grand jury which never really had a crime to investigate."

Former Solicitor General Theodore B. Olson, by then practicing law in Washington and stepping in at the eleventh hour to represent *Time* magazine and its reporter Cooper, wrote in even starker terms of how the combination of the vagueness of the law and the attitude of the special prosecutor were deadly for press freedoms: "If special prosecutors can be empowered to investigate allegations of conduct that isn't first established to be criminal, and to interrogate witnesses—especially reporters—about memories of distant conversations with sources regarding conduct that isn't plainly criminal, there is no politically motivated allegation that can't be turned into a criminal cover-up."[26]

The fallout from Miller's incarceration was predictably destructive. The Associated Press reported in July 2005 that the *Cleveland Plain Dealer* was holding back from publishing two stories that relied on leaked documents. The paper's editor, Doug Clifton, explained that it was the first time the paper felt pressed to take such a precaution.[27] On December 9, 2004, Jim Taricani, a reporter for a television station in Providence, Rhode Island, was incarcerated for his refusal to tell a federal judge the source of an FBI surveillance tape of a bribe being transacted. (The judge's one concession was to assign the 55-year-old reporter to home confinement in view of his having suffered a heart attack and received a heart transplant.) After being given permission by his source, a local lawyer, Taricani disclosed the source's identity and was let out of confinement. The lawyer, Joseph A. Bevilacqua, Jr., was prosecuted, convicted, sentenced to 18 months in prison, and disbarred.

There was something new about the atmosphere created by the Miller fiasco. The Reporters Committee for Freedom of the Press did a survey of pre-Miller press subpoenas and concluded that no American journalist spent "any significant amount of time behind bars" for refusing to obey a command to divulge a confidential source. Suddenly, noted Matt Welch in his *Reason* magazine column, there was a cascade of subpoenas. "Now journalists are joining their fellow citizens as targets," he noted ominously.[28] While "only 17 federal subpoenas were issued to unearth journalists' confidential sources between 1991 and September 6, 2001," wrote Welch, "that number may have been surpassed in 2004 alone, when…six reporters were found in contempt of court for refusing to name sources who cast aspersions on former Los Alamos scientist Wen Ho Lee." These contempt citations, Welch noted, were in addition to those emanating from criminal investigations. The trend, in other words, was not only to subordinate the journalist's privilege to government claims of exigency in criminal cases, but also to elevate the right of a private citizen in a civil defamation lawsuit to force the production of notes and testimony from reporters. The DOJ's assault on the press was having unforeseen consequences.

As Lucy Dalglish, publisher of *The News Media and the Law* and executive director of The Reporters Committee for Freedom of the Press, noted in the fall of 2004, "nearly every major media company in the country is fighting at least one subpoena from a federal prosecutor."[29] Agencies other than the DOJ began to get similar ideas. It was reported in February 2006 that the Securities and Exchange Commission "took the rare step of issuing a subpoena to two journalists…when it ordered columnists at two Dow Jones publications to provide information about conversations they had with stock traders and analysts." When it began to draw attention, the subpoena was withdrawn, "at least for the time being."[30]

Technically, refusal to comply with the vast majority of subpoenas issued to reporters and news organizations results in a finding of civil contempt. Civil contempt is meant to be coercive; the penalty is imposed until the recalcitrant witness relents and provides the testimony or documents demanded by the grand jury and prosecutor. The only limit to the length of a prison sentence is the life of the grand jury, which is 18 months. Upon the expiration of a grand jury's term, it is possible to renew it for an additional 18 months. Thus, it is theoretically possible to extend coercive punishment for a very long time unless the judge concludes that no amount of coercion will work with the witness. Even if a judge makes such a finding, he may then cite the witness for criminal contempt and impose a sentence of under six months without giving the reporter a jury trial. If the judge wants to impose more than six months, he must accord the reporter a jury trial, but in exchange for this benefit, the reporter then risks a criminal contempt sentence with no limit imposed by law. Courts have said that such contempt sentences should be "reasonable," but this term has not been defined. The potential for an effective tyranny over the press resulting from this contempt system is obvious—utterly vague standards for when a reporter can be ordered to comply, and unlimited fines and sentences for recalcitrance. The press lives under a veritable Sword of Damocles, all in a system that purports to have a free press.

A little recognized aspect of the contempt laws presents a news organization with another threat as potent as the jailing of its reporters and executives. Since a corporate news organization is not an entity that can be imprisoned, the punishment for corporate contempt typically is the imposition of monetary fines, often escalating daily as the news organization's recalcitrance continues. Such escalating coercive fines are well known in the labor relations arena when courts seek to end unlawful strikes by threatening to bankrupt the unions. During the grand jury probe into the Valerie Plame affair, for instance, a Washington, D.C., federal judge fined reporters Matt Cooper of *Time* and Judith Miller of *The New York Times* $1,000 per day each in addition to ordering them to jail until they testified. (The fines and sentences were stayed pending appeal.) Most such fines, when imposed on individual reporters, are typically paid by the news organizations for which they work. If it is the news organization itself that possesses the documents under subpoena, then the fines may be imposed directly on the corporation.

Since there is no limit to the fines that may be imposed, a judge has the power to bankrupt even the wealthiest media organization. When Matthew Cooper deviated from the path taken by Judith Miller and decided to testify, the cause was a decision by *Time* to turn over to the grand jury the notes and documents relating to Cooper's reporting. It was widely speculated at the time that the decision was based more on corporate financial considerations than on any sudden inclination of the magazine to do its patriotic duty and assist the grand jury. The director of the University of Minnesota's Silha Center for the Study of Media Ethics and Law, Jane Kirtley, told *Newsday* that "This [decision by *Time*] is sending a really dangerous message to prosectors [*sic*] and judges all over the country, who will now see the efficacy of imposing a fine on the news corporations."[31]

In short, the government's and the court's contempt powers are awesome. They not only can be imposed under the vaguest of circumstances and legal tests, but they are theoretically without limit in terms of the destruction that may be done to the recalcitrant reporter and media organization. If it is true, as the libertarian aphorism has it, that "the power to tax is the power to destroy," then it follows with even more force that the power of a court, sitting without a jury, to impose unlimited contempt sentences and endless escalating fines is the power to destroy any recalcitrant news organization. Thus is the free press, ostensibly protected by the First Amendment, no more secure from utter destruction than was the Arthur Andersen accounting firm.

• • ● • •

The *Pentagon Papers* case apparently did not cow *The New York Times* into never again disclosing state secrets. On December 16, 2005, the paper ran an exposé, written by reporters James Risen and Eric Lichtblau, telling the nation that shortly after the September 11 terrorist attacks President Bush had authorized the secretive National Security Agency (NSA) to eavesdrop, without legally required court approval, on massive numbers of telephone calls made from or to a foreign nation. Those familiar with the NSA's so-called data-mining techniques had known, or suspected, for years that the agency had the capability of monitoring any and all communications traffic in which it had a national security interest (and maybe even traffic in which it did not have any such legitimate interest). Still, the *Times* story landed like a bombshell. To some, the paper's disclosure was an act of patriotism and national service, as it unveiled a surveillance program of controversial legality (and constitutionality), that would provide far more eye-opening information to the American people than to its enemies. To others, publication of the story was an act of espionage (if not treason) in time of war. Under this theory, the *Times* was communicating to the nation's enemies highly classified information about the extent of the NSA's monitoring of their communications and activities, causing them to abandon such communications modes in favor of others not susceptible to this type of data-mining.

Political observer Jacob Heilbrunn wrote in a *New York Times* book review that "conservatives have been huffing and puffing about prosecuting *The New York Times* for treason" as part of a battle against perceived "liberal treachery." All true, perhaps, but Heilbrunn makes the mistake of dismissing the rant against the *Times* as "nonsense."[32] To the contrary, an indictment of the newspaper was a harrowing potential reality. Where the Nixon administration failed to dispatch its most irksome media critics under the espionage laws (primarily because of the intervening Watergate scandal), the Bush administration was making noises about following through.

Once again, the question arose whether the government could, and should, seek to prosecute the reporters, as well as the publisher, editors, and others who participated in putting out the story, including *The New York Times* Company itself. It was entirely possible, given the government's 30-year track record, that the administration just might want to make an example of the *Times* by going after publisher Arthur Sulzberger, Jr., executive editor Bill Keller, and the reporters themselves, namely, all those who were involved in either producing the stories or deciding to publish them.[33] The mere fact that it had not been done before would be cold comfort. The reach of federal statutes covering espionage, mail and wire fraud, dissemination of stolen government property, conspiracy with government officials to disseminate classified information, perhaps even treason, was dangerously uncertain, even without resort to the old standbys of mail and wire fraud. Perhaps the most comfort that the media parties could take from the situation in which they found themselves was that if the government were to indict, it would have to convince, beyond a reasonable doubt, 12 out of 12 jurors, likely sitting in either New York City (the *Times*'s hometown) or Washington, D.C. (not known for prosecution-oriented juries), the two districts where the "criminal" acts likely occurred, that the reporters and editors had done the nation a disservice by disclosing details of an arguably illegal and unconstitutional program.

Such a prosecution would not be without problems for still other reasons. It was not absolutely clear that the paper was telling people what many did not already know, since books had been written over the years about the NSA's inner workings.[34] Nor was it believable that terrorists did not have access to the same information the rest of us had. In a sense, the only thing truly new in the *Times* story, it might be said, was the revelation that this program was being conducted pursuant to a presidential order and without benefit of authorization by the secret national security court established in 1978 pursuant to the Foreign Intelligence Surveillance Act.[35]

If the only thing new about the story was indeed the disclosure that surveillance was being conducted unlawfully, could it be said that the newspaper was guilty of espionage or any other crime? This difficult question had to be considered by the reporters and the paper in making an educated guess beforehand as to what risk was entailed in publishing such a story. The article won a Pulitzer Prize, but the question lingered as to whether the administration, which swore to undertake a criminal investigation into the leaks as well as the publication, would follow through or would be satisfied simply to bluff. Yet whether an indictment would follow is beside the point. The Sword of Damocles, with its *in terrorem* impact on every move made by a reporter, newspaper, or other media outlet continues to hover over the head of journalism.

• • ● • •

The Boston Globe's Sacha Pfeiffer told an arresting tale in a piece she wrote for the paper's Sunday "Ideas" section in late 2007.[36] The reporter was trekking on a beaten path through the Himalayas in Nepal when she and her companion came across a checkpoint manned by Maoist insurgency guerillas who demanded a 300 rupee (approximately five dollars) fee for permission to pass. The State Department, however, had added this group to its terrorists list.

"In theory," wrote Pfeiffer, "this could expose me to prosecution, since multiple laws, including the USA Patriot Act and something called the International Emergency Economic Powers Act, prohibit US citizens from funding terrorism." When she returned, she found herself worried about the payment, and she began to make some phone calls "to ask about my legal status," including calls to the departments of Homeland Security, Justice, and State. "They squirmed a bit, told me Americans are advised not to travel to Nepal, mentioned the Maoists' terrorist status, and noted the relevant statutes." But what about the advice as to what to do this time, and in the future should the reporter face a similar situation? "Their underlying message was this: Don't worry about it." But, of course, this "advice" was not in writing and, besides, a reporter *does* have to worry about it if he or she comes back with a story critical of U.S. government policy or conduct. The more reporters involve themselves in covering the inner workings of those classified by the government as enemies of the nation, the more the reporters need to worry that they will be questioned about how much money they spent, on what and to whom. If government officials find themselves squirming when they are asked to interpret the laws they are tasked with enforcing, surely the Fourth Estate should squirm even more.

CHAPTER EIGHT

National Security: Protecting the Nation from Merchants, Artists, Professors, Students and Lobbyists for Non-Profits?

—— ●●● ——

Journalists aren't the only ones who run the risk of being accused of committing espionage and other crimes against state security in the course of doing their jobs. Over the past 30 years, so too have those working in a variety of professions, from artists and professors to merchants and lobbyists. When I first encountered the infinite malleability of the Espionage Act in the mid-1980s, while representing an East German academic, I assumed that the expanded use of the statute was the product of the U.S. government's Cold War mentality. Only later did I fully recognize that the kind of prosecutorial zeal that ensnared Professor Alfred Zehe was hardly limited to cases with an arguably real, even if vastly stretched, national security dimension. But national security was one of the early arenas where the feds pioneered the use of vaguely worded statutes to trap the innocent.

Securing the release of Jewish "refusenik" and human rights activist Anatoly Sharansky from the Soviet gulag had become a *cause celebré* in the late-1970s. The most promising strategy for freeing Sharansky involved arranging a trade of the high-profile prisoner in exchange for Soviet bloc prisoners held in the West, particularly convicted espionage agents in American prisons. Yet a serious problem stood in the way:

there was a dearth of such prisoners at that time. So the American intelligence establishment, in collaboration with the State Department, went about the task of fishing for "trade bait." All they needed was a Soviet bloc agent (or a reasonable facsimile), and a set of facts they could squeeze into the Espionage Act.[1]

The opportunity presented itself on November 4, 1983, when Professor Alfred Zehe, a prominent East German physicist, landed in Boston to attend a conference of the American Vacuum Society at the Massachusetts Institute of Technology. It came as a total shock when the professor was immediately arrested by federal agents and dragged to the U.S. District Court for Massachusetts, where he was charged with espionage. So much for the vacuum physics conference. The Americans, if they could convict their prey, had their trade bait. But why Zehe?

On the faculty of Dresden University, Zehe was a favored member of the academic East German elite. He was therefore given considerable leeway to travel, even to the West, and regularly spent a portion of each academic year teaching at the University of Puebla, in Mexico. Zehe made himself available as a technical consultant for the East German government whenever asked. It was hardly unusual on either side of the Iron Curtain. And so he developed a relationship with state security personnel.

When I was an undergraduate at Princeton in the 1960s, it was common knowledge on campus that certain professors consulted with and even recruited for the Central Intelligence Agency—a fact that was later borne out when former CIA director Allan W. Dulles's papers were released in 1998.[2] When I arrived at Harvard for law school, I learned that some faculty members were particularly tight with the Department of Defense. And doubtless a significant number of faculty members at the school down the road from Harvard, the Massachusetts Institute of Technology, served as consultants to national security and defense agencies. Indeed, the Dulles papers revealed that joining the Princeton group were professors from Harvard, M.I.T., Berkeley, Duke, and the Carnegie Institution. The difference, of course, was that American academics were not required to perform such services for their government to win the privilege to travel. They did it for the money, the prestige, or out of patriotic motives, but it was voluntary. In the Soviet bloc, cooperation with the government, especially by the elite, was expected.

Professor Zehe's involvement in what the Justice Department would later dub "espionage" and "conspiracy to commit espionage" began when U.S. Naval Intelligence selected some documents to use as bait which described long-obsolete submarine sonar technology that remained classified. The agency selected an employee working for a defense contractor in the Washington-Virginia corridor to work undercover to peddle the secret documents to an Eastern bloc agent. The undercover agent made a couple of stops along Embassy Row looking for a buyer. It was on his second attempt at the East German, or German Democratic Republic (GDR), embassy that he finally found an interested buyer.

The GDR agent who purchased the sonar technology documents insisted that they be delivered to the embassy in Mexico so that Professor Zehe could review them and advise his government concerning their meaning and value. Zehe, without being told the source nor the nature of the documents, was summoned from Puebla to Mexico City to meet with GDR officials to explain the documents. Zehe then returned to his teaching post. He thought nothing more of this rather routine incident until he was taken into custody by the FBI in Boston.

My law partners, Jeanne Baker and Nancy Gertner, and I were hired to represent Professor Zehe by the East German lawyer Wolfgang Vogel, the legendary "spy trader."[3] Vogel had arranged the repatriation of Francis Gary Powers, the American pilot who had flown an American U-2 high-altitude spy plane into Soviet airspace, only to be grounded and captured by the Soviets in 1960. It was the beginning of a long, if controversial, career for the suave lawyer who was the only member of his profession to belong to the bars of both East and West Berlin.

Vogel understood from the start that if Zehe were convicted, it would be up to him to figure out how to get the professor back. Vogel's (but not necessarily his government's) long-range plan, which ironically *depended* on the conviction of East Germans in U.S. custody, fit nicely into the Americans' desire to accumulate enough bait to secure the exchange of the high-profile Sharansky. My partners' and my role, however, was to represent Zehe to the best of our ability with the intention of securing his acquittal. Vogel fully understood this when he retained us, since we clearly explained to him the ethical obligations of American lawyers to represent their clients zealously and without conflicts of interest. Vogel may have been a "spy trader," but Zehe was not a spy. Still, Vogel retained us, likely assuming that if Zehe were in fact convicted, he would figure in a trade. If acquitted, Zehe would simply go home.

When we examined the factual and legal issues in the case, my partners and I discovered a very potent reason why the physicist should be acquitted and allowed to return to East Germany without the need of a trade: by any reasonable interpretation of the Espionage Act, Zehe had not committed a crime. After all, he was a non-citizen who had performed outside the United States the rather routine service for which he was indicted. If federal prosecutors' loose interpretation of the Espionage Act were allowed to stand in this instance, it would be extremely dangerous for a rather large number of foreign academics, scientists, and technical experts who occasionally consulted for their governments on issues of national security to set foot in the United States. Likewise, it would surely open the way for foreign governments, by way of retaliation, to treat American experts in a similar fashion when they traveled abroad for business or pleasure. It would be, in short, an absurd and ultimately self-defeating interpretation of the law, with disastrous consequences for those scholars who consult for their governments.

But this was the 1980s, the beginning of the "Silly Putty®" era of federal criminal law. The prosecution team, led by then-Assistant U.S. Attorney (and later director of the FBI) Robert S. Mueller, pushed the case forward, and so we filed a motion asking U.S. District Judge David S. Nelson to dismiss the indictment. We lost. Despite his admission that the Espionage Act did not state explicitly that it applied to non-citizens acting outside the United States, Judge Nelson concluded that it did so implicitly, however much the legislative evidence for such a conclusion was "sparse and at times ambiguous." It therefore covered Professor Zehe's scientific consultation at the GDR embassy in Mexico.[4]

The national security aura overhanging the case was powerful, to the extent at times of bordering on the comic. At one point I asked the judge to order the government to allow me to examine the sonar technology plans at the center of the case. I wanted to determine whether the defense team needed to call in an expert witness to assist in understanding the documents. Prosecutors objected to my having access to the sonar plans unless I obtained a security clearance. I lodged an objection to such a requirement. I was, after all, a native born American citizen and a member of the bar with no criminal record and nothing in my past to suggest disloyalty. I was asking to see the very same documents selected by Naval Intelligence and the FBI to pass along to the East German government. Those very documents were still sitting in some state security file in East Germany! Yet Judge Nelson sustained the prosecutors' objection. I refused, partly on principle and partly for tactical reasons, to undergo the security clearance procedure, not wanting to concede that the passing of the documents under any circumstances could be deemed injurious to national security, or that the obsolete documents were still properly classified. Eventually, the FBI backed down and the prosecution withdrew the motion demanding I obtain clearance. All the while, secretive back-channel trades were being discussed by East German and U.S. officials, without my or my colleagues' knowledge.

Prosecutors then suggested a way for Professor Zehe to avoid a conviction: end the prosecution by defecting and take up residence and an academic career in the United States. Professor Zehe, who was out on bail at the time and living in an apartment under the watchful eyes of both East German and FBI agents, decided he would agree to defect to the United States. He agreed to meet with two FBI agents in my office. The FBI agents slipped the professor out the back door of my office, unbeknownst to his East German escort (a humorless trench-coated character right out of central casting) waiting out front in his car. It turned out that the City of Boston's hard-fisted parking enforcement unit had forced the East German to stay outside, live parking, while Professor Zehe defected.

The U.S. government, however, threw an enormous monkey wrench into the works. It refused to accept Professor Zehe as a *bona fide* defector despite the fact that he had undergone a full debriefing, complete with a lie-detector test—the results of which did not meet with FBI approval. (Years later, Zehe suggested to me—and I now believe that he might well be right—that both he and his lawyers were naïve in believing that the government's defection suggestion was offered in good faith, since the feds had an overriding interest in using Zehe as trade bait rather than in bringing him over to the American side with a promise of permanent residence.) With only two options, either plead guilty and hope for a light sentence, or plead not-guilty and take his chances with the American legal system, Zehe decided to plead guilty. A few months later, he, along with some other Eastern bloc trade bait sitting in American jails, was exchanged for Anatoly Sharansky, who headed for Israel where he was received as a hero and commenced a new life as Natan (his Hebrew name) Sharansky. In contrast, when Zehe returned to East Germany, he found himself out of favor with the regime. When the GDR government fell and the Berlin Wall was torn down in 1989, Zehe left Germany and resumed his academic career in Puebla. The unified Germany was no kinder to him than either the East Germans or the Americans had been.

The precedent set by the Department of Justice, however, had legs. As tension between the West and Islamic radicalism began to grow in the increasingly contentious world that emerged after the collapse of Soviet Communism, the feds' Zehe escapade proved a worrisome harbinger of things to come. In October 2002, *Wall Street Journal* reporter Daniel Golden noted that ties between federal intelligence agencies and American universities had increased substantially after the terrorist attacks of September 11.[5] An increased number of academic political scientists and economists, he reported, were consulting with intelligence agencies, and the CIA's Intelligence Technology Innovation Center sponsored $2 million a year of "unclassified research by post-doctoral fellows" at 18 universities, including Harvard, Stanford, Carnegie Mellon, the University of Michigan, and Louisiana State University. What Golden didn't say was that the Zehe case put them at much greater risk.

Dual citizens, whose numbers among the professions have been growing during this era of increased globalization, are in even greater peril. On May 8, 2007, Iranian authorities arrested Haleh Esfandiari, a U.S.-Iranian dual citizen described as "a prominent Iranian-American academic who headed the Woodrow Wilson Center's Middle East programme in Washington."[6] She ended up spending more than 110 days in confinement and was questioned repeatedly by Iranian authorities before she was finally released. Former Congressman Lee H. Hamilton, president of the Wilson Center, said that he learned from his contacts in Iran that "her interrogations had focused almost entirely on activities of the Wilson Center."[7] Her detention, he exclaimed, was "an affront to the rule of law and common decency."[8]

Iranian intelligence continued its dragnet of U.S.-Iranian dual citizens. Just three days later, on May 11, authorities detained Kian Tajbakhsh, described by the Associated Press as "an urban planning expert who has also worked for the World Bank and is a senior research fellow at the New School in New York,"[9] and by June they had snared Ali Shakeri, described as "a peace activist and founding board member at the University of California at Irvine's Center for Citizen Peacebuilding."[10] These detentions, for reasons of Iranian "security," had followed the arrest of Parnaz Azima, an Iranian-American journalist-scholar working in Prague for the United States-financed Radio Farda, a Persian-language service of Radio Free Europe.[11] She was eventually released, but in March 2008, she was convicted and sentenced *in absentia* to one year in prison for "spreading anti-state propaganda." If she failed to return to serve her sentence, she would lose the deed to the home of her elderly mother, which was used to post bail.

It's a surprisingly dangerous world for academics, but the United States would be hard pressed to claim that it did not contribute to a body of precedents that make it easier to charge those engaged in what is perhaps most harshly characterized as "scholarly espionage" with serious national security crimes, and to do so for political rather than legally defensible reasons.

• • ● •

Just a few years after the Zehe case, the Department of Justice made clear the lengths to which it would go in the name of protecting national security, when my law firm and I became involved in a post-conviction appeal defending two people charged with assisting India's nuclear weapons program. "[T]he most troubling criminal proceeding over which I have presided in nearly seventeen years as a trial judge"—these were the words of Judge Douglas P. Woodlock, who presided over the trial. A Reagan appointee to the federal trial bench, Woodlock is one of those rare judges who cannot be pinned down as either pro-government or pro-defendant, "liberal" or "conservative," in criminal cases. His reputation is that of a cerebral, no-nonsense jurist who relishes the intellectual aspects of his cases. He has been known to think long and hard on difficult legal issues before rendering a decision, often to the dismay of court administrators who seem to value efficiency and "closed cases" statistics above all else.

Much about the prosecution was indeed disturbing, including, as we later learned, the fact that the government's position on the proper interpretation of the criminal statute and attendant regulations underlying the case contradicted its stance in other courts. But the more fundamental underlying problem was the utter inability of judges, lawyers, and experienced businessmen to figure out whether and how the federal export control regulations restricted the shipping of a certain piece of equipment manufactured by Walter L. Lachman, founder and chief owner-operator of two related companies (Fiber Materials, Inc. and Materials International) engaged in making high-technology materials and components mainly for the defense industry, and Maurice H. Subilia, Jr., his second-in-command.

Lachman and Subilia's long and arduous legal battle began in 1993 when they, along with their two companies, were indicted for allegedly selling equipment with military capabilities to India. In 1988 the two had arranged for a Swiss company to manufacture and ship to India a piece of equipment called a hot isostatic press, or HIP, which, due to its large size, would have required an export license had it been manufactured in and shipped from the United States. Lachman's company manufactured and shipped from the United States a smaller HIP that everyone agreed did not need an export license. (HIP devices subject materials to extreme heat and pressure, making them harder and more heat-resistant. Such technology is critical for a multitude of purposes, both industrial and military. The larger HIP, in particular, had uses in missile manufacture.) However—and here was the rub—Lachman's company also exported to India a control panel capable of operating *both* the smaller American-manufactured HIP and the larger Swiss-manufactured device. Was export of this panel prohibited without a license?

The political climate of the time played a large role in Lachman's and Subilia's indictment. During the late-1980s and early-'90s, Pakistan sought to bolster its nuclear arms program, aggravating an already hostile relationship with neighboring India. Prosecutors later claimed that the ability to super-harden materials used to manufacture the nose-tips of atomic missiles, and thus enhance their accuracy, was crucial to India's efforts to maintain its advantage in the arms race with Pakistan.

The export of certain materials and devices in this area was subject to two somewhat interlocking, but also conflicting, sets of regulations. One set of regulations issued by the Department of State ("State") dealt with controlling the export of items "specially designed" for military purposes, in hopes of both cooling the atomic arms race and maintaining American nuclear supremacy. To ship such specially designed equipment abroad, sellers would need export licenses. The other set of regulations, established by the Department of Commerce ("Commerce") for the purpose of encouraging American economic activity and a vibrant export sector, dealt exclusively with commodities having "dual" civilian and military uses. And so, while "specially designed" military-use materials and equipment clearly required an export license, "dual use" items were in somewhat of a twilight zone. Commerce insisted that it needed information when any "dual use" item was considered for shipment abroad so that it could examine the full context and decide whether to allow the shipment.

Needless to say, the sometimes overlapping jurisdictions and competing goals of these two agencies, one leaning toward limiting export of military technology, the other inclined toward stimulating export commerce, had the potential to squeeze business executives earnestly trying to accommodate both goals and appease both agencies.

The defendants shipped the HIP control panel without seeking or receiving an export license. While neither HIP apparatus was itself the issue, prosecutors contended that the control panel could not be shipped without the defendants' seeking an export license from Commerce, because that panel could operate the larger, as well as the smaller, HIP.

The determinative issue in the criminal case was whether the control panel was specially designed for a HIP of over five inches in diameter (which itself would have required an export license). The disagreement centered on the control panel that could operate both the larger and the smaller HIP and on the operative definition of the critical term "specially designed." Commerce claimed that the control panel shipped by the defendants from the U.S. was in effect part of the larger HIP and hence was subject to Commerce's export control regulations requiring an export license.

The indictment stunned Lachman and Subilia. After decades of experience in the defense industry, they thought they had a relatively firm grasp of Commerce's arcane regulations. They believed, with good reason, that the transaction was entirely legal. Giving the case an even deeper aura of unreality was the fact that the control panel that caused the whole imbroglio was a non-computerized, non-automated, off-the-shelf piece of equipment that could readily be obtained from multiple sources. Rarely, it seemed, had so much legal fuss been made over so little. Lachman, in particular, was incensed and offended. He was a devout American patriot. He took great offense at the implication that he would conduct business that would jeopardize the nation's security. The eventual recipient of the transaction was, after all, the Indian government—then and now the world's largest democracy and, despite its then-membership in the "non-aligned nations" camp, fundamentally an American ally. Some unscrupulous exporters will sell military equipment to the highest bidder and then wash their hands, but Walter Lachman was not one of them. Like many in his line of work, he viewed his profession as a noble cause. Now he found himself, his colleague, and his two companies charged with violations of export regulations supposedly fashioned to protect the nation's security. In 1995, the jury convicted.

Seeking to clear their names, Lachman and Subilia enlisted the counsel of attorney and Harvard Law School legal scholar Alan Dershowitz. I became involved through Dershowitz, as did three of my colleagues: Andrew Good and Philip Cormier of the Silverglate & Good firm, and Michael Schneider, former research assistant to Dershowitz and later a founding partner of the boutique criminal law firm of Salsberg & Schneider. While reviewing the charges against the various defendants and the trial transcript, the defense team discovered the troubling ambiguity in the Commerce provisions under which prosecutors charged and convicted Lachman and Subilia. The wording of the Commerce regulation left unanswered the critical question of whether it covered items that had dual uses and hence were not "specially designed" for military uses.

During the trial, long before we got involved in the case, Judge Woodlock had instructed jurors to follow the "plain meaning" definition of the term "specially designed." Woodlock observed that any apparatus built "so that it could have an end use in connection with ballistic missile components having a nuclear capability" would be considered "specially designed." This meant that even if the equipment had a dual use, it would nonetheless be considered "specially designed" for the military use and hence would be covered by the export control regulations. Using these definitions, the jury had convicted, since there was no question that the control panel was capable of dual uses. Indeed, the dual use capability of the panel was precisely the reason Lachman and Subilia did *not* seek an export license.

Just before sentencing, in August 2003, Lachman and Subilia's new defense team found and presented evidence that in other instances the Commerce Department itself, during the same period, often interpreted the "specially designed" language so as to exclude dual use items from the licensing requirement. We found statements made by the U.S. delegation at meetings with allied nations seeking to cooperate in controlling the export of strategic defense components, statements made by Commerce officials at educational seminars that were open to the public, and internal understandings among Commerce officials.

It was the evidence in the first category, official positions taken by the U.S. delegation to the Coordinating Committee on Multilateral Export Controls ("COCOM"), that was in many ways the most disturbing. It turned out that the U.S. delegation to COCOM conveyed to the nation's allies the American position on the meaning of "specially designed" as "equipment used solely for a particular purpose," thereby excluding dual use items from the export controls.[12] There was a reason, however, why Lachman's and Subilia's trial lawyers had no idea that the government had earlier asserted, as official American policy, a definition precisely the opposite of the incriminating one that it successfully urged upon Judge Woodlock and the jury at the trial: the COCOM proceedings were classified and hence not available to trial counsel.

The new defense team learned of this sleight-of-hand by happenstance, aided by some dogged investigative follow-through. The American position taken at COCOM, which would have ended the trial even before it began had it been made known to the court, was declassified in Germany, one of the participating COCOM nations, when it was used in a public trial in Darmstadt. Almost comically, the Justice Department insisted that it could not produce in Judge Woodlock's open court the original American version of this document because it remained classified in the United States, notwithstanding Germany's declassification and use in court in Germany of the translated version. The American document, therefore, had to be used in the Lachman/ Subilia post-conviction litigation on a classified basis.

The evidence of the position taken by government officials at industry seminars was almost as startling. Witnesses discovered by the new legal team revealed that Commerce Department officials, appearing at public educational seminars frequented by members of industry, taught that a "product or component is only specially designed for a certain product or purpose if it can only be used for that product or purpose."[13] The former Commerce officials who brought this revelation to the attention of the court told the judge that this "was the only meaning of the term 'specially designed' that was consistently used within" the Commerce Department.

The prosecutors were hardly pleased when confronted with the overwhelming evidence showing Commerce's double standards in export regulation. They tried to argue that the information contained in the classified COCOM minutes was "simply in error," and that the Commerce officials who spoke at public educational seminars were "not authorized to supply official definitions for terms." But Judge Woodlock would have none of it. He concluded that "there was no determinable definition for the term 'specially designed'…upon which a criminal proceeding could be mounted," and sided with Commerce's Inspector General who by then acknowledged the term to be ambiguous.

Judge Woodlock quoted a former Chief Justice of the United States, Morrison Waite, who wrote in 1876 that "it would certainly be dangerous if the legislature could set a net large enough to catch all possible offenders, and leave it to the courts to step inside and say who could rightfully be detained; and who should be set at large."[14] He concluded that Lachman and Subilia had not been given fair notice of what the law required, and tossed out the guilty verdict.

One of the opinions Woodlock cited as precedent for his decision was that of the Court of Appeals for the First Circuit in *United States v. Anzalone*,[15] the ultimately unsuccessful prosecution of the aide to then-Boston Mayor Kevin H. White, where the court had observed that "the

present ambiguity regarding coverage of the [cash transactions statute and regulations] has been created by the government itself." Were
Lachman and Subilia to appeal, after all, it would be that very court
that would decide the case, and presumably it would feel bound by its
earlier *Anzalone* opinion (discussed in Chapter One). Woodlock went
on to quote yet another precedent, Lewis Carroll's classic *Through the
Looking Glass*:

> "When *I* use a word," Humpty Dumpty said in a rather
> scornful tone, "it means just what I choose it to mean—
> neither more nor less."
>
> "The question is," said Alice, "whether you *can* make words
> mean so many different things."
>
> "The question is," said Humpty Dumpty, "which is to be
> master—that's all."[16]

The Department of Justice was not done with Lachman and Subilia,
however. Because the acquittal had been entered by the trial judge after
a conviction by the jury, the government had a right to appeal. And so
the case went to the same appellate court that had tossed out Theodore
Anzalone's money laundering conviction in 1985 on grounds that it
had been based on regulatory language that was too ambiguous. But
the times, as well as some members on the Court of Appeals for the
First Circuit, had changed.

The Court of Appeals issued its decision on October 25, 2004, 11 years
after Lachman and Subilia were indicted. It reversed Judge Woodlock.
"We hold," wrote the court, "that the applicable...regulation was not
unconstitutionally vague." After admitting that dictionary definitions
did not resolve the question, the First Circuit panel directed its attention to what it viewed as the purpose of the regulations. The regulatory
scheme, the court concluded, "was designed to ensure that exports do
not detrimentally affect the national security of the United States, while
not unduly restricting legitimate trade." The government's definition is
more in keeping with this goal, concluded the Court of Appeals, notwithstanding the evidence that Commerce itself had secretly interpreted the regulatory scheme (and had informally advised the industry) in

a manner that matched Lachman and Subilia's understanding and that Judge Woodlock finally adopted.

"We have concluded that the regulation is not ambiguous when construed in light of the statutory purpose," wrote the Court of Appeals. It deemed the classified material demonstrating the government's secret interpretation of the language to be irrelevant precisely because it was secret! It dismissed the Commerce members' public statements at industry seminars to be irrelevant because they were not "official." The regulation, the Court of Appeals concluded, "was reasonably susceptible to the construction that we have adopted" and hence "there is no basis for invalidating [the regulation] as failing to provide fair notice." It did not seem to matter that Lachman's and Subilia's interpretation was no less reasonable than that of the government, and was in fact more in keeping with Commerce's own long-held and often-expressed views. All that mattered was that the interpretation now being proffered by the government seemed more in keeping with America's security interests as now understood by the Departments of Commerce and Justice—all this without Commerce's being required to clarify the regulation, as it easily could have done, to cover "dual uses."

The Court of Appeals thus answered the question posed by Judge Woodlock and Humpty Dumpty: the government was to be master, and that ended the case. More than a decade after his indictment, Walter Lachman was sentenced to three years probation, the first of which was to be spent under house arrest. Maurice Subilia was sentenced to six months home confinement, probation, and a $250,000 fine. The government, dissatisfied with the sentences, appealed them. In October 2004, while the defendants' guilt was sealed, the defendants' long nightmare still was not quite over. The case finally ended in January 2008, after the government withdrew its appeal as a result of an intervening, unrelated Supreme Court decision upholding the kind of sentencing discretion exercised by Judge Woodlock.

The sentencing hearing yielded little insight into why the government brought the prosecution in the first place. For one thing, it was learned that there was no evidence whatsoever that the "carbon-carbon" technology embodied in the HIP devices was at all useful to India's atomic weapons program. The technology was relevant only in long-range intercontinental ballistic missiles, whereas the Indian program dealt in shorter-range delivery systems aimed at neighboring Pakistan and China. A government technical witness conceded that the HIP control panel that was at the heart of the prosecution was actually a very simple device (unlike the HIPs themselves which had been shipped lawfully) and could be made by any reasonably competent engineer. There was absolutely no national security-related reason to stretch the regulations to cover the shipment of such an easily manufactured, off-the-shelf, add-on device.

In finding the Commerce regulation "not ambiguous," the Court of Appeals had found clarity in language that an ordinary person of reasonable intelligence could not help but see as ambiguous. In that regard, the Court of Appeals was playing the King in another Lewis Carroll classic, *Alice's Adventures in Wonderland*. Alice cannot make sense of the White Rabbit's nonsensical charges, stated in rhyming verse, against the Knave, on trial for stealing the Queen of Heart's tarts:

> "If any one of them can explain it," said Alice.... "I'll give him sixpence. *I* don't believe there's an atom of meaning in it."

> The jury all wrote down on their slates, "*She* doesn't believe there's an atom of meaning in it," but none of them attempted to explain the paper.

> "If there's no meaning in it," said the King, "that saves a world of trouble, you know, as we needn't try to find any. And yet I don't know," he went on, spreading out the verses on his knee, and looking at them with one eye: "I seem to see some meaning in them, after all."[17]

• • ● • •

Given the liberties prosecutors and federal judges took with statutory interpretation during the Cold War, it stood to reason that in the wake of the terrorist attacks of September 11, the "Silly Putty®" approach would become even more deeply entrenched.

The feds launched one of the first such prosecutions against Steven Kurtz, member of the cutting edge, internationally known Critical Art Ensemble (CAE) and also art professor at the State University of New York at Buffalo (SUNY/Buffalo). Kurtz woke up on May 11, 2004, to find his wife Hope lying, apparently dead, in bed. He dialed 911 and paramedics soon arrived. One of them noted the presence of laboratory equipment in the house, including Petri dishes with live microorganisms. He notified the local police, who showed up to investigate. Kurtz, with his wife's body in the next room, demonstrated to the police the harmlessness of these biological specimens, explaining how he incorporated them into various pieces of his art. He even inserted his finger into the bright scarlet bacteria in one of the Petri dishes and put it in his mouth.[18]

It was all for naught. The police shortly notified the FBI. The next day, as he returned home from his late wife's funeral, Kurtz was confronted by three carloads of FBI agents and others dressed in hazardous materials suits. A full-scale bioterrorism scare was in progress, conducted cooperatively by five regional offices of the FBI, the Joint Terrorism Task Force, the Department of Homeland Security, the Department of Defense, the Buffalo police and fire departments, and the New York State Fire Marshall's office.[19] Kurtz and one of his colleagues, University of Pittsburgh genetics professor Dr. Robert Ferrell, had become the subject of a nationwide federal criminal terrorism investigation.

Much controversy ensued in the local and national press, and on Websites and blogs, as to whether the authorities had overreacted, especially once they discovered that the bacteria in Kurtz's Petri dishes were harmless organisms of the type found in profusion, for example, in the human gut. Kurtz had been using the bacteria, it turned out, in connection with a CAE project named "Gen Terra," which, according to a *New York Times* description, "looked at genetic engineering of organisms from the perspective of a fictional corporation."[20] Members of CAE employ somewhat more grandiose terms for the project, which they claim is "dedicated to exploring the intersections between art, technology, radical politics and critical theory."

Federal investigators, led by William J. Hochul, Jr., the lead terrorism prosecutor in the Buffalo U.S. attorney's office, interrogated other members of CAE and even looked into museums and other institutions that possessed artworks created by Kurtz. CNN reported, for example, the seizure of one Kurtz exhibit that "would allow gallery-goers to test for common genetic modifications in food."[21] The geographic reach of the investigation was determined largely by the success and renown of Kurtz's artwork, which, the CAE explained on its Website for raising a defense fund, "had been displayed in museums and galleries throughout Europe and North America."[22]

When the investigation was over, it was apparent that there was no prosecutable violation of the post-9/11 federal anti-terror statute under which the feds had been proceeding. Section 175 of the U.S. Biological Weapons Anti-Terrorism Act of 1989, enlarged in scope by Section 817 of the USA Patriot Act passed in the wake of the September 11 attacks,[23] outlaws the possession of "any biological agent, toxin, or delivery system of a type or in a quantity that, under the circumstances, is not reasonably justified by a prophylactic, protective, bona fide research, or other peaceful purpose."[24] Even the most creative stretching of this statute would not cover artworks made of common and harmless bacteria, clearly for a "peaceful purpose."

However, federal "catch-all" criminal statutes are always available to serve investigators' and prosecutors' agendas even when a particular activity does not fit within a more specific statute. Buffalo's Kurtz and his Pittsburgh colleague Ferrell soon found themselves named in a four-count indictment, two counts for mail fraud and two for wire fraud.[26] Because, the indictment alleged, the defendants used the instrumentalities of interstate commerce (a commercial interstate carrier for the mail fraud counts, and electronic computer communications for the wire fraud count) they were each subject to up to 20 years in prison (five years on each count).

How could this happen? According to the indictment,[26] the bacteria came from a non-profit corporation in Virginia, the American Type Culture Collection ("ATCC"), the principal business of which is "to supply biological materials and related products to registered customers." ATCC is both a manufacturer of lab organisms and a clearinghouse to which registered customers supply their own specimens. ATCC maintains accounts only for registered businesses and institutions (including colleges and universities), not for individuals. Hence, any person wanting to obtain a specimen must do so through an approved, registered institution. Registered customers have to demonstrate that they take certain precautions, including the employment of a bio-safety officer. In addition, customers are restricted from further transferring specimens obtained from ATCC; an ATCC Material Transfer Agreement provides that a registered customer "may make and use" the acquired biological material "for research purposes in your laboratory only."

The indictment acknowledged that the two types of organisms, *serratia marcescens* and *bacillus atrophaeus*, ordered through the University of Pittsburgh Human Genetics Laboratory, a registered customer of ATCC, posed no danger to public health.[27] But then the feds got creative. First the indictment regarded the organisms as "university property." Under the University of Pittsburgh's own regulations, any transfer of organisms from its lab to a third party was subject to a "material transfer agreement" to be kept on file at the university's Office of Research. The "scheme" to "defraud" occurred when Kurtz and Ferrell used the registered ATCC account of the University of Pittsburgh to order the bacteria, when in fact the intention was to transfer the bacteria from Pittsburgh to Kurtz. The idea was that, since it would have been impossible for Kurtz, an art professor rather than a scientist, to acquire the bacteria through SUNY/Buffalo, which also had an ATCC account, the defendants used "the mails and interstate wire communications" in the "furtherance of their scheme and artifice to defraud" when they arranged to move the bacteria to Kurtz via the University of Pittsburgh's account.

"I am absolutely astonished," commented Donald A. Henderson, Dean Emeritus of the Johns Hopkins University School of Hygiene and Public Health and a resident scholar at the Center for Biosecurity of the University of Pittsburgh Medical Center. "Professor Kurtz has been working with totally innocuous organisms." Henderson added that the two microorganisms involved in the case are not found on lists of substances of utility to biological terrorists. Addressing the precise assertion in the indictment (concerning the "fraudulent" nature of the transfer of innocuous organisms from one academic to another without the completion of detailed university departmental paperwork), University of California/San Diego Professor of Design Engineering Natalie Jeremijenko said that scientists engage in precisely this kind of cooperative and informal conduct with frequency. "I do it, my lab students do it. It's a basis of academic collaboration…. They're going to have to indict the entire scientific community."[28] SUNY/Buffalo Law Professor Stephen Halpern, a constitutional law specialist, agreed. The prosecution of Ferrell and Kurtz, he said, is "really going to have a chilling impact on the type of work people are going to do in this arena, and other arenas as well."[29]

While scientists expressed concern about the deadening effect this kind of prosecution would have on scientific collaboration and research, those engaged in literary and artistic pursuits focused more on its impact on First Amendment liberties. After all, as CAE explained, the project in which Professor Kurtz was involved was part of an artistic critique of the history of American involvement in germ warfare experiments. It was all too ironic (but, one naturally asks, was it really coincidental?) that this indictment was directed against political artwork concerned with bio-contamination resulting from government-funded research in germ warfare.[30] The PEN American Freedom to Write Committee sent a letter to the FBI supporting "strong, targeted laws to apprehend terrorists," but decrying what appears to be "the impulse to censor." Art needs to examine and bring public attention to biological research and "otherwise arcane bodies of knowledge."[31]

None of this is to say, of course, that some minor infraction was not committed. That is unclear. *The Buffalo News*, though assuming that there must have been some kind of legal violation, however trivial, got it about right when it editorialized: "Jaywalkers, beware."[32] But Professor Kurtz's defense attorney, the noted First Amendment lawyer Paul Cambria, Jr., got closer to the heart of the problem when he commented: "If the University of Pittsburgh feels that there was a contract breach, then their remedy is to sue Steve for $256 in a civil court" (the estimated value of the bacteria involved).[33] He was too restrained, however, when he referred to the indictment merely as "a stretch."[34] There is, or should be, a real question of whether the federal criminal fraud arsenal even applies to what, looked upon more dispassionately, is arguably a contract dispute between a non-profit organization, two universities, a professor, and an academic artist over $256 worth of benign bacteria.

The federal district judge to whom the case was assigned spent some time considering the matter. On April 21, 2008, he issued a 12-page decision dismissing the indictment.[35] Try as he might, he could not figure out how the case constituted wire or mail fraud. The ATCC from which the bacteria had been ordered was paid in full out of the University of Pittsburgh's account for its product, and hence there was no fraud on the seller; the ATCC had no particular interest in where the germs were directed by the University of Pittsburgh. Furthermore, Pittsburgh was not a victim since the indictment did not allege "any type of misrepresentation or fraudulent conduct directed toward [it] regarding the biological agents." The judge did, however, discuss a recent "no-sale theory of fraud" that was being developed by some federal prosecutors and courts in order to establish a mail or wire fraud where a failure to tell the seller precisely to whom it was selling could be seen as violating the statute, but he ruled that it did not apply in Kurtz's case, adding, ominously, that he gave no assurances that the indictment could not have been drawn up in a manner so as to survive the motion to dismiss.[36] One could easily conclude that the judge felt that Kurtz could in fact have been indicted under the almost infinitely malleable mail and wire fraud statutes, but that the court was giving him the benefit of the doubt this time in view, perhaps, of the overall ridiculous nature of the case.

• • ● • •

Sami Omar al-Hussayen was a 34-year-old doctoral candidate studying at the University of Idaho located—where else?—in Moscow, Idaho. This grad student "didn't exactly fit the profile" of a terrorist "when he was arrested in February 2003 and likened in court documents to

Osama bin Laden," as the press reported.[37] His troubles began when he used his computer skills to run a number of Websites for a Muslim charity. Even though the charity "on its face" engaged in normal and traditional religious teaching, prosecutors noted that if a Web surfer burrowed into the various sites linked to items appearing on al-Hussayen's sites, the surfer would encounter links containing "a handful of violent messages—written by others—encouraging attacks on the United States and donations to terrorist organizations."

The investigation started when a Moscow bank teller reported to the FBI that the Arab student engaged in a "suspicious" bank transaction. Al-Hussayen, the FBI learned, was from a prominent Saudi family. His father was a retired Saudi government education minister and his uncle was the president of the holy mosques at Mecca and Medina.[38] Al-Hussayen came to the United States in 1994 and obtained a master's degree from Ball State University in Muncie, Indiana. He arrived in Moscow in 1999 to get his doctorate in computer science from the University of Idaho. His wife and three children lived with him and the oldest two attended public school. At the time of the September 11 attacks, al-Hussayen was the president of the Muslim Student Association. Described by *The Seattle Times* as "the public face of Islam in Moscow,"[39] he organized a blood drive for victims of the attacks, participated in peace vigils, and wrote a letter on behalf of himself and other Muslim students condemning the attacks. None of this helped him very much with the FBI.

Al-Hussayen's federal indictment for providing "material support" and rendering "expert advice or assistance" to terrorists began with an FBI investigation into his rather public activities. Al-Hussayen was reportedly the first person to be indicted under the USA Patriot Act,[40] hurriedly enacted into law following the 9/11 terrorist attacks.[42] The new statute expanded the notion of "material support" for terrorism to include those who render "expert advice or assistance" to the terrorists and their cause. Because he was a skilled Webmaster and because Internet users could eventually access terrorist Websites by following the links from his site, al-Hussayen was seen as qualifying. "His fingerprints were intricately involved in the building of Websites that called on young people to go and kill themselves," argued Assistant U.S. Attorney Terry Derden to the jury. "Can you [lawfully] call on people to donate money to attack Americans?" he asked the 12 Idahoans sitting in judgment of the young Saudi student.

Various aspects of al-Hussayen's life and work had attracted the feds' suspicions. He had switched dissertation advisers in the middle of the school year, leading investigators to conclude that he was intentionally slowing down his graduate studies to prolong his stay in the United States. His courses included computer security. He moved his campus office from the computer science building to another building that previously contained the science department's nuclear reactor. According to one report, this led the FBI to believe that he might have been looking for radioactive material to make a "dirty bomb."[42] The feds got a national security wiretap of the student's phone, since there was not adequate "probable cause" to get a regular wiretap, and managed to snag about 20,000 emails and 9,000 phone calls during a year-long period. A team of 20 law enforcement officials followed him.

Providing "material support" to terrorism was not a new crime. In 1994 a law had been enacted under which, to secure a conviction, the government had to demonstrate some connection with an actual terrorist act. After the September 11 attacks, when Congress expanded the statute to cover "expert advice or assistance" to terrorist organizations, it did not bother to define the term. Georgetown University Law Professor David Cole, an expert on criminal law in the terrorism area, cited this particular provision as the "linchpin" of the DOJ's war on terror "precisely because it doesn't require proof that an individual engaged in any sort of terrorist act or even supported any terrorist activity."[43]

Notwithstanding the uncertain reach of the "material support" language of the statute, Judge Edward J. Lodge instructed the jury about the scope of the First Amendment's protection of free speech. "Freedom of speech," the judge noted, relying on traditional legal understanding that became shakier with each passing year of the war on terror,[44] "protects an individual's or a group's right to advocate their beliefs even if those beliefs advocate the use of force or violation of law unless the speech is directed to inciting or producing imminent lawless action and is likely to incite or produce such action."[45] This jury instruction, the formulation of the line to be drawn between free speech and unlawful incitement to violence, led the jury to acquit the grad student of the terrorism-related charges "in two or three hours," according to one of the jurors.[46] (One juror explained that the evidence "showed he was involved in what he was doing, but it seemed rather innocent, the stuff he was talking about."[47]) The case did little to clarify the meaning of "expert advice or assistance," however. What it did do was confirm the breadth of the First Amendment's protections in this particular case, where the "assistance" consisted of maintaining or linking to mere Websites. The loose statute remained on the books.

The jury deadlocked, however, on relatively minor charges that he had violated immigration laws by engaging in visa fraud. After his acquittal of the more serious charges, al-Hussayen's lawyer negotiated a deal with the government. He agreed not to contest the student's deportation, and in exchange the prosecutors agreed not to retry him on the deadlocked counts. He was deported to Saudi Arabia a few weeks after the trial ended. Mr. al-Hussayen settled in Riyadh where he worked as an instructor at a technical university. His wife took employment as a kindergarten teacher.

• • ● • •

Until his 2005 criminal indictment, Emadeddin Z. Muntasser was living the American dream. He came to the United States from Libya in 1981 at the age of 16 to attend school. After graduating from college in 1986, Emad, as he was known to friends, decided he liked what he saw of American life and settled down. He founded a successful retail furniture business, married, and started a family.

Muntasser, a legal permanent resident, filed an application for citizenship in October 2002, and was exasperated at the long delays in having his case processed. Even after the terrorist attacks of September 11, when suspicion suddenly seemed to focus on foreign-born Muslims,

Muntasser didn't foresee the hurdles he would encounter in trying to become a citizen.

It turned out that federal authorities had for some time been keeping track of Muntasser and some of his friends and associates, who in 1993 had organized a Muslim charity in Massachusetts named Care International, Inc. They referred to their organization as "Care," though it had no affiliation with the multinational anti-poverty charity *CARE*. Its purpose was to help Muslims made destitute in war-torn areas of the world, primarily in Afghanistan and Bosnia. Prosecutors during Muntasser's later criminal trial tried to make it appear that Care's efforts were focused on helping only the injured "mujahideen," or holy warriors, and the families of deceased fighters. In fact, the beneficiaries of Care's charitable efforts were the "martyrs" of the conflict, a much broader concept in Islam, as it covered anyone killed in the Afghan conflict.

Muntasser's charitable efforts ran into a rather sudden change in American policy in that tumultuous region. Ronald Reagan had called these Muslims "freedom fighters,"[48] and the U.S. government had supported them with guns and money in their resistance to the Soviet invasion (as readers might recall from the Tom Hanks movie *Charlie Wilson's War*), but American opinion gradually turned against the mujahideen through the early-1990s. By 1996, when the Taliban took over control of Afghanistan, the CIA and other orientalists in the American foreign policy establishment were recognizing that some of the American-funded Afghani mujahideen who fought the Soviets were allying with the radically conservative Taliban and turning on their erstwhile American sponsors and other Western interests. Suddenly anyone in the United States who continued to support, among others, the dead and injured fighters and their families became suspect. Despite the fact that Muntasser had left Care in 1996, he became a victim of these changing alliances.

When Muntasser tired of waiting for the Immigration and Naturalization Service, which by then had morphed into the U.S. Citizenship and Immigration Services (part of the Department of

Homeland Security), to approve his application for citizenship, he filed a civil lawsuit in the federal district court in Boston in June 2004, asking Judge Rya Zobel to order the INS to process it. He survived the preliminary skirmishes in which the government sought to get his lawsuit dismissed, and Zobel set a hearing at which, Muntasser and his immigration lawyer felt, she was likely to allow his application.

The Department of Justice apparently had a similar sense of what Judge Zobel was going to do. In May 2005, the day before Muntasser's hearing, the U.S. attorney in Boston unveiled an indictment against him reeking of hints that he was sympathetic to terrorism. The accusations necessarily were indirect, based upon political and religious views, since there was no evidence of participation in, nor material support for, any terrorist activity, nor any evidence that Care had ever provided aid to fighters.[49] The next day the U.S. attorney asked Judge Zobel to dismiss the citizenship application in light of the indictment. Perhaps smelling a rat, Zobel refused to dismiss the case but put it on hold pending resolution of the indictment.

The heart of the somewhat rambling indictment charged that, in 1993, when Muntasser filed an application seeking to have the Internal Revenue Service's exempt organizations office declare Care qualified as a charitable, non-profit, tax-exempt organization, he omitted crucial information supposedly called for in the application. Similar "material omissions," the indictment charged, characterized Care's annual filings with the IRS after the group was granted its tax exemption.

An application for tax-exempt status is supposed to make the case for why the organization's work qualifies (or, in the case of a new organization, will qualify) as charitable or educational within IRS guidelines. Taxpayers donating to a qualified organization may deduct such payments as charitable contributions on their tax returns. An organization devoted to supporting victims, including widows and orphans of violence and other "man-made disasters" (the phrase used in Care's application)[50] in Afghanistan, Bosnia, Chechnya and other countries caught up in sectarian violence then as now, would clearly qualify for tax-exempt status under applicable guidelines.[51] But, said the indictment, Muntasser had failed to disclose certain other facts about Care that, were it known to the IRS, could have led the agency to question, perhaps even deny, tax-exempt status.

The government's tax prosecution theory, as simply stated as possible, was that if the organizers and officers of Care had been more explicit in including in its application for tax-exempt status, and in its annual reports, more "material" information about the objects of Care's charitable undertakings, the IRS might have denied the exemption application altogether. The indictment charged: "The defendants did not disclose to IRS that Care was engaged in activities involving solicitation and expenditure of funds to support and promote the mujahideen and jihad, including the printing and distribution of pro-jihad publications."

There were those words again, alluding to terrorism where there was not any evidence whatsoever of material support for terrorism. But strip away the scare tactics, and the prosecution's case evaporated. Muntasser was indicted not for something false that he said, but, rather, for failing to say something deemed relevant ("material") by the government, looking back. It's dangerous to have such an ill-defined concept of "material omission." Indeed, trial Judge F. Dennis Saylor IV, in throwing out the jury's guilty verdict, described the indictment as "a somewhat creative approach," adding that while prosecutors can at times be "creative," those efforts must be exercised "within reason."[52]

New organizations filing for tax-exempt status for the first time might not have a full understanding of all the activities that they will eventually undertake, so what would be considered "material" might require prefiguring the organization's future. The material omissions statute is even more dire for organizations that are already up and running, and which might carry out myriad administrative, fundraising, and other activities that are secondary and derivative of the primary mission. Since the amount of information and documentation supporting such an application could, in theory, be virtually unlimited (in theory, filers could provide all information to the IRS out of an excess of caution against making a material omission, but this is obviously impracticable and would, in any event, overwhelm the agency), this provision constitutes a veritable slippery slope for applicants and their lawyers. Surely every filer could be found to have left out *something* that a bureaucrat, or prosecutor, might after the fact deem arguably "material."

What's more, Care and its founders and officers clearly had a First Amendment right to voice their political and religious views in their newsletters and on their Website. (This is one reason why the indictment did not charge him, directly, for his and Care's views.) The IRS is not permitted to deny tax exemption because of the viewpoints expressed in an organization's newsletters. So an indictment claiming that this "material" information was not provided (note, too, that it was not specifically asked for) is legally dubious.

The conclusion one draws is that the government fashioned the prosecution as a "material omission" tax case because it was unable to find any evidence to justify a "material support of terrorism" prosecution. As Judge Saylor wrote in a post-verdict opinion tossing out all but one of the charges on which the jury found Muntasser guilty (a relatively minor one alleging a tenuously related false statement made by Muntasser in an interview by the FBI, concerning his travel, which Muntasser appealed), there was no evidence presented at the trial that any actual money was given to fighters, let alone to terrorists.[53] If the feds could get Muntasser convicted for some fraudulent activity, they would likely achieve what they were trying to do when they interrupted his lawsuit the day before his citizenship hearing. If you're not yet a citizen when you're convicted, you may get kicked out of the country and never become a citizen.

One of the defense team's expert witnesses, Marcus Owens, a tax lawyer and himself a former head of the IRS exempt organizations branch, told Muntasser's lawyers that Muntasser's case was the first prosecution of its kind under the material omissions statute. Because of the slippery slope in the "material facts" definition, the unprecedented application of the statute against a non-profit organization that the federal government simply didn't like should be enough to make any non-profit concerned about what it might not have disclosed to the IRS.

Additionally, Owens, when he took the stand for the defense, explained that, with regard to Care's newsletters, "the IRS had a rather clear position, that it was not going to probe religious speech. And decisions on whether an organization qualified for a tax exemption would be made on the basis of its activities, in particular, what it did with its money, was the money used for charitable purposes or not."[54]

However, the IRS apparently got all the information it needed in order to process Care's application. The bureaucrats in the IRS regional office covering Boston who initially reviewed Care's application actually noted the connection to relief activities in Afghanistan and Bosnia, which were considered areas of special foreign policy interest to the United States government, and they asked the national review office in Washington, then headed by Marcus Owens, to review it.[55] Thus, the material disclosed in Care's application was obviously sufficient to trigger this higher and more intensive level of IRS review. Even assuming that the government was correct in alleging that Muntasser had omitted material facts relevant to the IRS's review process (which Owens disputed), the national Exempt Organizations Division was in fact put on notice by the regional office of possible questions raised due to the nature of the activities and the area of the world in which they were to be carried out. The IRS agents could, obviously, have then asked Care more questions if they were concerned about anything in the filings. But the national-level bureaucrats saw what lower-level reviewers had flagged and concluded that they had seen enough; they decided not to ask Care any additional or clarifying questions.

Since Care's application was sufficient to trigger a higher level of review for its application, and the IRS staffers in Washington chose not to ask further questions, how can it be said that the application lacked sufficient material disclosures to put the IRS on notice? The case raises in bold relief the question of how a filer is supposed to figure out what would be a material omission in such a filing for tax-exempt status, and when such an application, which contains sufficient information to prompt a special review by, but no further questions from, the IRS, would be deemed criminally misleading. The lawyers on Muntasser's defense team,[56] and the former government officials and other experts consulted by Muntasser's lawyers, scratched their heads on this question throughout the entire case. The jury nonetheless convicted, and Muntasser was held in prison for five months until Judge Saylor, before sentencing, threw these particular charges out. (The government appealed.)

The government's use of the tax exemption application in a material omissions indictment was sufficiently worrisome that Owens discussed the issue at a February 2008 Washington Non-profit Legal and Tax Conference. His advice to other non-profits was reported in the widely read *Health Law Reporter*:

> The case, Owens continued, raises the stakes for exempt health care organizations, who are faced with completing the new Form 990 and who may inadvertently omit material or make a mistake answering an ambiguous question. "The problem is that we do not know where the government is going to go with this," he added.[57]

The challenge facing non-profits is, however, even more perplexing than Owens asserts. As the Muntasser prosecution makes clear, one can be indicted even when one's omission in failing to answer "an ambiguous question" is not at all "a mistake," but simply a logical, common, and almost predictable result of seeking to comply, in good faith, with such ambiguous questions and requirements.

"The government," wrote Judge Saylor with admirable candor when he threw out the conviction, "has had substantial difficulty articulating a clear theory of the case and explaining why the evidence and the law support their theory."[58] One of the most interesting aspects of Judge Saylor's decision to toss out almost the entirety of the jury's guilty findings was the primary legal precedent that he cited. Judge Saylor wrote that "a person can only be prosecuted where the person has a duty to disclose a particular matter to the government and failed to do so."[59] This requirement that prosecutors demonstrate that the person accused actually had such a duty was established, wrote Judge Saylor, by the opinion of the Court of Appeals for the First Circuit in *United States v. Anzalone*.[60]

This citation of the *Anzalone* case as the operative precedent was a particularly sweet vindication of the rule of law to two members of the Muntasser defense team who had served on the legal team that more than two decades earlier had convinced the First Circuit to overturn the money-laundering conviction of Theodore Anzalone (see Chapter One, concerning harassment of politicians), namely former Stanford Law School dean Kathleen Sullivan and me. The big question, of course, was whether the Court of Appeals would have the integrity to adhere to its own precedent when faced with the government's appeal of Judge Saylor's ruling.

• • ● • •

"Although the government undoubtedly has an interest in ensuring national security—an interest that might sometimes entail prosecuting transmitters and recipients of information whose behavior implicates the First Amendment—the Espionage Act, as written, is an unconstitutional vehicle through which to pursue such an interest." With these words, the *Harvard Law Review*, that bastion of the academic legal establishment, lambasted a U.S. district judge's refusal to dismiss a 2005 espionage indictment against two lobbyists for the American Israel Public Affairs Committee (AIPAC), a non-profit advocacy organization. "Much uncertainty," the *Review* noted with its characteristic understatement, "surrounds the government's right to criminally prosecute lobbyists, members of the press, and others who traffic in information deemed harmful to national security." "This uncertainty," concluded the editors, "stems largely from the incomprehensible nature of the espionage statutes."[61]

The reason why the Department of Justice brought such a strained prosecution was precisely because legal developments of the past quarter century have made it easy to twist old statutes to serve new purposes. Suddenly, activities long considered par for the course for the likes of Beltway insiders morphed into federal felonies of the utmost gravity, all without any action by Congress to change the wording of the Espionage Act.

Steven J. Rosen and Keith Weissman were classic issues specialists and lobbyists. They schmoozed with government sources about the status of issues important to AIPAC, and exchanged information with them as well as with members of the news media in an effort to influence public opinion and government action. There was nothing remarkable about them, except that they ended up indicted for espionage.

As the investigation leading up to their indictment quickened, both Rosen and Weissman left their jobs with AIPAC, an organization that long has been admired (or reviled, as the case may be, in some quarters) for its success in lobbying the United States government regarding the nation's policies in support of Israel. The highly respected *National Journal* in 2005 listed AIPAC as the second most powerful and effective lobby, after the National Rifle Association and on a par with the American Association of Retired Persons.[62]

Unlike many lobbyists who concentrate on influencing congressional opinion, Rosen and Weissman focused on members of the executive branch. In the course of doing their work, they had cultivated relationships with executive branch officials as well as other sources of information concerning the Middle East. One such relationship was with eventual co-defendant Lawrence A. Franklin. Franklin was employed by the Department of Defense and held a Top Secret security clearance with access to sensitive information about, among other matters, Iran, Franklin's major foreign policy interest and obsession. The indictment describes breakfast and lunch meetings at which policy issues were discussed and information from secret policy documents passed to the lobbyists. Rosen, in turn, passed along some of that information to members of the press, touting it as "a considerable story," as well as to a couple of Israeli diplomats. Rosen was also alleged to have called a senior fellow at a Washington think tank to discuss some of the information he'd received from Franklin. At one point, alleges the indictment, Franklin disclosed to Rosen and Weissman classified information concerning potential attacks on American forces in Iraq.

The first count of the indictment alleged a conspiracy to transmit information relating to the national defense to people not entitled to receive it. Franklin was charged with conveying information to Rosen and Weissman as well as to a foreign diplomat (said to be an Israeli), while Rosen and Weissman had conveyed information to journalists, diplomats, and others at AIPAC.

The provision of the Espionage Act used to indict Franklin related to the possession of confidential defense-related information by an official authorized to possess it. Franklin's guilt was fairly clear-cut. He was, after all, a government employee with certain secrecy obligations that he had voluntarily undertaken in connection with this job. He agreed to plead guilty even before he was indicted and to wear a secret "bug" while working with government agents to collect evidence against Rosen and Weissman. It was the portion of the indictment directed against the two non-government employees, Rosen and Weissman, that raised troubling questions about abuse of the statute's language, intent, and historical application:

> Whoever having unauthorized possession of [any document] relating to the national defense, or information relating to the national defense which information the possessor has reason to believe could be used to the injury of the United States or to the advantage of any foreign nation, willfully communicates...the same to any person not entitled to receive it...shall be fined...or imprisoned not more than ten years, or both.[63]

The application of this statute to two private citizens who were not working for the government and who did not have security clearances (and who therefore were not violating the agreed terms of confidentiality agreements such as existed between Franklin and the government) sent shockwaves through the world of private sector security analysts, lobbyists, and others. It is the mother's milk of lobbying, after all, for otherwise disparate groups of Americans to band together and pressure the government to favor their particular ethnic, racial, religious, occupational, political, or cultural groups. The process involves, in part, an exchange of information—often quite sensitive information. Many Irish-American citizens might recall similar exchanges of information from the days of tension and veritable political and religious warfare in Ireland.

The sudden notion that it constituted espionage to receive and disseminate confidential information on such matters in that cauldron of leaked information known as Washington startled many. Rosen, for one, was thrown for a loop: "I'm being looked at for things I've done for twenty-three years, which other foreign-policy groups, hundreds of foreign-policy groups, are doing."[64] A former chief privacy officer of the CIA, Leo Strickland, underscored how central these kinds of leaks were to reporting on the day's events: "Twice in the Clinton Administration we had proposals to broaden the [espionage] statute to include the recipients, not just the leakers, of classified information. *The New York Times* and *The Washington Post* went bat-shit about this legislation. They saw it as an attempt to shut down leaks."[65] And so Congress did nothing to amend the vague statute.

That didn't stop the feds from using it to go after Rosen and Weissman, and Virginia-based U.S. District Court judge T.S. Ellis III accepted their interpretation of the Espionage Act. He refused to dismiss the indictment.[66]

Judge Ellis understood the nature of the defendants' dilemma. He characterized the first leg of Rosen and Weissman's "constitutional challenge" as being "based on the principle that the Due Process clause of the Fifth Amendment prohibits punishment pursuant to a statute so vague that men of common intelligence must necessarily guess at its meaning and differ as to its application." While he agreed that "the phrase 'information relating to the national defense'" was "potentially quite broad," he ruled that the phrase "is limited and clarified by the requirements that the information be a government secret, i.e., that it is closely held by the government, and that the information is the type which, if disclosed, could threaten the national security of the United States." Because of these limitations, he ruled, the phrase actually "provides fair notice of what it encompasses and is also an adequate safeguard against arbitrary enforcement." One somehow doubts that a poll of typical Washington lobbyists and policy analysts would produce a similar conclusion about "fair notice."

The second prong of the defendants' vagueness challenge ("that they lacked constitutionally adequate notice as to who was 'entitled to receive' the national defense information") was similarly disposed of by Judge Ellis. He admitted, as he had to, that "the statute itself provides no definition of the phrase 'entitled to receive,' nor does it expressly delegate to the executive branch the authority to determine who is entitled to receive national defense information." He ruled, however, that other court decisions somehow clarified the statute by incorporating "the executive branch's classification regulations." He cited, as precedent for this conclusion, the 1984 case involving the prosecution of Samuel Loring Morison, a government employee working for Naval Intelligence with a security clearance who had signed a non-disclosure agreement. Morison had recognized that improper disclosure of secret information and documents would open him to prosecution, but nonetheless he had sold clearly classified photographs to the publication *Jane's Defence Weekly*.[67] Judge Ellis did not make clear how and why it was that two civilian lobbyists, not subject to a government confidentiality agreement or security clearance, were supposed to think that they were bound by the same rules as a government employee working for an intelligence agency pursuant to a clear confidentiality agreement.

Judge Ellis then evaluated Rosen's and Weissman's claim that the prosecution violated the First Amendment's guarantee of free speech. Ellis agreed that the case did raise First Amendment concerns. "In the broadest terms," he recognized, "the conduct at issue—collecting information about United States' foreign policy and discussing that information with government officials (both United States and foreign), journalists, and other participants in the foreign policy establishment—is at the core of the First Amendment's guarantees." He went even further, admitting that "even under a more precise description of the conduct—the passing of government secrets relating to the national defense to those not entitled to receive them in an attempt to influence United States foreign policy—the application of [the espionage statute] to the defendants is unquestionably still deserving of First Amendment scrutiny." He agreed that "the analysis of the First Amendment interests" depends upon the class of persons involved. Government employees and defense contractors, the judge noted, possess their access to information as a result of government rules and contractual agreements made known to them. Ellis recognized that Rosen and Weissman belong to quite a different class: "those who have not violated a position of trust with the government to obtain and disclose information, but have obtained the information from one who has." Astonishingly, however, he still agreed with the government's argument that the Espionage Act, by implication, could be applied to private citizens such as Rosen and Weissman, and concluded that the two lobbyists were subject to the statute.

Judge Ellis was not cavalier in ruling as he did. He was clearly disturbed. "In the end, it must be said that this is a hard case," he admitted at the conclusion of his 68-page opinion. But, of course, it is a harder case for the two defendants who were indicted under a radical expansion of the Espionage Act and ordered to stand trial, facing decades in prison for doing what many lobbyists and private policy analysts in the nation's capital consider to be their jobs. When the Court of Appeals added to the DOJ's burden of demonstrating unlawful intent, however, the new administration gave up the ghost and sought dismissal of this beleaguered indictment.[68]

Meanwhile, Congress, which has the authority to rewrite the espionage statute to clarify its boundaries and terms, has remained silent. The Department of Justice remains the primary arbiter of how far the statute should be expanded, and the judiciary seems loath, in an "age of terror," to second-guess or otherwise interfere.

The lesson of all of these cases, and countless others like them, is clear enough, even if the statutes are not. The Department of Justice has the tools to charge a wide range of members of civil society with serious national security-related violations, even when those alleged violations do not, by any reasonable stretch of the imagination, truly pose a danger to the nation's security. More striking, however, is the fact that these statutory and regulatory tools do not tell the average citizen quite what it is that they need to avoid doing in order to stand clear of the government's snare.

For Whom the Bell Tolls

———•••———

Creativity and inventiveness are honored and valued in many areas of life. Crafting innovative legal theories to ground criminal prosecutions should not be one of them. Congress should muster the political will to create whatever cutting-edge criminal statutes it deems essential that reflect contemporary conditions and needs. But it is unacceptable, meanwhile, to tease prosecutions out of statutes that do not clearly proscribe the conduct involved. New wine should be put into new, not old, bottles. Liberty and fairness are at stake.

In a special section on white collar crime published in *The National Law Journal* in July 2005, co-authors and attorneys Stephen G. Sozio and Earnest B. Gregory noted an "emerging trend."[1] Federal prosecutors were suddenly bringing criminal cases "against corporations and their managers in connection with work-place injuries and deaths." Having previously reserved criminal liability "for conduct showing the most flagrant disregard for worker safety," the feds were now prosecuting a broader array of conduct. The same trend has been seen in state enforcement of workplace safety, the authors noted, but only because state legislatures have amended old laws or passed new ones that redefine criminal behavior in the workplace. In contrast, federal prosecutors were seeking "to marshal a spectrum of existing laws that carry considerably stiffer penalties than those governing workplace safety alone," wrote Sozio and Gregory, citing a *New York Times* report.[2]

In other words, the statutes enacted by the Congress to deal with workplace safety issues were not sufficiently all-encompassing and onerous for the taste of federal prosecutors. So they have proceeded to do precisely what former Attorney General Robert Jackson, in 1940, warned his U.S. attorneys against: "pick people that he thinks he should get" and "then [search] the law books…to pin some offense on him."

It is not that Congress is unable to enact legislation tightening the criminal law governing workplace safety to carry a heavier penalty. A Wrongful Death Accountability Act, doing just that, was brought before Congress in 2003 and again in 2005, but it was going nowhere.[3] The Justice Department, in the meantime, did not feel the need to await passage of new legislation. Federal prosecutors simply combed the federal criminal code for an existing vehicle sufficiently vague (and severe) to arguably cover the targeted offense. And this, of course, lowered Congress's incentive to get its legislative act together.

It is tempting to see such prosecutorial zeal as heroic in its effort to compensate for weaknesses or paralysis in the legislative branch. But it also enhances the power of the executive branch in ways too few Americans, who over the past 30 years have been preoccupied with other forms of executive overreaching, fully grasp. This particular form of empowerment of the executive would have alarmed the nation's founders, to whom the power to indict, convict and punish was rightly seen as a potential engine of oppression.

Law under our chosen system performs its highest purpose when it limits government power, since history and experience show that governments tend to overuse their perceived authority. The King of England obtained his powers through divine anointment, aided by the accident of lineal succession. It was a crucial turn in the history of civilization and the rule of law when the English barons imposed the *Magna Carta* on King John in 1215, thereby circumscribing executive power and endowing the people with fledgling civil liberties. When it came time for the Americans to draw up their own constitutional charter, they too stressed the limitations on federal authority.

The assertion of federal criminal jurisdiction over a wide variety of matters, including those thought to be quintessentially local, has provoked something of a backlash among those who describe themselves as "federalists." However, federalists, who are primarily concerned with empowering states and regions while reducing the federal government's role, attend to those areas where federal jurisdiction is often clear (even if onerous) and where federal mandates are set forth in language all-too-readily understood by those subject to regulation. For their part, "libertarians" concern themselves primarily with the breadth and depth of both state and federal control over too many aspects of life. What has received little attention, however, are those areas where the Justice Department has asserted, on the basis of the vaguest provisions of federal law, the authority to severely punish conduct either not intuitively malignant or that state authorities should pursue, if at all, via civil or administrative proceedings.

Our Constitution includes a substantial number of procedural rights that guarantee a fair trial: representation by legal counsel, trial by jury, trial before an independent judiciary, and the right of a defendant not to self-incriminate. But all the procedural rights in the world are for naught if the defendant is unable to understand what it is for which he or she stands indicted.

• • ● • •

The more subtle theme of this book, which deserves greater stress here, is that over the years the federal judiciary has acted too often as a handmaiden to federal prosecutors in their misguided efforts to nail their targets with vague, outmoded statutes badly in need of clarification or revision. Perhaps no other case better illustrates the point than that of Bradford C. Councilman, who was tried before the U.S. District Court for Massachusetts on wiretap charges. This was the same court that heard the Anzalone cash transaction reporting case in 1984, and saw through the feds' strategy to prosecute conduct that Congress had not yet outlawed. After a long, expensive battle, Anzalone was finally exonerated, thanks to the federal appellate bench that then sat in Boston. Nearly twenty years later, Councilman found himself in the maw of a changed court (and a changed judicial culture) and wasn't so fortunate.

Councilman was vice-president of Interloc, Inc., a company based in Greenfield, Massachusetts, that provided an online listing service for rare and out-of-print books. Interloc supplied a number of its book-dealer customers with electronic mail addresses (ending in @interloc.com) and acted as an Internet service provider (ISP) for those customers.[4]

Councilman was charged in 2001 with making, without his customers' knowledge, extra copies of email messages passing on the Interloc system between book dealers and Amazon.com, the giant Internet bookstore. The government charged that Councilman had made the extra copies to learn what the dealers were doing, in terms of pricing and such, which gave him and his company an unfair commercial advantage. In other words, Councilman and his company allegedly took advantage of their role as ISP in order to secretly gain a commercial advantage in their role as book dealers. Councilman maintained that he never read the messages and that those copies that were made would have been made solely for back-up storage purposes.

The two issues in the case were whether Councilman was indeed the person who made the copies of the emails (the *factual* question) and, if so, whether that conduct violated federal criminal law (the *legal* issue). The DOJ claimed that Councilman's alleged actions violated the federal wiretap statute, which outlawed the unauthorized interception and disclosure of electronic communications. All parties to the case, as well as District Judge Michael Ponsor, agreed that the determinative legal question was whether the conduct, attributed by the government to Councilman, violated the Wiretap Act.

This seemingly simple question proved anything but. The federal wiretap laws (originally written before the dawn of the Internet, often amended, not always clear, and frequently lagging behind the whip-crack speed of technological change) contained an apparent exception. Both sides agreed that the communications had been intercepted and copied while the messages were in temporary storage on Interloc's computer system on their way from sender to receiver, not while streaming through wires. Interloc's computer system, in other words, was a way station where a message stopped briefly during its journey from sender to recipient. The message would be in Interloc's system completely properly. Councilman argued that any copy made there, for whatever reason, was not the product of an unlawful interception or "wiretap." And here was the rub.

Councilman's lawyer, my then-law partner Andrew Good, moved to dismiss the indictment for failure to charge an activity that amounted to a crime. Councilman's position was that because the government agreed that the communications were in electronic storage rather than in electronic transit when the extra copies were made, no wiretap had occurred. The government argued that a violation of the Wiretap Act had occurred even though the communications were not traveling in a "wire" when intercepted.

It was the fabled question of "how many angels can dance on the head of a pin?"—a quintessential technicality. But it was a crucial technicality, for the answer determined whether the routine making of such extra copies, by Councilman or by thousands of other ISPs, even for a perfectly benign purpose, violated a serious federal criminal statute. Yet there was another consideration that should have been taken into account: Was the correct interpretation of the statute (whatever that might be) obvious enough that Councilman could be said to have knowingly and intentionally violated the law?

It is crucial to understand that Councilman, working for an Internet service provider, was not in the same position as an outside party seeking to tap into the line and intercept the emails involved. Such interception by a stranger would easily be deemed wiretapping; it would clearly violate the statute but also would be intuitively wrong. In contrast, Councilman argued that the law enabled him, as an ISP, to have lawful access to the emails while in electronic storage. Interloc and its employees did, after all, have lawful access to the messages in order to perform their assigned ISP task of sending the messages further along. The question was whether the interception statute was violated by Councilman's allegedly making extra copies of the contents of messages while they were momentarily, and lawfully, in his custody.

Furthermore, there would have been a perfectly reasonable purpose for making extra copies of the transmitted messages—to provide back-up in the event of a system failure. If such an action were to be declared a crime, it should be done by clear statute, not by twisting an existing law to perform a function for which it was not obviously meant. It was particularly dangerous to seek to stretch the wiretap law to cover such a ubiquitous and seemingly proper practice, where an ISP would have no clue that it was committing what the DOJ deemed a felony.

The difficulty of the question threw the federal judicial system in Boston into almost comic paroxysms of confusion and disagreement. Judge Ponsor, an intelligent and conscientious trial judge, initially ruled in July 2002 that Councilman's alleged conduct, at the very least, violated the spirit of the statute. He denied the motion to dismiss the indictment filed by Good and scheduled a trial.

But then, as Judge Ponsor was preparing to conduct the trial, he learned that the U.S. Court of Appeals for the Ninth Circuit, which has jurisdiction over a number of states on the West Coast, decided a case (*Konop v. Hawaiian Airlines*[5]) involving the interpretation of the same provision of the Wiretap Act, and ruled in favor of the position advanced by Councilman's lawyers in Boston. The *Konop* case involved a civil dispute between an employee and the company for which he worked. The employee claimed that the employer unlawfully gained access to his secure Website and disclosed the contents of that Website, in violation of the Wiretap Act and the Stored Communications Act. Admitting that the statutory scheme was "a confusing and uncertain area of the law" because technology had gotten so far ahead of Congress, the Ninth Circuit concluded that it did not constitute "wiretapping" for a party to access online communications after they were no longer in transit but instead had landed in storage.

Judge Ponsor reversed himself and dismissed Councilman's indictment in February 2003.[6] The Boston federal prosecutors disagreed vehemently, even though in the *Konop* case the Justice Department, appearing as a non-party "friend of the court," had informed the court that it was the government's view that the Wiretap Act did *not* cover stored messages.

There was some speculation, particularly among privacy advocates and civil libertarians, that in *Konop* the government may have *narrowly* read the statute in order to protect government agents from being sued for post-9/11 intrusions into stored messages, while on the East Coast it was trying to convict a private citizen under a *broad* reading.

Judge Ponsor would not tolerate these double standards.[7] He concluded that the DOJ and the legal system could have only one interpretation of the statute, that the Ninth Circuit opinion seemed correct, and hence there was no illegal "interception" of email in Councilman's case.

Unsurprisingly, the Justice Department appealed, but a three-judge appeals court panel affirmed Judge Ponsor's decision. By a vote of 2-1, a panel of judges on the United States Court of Appeals for the First Circuit agreed with Judge Ponsor's legal analysis. The dissenting judge, after a long and complex analysis of both the law and the technology involved, concluded, remarkably, that the statute did apply to Councilman's conduct largely because "I find it inconceivable that Congress could have intended such a result" that would exclude such conduct from the statute's ambit. Congressional intent, in other words, should trump what lawmakers actually say in the text of a statute, an odd notion if citizens are supposed to be able to figure out their legal obligations when their liberty is at stake. Under this tortured logic, the citizen is supposed to see into the minds of legislators, rather than to follow the statute's words.[8] The other two members of the court panel did not buy it and ruled in Councilman's favor.

The panel's decision set off an uproar. Prosecutors, political figures, *The New York Times*, *The Washington Post*, industry officials, and privacy activists decried such a narrow reading of the Wiretap Act. Many filed friend-of-the-court briefs supporting the DOJ's position, urging the First Circuit to reconsider the three-judge panel's majority view. Vermont Senator Patrick Leahy, one of the key sponsors of the 1986 Electronic Communications Privacy Act, denounced the decision on the Senate floor. "If allowed to stand, this decision threatens to eviscerate Congress's careful efforts to ensure that privacy is protected in the modern information age," he charged. (Obviously, those "careful efforts" were not sufficiently careful so that ordinary people, or even extraordinary judges, could agree on what Congress meant and what the statute required.) The Electronic Privacy Information Center (EPIC), one of the nation's premier Internet-privacy advocacy groups, warned that the First Circuit's ruling would encourage ISPs to feel "free to monitor their customer's email for their own competitive advantage."

Interestingly, the ambiguity of the statute put civil libertarians, in particular, at odds. Those who emphasized privacy protection were outraged by the panel's decision. Those more concerned with the "due process" need for clear statutes before convicting citizens, saw it as something of a victory. And it surely created some unease that the Department of Justice took one position in the Ninth Circuit when it feared its agents being accused of invasion of a citizen's privacy, but an opposite position in the First Circuit when the government was the accuser against the citizen.

Under intense public and congressional pressure, the First Circuit agreed to reconsider the case *en banc* (that is, by the full membership of the court), and on August 11, 2005, the full court reversed the decision of the three-judge panel. The court's *en banc* opinion pivoted on a question central in the criminal law: "whether Councilman had fair warning that the Act would be construed to cover his alleged conduct in a criminal case, and whether the rule of lenity or other principles require us to construe the act in his favor." The five-judge majority of the court claimed to "find no basis to apply any of the fair warning doctrines." Nor did they see fit to apply the "rule of lenity," which would hold, essentially, that if there were reasonable doubt over the interpretation of a criminal statute, the defendant had to be given the benefit of that doubt.

The court's analysis was remarkable for the degree to which it dismissed all of the doubts previously expressed about the meaning and reach of the Wiretap Act. In response to Councilman's argument that the "plain text" of the statute did not cover his actions, the majority said: "As often happens under close scrutiny, the plain text is not so plain." But this lack of clarity, rather than working for Councilman, somehow worked against him. The majority claimed to resolve "this continuing ambiguity" in the statute's language by looking to the legislative history of the enactment, a notoriously difficult task under the best of circumstances. Congress intended to give "broad" protection to electronic communications, they concluded, and so the panel's prior *Councilman* decision was flawed.

The majority of First Circuit judges must have been a bit self-conscious about reinstating an indictment that was so controversial and that had perplexed so many fine judicial minds on both coasts. The court thus could not entirely deny that there was *some* degree of ambiguity here. But the rule of lenity, the majority intoned, applies only in cases of "grievous ambiguity in a penal statute." In this case, the majority remarked in one of its more bizarre formulations, there was only "garden-variety, textual ambiguity." "The Wiretap Act is not unconstitutionally vague in its application here," concluded the majority. "From its text, a person of average intelligence would, at the very least, be on notice" that Councilman's activity was covered.

It was this last part of the majority's opinion reinstating the indictment that drew the seeming ire of Circuit Judge Juan Torruella, who issued a stinging, and illuminating, dissent, with which only one fellow judge agreed. Judge Torruella called the majority's interpretation of the statute "an unfortunate act of judicial legislation," and pointed out that the defect in the law can only be addressed by Congress's rewriting the statute. "It is not by coincidence that every court that has passed upon the issue before us has reached a conclusion opposite to that of the *en banc* majority," he wrote. Even if the majority's interpretation of the statute were correct, the rule of lenity surely must be applied in this case: "Councilman is being held to a level of knowledge which would not be expected of any of the judges who have dealt with this problem," to say nothing of "men and women of common intelligence." "If the issue presented be 'garden-variety,'" as the majority decision had claimed, "this is a garden in need of a weed killer."

Nine years after his alleged criminal acts, Bradford Councilman was finally put to trial before a jury of his peers to determine the factual question of the case—whether he was the person who copied the stored emails and thereby committed what the Court of Appeals said would be a federal felony. At Councilman's trial, a government witness conceded that the email copies were periodically purged because the accumulation of duplicate copies intermittently overloaded the system. This fact made it more likely that the copies were made routinely by someone at the company to supply a temporary back-up in the event of accidental deletion of the original message before it arrived at its destination. An FBI agent testified at the trial that when a cooperating witness tried to explain this to the prosecutor during a trial preparation session, the prosecutor balked and asked the witness and his lawyer to confer, whereupon the witness retracted the innocuous explanation for the back-up procedure. The jury returned a verdict of "not guilty" on February 6, 2007. Jurors have their own way, sometimes, of clearing weeds.

So the Court of Appeals for the First Circuit completed the journey from the principled jurisprudence of the *Anzalone* case to upholding, at all costs, the 1995 convictions of Walter Lachman and Maurice Subilia (discussed in Chapter Eight), and the indictment against Bradford Councilman. It marked a new age. The legal devices that the *Anzalone* court said were symbolic of the Soviet Union's legal system (where prosecutors would go after citizens armed with the nearest arguably analogous criminal statute if none covering the defendant's precise activity is available) have gained respectability and, indeed, the status of legal precedent. Of course, increased judicial cooperation with Justice Department prosecutions is not limited to Boston. Nor is it restricted to white collar prosecutions in the areas of export control and the Internet. Rather, the garden of federal criminal law is overrun with weeds throughout the landscape.

• • ● • •

Wrongful prosecution of innocent conduct that is twisted into a felony charge has wrecked many an innocent life and career. Whole families have been devastated, as have myriad relationships and entire companies. Indeed, one of the most pernicious effects of the Justice Department's techniques—too often given warrant by the courts—is that they wreck important and socially beneficial relationships within civil society. Family members have been pitted against one another. Friends have been coerced into testifying against friends even when the testimony has been less than honest. Corporations have turned against employees and former partners to save the companies from obliteration, following scripts entirely at odds with the truth and subject to the sole approval of federal prosecutors. Newspaper reporters have been pitted against confidential sources. Artists, including those critical of the government, have been subjected to Kafkaesque harassment. Lawyers and clients have found themselves adversaries, as have physicians and patients, where enormous pressure has been placed on the ill to turn against those in whose capable professional hands they placed themselves in search of treatment. No society can possibly benefit from having its government so recklessly attack and render asunder such vital social and professional relationships.

But the damage extends beyond individual lives. We as a society face collective fallout from the proliferation of these dark practices. The Founders' idea of separation of powers, in which abuse of power would be checked by inter-branch monitoring and even rivalry, was to be supplemented by a vibrant civil society that would also check excessive government power. Over the past 30 years, federal prosecutors' efforts to divide us have served to both increase executive power (aided and abetted by a largely quiescent judiciary) and deflate the capacity of civil society to check executive overreach. You might say it's a twofer.

Historically, the independent bar has acted as a counterweight to government power. In recent decades, however, it has been subject to increasing pressure and intimidation under formless statutes applied recklessly to the lawyer's craft. Thus far, the independent bar has survived, but its vulnerability is palpable.

Consider the recent imbroglio over the federal government's attempt to intimidate lawyers representing "war on terror" prisoners held by military authorities at Guantánamo Bay, Cuba. During a January

11, 2007, radio interview, Charles "Cully" Stimson, then the deputy assistant secretary of defense for detainee affairs, declared that he was shocked that lawyers at some of the nation's preeminent law firms were donating legal services to the detainees. "I think, quite honestly," he said, "when corporate CEOs see that those firms are representing the very terrorists who hit their bottom line back in 2001, those CEOs are going to make those law firms choose between representing terrorists or representing reputable firms."[9] Stimson, speaking with what many sophisticated observers felt was the support of Bush administration higher-ups, appeared to be suggesting an industry boycott of firms donating legal services to the suspected terrorist detainees.[10]

Stimson may have expected his barely veiled threat to intimidate lawyers into steering clear of Guantánamo. Instead, the legal community and corporate sector loudly and clearly supported the independent bar's long tradition of representing *pro bono publico* (for the public good) those accused of even the most heinous crimes. The outcry caused military and administration officials to distance themselves from Stimson's remarks. Stimson was thrown overboard and soon resigned. The Bar Association of San Francisco, it was reported, even launched an investigation (probably an ill-considered overreaction) into whether Stimson violated legal ethics by suggesting a boycott of law firms for performing such a service.[11] The government's unhappiness with the independence of the private bar was evident, but the administration chose not to make its stand on an issue as deeply ingrained in our legal culture as the right of even the most unpopular defendant to a skillful defense. Civil society won this skirmish.

But the question is whether the independence of the bar will flourish as vibrantly in the future as it has in the past, especially when threatened with prosecution. One need not agree with the activities engaged in nor positions taken by the private bar or any of the professions or professionals discussed in this book to understand why their health and independence are essential to both American freedom and the system of checks and balances that underlies constitutional liberty. It is this balance that is at risk when any citizen or group within civil society can be dubbed criminal by an inflated executive branch for engaging in ordinary activities common to their respective professional missions. When one is attacked, all should feel attacked, as the liberty of all is put at risk.

• • ● • •

What is to be done?

My teacher, colleague, and friend Alan Dershowitz has suggested in his Foreword that the problem is essentially structural and might be ameliorated by separating the prosecutorial from the political functions of the office of the attorney general. While there is some validity to Dershowitz's concern about the relationship between presidents and their attorneys general, I am skeptical that such a reform would accomplish much. Although a culture dangerous to American liberty has developed within the Justice Department, my view is that the problem lies principally with the history of federal criminal law itself, which has become increasingly unmoored from traditional common law notions of criminal intent and the clarity of criminal statutes. Federal prosecutorial culture has indeed been driven by the twin forces of politics and ambition, but those human vices (if vices they be) are present as well in state prosecutors. As the parable of Eliot Spitzer and Hank Greenberg demonstrates, even the most ambitious state prosecutors are loath to risk using state criminal law in the same fashion as the DOJ uses federal law. For one thing, state prosecutors have to deal with state judges who function in the common law tradition, where guilt combines legal and moral components. For another, state statutes, more often than not, are comprehensible.

If I am right, we must foster the realization that the Justice Department's tactics too often are employed not to protect, but to attack law-abiding society. While it is true, as Dershowitz posits, that sometimes creative criminal "miscreants" cleverly get around the letter of the law (especially laws that have become obsolete) and therefore tempt equally creative prosecutors to stretch the law, it is also true that too many ordinary, well-meaning, and innocent people get caught in the maw of the Department of Justice's prosecutorial machinery. For them, life becomes nightmarish, like an episode in a Franz Kafka novel.

Too often, the DOJ has successfully convinced the public, and an often all-too-gullible press, that its prosecutors are acting to clean up some nest of corruption or dire threat to the nation. In the kinds of crusades to which we have become accustomed and find far too comforting, the DOJ has often managed to enlist the press as a cheering section rather than as an appropriately skeptical Fourth Estate. Reporters are too willing to sit down with their prosecutorial sources to learn about the evil-doers in the dock, without doing the hard work of understanding why and how the government claims their conduct broke the law, or even why and how they are supposedly bad people. Reporters must begin to enlist the aid of defense lawyers, as well as the few academics who understand these prosecutions, to offer sophisticated and critical reporting of federal prosecutions. Reporters who cover legal stories might also spend some time in law school and in apprentice legal practice.

All of this is not to say, of course, that many of those prosecuted are not real criminals who engaged in real crimes defined by clear and reasonable laws. But the growing exceptions are far too numerous to miss, and the burgeoning phenomenon of prosecuting the innocent on the basis of undecipherable statutes and regulations is too dangerous to ignore. Reporters should spend less time rushing to cover such photo-ops as the traditional "perp walk," the public walk-of-shame, perfected by Rudolph Giuliani, former United States Attorney for the Southern District of New York, and more time learning the realities of our increasingly troubled and troubling federal criminal justice system.

Of course, criminal defense lawyers, especially in the area of white collar crime, are not always helpful to reporters seeking to learn whether a particular prosecution is real or faux. A growing percentage of members of the criminal defense bar are alumni of the Department of Justice, and far too many, though hardly all, have imbibed the culture of the DOJ and carry it into their white collar defense careers. Too many feel that if their clients have been indicted, they must have violated the law, and that if they are being prosecuted by the DOJ, they are likely to be convicted. Such lawyers all too often do not believe in the innocence of even their innocent clients, and, in any event, think that an effective defense is rarely available in a federal prosecution. Hence, plea bargaining, rather than vigorous defense, becomes the order of the day. With plea bargaining comes the pernicious practice (to borrow again Professor Dershowitz's seemingly cynical but all-too-accurate phrase) of teaching the witness not only to sing, but also to compose.

Journalists also should be far more skeptical when reporting, as truth, the testimony of witnesses who have been pressured, with threats and/or rewards, to suddenly turn on former colleagues and claim that activities that they themselves engaged in and defended for a long time suddenly appear to be criminal. Testimony and sentencing deals must be scrutinized by an independent press, not by Fourth Estate lackeys. Rewards given to witnesses by prosecutors, often carried out by sentencing judges, in exchange for testimony against others should be viewed as bribery or threats. Indeed, the practice should be abolished altogether, either by court rule or congressional legislation. Shouldn't the press be aiding that effort? After all, no self-respecting legal system, especially one plagued by vague laws, can tolerate such tactics and still claim to value truth and justice.

Criminal defense attorneys must begin to view themselves, especially in cases such as those discussed in this book, more as civil liberties lawyers. Their job should be to protect liberty itself, as well as their clients. At the deepest level, those two goals can and should be seen as complementary. Many lawyers are reluctant to talk publicly about the unfairness of the prosecutions against their clients, concerned about ubiquitous court rules restricting pre-trial publicity that supposedly might influence a future jury. Such rules, when applied too broadly, are also likely unconstitutional, as prior restraints on speech that defeat rather than promote justice. Besides, the typical justification for such pre-trial publicity rules is that they are meant to protect potential jurors from being prejudiced. Yet such a justification is entirely irrelevant after a trial when all that is left is an appeal before appellate judges.

The application of these rules, as well as judicial "gag orders" imposed under their authority, should be challenged by defense lawyers in appropriate cases. After all, under the current circumstances, many an innocent man, woman, organization, and company will end up forgoing a jury trial. A vicious circle has developed: Lawyers are constrained against fighting for their innocent clients in the court of public opinion, making it more likely that such clients will end up pleading guilty to avoid the risk of staggeringly long sentences meted out to those convicted after often unfair jury trials.

Judges play an important role in perpetuating a system that is becoming increasingly corrupt. They pretend to believe witnesses whose testimony has been forged under enormous undue pressure, and they even praise and reward those witnesses with reduced sentences for their "cooperation," even when that cooperation has been directed to prosecutors rather than to justice. If judges continue to allow bought or coerced testimony, then pressure must be brought to bear on Congress to enact legislation outlawing the practice. Judges who go along with this system are undermining justice, not administering it, and they should be treated as such rather than honored for their "public service." The proverbial emperor, though donning a black robe, in reality has no clothes and should not be treated otherwise.

As every judge on the federal bench knows, there is a clause in the body of the Constitution, less well known than the various amendments in the Bill of Rights, that prohibits Congress from enacting "any ex post facto Law."[12] *Black's Law Dictionary*, the standard work in the field, defines such a law as one "that impermissibly applies retroactively, [especially] in a way that negatively affects a person's rights, as by criminalizing an action that was legal when it was committed."[13] That clause is too rarely used in the modern era. It should be reinvigorated. If a prosecution is brought on the basis of a vague statute, and if there was no reasonable warning to the defendant that he was committing a crime, the indictment should be dismissed. Judges should not twist themselves, and the statutes they are charged with enforcing, utterly out of shape in order to do the DOJ's bidding.

Yet another provision of the Constitution should be reinvigorated in the battle against vague statutes. At one point in American history, as discussed in Chapter One, the federal courts more carefully enforced the "due process" clauses of the Fifth Amendment (applying to the federal government) and Fourteenth Amendment (applying to the states) in order to invalidate criminal convictions based on statutes that are so vague that people of ordinary intelligence cannot understand what conduct is proscribed. The federal courts need to take this constitutional right more seriously. Where not only ordinary citizens but even federal judges disagree about the meaning of a statute, as happened in the Bradford Councilman case, it does not take a legal genius to recognize that the law is hopelessly ambiguous.

Alone among the Supreme Court justices, Antonin Scalia has figured out precisely how dangerous a tool for intimidating public officials the Congress, abetted by a pliant judiciary, has handed to federal prosecutors. Justice Scalia's insight and concern were voiced most clearly and urgently in a 2009 case involving the "mail fraud" prosecution of lower-echelon Chicago city employees who, in Scalia's words, "received no direct personal benefit from the patronage they doled out on behalf of their political masters."[14] The prosecution was brought under a legislative expansion of the mail fraud statute to include any "scheme or artifice to deprive another of the intangible right of honest services."[15] (Ironically and almost comically, this phrase had been added by Congress to the mail fraud statute in response to an earlier Supreme Court decision refusing to expand the scope of the statute, as prosecutors had sought to do, without a legislated amendment.[16]) Scalia dissented from the court's refusal to review the Court of Appeals' affirmance of the city workers' conviction.

> If the "honest services" theory—broadly stated, that officeholders and employees owe a duty to act only in the best interests of their constituents and employers—is taken seriously and carried to its logical conclusion, presumably the statute also renders criminal a state legislator's decision to vote for a bill because he expects it will curry favor with

a small minority essential to his reelection; a mayor's attempt to use the prestige of his office to obtain a restaurant table without a reservation; a public employee's recommendation of his incompetent friend for a public contract; and any self-dealing by a corporate officer.

While "it is one thing to enact and enforce clear rules against certain types of corrupt behavior," noted Scalia, it is "quite another to mandate a freestanding, open-ended duty to provide 'honest services'—with the details to be worked out case-by-case." Scalia decried the improper role that federal prosecutors assumed "to define the fiduciary duties that a town alderman or school board trustee owes to his constituents." He further complained about the potential for "abuse by headline-grabbing prosecutors in pursuit of local officials, state legislators, and corporate CEOs who engage in any manner of unappealing or ethically questionable conduct."

Scalia discerned the heart of the matter when he warned: "It is simply not fair to prosecute someone for a crime that has not been defined until the judicial decision that sends him to jail." And he ended his short, six-page dissent decrying the Court for refusing to review the "expansion of criminal liability that this case exemplifies," concluding: "Indeed, it seems to me quite irresponsible to let the current chaos prevail." But, of course, the chaos and the unfairness are destined to prevail until at least five justices, not just one, see and act on the problem. Still, it is refreshing to have a Supreme Court justice worry not only that the application of the statute might have been unconstitutionally vague, but that the prosecution was patently unfair.

• • ● • •

If we desire to effectuate such changes in practice and attitude, how would we begin? Recently, I found the key to answering this question while reading a Supreme Court brief filed in an important free speech case. The case was *Scheidler v. National Organization for Women (NOW)*, decided by the high court in February 2006.[17] The question before the Court was whether anti-abortion protesters could be punished as "racketeers" under the incredibly loosely worded Racketeer Influenced and Corrupt Organization (RICO) Act. RICO was originally enacted to prosecute "organized crime" and to deprive its members of their ill-gotten gains. It was eventually turned against a wide spectrum of citizens: business executives, political activists, and others.

In *Scheidler*, NOW tried to adapt the civil provisions of RICO as well as the federal extortion laws to obtain a ruinous money judgment against national anti-abortion groups. NOW wanted to punish and deter protests aimed at preventing the operation of abortion clinics. Also at stake was whether the federal court could issue a nationwide injunction barring certain types of anti-abortion protests. Had the pro-choice groups succeeded, there would have been an extraordinarily dangerous precedent that would have lumped together perfectly legitimate exercises in the constitutionally protected rights of free speech and assembly, along with criminal activities involving violence.

The case divided not only pro-choice and anti-choice groups, but also political progressives who were in favor of the right to choose an abortion, and civil libertarians who were pro-choice but were unwilling to destroy the First Amendment in the process. It was an extraordinary case that sorely tested political alliances as well as the idea of principled, viewpoint-neutral adherence to civil liberties.

Suddenly, I came across a friend-of-the-court brief filed by, of all organizations, the AFL-CIO. For what possible reason, I asked myself, would the nation's premier labor union want to file a brief in an abortion case? While the union tended to be sympathetic to the right to choose, it was officially agnostic on the question since abortion was not one of labor's pressing issues. I decided to make some inquiries of the union's legal counsel, and my question was answered. AFL-CIO lawyers were concerned that a victory for the pro-choice plaintiffs would create a precedent enabling businesses to file lawsuits and obtain injunctions, based on the federal racketeering and extortion statutes, that would interfere with labor strikes, protests, and pickets. If Operation Rescue and the Pro-Life Action League could be penalized under such vague laws for engaging in vehement demonstrations against abortion clinics, then, reasoned the AFL-CIO lawyers insightfully, any labor union could similarly be put out of business for aggressive picketing activities. And if the civil RICO provisions, combined with extortion law, were to apply to such conduct, there was no principled reason why, the next time, the criminal provisions could not be invoked in a ruinous indictment against participating labor organizations and individuals.

The labor movement thus came to the aid of organizations for which it otherwise had no particular sympathy and with which it did not politically or ideologically identify. It was, I thought, a brilliant and principled move, the kind of broad strategic thinking few advocacy organizations are known for. The union's move demonstrated how, when it comes to rights, *all* sectors of civil society have precisely the same interest in preserving the protections conferred by law, properly understood. As the free speech civil libertarian Nat Hentoff recognized in the title of one of his First Amendment books, "free speech for me but not for thee" is not a winning maxim for a free society.

What this teaches us is that, when it comes to protecting the constitutional right to be free from prosecution under vague statutes that the average citizen cannot understand, all sectors of civil society have a stake in vindicating that interest. Filing friend-of-the-court briefs, lobbying for legislative or regulatory change, writing newspaper op-ed columns or letters to the editor, and other such advocacy should not be limited to supporting only one's self and one's own kind. Rather, such activities should be directed toward supporting the legal principles that protect us all. Americans need a new sense of the nature of true community, a common interest in protecting the rights even of those toward whom we might have no keen identification nor special affection.

The battle to restore proper balance between the power of federal prosecutors and civil society cannot be fought along lines separating liberals from conservatives, law-and-order advocates from libertarians, populists from industry leaders, reporters from moguls, or any of the other categories into which our increasingly fractious society sorts us. In this arena, the divide between self-interest and the interest of others disappears. When the feds appear on the scene, claiming to represent the public interest by going after some citizen who had no reasonable way of knowing that his or her conduct could be deemed a felony, do not ask for whom the bell tolls. It tolls for all.

ACKNOWLEDGMENTS

This project has been a near obsession since the week in October 1990 when I sat down and spewed out an initial 30-page outline that encapsulated my thinking about the changes in federal prosecutions that were accounting for an increasing number of people being sent to prison for doing things—often rather ordinary and intuitively acceptable things—that I did not believe violated any federal criminal statute. I've spent many years since then talking with friends, clients, associates, and others about this disturbing phenomenon. Many of them have been exceedingly generous with their time, intelligence, insights, experiences, good judgment, and patience. It has proven impossible for me to remember the names of all of those who have helped me along the way, but when it became obvious that I was going to undertake this book, I started doing my best to keep track.

Samuel Abady, whose experience in criminal law and generosity with his time and skill proved invaluable.

Jeanne Baker, friend and former law partner, with whom I went through some of the experiences chronicled in this book.

Charles "Buzzy" Baron, the quintessential teacher, whose insights were generously shared.

John "Jay" Barter, skillful lawyer and colleague, who shared with me his analyses.

Peter Berkowitz, fighter in the academic and cultural trenches, whose wide-ranging intellect is as bothered by prosecutorial excess as by academic idiocy.

David Boaz, freedom fighter extraordinaire, who, from his perch at the Cato Institute, was one of the earliest in the political and publishing arenas who, at crucial moments, encouraged me to proceed with this project.

Walter G. Bradley, who urged me to do what he has been doing— synthesizing a lifetime of experiences and insights to be picked up and acted upon by others.

Bob Chatelle, who gave me his views that were always informed by his passion for justice.

Laurie P. Cohen, former investigative journalist of great skill, who encouraged and advised me from the earliest stages.

Philip G. Cormier, colleague and lawyer, who always had the right detail handy.

Alan Dershowitz, fellow Brooklyn expatriate, extraordinary teacher, then colleague, and finally devoted friend, with whom I've lived so many professional and personal experiences, and who has acted as a sounding board for me over these many decades.

Elsa Dorfman, my beloved and adored wife, portrait photographer, who has helped me see more than merely what I look like, and who has encouraged me to complete this long-gestating project despite the sacrifices in so many aspects of our lives together, particularly in the past four years.

Nancy Neveloff Dubler, dear friend since we met in law school, on whose wisdom and judgment I've come to rely in so many areas.

David Duncan, lawyer, on whose judgment and generosity I can always rely.

Susan Estrich, law teacher, activist, writer, polemicist, lawyer, whose friendship and encouragement and good judgment have been so important on this project.

Louis Fischer, former government lawyer, now in private practice, for his wise insights.

Cathy Fleming, "white collar" defense lawyer, who does it right and was generous with her insights.

Maurie Fox-Warren, whose accounting skill and judgment not only keeps me on the safe side of the tax man, but whose assistance on the accounting issues was generously provided.

Nancy Gertner, dear friend and colleague since we met after her Seventh Circuit clerkship, with whom I shared some of the most formative experiences recounted in this book, for her always-appreciated judgment and encouragement.

Sally Goodson, for her insight into her physician brother's outrageous case.

Malick W. Ghachem, legal scholar and practitioner, and civil libertarian, who has been so supportive of this project.

Andrew Good, long-time law partner, lawyer of consummate skill and tenacity, who litigated several of the cases discussed in this book.

Michael Greco, tireless fighter, from within the legal establishment, for justice and decency.

Kenneth Hausman, for sharing with me details of the Frank Quattrone case that he so skillfully litigated.

Jon Hiatt, attorney with the AFL-CIO, who was generous in providing documents and insight.

Suzanne D. Hill, extraordinary office manager of the Silverglate & Good law firm (now Good & Cormier), who helped keep me organized and who made many salutary suggestions essential to the success of this project.

Edward S. Hochman, lawyer and extraordinary intellectual gadfly, who encouraged me in this project and always let me know when he disagreed.

N. Richard "Dick" Janis, one of those relatively rare former federal prosecutors with the insight and skill to put his talents to work in the cause of justice.

Peter Kadzis, my long-time editor at *The Boston Phoenix,* on whose wisdom and good judgment I've always been able to count.

Ralph Kaplan, who was very helpful in my discussion of certain business and investment practices.

Roger Kimball, head of Encounter Books, whose infectious enthusiasm for and understanding of this project, and whose intuitive grasp of the importance of liberty from government overreaching caused me to choose him to publish this book the minute I sat down in his office, face-to-face, for the first time.

Katie Leishman, investigative reporter extraordinaire, who encouraged me to write this from the first day she heard about it.

Anthony Lewis, whose example for writing about law in readable English has been an inspiration to generations and has made law accessible to the general public, for reading an early version of my proposal and encouraging me to proceed.

Dustin A. Lewis, my research assistant for two crucial years when this project got really serious, who became a trusted friend, and who understood intuitively, from the first day, why this book had to be written. His assistance and encouragement came at a crucial moment in this project, and I will never forget that loyalty and skill. His devotion to pursuing a career in human rights will much benefit society.

Greg Lukianoff, lawyer and now president of The Foundation for Individual Rights in Education, whose legal brilliance was matched by his encouragement.

Timothy Lynch, Director of the Project on Criminal Justice at the Cato Institute, who saw the value of this project the day he learned about it, and whose encouragement and judgment have been indispensable.

Jennifer Lyons, loyal agent, who has supplied to this project the kind of publishing industry knowledge I lack.

Paul McMasters, former First Amendment Ombudsman at The Freedom Forum, for his wise advice in all matters relating to free speech and the press.

Michael Meyers, blunt, articulate, brilliant and fearless fighter for liberty, who could be counted on to give unvarnished advice.

Scott Michel, for his advice on complex tax matters.

Tracey Miner, skilled white collar defense lawyer, who was unstinting with her time.

Errol Morris, extraordinary documentarian and friend, who was generous with his time and encouragement, and his wife **Julia Sheehan**, wise partner in Errol's work and sage advisor generally.

Norman and Jane Moscowitz, extraordinarily talented team of criminal defense lawyers, whom I've known since the very earliest days of their entry into the legal field, and who were kind enough to review drafts and supply me with valuable information and insights.

Ethan Nadelmann, warrior against the drug warriors, who was helpful in my chapter on pain doctors.

Cono Namorato, essential godfather in all matters relating to the tax code, who was helpful and encouraging at a crucial point.

Daphne Patai, friend and valued cohort in the battle for liberty, who was as generous as she was wise in all that she did to help me along.

Chris Perez, who read and commented on portions of the manuscript.

Petsi's Pies Bakery & Café in Cambridge, which allowed me at crucial points to escape/hide there for hours at a time when I had to get away from the pressures of law practice and my other assorted activities and obligations, in order to read, think, write and revise a difficult section of this book.

Steven Pinker, friend of liberty in all its manifestations, who generously read the manuscript and even did a jacket blurb.

Ellen S. Podgor, law professor, blogger, and criminal defense practitioner of unusual skill and insight, an essential resource for the legal world, who understood this project perfectly.

Daniel Poulson, research assistant, now young lawyer, who was so helpful during his tenure working for me.

Dorothy Rabinowitz, extraordinarily talented and effective columnist, without whose encouragement it is not clear this project would have been completed, whose instincts are so often right on the mark, and whose generosity with her time and skill has been *sine qua non* for the completion of this book.

Helen Rees, whose advice on and experience in the book business were so generously shared.

Siobhan Reynolds, President of the essential Pain Relief Network, fighter extraordinaire for the rights of physicians and their patients to function without the heavy hand of the federal drug warriors, and her lawyer comrade-in-arms, **Laura Cooper.**

Jennifer Roberts, book editor, whose advice proved ever useful.

Howard Rubenstein, New York's legendary public relations guru, who was one of the first people I consulted about the viability of this project and who urged me unequivocally to proceed with it.

Richard Sandler, friend and lawyer to Michael Milken, with whom I worked on that extraordinary case, and whose generosity with his time and insights is much appreciated.

Jennifer Schneider, M.D., who spent much time discussing with me the deleterious impact that the drug warriors have on the work of pain doctors and on the welfare of their patients.

Michael Schneider, skillful criminal defense advocate and long-time colleague, who spent considerable time helping me explain the complex details of the extraordinary saga of his client Walter Lachman.

Daniel Shuchman, money manager and warrior for liberty and decency, who spent endless hours reading drafts and giving me his sage advice on how to direct this book to the audience where it would do the most good for the nation.

Isaac Dorfman Silverglate, my talented son, whose skill as a creative writer for an innovative advertising agency helped me in crucial ways to focus this book and refine the concept.

Harry Skoyles, energetic research assistant one summer.

Kyle Smeallie, who picked up the baton late in the game and, with consummate skill, great devotion to the enterprise, and utterly essential resolve, helped me see this project through to the end.

G. Richard Strafer, who worked for me decades ago while a student and who now is an extraordinary and persistent criminal defense lawyer, whose help was essential in my writing about the saga of his client Raul Martinez.

Kathleen Sullivan, who worked with Nancy Gertner and me in the very early stages of all of our careers, and who went on to become a law teacher and law school dean of uncommon skill before returning, more recently, to the practice of appellate law.

John Swomley, trial lawyer of exceptional talent and grit, who has listened to my rants for years and whose feedback was always direct and helpful.

Carl Takei, research assistant in the early days of this project, now a civil liberties lawyer, whose work was foundational.

Peter Tannenwald, law school classmate and communications lawyer, for his advice in his field.

Stuart Taylor, Jr., lawyer turned writer, whose extraordinary ability to straddle the worlds of law and journalism was so generously shared with me.

James F. Tierney, research assistant toward the crucial conclusion of this project, whose insights into law much belied the fact that he had not yet commenced going to law school.

Cathy Tumber, editor extraordinaire, whose remarkable skill as my editor for years at *The Boston Phoenix* caused me to have the good judgment and equally good luck to retain her services to help me revise and rearrange the manuscript so as to turn it into a book that intelligent and engaged laymen, not only lawyers, could appreciate.

Martin Weinberg, criminal defense lawyer of remarkable skill and persistence, who was generous with his time and insights.

Craig R. Whitney, journalist and editor of rare skill, whom I met when he was writing his extraordinary book about the adventures of Wolfgang Vogel, the "spy trader" of considerable Cold War fame, and of my client Alfred Zehe, and whose willingness to spend time discussing the Zehe case with me and sharing insights is much appreciated.

Jan N. Wolfe, my research assistant for the final two years of the writing of the manuscript, was one of those people whose contributions to the completion of this project, and whose loyalty, devotion, skill and insights, were essential. The nation is fortunate that he is now supplementing his extraordinary literary and reportorial judgment by attending law school.

Robert L. Wyatt was generous in sharing with me details of his physician clients who were indicted.

Norman S. Zalkind, close friend of forty years, first law partner, jury trial lawyer extraordinaire, insightful student of the evolution of the criminal justice system, who generously shared his insights with me and who reviewed certain portions of the manuscript.

Susan Zalkind, who did skillful research and editing during one crucial summer.

And thanks and a salute to my many clients who went through the torments of hell because of the problems discussed in this book.

ENDNOTES

Preface to the Paperback Edition:

1. The full account of Dr. Hurwitz's entanglement with federal drug warriors is recounted in Chapter Two.

2. Adam Liptak, "Outspoken Activist's Case Becomes Tangled in Secrets," *The New York Times*, November 1, 2010, available at http://www.nytimes.com/2010/11/02/us/02bar. html.

3. Radley Balko, "The Worst Kind of Ham Sandwich: The vindictive grand jury investigation of pain-relief advocate Siobhan Reynolds," *Slate*, December 21, 2010, available at http://www.slate.com/id/2278244/.

4. Petition for Writ of Certiorari in the United States Supreme Court, *In re Grand Jury Proceedings (Siobhan Reynolds and Pain Relief Network, Inc.)*, September 17, 2010, available at http://reason.com/assets/db/1288288059364.pdf.

5. Email message to the Pain Relief Network Community from Siobhan Reynolds, December 29, 2010.

6. For an analysis of the Gleason prosecution, see Chapter Two.

7. For an expanded discussion, see Chapter Seven.

8. *U.S. v. Aleynikov* (S.D.N.Y., Sept. 3, 2010, quoting *In re Vericker*, 446 F.2d 244, 248 (2d Cir. 1971)).

9. Glenn Greenwald, "Government-created climate of fear," *Salon*, January 10, 2011, available at http://www.salon.com/news/opinion/glenn_greenwald/2011/01/10/fear/index.html.

10. Lyle Denniston, "Analysis: Anti-terrorism case not an easy one," SCOTUSblog, February 23, 2010, available at http://www.scotusblog.com/2010/02/analysis-anti-terrorism-case-not-an-easy-one/.

11. Adam Liptak, "Before Justices, First Amendment and Aid to Terrorists," *The New York Times*, February 24, 2010, available at http://www.nytimes.com/2010/02/24/us/24scotus.html.

12. Wendy Kaminer, "'Material Support' Bans and the Criminalization of Political Advocacy," *The Atlantic*, June 21, 2010, available at http://www.theatlantic.com/national/archive/2010/06/material-support-bans-and-the-criminalization-of-political-advocacy/58469/.

13. *Holder v. Humanitarian Law Project*, 561 U.S. ___ (2010) at 2720.

14. David Cole, "Chewing Gum for Terrorists," *The New York Times*, January 2, 2011, available at http://www.nytimes.com/2011/01/03/opinion/03cole.html.

15. "Honest services" fraud, in particular Justice Antonin Scalia's critique thereof, is discussed in the Conclusion of this book.

16. *Skilling v. United States*, 561 U.S. __ (2010) at 2935 (Scalia, J., concurring in part).

17. See Harvey A. Silverglate and Monica R. Shah, "The Degradation of the 'Void for Vagueness' Doctrine: Reversing Convictions while Saving the Unfathomable 'Honest Services Fraud' Statute," *Cato Supreme Court Review 2009–2010*, available at http://www.cato.org/pubs/scr/issue.php?year=2010.

18. Jonathan Saltzman, "Wilkerson receives 3½ years in prison," *The Boston Globe*, January 7, 2011, available at http://www.boston.com/yourtown/boston/roxbury/articles/2011/01/07/wilkerson_receives_3_years_in_prison/.

19. Michael Grunwald, "'Only the speaker and God know the total truth'; No quid pro quos tied to Flaherty, but what of subtle choreography?" *The Boston Globe*, March 30, 1996. Former U.S. attorney William Weld, who led the prosecution against longtime Boston mayor Kevin White (discussed in Chapter One), was skeptical of the charges against Flaherty, telling *The Boston Globe* in 1995 that "he does not believe there is enough evidence to charge House Speaker Charles F. Flaherty with accepting illegal gratuities." Weld went on to say that "he, too, has accepted hospitality from friends, and joked that he could end up in a federal penitentiary." Shelley Murphy, "Weld doubts Flaherty indictment," *The Boston Globe*, November 17, 1995.

20. *Skilling v. United States*, 561 U.S. __ (2010).

21. Peter Burrows, "He's Making Hay as CEOs Squirm," *Bloomberg Businessweek*, January 15, 2007, available at http://www.businessweek.com/magazine/content/07_03/b4017075.htm.

22. An investigative series in *The Wall Street Journal* on options backdating was awarded the 2007 Pulitzer Prize for Public Service. See http://www.pulitzer.org/citation/2007-Public-Service.

23. Peter Lattman, "Prosecutions in Backdating Scandal Bring Mixed Results," *The New York Times*, November 12, 2010.

24. *Id.*

25. Holman W. Jenkins, Jr., "The Backdating Embarrassment," *The Wall Street Journal*, November 17, 2010.

26. 18 U.S.C. § 1001 (making false statements to a federal official); Lattman, "Prosecutions in Backdating Scandal Bring Mixed Results."

27. Stuart Pfeifer and E. Scott Reckard, "Judge dismisses charge against Broadcom co-founder," *The Los Angeles Times*, December 10, 2009, available at http://articles.latimes.com/2009/dec/10/business/la-fi-samueli10-2009dec10.

28. Amanda Bronstad, "Judge Says Government 'Distorted the Truth-Finding Process' in Broadcom Case," *The National Law Journal*, December 16, 2009, available at http://www.law.com/jsp/article.jsp?id=1202436371130.

[29.] Reporter's Transcript of Proceedings, *United States v. William J. Ruehle*, U.S. District Court, Central District of California, Southern Division, December 15, 2009, at 5201.

[30.] Stuart Pfeifer, "Former KB Home CEO Bruce Karatz sentenced to five years' probation," *The Los Angeles Times*, November 11, 2010, available at http://articles.latimes.com/2010/nov/11/business/la-fi-karatz-sentence-20101111.

[31.] Zachary A. Goldfarb, "Task force to take up financial fraud cases," *The Washington Post*, November 18, 2009, available at http://www.washingtonpost.com/wp-dyn/content/article/2009/11/17/AR2009111703980.html.

[32.] Fairness dictates that I disclose that I played a paid advisory and strategy role in Goyal's appeal.

[33.] *U.S. v. Prabhat Goyal* (9th Cir., 2010) (Kozinski, C.J., concurring), at 19761–19762.

[34.] See Brian W. Walsh and Tiffany Joslyn, "Without Intent: How Congress Is Eroding the Criminal Intent Requirement in Federal Law," The Heritage Foundation and National Association for Criminal Defense Lawyers, May 2010, at 13, available at http://www.nacdl.org/withoutintent.

[35.] Schmidt wrote op-eds in both *The New York Times* and *The Wall Street Journal*. See Yuri Schmidt, "Khodorkovsky and the Rule of Law," *The New York Times*, December 27, 2010, available at http://www.nytimes.com/2010/12/28/opinion/28iht-edschmidt28.html; Yuri Schmidt, "The Show Trial of Mikhail Khodorkovsky," *The Wall Street Journal*, May 20, 2010, available at http://online.wsj.com/article/SB10001424052748703957904575252352874291616.html.

[36.] See Leon Aron, "Frenemies: Putin and Medvedev are fighting behind the scenes of the Khodorkovsky trial," *The New Republic*, December 3, 2010, available at http://www.tnr.com/article/world/79600/frenemies-putin-medvedev-khodorkovsky-russia; Gregory L. White, "A Tycoon Who Took On the Kremlin," *The Wall Street Journal*, December 30, 2010, available at http://online.wsj.com/article/SB1000142405274870390990457605161213012494.html; Joe Nocera, "Guilty Verdict for a Tycoon, and Russia," *The New York Times*, January 1, 2011, available at http://www.nytimes.com/2011/01/01/business/01nocera.html.

[37.] See, for example, Harvey A. Silverglate, "Federal Criminal Law: Punishing Benign Intentions," along with other essays published in *In the Name of Justice: Leading Experts Reexamine the Classic Article "The Aims of the Criminal Law,"* ed. Timothy Lynch (Cato Institute, 2009).

Introduction:

[1.] *Morissette v. United States*, 342 U.S. 246, 247-250 (1952); further details are available from the Court of Appeals opinion affirming Morissette's conviction, *Morissette v. United States*, 187 F.2d 427 (6th Cir. 1951).

[2.] See, generally, Ford W. Hall, *The Common Law: An Account of Its Reception in the United States*, 4 Vand. L. Rev. 791 (1951).

[3.] Justice Douglas concurred in the result without signing onto Justice Jackson's opinion, and Justice Minton took no part in the decision of the case.

4. Robert H. Jackson, "The Federal Prosecutor," April 1, 1940, delivered at the second Annual Conference of United States Attorneys, in Washington, D.C., reproduced at 31 Am. Inst. Crim. L. & Criminology 3 (1940-1941).

5. John S. Baker, Jr., *Measuring the Explosive Growth of Federal Crime Legislation*, Federalist Society for Law and Public Policy Studies White Paper, May 2004. The Federalist Society commissioned this study, the report says, "to ascertain the current number of crimes in the United States Code, and to compare that figure against the number of federal criminal provisions in years past." The report analyzed legislation enacted between 1997 through 2003. Updated on June 16, 2008. Available at http://www.heritage.org/Research/LegalIssues/lm26.cfm.

6. When Congress enacts a general statute, it sometimes assigns to some administrative agency the authority to write detailed or explanatory regulations that put flesh on the statutory skeleton. Thus, the federal statute that outlaws securities fraud assigns to the Securities and Exchange Commission the authority to write regulations detailing various kinds of securities fraud. Violation of a regulation thus becomes the equivalent of violation of the underlying statute.

7. See *United States v. Hudson & Goodwin*, 11 U.S. (7 Cranch) 32 (1812) (unlike state courts, federal courts cannot exercise common law criminal jurisdiction); *Erie R. Co. v. Tompkins*, 304 U.S. 64 (1938) (there is no general federal common law, even in civil matters); *Whalen v. U.S.*, 445 U.S. 684, 698 (1980) (the power to define crimes and punishments "resides wholly with the Congress"); *Dixon v. United States*, 126 S.Ct. 2437, 2439 (2006) ("Federal crimes are solely creatures of statute") (citing *Liparota v. United States*, 471 U.S. 419, 424 [1985]). This may have been because "[t]he Framers...recognized that the diverse development of the common law in the several States made a general federal reception impossible." *Seminole Tribe of Florida v. Florida*, 517 U.S. 44, 139-140 (1995) (Souter, J., dissenting).

8. *Dowling v. U.S.* 473 U.S. 207, 213 (1985).

9. *Cox v. Louisiana*, 379 U.S. 536 (1965).

10. *Edwards v. South Carolina*, 372 U.S. 229 (1963).

11. See *Cox v. Louisiana*, 379 U.S. 559 (1965); *Raley v. Ohio*, 360 U.S. 423 (1959).

12. See *Papachristou v. City of Jacksonville*, 405 U.S. 156 (1972); *Edwards v. South Carolina*, 372 U.S. 229 (1963).

13. *Connally v. General Construction Co.*, 269 U.S. 385, 391 (1926).

14. *United States v. Garber*, 607 F.2d 92 (5th Cir. 1979) (*en banc*).

15. *Id.* (emphasis added).

16. Proceedings of the 17th Annual National Institute on White Collar Crime, March 6, 2003, quoted in John Gibeaut, *Junior G-Men*, 89 A.B.A. J. 46, 48 (June 2003).

17. Professor Dershowitz has used this formulation on numerous occasions in his Harvard Law School classes. See Harvey A. Silverglate, "Ashcroft's big con: False confessions, coerced pleas, show trials — the Justice Department's reliance on Soviet-style tactics has turned the war on terror into a Potemkin village," *The Boston Phoenix*, June 25, 2004, available at http://bostonphoenix.com/boston/news_features/top/features/

documents/03936976.asp. See also Paul Craig Roberts, "Fake Crimes," Feb. 4, 2004, available at http://www.lewrockwell.com/roberts/roberts29.html.

[18.] *Giglio v. U.S.*, 405 U.S. 150 (1972).

[19.] 18 U.S.C. § 201(c)(2): "Whoever directly or indirectly gives, offers, or promises anything of value to any person, for or because of the testimony under oath or affirmation given or to be given by such person as a witness upon a trial, hearing, or other proceedings, before any court…or for or because of such person's absence therefrom, shall be fined under this title or imprisoned for not more than two years, or both."

[20.] *United States v. Singleton*, 144 F.3d 1343 (10th Cir. 1998, panel opinion).

[21.] *United States v. Singleton*, 165 F.3d 1297 (10th Cir. 1999, *en banc*).

[22.] *North Carolina v. Alford*, 400 U.S. 25, 28 (1970).

[23.] Tim Wu, "American Lawbreaking: Illegal Immigration," Slate.com, October 14, 2007, available at http://www.slate.com/2175730/entry/2175733/.

Chapter One:

[1.] Carl Hiaasen, "Try Martinez Again? It's Not Worth It," *The Miami Herald*, March 28, 1996.

[2.] Much of the background information about Raul Martinez's career has been graciously and helpfully provided by one of Martinez's attorneys, R. Richard Strafer, who years earlier had worked for me while he was attending law school in the Boston area.

[3.] Alfonso Chardy, "Sources: Lehtinen rushed probe after Pepper fell ill," *The Miami Herald*, February 17, 1991.

[4.] Jeff Leen, "Sources: Lehtinen was a 'ticklish' problem; controversies, temper overbalance talent," *The Miami Herald*, January 19, 1992.

[5.] Jeff Leen, "Tyrant or Target?," *Tropic*, February 24, 1991.

[6.] T. D. Allman, *Vanity Fair*, February 1991.

[7.] 18 U.S.C. § 1951.

[8.] Testimony of Silvio Cardoso, trial transcript in *United States v. Martinez*, February 12, 1991, at 40.

[9.] The Hobbs Act (18 U.S.C. § 1951) provides that:

> (a) Whoever in any way or degree obstructs, delays, or affects commerce or the movement of any article or commodity in commerce, by robbery or extortion or attempts or conspires so to do, or commits or threatens physical violence to any person or property in furtherance of a plan or purpose to do anything in violation of this section shall be fined under this title or imprisoned not more than twenty years, or both.
>
> (b) As used in this section—
>
> > (1) The term "robbery" means the unlawful taking or obtaining of personal property from the person or in the presence of another, against his will, by means of actual or threatened force, or violence, or fear of injury, immediate or future, to his person or property, or

property in his custody or possession, or the person or property of a relative or member of his family or of anyone in his company at the time of the taking or obtaining.

(2) The term "extortion" means the obtaining of property from another, with his consent, induced by wrongful use of actual or threatened force, violence, or fear, or under color of official right.

(3) The term "commerce" means commerce within the District of Columbia, or any Territory or Possession of the United States; all commerce between any point in a State, Territory, Possession, or the District of Columbia and any point outside thereof; all commerce between points within the same State through any place outside such State; and all other commerce over which the United States has jurisdiction.

10. The 11th Circuit also found that jurors had improperly considered outside materials, which contributed to its decision to reverse the lower court's verdict and grant Martinez a new trial. See *United States v. Martinez*, 14 F.3d 543 (11th Cir., 1994). Unfortunately, the Court of Appeals, relying upon Supreme Court opinions in the cases *McCormack v. United States*, 500 U.S. 257 (1991) and *United States v. Evans*, 504 U.S. 255 (1992), was little clearer on the definition of extortion than was Judge Kehoe. See *Martinez*, 14 F.3d at 552-553.

11. Chris Cillizza, "The Best House Ads," The Fix (Washingtonpost.com blog), November 11, 2008, available at http://voices.washingtonpost.com/thefix/2008/11/the_best_house_ads.html.

12. Jonathan Kaufman, "Serving the public – or themselves? Official corruption here reaches dizzying heights," *The Boston Globe*, June 24, 1984, p. A21.

13. Mark L. Wolf helped orchestrate the operation. Weld's top deputy who nearly became the U.S. attorney instead of Weld, Wolf had cut his teeth as a top assistant to Attorney General Edward H. Levi – the former law professor tapped by Gerald Ford to clean up the discredited Department of Justice and FBI in the wake of the Watergate scandal. Levi's predecessor as attorney general, John N. Mitchell, left the office in disgrace, eventually serving a prison term for obstruction of justice and related crimes. Well-known then and later (he was eventually named a federal district judge, a position he has served with distinction) for a low tolerance for corruption, Wolf was the ideal post-Watergate DOJ policymaker and administrator. For the same reason, he seemed a natural for helping Weld root out corruption in Boston's City Hall. Rounding out the top team were Robert J. Cordy, a former Dartmouth football player, public defender and later private practitioner who went on to a seat on the Supreme Judicial Court of Massachusetts (appointed by Governor Paul Cellucci, Weld's protégé, in 2001), and Daniel I. Small, who eventually left the U.S. attorney's office for a successful career as a white collar criminal defense lawyer and sought-after continuing legal education lecturer.

14. *United States v. Anzalone*, 766 F.2d 676, 1985 U.S. App. LEXIS 20143 (1985).

[15.] Quoting the former totalitarian Communist state's Criminal Code, the court drove the point home:

> If any socially dangerous act has not been directly provided for by the present Code, the basis and extent of liability for it is determined by applying to it those articles of the Code which deal with the offences [sic] most similar in nature.

[16.] The new crime of the depositor's structuring a transaction in order to evade the bank's reporting obligations was created on October 27, 1986. See 31 U.S.C. § 5324.

[17.] American Bar Association Committee on Government Standards, "Keeping Faith: Government Ethics and Government Ethics Regulation," 45 Admin. L. Rev. 287, 304-305 (1993).

[18.] "The Political Profiling of Elected Democratic Officials: When Rhetorical Vision Participation Runs Amok," EPluribus Media, February 18, 2007.

[19.] "An Investigation of Allegations of Politicized Hiring by Monica Goodling and Other Staff in the Office of the Attorney General," The DOJ Office of Professional Responsibility and the DOJ Office of the Inspector General, July 28, 2008. Available at: http://www.usdoj.gov/oig/special/s0807/final.pdf.

[20.] Scott Horton, "Vote Machine: How Republicans Hacked the Justice Department," Harper's, March 2008.

[21.] "Petition in Support of Governor Siegelman." July 13, 2007. Available at http://don-siegelman.net/files/letter_from_44.pdf; last accessed May 4, 2009.

[22.] Adam Cohen, "The Strange Case of an Imprisoned Alabama Governor," The New York Times, September 10, 2007.

[23.] Adam Nossiter, "Freed Ex-Governor of Alabama Talks of Abuse of Power," The New York Times, March 29, 2008.

[24.] Id.

[25.] 18 U.S.C. §§ 2 & 666(a)(1)(B), federal funds bribery.

[26.] 18 U.S.C. § 371.

[27.] 18 U.S.C. §§ 2, 1241 & 1346.

[28.] 18 U.S.C. § 1951 (extortion under color of official right).

[29.] RICO, 18 U.S.C § 1962(c).

[30.] Scott Horton, "Vote Machine: How Republicans Hacked the Justice Department," Harper's, March 2008.

[31.] Julian McPhillips, "Alabama Voices," The Montgomery Advertiser, June 20, 2007.

[32.] Scott Horton, "Vote Machine: How Republicans Hacked the Justice Department," Harper's, March 2008.

[33.] United States v. Siegelman, No. 07-13163-B (11th Cir., 2008) (Black and Marcus, Circuit Judges), Order dated March 27, 2008.

[34.] According to The Boston Globe in 1993, "the fact that State Representative Thomas Finneran (D-Mattapan), an Irish-Catholic politician who lives in a district that is majority minority, wins re-election easily is often cited as evidence that the black leadership has failed to maximize its opportunities." See Chris Black, "Minorities left on outside of citywide office," *The Boston Globe*, November 15, 1993, p. B1.

[35.] In a 1998 *Boston Globe Magazine* profile, columnist Adrian Walker wrote that "though Rushing, a textbook liberal, differs politically from the more conservative Finneran, they've always respected each other's intellect and integrity." See Adrian Walker, "House Rules," *Boston Globe Magazine*, June 28, 1998, available at http://graphics.boston.com/globe/magazine/1998/6-28/featurestory/.

[36.] Harvey A. Silverglate, "Finneran's Wake," *The Boston Phoenix*, June 24, 2005.

[37.] *Black Political Task Force v. Galvin*, 300 F.Supp.2d 294 (2004).

[38.] J.M. Lawrence, "Common Cause Took Aim at Tom," *The Boston Herald*, June 8, 2005.

[39.] 18 U.S.C. §1001, the so-called "false statement" statute, provides:

> Whoever...knowingly and willfully—
>
>> (1) falsifies, conceals, or covers up by any trick, scheme, or device, a material fact;
>>
>> (2) makes any materially false, fictitious, or fraudulent statement or representation; or
>>
>> (3) makes or uses any false writing or document knowing the same to contain any materially false, fictitious, or fraudulent statement or entry;
>
> shall be fined under this title, imprisoned not more than 5 years or...both.

[40.] There was an obstruction of justice charge that Finneran had failed to produce certain documents and lied about their existence. It was dismissed as part of the later plea bargain.

[41.] A federal appellate court once described a perjury trap in the following terms:

> A perjury trap is created when the government calls a witness before the grand jury for the primary purpose of obtaining testimony from him in order to prosecute him later for perjury. *United States v. Simone*, 627 F.Supp. 1264, 1268 (D.N.J., 1986) (perjury trap involves "the deliberate use of a judicial proceeding to secure perjured testimony, a concept in itself abhorrent"). It involves the government's use of its investigatory powers to secure a perjury indictment on matters which are neither material nor germane to a legitimate ongoing investigation of the grand jury. *United States v. Chen*, 933 F.2d 793, 797 (9th Cir., 1991).

The investigation and prosecution of former White House vice-presidential advisor during the George W. Bush administration, I. Lewis "Scooter" Libby, is a case in point. There, a special prosecutor indicted, tried and convicted Libby for lying to federal investigators and to the grand jury about an incident in which, it turned out, several administration operatives leaked to the news media apparently confidential information about the identity of a CIA operative, Valerie Plame Wilson. No one was ever prosecuted for the leak, and indeed it was never firmly established that the leaking itself was a crime.

However, as is becoming more and more the case in the federal system, if the underlying crime (if, indeed, it be a crime at all) doesn't get you, surely the cover-up will.

[42.] Harvey A. Silverglate, "Finneran's Wake: U.S. Attorney Michael Sullivan is Riding High on the Former House Speaker's Perjury Indictment. Too Bad It's Misguided," *The Boston Phoenix*, June 24, 2005.

[43.] I thank Samuel Abady for pointing out to me that this memorable statement comes from Sol Wachtler, the former Chief Judge of the Court of Appeals of New York, who himself later went to federal prison for harassing his girlfriend, Joy Silverman, by using the facilities of interstate communications, a case seen by some at the time as a dubious extension of the federal statute. Wachtler made the statement about grand juries in general, both state and federal, in an interview with *The New York Daily News*, in which he proposed abolishing grand juries entirely and allowing prosecutors to bring charges, since grand juries in the modern age were no longer serving their original protective function of checking the power of prosecutors to bring charges. See Frank Lombardi & Marcia Kramer, "New top state judge: Abolish grand juries & let us decide," *The New York Daily News*, January 31, 1985, p. 3.

[44.] Shelley Murphy & Stephanie Ebbert, "'The wound…will hurt for the rest of my life,'" *The Boston Globe*, January 6, 2007, p. 1.

[45.] Plea and disposition transcript, *United States v. Thomas M. Finneran*, Criminal Action No. 05-10140-RGS, January 5, 2007, at p. 19.

[46.] Laurel Sweet, "Witness says Finneran was victim of 'witch hunt,'" *The Boston Herald*, December 19, 2007.

Chapter Two:

[1.] Maia Szalavitz, "Dr. Feelscared: Drug warriors put the fear of prosecution in physicians who dare to treat pain," *Reason Online*, http://www.reason.com/0408/fe.ms.dr.shtml.

[2.] Disclosure: The law firm to which the author is "of counsel" represented one of Purdue Pharma's executives.

[3.] According to pain therapists and *The Diagnostic and Statistical Manual of Mental Disorders*, people who suffer from addiction exhibit: (1) loss of control over use of the drug, (2) continued use despite adverse life consequences, and (3) obsessive preoccupation with obtaining the drug and with its physical and psychic impact. A patient who makes fraudulent representations to the physician in order to obtain narcotics to "get high" is likely addicted, so that the withdrawal of the drug itself causes intense physical and psychological pain.

[4.] Interview via email exchanges with pain expert Jennifer Schneider, M.D., in July 2007. Dr. Schneider is an internal medicine, addiction medicine, and pain management specialist, certified by the American Board of Internal Medicine and the American Society of Addiction Medicine.

[5.] Lester Grinspoon & James Bakalar, *Marihuana: The Forbidden Medicine*, Yale University Press, 1997.

[6.] See *Gonzales v. Raich*, 545 U.S. 1 (2005), concerning the DEA's war against medical uses of marijuana.

[7.] Jerry Markon, "Virginia Doctor Defends Prescribing Pain Pills," *The Washington Post*, December 7, 2004.

[8.] Ronald T. Libby, "Treating Doctors as Drug Dealers: The DEA's War on Prescription Painkillers," *Policy Analysis*, No. 545, June 16, 2005 (CATO Institute), p. 7.

[9.] John Laidler, "Grants to help combat drug use: Local programs expected to target OxyContin, heroin," *The Boston Globe*, August 8, 2004.

[10.] Quoted in Ronald T. Libby, "Treating Doctors as Drug Dealers," at p. 12.

[11.] Prescription Pain Medications: Frequently Asked Questions and Answers for Health Care Professionals, and Law Enforcement Personnel, 2004. Archived versionAvailable at http://www.painfoundation.org/eNews2004/0904/PainMedLegalFAQ.pdf; last accessed June 2, 2008.

[12.] Maia Szalavitz, "Dr. Feelscared: Drug warriors put the fear of prosecution in physicians who dare to treat pain," *Reason Online*, http://www.reason.com/0408/fe.ms.dr.shtml.

[13.] Jerry Markon, "Pain Doctor 'Cavalier,' Jury Foreman Says," *The Washington Post*, December 21, 2004.

[14.] Jacob Sullum, "Chilling Conviction," *The Washington Times*, December 26, 2004.

[15.] *United States v. Hurwitz*, 459 F.3d 363, (4th Cir. 2006).

[16.] Tina Rosenberg calls Dr. Portenoy "a leading authority on the treatment of pain" in her article "When is a Pain Doctor a Drug Pusher?" *The New York Times Magazine*, June 17, 2007.

[17.] John Tierney, "At Trial, Pain Has a Witness," *The New York Times*, April 24, 2007.

[18.] John Tierney, "Dr. Hurwitz Convicted on 16 Counts of Drug Trafficking," *NYTimes* blog, April 27, 2007, available at http://tierneylab.blogs.nytimes.com/2007/04/27/dr-hurwitz-convicted-of-16-drug-trafficking-charges/.

[19.] John Tierney, "Hurwitz Jurors Explain Their Verdict," *NYTimes* blog, April 30, 2007, available at http://tierneylab.blogs.nytimes.com/2007/04/30/hurwitz-jurors-explain-their-verdict/.

[20.] *Id.*

[21.] Ronald T. Libby, "Treating Doctors as Drug Dealers: The DEA's War on Prescription Painkillers," *Policy Analysis*, No. 545, June 16, 2005 (CATO Institute), pp. 20-21.

[22.] Gary Langer, "Poll: Americans Searching for Pain Relief," ABC News Online, May 9, 2005, available at http://abcnews.go.com/Health/PainManagement/story?id=732395.

[23.] Tina Rosenberg, "When is a Pain Doctor a Drug Pusher?" *The New York Times Magazine*, June 17, 2007.

[24.] R. Morgan Griffin, "Safe Pain Relief With Aspirin Therapy," *WebMD* (peer reviewed article), available at http://www.webmd.com/heart-disease/features/safe-pain-relief-aspirin-therapy?page=2.

[25.] Maia Szalavitz, "The Pain Police: Hurwitz Case Shows Doctors Can Be Healers or Cops – Not Both," *Huffingtonpost.com*, April 30, 2007, available at http://www.huffing-tonpost.com/maia-szalavitz/the-pain-police-hurwitz_b_47263.html.

[26.] Maia Szalavitz, "Dr. Feelscared: Drug warriors put the fear of prosecution in physicians who dare to treat pain," *Reason Online*, http://www.reason.com/0408/fe.ms.dr.shtml.

[27.] "Dr. Cecil Knox Surrenders Medical License and DEA Registration Number; Sentenced to Five Years Probation," U.S. Department of Justice Press Release, January 20, 2006, available at http://www.usdoj.gov/usao/vaw/press_releases/knox_20jan2006.html.

[28.] Dr. Jennifer P. Schneider, who was an expert witness in Dr. Hassman's case, reports that, in the end, the prosecutor recognized that the charges were absurd and settled, instead, for a plea bargain to four new, unrelated counts that charged, essentially, that Dr. Hassman did not report patients who had admitted to her that they had given to or taken from a family member an opioid pill—a practice engaged in millions of times a year by pain patients. The charges concerning the physician's duty to report what the patient told her were so dubious that, reports Dr. Schneider, "her lawyer and the government lawyer were worried that the judge would realize that these weren't real felonies and would throw out the plea agreement, but it seems the judge didn't realize this and accepted it." Email interview of Dr. Schneider, dated July 8, 2007.

[29.] Maia Szalavitz, "Dr. Feelscared: Drug warriors put the fear of prosecution in physicians who dare to treat pain," *Reason Online*, http://www.reason.com/0408/fe.ms.dr.shtml.

[30.] Timothy E. Quill, M.D., & Diane E. Meier, M.D., "The Big Chill – Inserting the DEA into End-of-Life Care," *The New England Journal of Medicine*, January 5, 2006.

[31.] George J. Annas, "Congress, Controlled Substances, and Physician-Assisted Suicide – Elephants in Mouseholes," *The New England Journal of Medicine*, March 9, 2006.

[32.] *Gonzales v. Oregon*, 126 S.Ct. 904, 2006 U.S. LEXIS 767 (2006).

[33.] The Pain Relief Network, more than any other group, has sought to expose and combat this *de facto* establishment of a national law enforcement, rather than a state medical standard, for treatment of pain. See www.painreliefnetwork.org.

[34.] 21 U.S.C. §§ 301 *et seq.*

[35.] Alex Berenson, "Indictment of Doctor Tests Drug Marketing Rules," *The New York Times*, July 22, 2006.

[36.] A familiar example of this phenomenon of secondary therapeutic uses is aspirin, a drug that does not require any prescription. Aspirin is typically used to treat pain or high fever and has been so used for well over a century. However, in more recent years physicians have been recommending that their middle-aged patients take aspirin daily to thin out their blood and thereby prevent heart attacks resulting from blood clots. Were aspirin a prescription drug, the manufacturers would not be allowed to recommend it as a heart-attack preventative unless and until they convinced the FDA to include such a use on the label. Yet physicians would be free, based upon their own treatment experience and medical judgment, to recommend or prescribe it to their patients regardless of the restrictions that the labeling rules impose on the manufacturer.

[37.] Email from Jennifer P. Schneider, M.D., to Harvey A. Silverglate, dated July 8, 2007.

38. *Black's Law Dictionary* defines a conspiracy as "an agreement by two or more persons to commit an unlawful act, coupled with an intent to achieve the agreement's objective."

39. "Federal Justice Statistics," U.S. Department of Justice, Bureau of Justice Statistics. Available at http://www.ojp.usdoj.gov/bjs/fed.htm; last accessed February 23, 2009.

40. Dr. Gleason's sentencing was pending as of publication.

41. Carey Goldberg, "'No' to drug money: Dr. Daniel J. Carlat wants to limit corporate sway over psychiatry," *The Boston Globe*, May 7, 2007.

42. Dr. Jerome P. Kassirer, *On the Take* (New York: Oxford University Press, 2004).

43. *United States v. Migliaccio* and *United States v. Avery*, cases consolidated on appeal, reported at 34 F.3d 1517, 1994 U.S. App. LEXIS 24278 (10th Cir., 1994).

44. Indeed, Robert Wyatt, the trial attorney for the two doctors, who represented only Dr. Avery on appeal, showed the jury four medical dictionaries in which "salpingoplasty" was listed as one of the terms used for reversal of tubal ligations, but the government claimed that it was an obscure rather than commonly used term and hence was used to mislead the CHAMPUS personnel who reviewed the applications for payment. (Telephone interview of Attorney Robert Wyatt, Wyatt Law Office, Oklahoma City, OK, on December 14, 2007.)

45. One of the most serious threats to pain doctors is the DEA's technique of squeezing vulnerable patients to turn against their physicians. The phenomenon is well known to criminal defense lawyers and is amply described in a June 2005 Cato Institute policy analysis by Professor Ronald T. Libby of the University of North Florida.

46. Telephone interview of Attorney Robert Wyatt on December 14, 2007.

Chapter Three:

1. 21 U.S.C. §§ 360 *et seq.*

2. 21 U.S.C. §§ 360c *et seq.*

3. Indicted with Leichter were John F. Cvinar, David W. Prigmore, George Maloney, Janice Piasecki, and Kenneth Thurston. Maloney and Thurston were acquitted by the jury and hence were not involved in the appeal. Piasecki was acquitted by Judge Tauro midway through the trial.

4. See *United States v. Prigmore*, 243 F.3d 1, 2001 U.S. App. LEXIS 3977 (1st Cir. 2001).

5. 21 U.S.C. § 360e(d)(2).

6. 21 C.F.R. § 860.7(d)(1).

7. The FDA maintains a database known as Manufacturer and User Facility Device Experience ("MAUDE") that collects reports of adverse experiences with Class III medical devices. The purpose of this facility is to allow for constant feedback from, and sharing among, users of these devices, including physicians and hospitals. See http://www.fda.gov/cdrh/maude.html.

8. The company was sentenced on April 4, 1994 and ordered to pay a fine of $61 million, along with a special assessment of $78,200.00. This payment represented all revenues that USCI obtained from the sale of the catheters in question.

9. Janice Piasecki was acquitted by Judge Tauro at the close of the government's evidence. George Maloney and Kenneth Thurston were acquitted by the jury.

[10.] *United States v. Prigmore, supra.*

[11.] See discussions of the Lachman case in Chapter Eight (National Security) and the Councilman case in the Conclusion.

[12.] *United States v. Prigmore,* 243 F.3d at 22-23.

[13.] Much of the information about the Health Care Fraud Unit's history, and its pursuit of TAP Pharmaceuticals and its employees, appeared in abbreviated form in Harvey A. Silverglate, "Beantown Shakedown," *The Wall Street Journal,* June 23, 2005.

[14.] See 21 *Corporate Crime Reporter* 47, November 27, 2007, available at http://www.corporatecrimereporter.com/capitals112707.htm (quoting Russell Mokhiber) ("Federal prosecutors in Boston have developed perhaps the premier health care fraud prosecution team in the country—outside of Washington.").

[15.] Leichter pled guilty to 21 U.S.C. § 331(a) (prohibiting "[t]he introduction or delivery for introduction into interstate commerce of any food, drug, device, or cosmetic that is adulterated or misbranded"), with a corresponding penalty under 21 U.S.C. § 333(a)(1) (setting the maximum prison sentence as one year, and the maximum fine as $1,000).

[16.] See discussion of the prosecution of the KPMG tax shelter case, Chapter Five.

[17.] Alice Dembner, "Prosecutors Here Lead in Health Fraud Cases," *The Boston Globe,* May 13, 2003.

[18.] Jonathan Saltzman & Liz Kowalczyk, "Drug firm, subsidiary settle suits for $515M," *The Boston Globe,* September 29, 2007.

[19.] The federal False Claims Act, 31 U.S.C. §§ 3729 *et seq.,* originally enacted in 1863 to prosecute profiteers during the Civil War, was substantially amended in 1986 by the False Claims Amendments Act. Under this legislation, not only was the government's ability to recoup losses sustained from fraud committed against the United States enhanced, but the whistleblower provisions gave private persons a huge incentive to report such fraud. The government may sue to recoup three times the amount of the fraud, but individuals with knowledge of such frauds may bring suit in the government's name and against the malefactors. Such *qui tam* suits are initially filed secretly, with the government being notified and given an opportunity to decide whether to join in and take over control of the civil lawsuit. When such lawsuits yield monetary judgments or settlements against the defrauders, the whistleblowers are entitled to a substantial portion of the recovery.

[20.] Under applicable legal principles, a conviction in a criminal case can have the effect of precluding relitigation of the underlying question of responsibility in a related civil suit. Thus, if an individual is convicted or pleads guilty in the criminal case, he normally would be unable to claim a lack of responsibility in a civil suit for monetary damages. The reverse is not true, however: A loss in a civil suit is not admissible in a criminal case to prove guilt. The underlying reason for this is that guilt in a criminal case must be proven beyond a reasonable doubt, while responsibility in a civil suit can be determined by a mere preponderance of the evidence (that is, that responsibility is more likely than not).

[21.] Indictment in *United States v. Alan MacKenzie et al.,* No. 01-CR-10350 (D.Mass.), p. 26.

[22.] In one illustrative allegation in the indictment, the prosecutors charged that in November 1995, a sales rep reporting to one of the defendants "sought approval to give a urology practice located on Cape Cod $200 to support the practice's annual Christmas Party." The medical group was a Lupron purchaser. Continued the indictment about this heinous disguised bribe: "In requesting this money as an 'educational grant' the sales representative stated that she would ask one of the doctors 'to talk about Lupron and prostate cancer at the party to justify the donation, ha-ha.'" Indictment in *MacKenzie* at p. 34. The defendant approved the "educational grant" that the indictment sarcastically put into quotation marks.

[23.] That defendant's lawyer, Tracy A. Miner, noted that the TAP case and others like it "could be brought anywhere in the country, but are brought here [in Boston] because of the aggressive U.S. Attorney's Health Care Fraud Unit." Boston had become the Mecca for such cases. It created, admitted Miner, a partner at a major Boston law firm with a substantial white collar criminal defense practice, a growth industry for the Boston legal community. Phone interview with Miner.

[24.] To the extent the government should have learned a lesson from the case, the prosecution's most astute epitaph came from a Philadelphia lawyer, Marc Raspanti, who represents whistleblowers but who was not involved in the TAP case: "The government did very well in its civil case against TAP, brought by a whistle-blower," he told *The Boston Globe*. "It may have over-reached when it brought a criminal case" against individual employees. See Shelley Murphy and Alice Dembner, "All acquitted in drug kickback case," *The Boston Globe*, July 15, 2004.

[25.] Criminal Information, *United States of America v. Serono Laboratories, Inc.*, 05 CR 10282 (RCL) (D. Mass.), paragraph 6.

[26.] The government's intent in bringing this and similar cutting-edge indictments was discussed in an article in *The National Law Journal*. See Robert Brady, Meredith Manning, & Peter Spivack, "Crackdown on 'off-label' pitches: Pharmaceutical companies have been penalized for pushing their products for unapproved uses," *The National Law Journal*, March 20, 2006. The authors were partners at the major Washington firm of Hogan & Hartson, which does substantial white collar criminal defense work. One of the authors previously held several leadership positions at the FDA. The article is not explicitly critical of the Department of Justice, but simply reports that the department sought "to expand the nature and extent of company conduct it will investigate." The article cited one case, a 2004 prosecution of Pfizer, Inc., settled with a $430 million payment for the company's having, according to the authors, "illegally promoted its anti-epileptic drug, Neurontin, for an array of unapproved uses, including pain and bipolar disorder." "The Neurontin case," continued the article, "stands for the novel proposition that a company's off-label promotion is a violation of the FDA if the promotion results in submission of an off-label claim for reimbursement to a federal health care program." The prosecution "may have established a new standard." Similar cases were cited that were brought against other pharmaceutical companies. Thus was the government expanding the array of violations that off-label promotion might produce, such expansion accomplished by simply expanding its theories of prosecution rather than establishing, by new regulatory language, where the government would draw the line between acceptable and criminal conduct. In one of those cases, Eli Lilly & Co. agreed to plead guilty and pay a $36 million fine in connection with sales practices for its drug Evista, for which the company sought to enlarge the market "by promoting it for unapproved uses." When discussing the Serono case, the authors cited it as further proof of the intention of the DOJ to "thoroughly examine marketing efforts such as Serono's efforts…to convince physicians to use a drug in a wider patient population." This prosecution "is the first known instance of the DOJ asking a company to evaluate or assess incentive compensation" as a cause of overly vigorous sales efforts, while the Eli Lilly case was "the first in which the DOJ has addressed market research as a potential promotional tool."

[27.] North Carolina Bar Association, Brochure for Continuing Legal Education (CLE) conference in Aspen, Colorado, Jan. 5-10, 2007, available at https://www.ncbar.org/cle/brochures/291.pdf.

[28.] Eric Lichtblau, "Settlement in Marketing of a Drug for AIDS," *The New York Times*, Oct. 18, 2005.

[29.] Denise Lavoie, Associated Press, "Former Serono executives acquitted of offering kickbacks," *The Boston Globe*, May 3, 2007.

[30.] Alex Berenson, "Indictment of Doctor Tests Drug Marketing Rules," *The New York Times*, July 22, 2006. This case is also discussed in the chapter on the harassment of physicians, Chapter Two.

[31.] Jazz Pharmaceuticals by this time had acquired Orphan Medical, Inc.

[32.] Alex Berenson, "Indictment of Doctor Tests Drug Marketing Rules," *The New York Times*, July 22, 2006. This case is also discussed in the chapter on the harassment of physicians, Chapter Two.

[33.] *Id.*

Chapter Four:

[1.] Telephone interview with a Milken attorney, who requested anonymity (June 2007).

[2.] Michael Powell, "A Crime Buster, With His Eye on the Future," *The New York Times*, December 10, 2007.

[3.] Liman's predecessor as Milken's lead counsel was the legendary and considerably scrappier Washington lawyer Edward Bennett Williams, who died of cancer before Milken was indicted.

[4.] Daniel Fischel, *Payback: The Conspiracy to Destroy Michael Milken and His Financial Revolution* (New York: HarperBusiness, 1995). Material and analyses from Professor Fischel's book have proven invaluable in corroborating and supplementing portions of this chapter.

[5.] Roughly, here is how the "scheme" worked: Solomon in 1985 asked Milken and Rosenthal if Drexel could assist him in obtaining short-term capital losses that he could use on his tax return for that year to offset gains in his account. The type of transaction suggested would have the effect of delaying any tax due by one year. (Wage earners pay income tax on their annual earnings. Investors, on the other hand, pay capital gains taxes on profits realized from the sale of their investments. If a sale is made within a short period of time from the date of purchase, it is considered a "short-term capital gain" and subject to a higher tax rate. In contrast, if the investment is held longer, the tax rate is that for "long-term capital gains," which is lower.) Since the transaction involved an actual loss, Milken promised Solomon that he would keep Solomon in mind when a good investment came up in the following year. That way, Solomon could make up the loss. And since that "make up" investment, if held for more than six months, would produce a long-term capital gain, it would be taxed at a lower rate than either ordinary income or a short-term capital gain.

6. Editorial, "Explanation in Order," *The Wall Street Journal*, June 12, 1992.

7. Ronald Sullivan, "Former Protégé of Milken Convicted for a Kickback," *The New York Times*, June 11, 1992 ("Lawyers on both sides said Mr. Milken, who is eligible for parole in 25 months, did not greatly help his chances of reducing his term because his testimony was seen as helping as much as hurting Mr. Rosenthal.").

8. *United States v. Quattrone*, 441 F.3d 153 (2d Cir., 2006).

9. Per interview with Quattrone's legal counsel, Kenneth Hausman, June 13-14, 2007.

10. It is worth quoting Char's email in full:

> With the recent tumble in stock prices, and many deals now trading below issue price, the securities litigation bar is expected to [sic] an all out assault on broken tech IPOs.
>
> In the spirit of the end of the year (and the slow down in corporate finance work) we want to reminding [sic] you of the CSFB document retention policy. The full policy can be found at http://intranet.csfb.net/GlobalIBD/Lcd/doc_retention_us.html The relevant text is:
>
> "For any securities offering, the Designated Member should create a transaction file consisting of (i) all filings made with the SEC in connection with an SEC registered offering or, in an unregistered offering, the final offering memorandum used in a Rule 144A offering or other form of private placement, (ii) the original executed underwriting or placement agent agreements, (iii) the original executed comfort letters from accountants, (iv) the original executed opinions of counsel and (v) a completed document checklist (see Exhibit B hereto). In order to avoid confusion and ensure greater compliance with these policies, no file categories other than those set forth in Exhibit B may be created in connection with any CSFB managed securities offering without the approval of your team leader and a lawyer in the IBD Legal and Compliance Department or the CDC manager."
>
> So what does it mean? Generally speaking, if it is not (i) – (v), it should not be left in the file following completion of the transaction. That means no notes, no drafts, no valuation analysis, no copies of the roadshow, no markups, no selling memos, no IBC or EVC memos, no internal memos.

Note that if a lawsuit is instituted, our normal document retention policy is suspended and any cleaning of files is prohibited under the CSFB guidelines (since it constitutes the destruction of evidence). We strongly suggest that before you leave for the holidays, you should catch up on file cleanup.

Quoted from *United States v. Quattrone*, 441 F.3d 153 [slip op. at p. 11].

[11.] Andrew Ross Sorkin, "NASD Ends Case Against Quattrone," *The New York Times*, June 2, 2006.

[12.] Randall Smith, "Regulators Drop Civil Case Against Frank Quattrone," *The Wall Street Journal*, June 2, 2006.

[13.] Andrew Ross Sorkin, "NASD Ends Case Against Quattrone," *The New York Times*, June 2, 2006.

[14.] Editorial, "Quattrone's Intent," *The Wall Street Journal*, March 22, 2006.

[15.] Roger Parloff, "Why Quattrone Deserves to Walk," *Fortune*, March 21, 2005.

[16.] Interview of Kathleen Ridolfi by Harvey A. Silverglate.

[17.] Andrew Ross Sorkin, "NASD Ends Case Against Quattrone," *The New York Times*, June 2, 2006 ("Mr. Quattrone's lawyers argued that NASD did not adopt rules governing the practices in question until 2002."); see also Randall Smith, "Regulators Drop Civil Case Against Frank Quattrone," *The Wall Street Journal*, June 2, 2006 ("But Quattrone's lawyers argued that the rules in effect at the time, since bolstered, didn't bar his actions.").

[18.] According to Quattrone's attorney, NASD did not propose rules addressing the long-standing and widespread industry practices challenged in its action against Quattrone until 2002, well after the period on which the charges were based (1999-2001). A new rule concerning IPO allocations to executives of investment banking clients (Rule 2712), which was proposed in 2002, still has not been approved. A new rule governing research analysts' compensation and interactions with bankers and corporate clients (Rule 2711) was adopted in May 2002, and even then allowed firms a several-month grace period to develop procedures to comply with the sweeping changes of the new regime.

[19.] Pamela A. MacLean, "Limited fallout from 'Quattrone': Broader language in Sarbanes-Oxley will ease way for prosecutors," *The National Law Journal*, March 27, 2006.

[20.] Stewart completed her sentence in March 2005.

[21.] 18 U.S.C. § 1001.

[22.] Commentators have marveled at such a situation: It is a felony to lie to any one of the many hundreds of thousands of federal officials strewn throughout the country about any matter arguably within their jurisdiction to inquire about, even if the person making the statement is not put under oath. Because the typical reasonably educated citizen knows that it is a crime (perjury) to lie under oath (such knowledge of the law being common and intuitive, given the formality of the administration of the oath), that same citizen would likely find it counterintuitive that the oath is in fact largely irrelevant, and that it is a felony to lie to government officials even when not sworn to tell the truth.

[23.] Securities Exchange Act of 1934, Section 10(b).

24. The SEC thus enacted Rule 10b-5, which provides:

It shall be unlawful for any person, directly or indirectly, by the use of any means or instrumentality of interstate commerce, or of the mails or of any facilities of any national securities exchange,

a. To employ any device, scheme, or artifice to defraud,

b. To make any untrue statement of a material fact or to omit to state a material fact necessary in order to make the statements made, in the light of the circumstances under which they were made, not misleading, or

c. To engage in any act, practice, or course of business which operates or would operate as a fraud or deceit upon any person,

in connection with the purchase or sale of any security.

25. Daniel Fischel, *Payback: The Conspiracy to Destroy Michael Milken and His Financial Revolution* (New York: HarperBusiness, 1995) 57-58.

26. *Id*. at 59.

27. Michael McMenamin, "St. Martha: Why Martha Stewart should go to heaven and the SEC should go to hell," *Reason*, October 2003 ("But open-endedness has its advantages. It allows the SEC to ignore, condone, or even facilitate insider trading when it chooses and then go after a juicy target like Martha Stewart, whose alleged insider trading is well outside anything recognized as such by the Supreme Court.").

28. "Martha Stewart will pay $195K to settle civil insider trading charges with SEC," Associated Press, August 7, 2006.

29. "Stewart convicted on all charges," *CNNMoney.com*, March 10, 2004.

30. Indeed, when Lay died before his appeal was decided, he in a sense got his final revenge, since the conviction had to be vacated, as is the ordinary federal practice when a conviction is under appeal at the time the appellant dies.

31. Alexei Barrionuevo & Kurt Eichenwald, "The Enron Case That Almost Wasn't," *The New York Times*, June 4, 2006.

32. Ellen S. Podgor, "Overcriminalization," *Conglomerate: Business, Law, Economics, Society*, June 1, 2006, available at http://www.theconglomerate.org/2006/06/overcriminaliza.html.

33. Malcolm Gladwell, "Open Secrets: Enron, intelligence, and the perils of too much information," *The New Yorker*, January 8, 2007,Available at http://www.newyorker.com/reporting/2007/01/08/070108fa_fact_gladwell.

34. Weil's column ran in the Texas regional edition of *The Wall Street Journal*, in the "Heard in Texas" feature, on September 20, 2000.

Chapter Five:

1. Carrie Johnson, "Charge Against KPMG Dropped: Firm Cooperated Over Tax Shelters, Prosecutors Say," *washingtonpost.com*, January 4, 2007.

2. Lynnley Browning, "Ernst & Young Won't Face Criminal Charges," *The New York Times*, May 31, 2007.

3. The nation's top international accounting firms (the ones large enough to conduct audits of the largest corporations) were, not so many years ago, dubbed "the Big Eight" which, after various mergers, became in 2002 "the Big Five." They were: Arthur Andersen; Deloitte & Touche; KPMG; Ernst & Young; and PricewaterhouseCoopers.

4. Robert A. Mintz, "Too Late for Arthur Andersen," *Legal Times*, June 6, 2005. Mintz was at the time head of the securities litigation, government investigations, and white collar criminal defense practice group at Newark, New Jersey's McCarter & English law firm.

5. *Id.* at p. 70.

6. This "usually indicates," wrote *The New York Times*'s savvy Supreme Court analyst Linda Greenhouse, in reporting the unexpected grant of the petition, that "the government considers an appeal to be frivolous or inconsequential." See Linda Greenhouse, "Supreme Court Will Review Conviction of Arthur Andersen," *The New York Times*, January 8, 2005.

7. In this context, such a charge against earnings is a non-recurring charge-off made by the company that reduces its earnings for the reportable period, but does not indicate a recurring or regular pattern. In other words, the reader is supposed to assume that while some event caused this particular charge, it would not necessarily be a regular or recurring event. In contrast, normal expenses of doing business are expected to recur in each reporting period. Corporations are thought to have an incentive to classify charges as non-recurring, where possible, in order to make current financial results seem more positive, or at least indicative of a more positive future. Enron was thought to have classified many normal costs of doing business as one-time non-recurring charges, thereby overstating the company's financial health.

8. Tony Mauro, "One little e-mail, one big legal issue," *The National Law Journal*, April 25, 2005, p. 7.

9. It is the role of the jury to determine the facts. The judge instructs the jury as to the legal principles that govern the case. The jury, once instructed on the law, then proceeds to decide how the facts fit within the legal framework, and whether they require a verdict of guilty or not guilty.

10. *Arthur Andersen LLP v. United States*, 544 U.S. 696 at 706 (2005).

11. Jess Bravin, "Supreme Court Hints at Curbing Strategy on White-Collar Crime," *The Wall Street Journal*, April 28, 2005.

12. Two KPMG leaders testified to Congress in 2003, defending the shelters by making four arguments, which can be viewed in detail at http://www.pbs.org/wgbh/pages/frontline/shows/tax/schemes/testimony.html. In his prepared statement, Jeffrey Eischeid offered a four-part defense of KPMG: that the firm no longer markets aggressive sheltering strategies such as FLIP, OPIS, BLIPS or SC2; that when it did offer such strategies, they were "consistent with the laws in place at the time;" that the strategies underwent "intensive and thorough" internal review, which often resulted in "vigorous, sometimes even heated, debate"; and that KPMG has changed over the past three years as "the regulatory environment and marketplace conditions have changed." Eischeid also noted that no court had ruled against any of these four strategies. Under questioning from Sen.

Carl Levin (D-Mich.), he insisted that the shelters were not marketed as tax reduction strategies, but rather as investment strategies with tax benefits.

13. *Jacobellis v. Ohio*, 378 U.S. 184 (1964).

14. Robert Weisberg & David Mills, "A Very Strange Indictment," *The Wall Street Journal*, Review & Outlook, October 12, 2005. Weisberg is Edwin E. Huddleson, Jr. Professor of Law and director of the Criminal Justice Center at Stanford University. Mr. Mills is senior lecturer at Stanford Law School. Together, they have taught a course in white collar crime at Stanford Law School.

15. Editorial, "Congress and KPMG," *The Wall Street Journal*, August 30, 2005.

16. *Id.*

17. *Id.*

18. In 2005, the Supreme Court declared that the sentencing guidelines, up to that point mandatory, were merely advisory, leaving to trial judges considerable discretion in imposing sentences on defendants. Subsequent appellate case law, however, made clear that the guidelines were to be given substantial deference by trial judges, although they were empowered to articulate specific reasons for departing from them in a particular case.

19. Memorandum to All Component Heads and United States Attorneys re: "Bringing Criminal Charges Against Corporations," from Eric H. Holder, Jr., Deputy Attorney General, June 16, 1999. Available at http://www.usdoj.gov/criminal/fraud/docs/reports/1999/chargingcorps.html. Holder suggested that cooperation was partially defined by whether a company agreed to waive the legally protected attorney-client and work-product privileges. He further suggested that cooperation would be determined by "whether the corporation appears to be protecting its culpable employees and agents" by advancing or paying those individuals' attorney fees.

20. "Principles of Federal Prosecution of Business Organizations," Deputy Attorney General Larry D. Thompson to Heads of Department Components of U.S. Attorneys, January 20, 2003, Office of the Deputy Attorney General.

21. Former federal prosecutor and now scrappy defense lawyer N. Richard Janis has been relentless in exposing the unfairness of the Thompson Memorandum and its successors, and some progress has been made, but the DOJ's approach remains essentially the same. See, for example, N. Richard Janis, "Taking the Stand: The McNulty Memorandum: Much Ado About Nothing," *Washington Lawyer*, February 2007.

22. Lynnley Browning, "Document Could Alter KPMG Case," *The New York Times*, Sept 15, 2006.

23. Subsequent litigation on these shelters did indeed go in favor of the government's position.

24. Laurie P. Cohen, "Prosecutors' Tough New Tactics Turn Firms Against Employees," *The Wall Street Journal*, June 4, 2004.

25. Ms. Martin was quoted by Laurie Cohen in the *WSJ* as saying that Mr. Bennett was a "pleasure" to work with. This symbiotic and perhaps even pleasurable relationship appeared to continue in the KPMG case.

[26.] Jonathan Weil, "KPMG's Settlement Provides for New Start," *The Wall Street Journal*, August 29, 2005.

[27.] Floyd Norris, "KPMG, a Proud Old Lion, Brought to Heel," *The New York Times*, August 30, 2005.

[28.] Deborah Solomon & Ann Marie Squeo, "Crackdown Puts Corporations, Executives in New Legal Peril," *The Wall Street Journal*, June 20, 2005.

[29.] Jonathan Glater, "Indictment Broadens In Shelters At KPMG," *The New York Times*, October 18, 2005.

[30.] Lynnley Browning & Colin Moynihan, "A Surprise In Tax Case On KPMG," *The New York Times*, March 28, 2006.

[31.] Lynnley Browning, "Guilty Plea Made in Trial Over Shelters From KPMG," *The New York Times* (New England Edition), December 22, 2006, at C3.

[32.] Paul Davies, "Defendant in KPMG Tax Case Pleads Guilty, Agrees to Cooperate," *The Wall Street Journal*, September 11, 2007.

[33.] Memorandum to United States Attorneys re: "Principles of Federal Prosecution of Business Organizations," from Larry D. Thompson, Deputy Attorney General, January 20, 2003.

[34.] In July 2007, Judge Kaplan dismissed the charges against 13 of the defendants, saying that the government's deferred prosecution agreement with KPMG violated the individual defendants' Sixth Amendment right to counsel and their right to due process. *U.S. v. Jeffrey Stein, et al.* (S.D.N.Y., July 16, 2007). Available at http://online.wsj.com/public/resources/documents/stein.pdf. This significant ruling was upheld in August 2008 by the Court of Appeals for the Second Circuit. In December 2008, a jury found three of the remaining defendants guilty on multiple counts of tax evasion, while acquitting a former KPMG tax partner.

[35.] Deborah Solomon, "SEC Brings New Federal Oversight To Insurance Industry With Probes," *The Wall Street Journal*, April 1, 2005.

[36.] See letter written by Greenberg's lawyer, David Boies, to AIG's law firm, dated March 28, 2005, reported in *Insurance Journal*, March 29, 2005, available at http://www.insurancejournal.com/news/national/2005/03/29/53099.html.

[37.] Ian McDonald, Theo Francis & Deborah Solomon, "AIG Admits 'Improper' Accounting," *The Wall Street Journal*, March 31, 2005.

[38.] "Ex-AIG chief assails move to restate results," *The Boston Globe*, Associated Press, August 5, 2005.

[39.] Jenny Anderson, "Suit Against A.I.G. Figure May Expand," *The New York Times*, November 26, 2005.

[40.] *Id.*

[41.] *Id.*

[42.] Jenny Anderson, "Indictments Raise Pressure In Insurer Case," *The New York Times*, February 3, 2006.

[43.] Gretchen Morgenson, "A.I.G. Apologizes and Agrees to $1.64 Billion Settlement," *The New York Times*, February 10, 2006.

44. "Hank Greenberg at War," *Business Week*, March 27, 2006.

45. *Id.*

46. Email message to Harvey A. Silverglate from Professor Susan R. Estrich, July 18, 2007.

47. Roddy Boyd, "New battle for Hank Greenberg," *Fortune/CNN Money*, May 21, 2008, available at http://money.cnn.com/2008/05/21/magazines/fortune/fortune500/Boyd_Greenberg.fortune/index.htm?postversion=2008052113.

Chapter Six:

1. John Christoffersen, Associated Press, "Arrest sparks worries over implications of corporate law," *The Houston Chronicle*, March 4, 2007.

2. Sarah Johnson, "Sarbox May Extend to Child Pornography," *CFO.com*, March 16, 2007.

3. *United States v. Philip D. Russell*, Docket No. 3:07CR31(AHN), U.S.D.C., Dist. of Connecticut, Ruling on Motions to Dismiss Indictment, filed August 22, 2007.

4. Sarah Johnson, "Sarbox May Extend to Child Pornography," *CFO.com*, March 16, 2007.

5. Martin B. Cassidy, "Legal world focused on lawyer prosecution," *Greenwich Time*, March 4, 2007.

6. Martin B. Cassidy, "Child porn case has attorneys worried," *The Stamford Advocate*, March 4, 2007.

7. John Christoffersen, Associated Press, "Arrest sparks worries over implications of corporate law," *The Houston Chronicle*, March 4, 2007.

8. Martin B. Cassidy, "Legal world focused on lawyer prosecution," *Greenwich Time*, March 4, 2007.

9. "Government's Omnibus Response to the Defendant's Motions to Dismiss Counts One and Two of the Indictment," filed in *United States v. Philip D. Russell*, Criminal Indictment No. 3:07CR31(AHN), at page 14.

10. Government's brief at 14, citing *United States v. Iho*, 465 F.Supp. 2d at 635-36.

11. *Rogers v. State*, 113 S.W. 3d 452, 458-59 (Tex.App. 2003), cited in Russell's "Memorandum in Support of Motion to Dismiss Count Two" at page 9.

12. Glenn Puit, "Arrest Threat: Child Porn Copies Lead to Conflict," *The Las Vegas Review Journal*, July 28, 2003, cited in Russell's "Memorandum in Support of Motion to Dismiss Count Two" at page 9.

13. 18 U.S.C. § 4.

14. *Roberts v. United States*, 445 U.S. 552, 558 n. 5 (["The misprision statute] has been construed to require 'both knowledge of a crime and some affirmative act of concealment.'"). See generally Gabriel Ciociola, "Misprision of Felony and its Progeny," 41 Brandeis L.J. 697, 699 (2003).

15. This phenomenon is discussed further in Chapter Seven, concerning the press.

16. The obstruction statute under which Cintolo was indicted provided:

> Whoever...corruptly or by threats or force, or by any threatening letter or communication, influences, obstructs, or impedes, or endeavors to influence, obstruct, or impede, the due administration of justice, shall

be fined not more than $5,000 or imprisoned not more than five years, or both. 18 U.S.C. § 1503.

[17.] EC-7-8, *ABA Model Code of Professional Responsibility* (1982).

[18.] *Smith v. Anderson Tully*, 608 F.Supp, 1143, 1146-47 (D. Miss. 1985).

[19.] "Cintolo's only response to this grisly piece of news," the Court of Appeals said, "was to mention calmly [to Angiulo] that he had instructed LaFreniere to talk with no one, and to refer all calls to him." *United States v. Cintolo*, 818 F.2d 980 (1st Cir., 1987). Some criminal defense lawyers might have handled this delicate situation differently, but, all factors considered, the Massachusetts Association of Criminal Defense Lawyers and the National Network for the Right to Counsel were right on the mark in urging the Court of Appeals to take a realistic, functional view of Cintolo's role, plight, and judgments.

[20.] *United States v. Cintolo*, 818 F.2d 980 (1st Cir., 1987).

[21.] The Court of Appeals, moreover, did not internalize its own reasoning from its conclusory review of the wiretap tapes. "This particular conversation," wrote the court, "concluded with Angiulo instructing Cintolo to meet with LaFreniere again and 'to evaluate [the situation] very carefully.'" In other words, it appeared that the Angiulos might be prepared to back off the plan to "hit" LaFreniere, having been tempered by Cintolo's assurances that he was trying to keep his client calm. Any criminal lawyer would have understood how and why Cintolo handled this dangerous and delicate problem in the way he did, even if some would have taken a more prosecutor-friendly path and thereby exposed their client to mortal danger. But to the Court of Appeals, as to the Department of Justice, all of this signified a lawyer gone bad, notwithstanding the assurances from the *amici*, experienced defense lawyers, that Cintolo handled himself about as well as could be expected (or at least perfectly acceptably) under extraordinarily difficult circumstances. That the Court of Appeals continued, throughout its opinion, to refer to LaFreniere as Cintolo's "client" (encasing the word "client" in quotation marks on each occasion) betrayed the court's naïve, or perhaps cynical, view that Cintolo at no time acted with LaFreniere's, rather than Angiulo's, interests in mind.

[22.] *United States v. Cintolo*, 818 F.2d 980, 990 (1st Cir., 1987).

[23.] "Blue-ribbon task force finds President Bush's signing statements undermine separation of powers," ABA Press Release, July 24, 2008.

[24.] Telephone discussion and email exchanges between Michael Greco and the author at various times in 2007.

[25.] "DOJ Alleges American Bar Association Violates Antitrust Consent Decree," *Antitrust Lawyers Blog*, June 23, 2006, available at http://www.antitrustlawyerblog.com/2006/06/doj_alleges_american_bar_assoc.html.

[26.] "Court order brings ABA consent decree to conclusion," American Bar Association, available at http://www.abanet.org/media/youraba/200606/article02.html.

[27.] Department of Justice Press Release, "Justice Department and American Bar Association Resolve Charges that the ABA's process for accrediting law schools was misused," June 27, 1995, available at http://www.usdoj.gov/atr/public/press_releases/1995/0257.htm.

[28.] "Redacted" documents are documents where certain information is omitted. For example, some documents might be redacted by deleting the names of individuals, either to protect their privacy or to refrain from notifying them that they are under surveillance or investigation. Other documents might be redacted in order to protect the identity of informants or undercover operatives.

29. Memorandum "To: All ACLU, ACLU Foundation and ACLU Affiliate Staff" from Ann Beeson, dated August 26, 2005, "re: URGENT: Restrictions on Information Regarding *ACLU v. Gonzales*, Our Legal Challenge to the National Security Letter Issued to an Organization with Library Records."

Chapter Seven:

1. Meghan Martin & Larry Larsen, "A Guide to Journalist Shield Laws," *Poynter Online*, available at http://www.poynterextra.org/shieldlaw/states.htm (accessed June 5, 2008).

2. Portions of the discussion of the Jared Paul Stern case have appeared previously in Harvey A. Silverglate, "Sleazy? Yes. Criminal? Probably not," *The Boston Phoenix*, April 12, 2006.

3. Title 18 U.S.C. sec. 875(d) states in relevant part:

> Whoever, with intent to extort from any person, firm, association, or corporation, any money or other thing of value, transmits in interstate or foreign commerce any communication containing any threat to injure the property or reputation of the addressee or of another or the reputation of a deceased person or any threat to accuse the addressee or any other person of a crime, shall be fined under this title or imprisoned not more than two years, or both.

4. *United States v. Jackson*, 180 F.3d 55, 70 (1999).

5. Here's the text of this bit of Silly Putty®, codified at 18 U.S.C. § 1343:

> Whoever, having devised or intending to devise any scheme or artifice to defraud, or for obtaining money or property by means of false or fraudulent pretenses, representations, or promises, transmits or causes to be transmitted by means of wire, radio, or television communication in interstate or foreign commerce, any writings, signs, signals, pictures, or sounds for the purpose of executing such scheme or artifice, shall be fined under this title or imprisoned not more than 20 years, or both.

6. The courts have interpreted this "honest services" language broadly, typically holding that a violation occurs when an "employee of a private entity (or a person in a relationship that gives rise to a duty of loyalty comparable to that owed by employees to employers) purporting to act for and in the interests of his or her employer (or of the other person to whom the duty of loyalty is owed) secretly act[s] in his or her or the defendant's own interests instead, accompanied by a material misrepresentation made or omission of information disclosed to the employer or other person." *United States v. Rybicki*, 354 F.3d 124, 141-42 (2d Cir. 2003) (reaffirmed *en banc*) (cert. den. Oct. 4, 2004).

7. Adam Goldman, "No Charges for N.Y. Tabloid Scribe," *The Washington Post*, January 24, 2007, available at http://www.washingtonpost.com/wp-dyn/content/article/2007/01/24/AR2007012400292.html.

8. *Near v. Minnesota*, 283 U.S. 697 (1931).

9. The relevant section, 18 U.S.C. § 798, provides:

> Disclosure of Classified Information.
>
> > (a) Whoever knowingly and willfully communicates, furnishes, transmits, or otherwise makes available to an unauthorized person, or publishes, or uses in any manner prejudicial to the safety or interest of the United States or for the benefit of any foreign government to the detriment of the United States any classified information—
> >
> > > (1) concerning the nature, preparation, or use of any code, cipher, or cryptographic system of the United States or any foreign government; or
> > >
> > > (2) concerning the design, construction, use, maintenance, or repair of any device, apparatus, or appliance used or prepared or planned for use by the United States or any foreign government for cryptographic or communication intelligence purposes; or
> > >
> > > (3) concerning the communication intelligence activities of the United States or any foreign government; or
> > >
> > > (4) obtained by the processes of communication intelligence from the communications of any foreign government, knowing the same to have been obtained by such processes—
> >
> > Shall be fined not more than $10,000 or imprisoned not more than ten years, or both.

10. *New York Times Co. v. United States*, 403 U.S. 713, 1971 Lexis 100 (1971).

11. Sanford J. Ungar, *The Papers & The Papers: An Account of the Legal and Political Battle Over The Pentagon Papers* (New York: E. P. Dutton & Co., Inc., 1972). Disclosure: I represented Sanford Ungar, in his capacity as a *Washington Post* reporter, during the *Pentagon Papers* episode.

12. Whitney North Seymour, *United States Attorney* (New York: William Morrow and Co., 1975), p. 204.

13. My analysis of the Supreme Court's *Pentagon Papers* opinion (*New York Times Co. v. United States*) and discussion of subsequent efforts by the Nixon administration to indict the newspapers appeared for the first time in my regular *Boston Phoenix* column. See Harvey A. Silverglate, "The Gray Lady in Shadow: Could publication of the domestic-spying story lead to indictment of *The New York Times?*" *The Boston Phoenix*, January 6, 2006, available at http://bostonphoenix.com/boston/news_features/other_stories/multi_5/documents/05188679.asp.

14. See, e.g., Daniel Ellsberg, *Secrets: A Memoir of Vietnam and the Pentagon Papers* (New York: Penguin, 2003), pp. 455-57; John Prados & Margaret Pratt Porter, eds., *Inside the Pentagon Papers* (Lawrence, Kansas: University Press of Kansas, 2004), p. 89.

15. Gabriel Schoenfeld, "Has *The New York Times* Violated the Espionage Act?" *Commentary*, March 2006.

[16.] The Classified Information Procedures Act (CIPA), which was promulgated in 1980 and amended since, designates what types of classified information and materials a defendant may seek. 18 U.S.C. app. III.

[17.] Harold Edgar & Benno C. Schmidt, Jr., "The Espionage Statutes and Publication of Defense Information," *Columbia Law Review*, Vol. 73, No. 5 (May 1973). The quote is at p. 930.

[18.] *Branzburg v. Hayes*, 408 U.S. 665 (1972).

[19.] "The Reporters' Privilege Compendium: An Introduction," Reporters' Committee for Freedom of the Press, available at http://www.rcfp.org/privilege/item.php?pg=intro (last accessed June 5, 2008). At the time of the *Branzburg* decision, only 17 states had reporter shield statutes. Steve Montiel, 'Triumph of black journalists' – shield law lesson for today, *San Francisco Chronicle*, October 30, 2005, available at http://www.sfgate.com/cgi-bin/article.cgi?file=/chronicle/archive/2005/10/30/INGH1FEJRG1.DTL.

[20.] 28 C.F.R. § 50.10 and the United States Attorney's Manual, § 9-2.161. Among other things, the guidelines provide that the Attorney General must approve subpoenas for testimony by news media, and that the subpoenas should be used to obtain only essential, not peripheral or speculative, information. The guidelines further state that all reasonable efforts to obtain the information from alternative sources must first be made.

[21.] *United States v. Progressive*, Inc., *et al.*, 467 F. Supp. 990 (W.D. Wisc., 1979).

[22.] *United States v. Progressive*, Inc., *et al.*, 486 F. Supp. 5, 8 (W.D. Wisc., 1979) (decision on defendants' motion to reconsider and vacate prior restraint); see also Howard Moreland, "On the Progressive Case," Presentation at Cardozo School of Law, March 2, 2004, available at http://www.fas.org/sgp/eprint/cardozo.html.

[23.] *Ibid.*, 486 F. Supp. at 7.

[24.] Letter Bomb: Printing atomic 'secrets', *Time*, October 1, 1979, available at http://www.time.com/time/magazine/article/0,9171,947479-1,00.html.

[25.] David Rivkin & Bruce Sanford, "Outing Operatives, Jailing Journalists," *The Wall Street Journal*, Dec. 14, 2004.

[26.] Theodore B. Olson, "Scandal," *The Wall Street Journal*, Oct. 31, 2005.

[27.] Associated Press, "Fearing Legal Battle, Ohio Newspaper Holds Stories," *The Los Angeles Times*, July 9, 2005, available at http://www.latimes.com/news/nationworld/nation/la-na-cleveland9jul09,1,4605149.story. See also David Cay Johnston, "Most Editors Say They'd Publish Articles Based on Leaks," *The New York Times*, July 11, 2005.

[28.] Matt Welch, "Taking the Fifth: When journalists threaten our right to remain silent," *Reason*, March 2005.

[29.] Lucy Dalglish, "Back to square one, 34 years later," *The News Media and the Law*, Fall 2004, Volume 28, Number 4, at 1.

[30.] Stephen Labaton, "U.S. Subpoenas 2 Dow Writers, Then Backs Off," *The New York Times*, Feb. 25, 2006, at A1.

[31.] Tom Brune, "Time Inc. gives up reporter's notes," *Newsday*, July 1, 2005, available at http://www.newsday.com/news/nationworld/nation/ny-usleakq4326425jul01,0,1931787.story.

[32.] Jacob Heilbrunn, "Start Me Up," *The New York Times Book Review*, November 26, 2006 (reviewing *Unanimous, I Hate Ann Coulter!*, Simon Spotlight Entertainment, 2006).

[33.] Harvey A. Silverglate, "The Gray Lady in Shadow," *The Boston Phoenix*, January 6, 2006.

[34.] See, for example, James Bamford, *The Puzzle Palace: A report on America's most secret agency* (Boston: Houghton Mifflin, 1982); James Bamford, *Body of Secrets: Anatomy of the ultra-secret National Security Agency: from the Cold War through the dawn of a new century* (New York: Doubleday, 2001); and Patrick Radden Keefe, *Chatter: Dispatches from the secret world of global eavesdropping* (New York: Random House, 2005).

[35.] Foreign Intelligence Surveillance Act of 1978, 50 U.S.C. §§ 1801 *et seq.*

[36.] Sacha Pfeiffer, "Extreme Souvenir: How I handed money to Maoist insurgents, and lived to worry about it," *The Boston Sunday Globe*, "Ideas" section, December 30, 2007.

Chapter Eight:

[1.] The Espionage Act, 18 U.S.C. §§ 792-99.

[2.] John Cavanagh, then-director of the Institute for Policy Studies, wrote in an article published in 1980 that throughout the 1960s and possibly beyond "at least five Princeton professors worked secretly as high-level consultants for the CIA," a fact discovered from the personal papers of former CIA Director (and Princeton alumnus) Allen W. Dulles. Dulles's papers indicated that Princeton was far from alone among American universities in providing academic consultation to American intelligence specialists. And not all of these activities were even kept secret. One of the Princeton Professors, renowned Russian scholar James Hadley Billington, later the Librarian of Congress, admitted in 1968 to the undergraduate newspaper, *The Daily Princetonian*, that he consulted for the CIA's Office of National Estimates "two or three times a year." He described the papers submitted by him and his faculty cohorts as "broad and scholarly." Fellow Princeton historian Cyril Black, who in 1976 had denied to the campus newspaper that he had ever been in the CIA's "employ," admitted to Cavanagh in 1980 (when Cavanagh gained access to the Dulles papers and the truth had emerged) that he had been a paid consultant. "Nobody ever asked me if I was a consultant," Black explained, thus giving himself the leeway to deny the rumors that he was an "employee." Rounding out the group were Professors Klaus Knorr, Joseph Strayer, and T. Cuyler Young, who met with Dulles four times a year "to assist with intelligence assessments for the CIA's Office of National Estimates," according to Cavanagh. Then-university President Robert F. Goheen knew of this, so it was not exactly a complete secret.   John Cavanagh, "Dulles Papers Reveal CIA Consulting Network," *Forerunner*, April 29, 1980, http://www.cia-on-campus.org/princeton.edu/consult.html. Many thanks to Craig R. Whitney for calling this piece to my attention. See also Tim Weiner, *Legacy of Ashes—The History of the CIA* (New York, Doubleday, 2007), discussing the role of numerous Ivy League academics in the work of the CIA.

[3.] Craig R. Whitney, *Spy Trader: Germany's Devil's Advocate & the Darkest Secrets of the Cold War* (New York: Times Books/Random House, 1993). Readers interested in more details of the Alfred Zehe prosecution and its diplomatic entanglements, as well as more generally of the remarkable career of Wolfgang Vogel, are directed to Mr. Whitney's invaluable and fascinating volume, some details of which, however, Professor Zehe would disagree with. Whitney was the long-time European diplomatic correspondent for *The New York Times*.

4. *United States v. Zehe*, 601 F.Supp. 196, 1985 U.S. Dist. LEXIS 23053 (D. Mass. 1985). In an odd aside, Judge Nelson observed: "Finally, the defendant questions the policy implications of applying the Act to noncitizens who might merely have reviewed defense documents supplied to them by their respective governments. The Court does not find the defendant's scenario likely. Under the statutorily defined crimes of espionage in sections 793 and 794, noncitizens would be subject to prosecution only if they actively sought out and obtained or delivered defense information to a foreign government or conspired to do so." *Zehe*, 601 F.Supp. at 201. Of course, an academic who has an agreement with his government that he would make himself available to advise his government and help his government understand technological issues relating to national security would almost certainly be seen as a "conspirator" in any act of espionage engaged in by his government's secret agents. The federal conspiracy laws, after all, are even broader and more vague than the espionage laws.

5. Daniel Golden, "After Sept. 11, the CIA becomes a force on campus," *The Wall Street Journal*, October 7, 2002.

6. Guy Dinmore, "Pominent US scholar detained in Iran," *The Financial Times*, May 9, 2007.

7. *Id*.

8. Ali Akbar Dareini, Associated Press, "Iran charges a noted scholar, 2 others from US with spying," *The Boston Globe*, May 30, 2007.

9. Associated Press, "3rd Iranian-American Detained by Tehran, Which Hints at a Treason Plot," *The New York Times*, May 24, 2007.

10. Katarina Kratovac, Associated Press, "Groups urge Iran to release detainees," *The Boston Globe*, June 1, 2007.

11. "Iran: Another Iranian-American Scholar Detained; Crackdown Against Iranian Civil Society Intensifies," *Human Rights Watch*, http://hrw.org/english/docs/2007/05/24/iran15993_txt.htm.

12. *United States v. Lachman*, 278 F.Supp. 2d 68, 2003 U.S. Dist. LEXIS 14636 (August 14, 2003).

13. *Id*. at 82.

14. *Id*. at 91 (quoting *United States v. Reese*, 92 U.S. 214 (1876)).

15. *United States v. Anzalone*, 766 F.2d 676, 681 (1st Cir. 1985); see also the discussion of the case of Theodore Anzalone in Chapter One.

16. Lewis Carroll, *Through the Looking Glass*, What Alice Found There (1986) (emphasis in the original), quoted by Judge Woodlock in footnote 45 of his Lachman opinion.

17. Lewis Carroll, *Alice's Adventures in Wonderland* (Forum Books, New York, 1963), p. 159.

[18.] "This is right out of Hitler's handbook," *The Guardian*, Guardian Unlimited Website, October 20, 2005, http://arts.guardian.co.uk/features/story/0,11710,1596029,00.html.

[19.] *Id.*

[20.] David Staba, "Use of Bacteria in Art Leads to Investigation," *The New York Times*, June 7, 2004.

[21.] Al Matthews, "SUNY Buffalo art: It's not bio-terror, but is it illegal anyway?," *CNN Headline News*, July 12, 2004, available at http://www.cnn.com/2004/SHOWBIZ/07/12/buffalo.art.

[22.] Critical Art Ensemble Defense Fund, "Frequently Asked Questions," available at http://www.caedefensefund.org/faq.html.

[23.] 18 U.S.C. § 175 (Prohibitions with respect to biological weapons).

[24.] David Staba, "Use of Bacteria in Art Leads to Investigation," *The New York Times*, June 7, 2004.

[25.] 18 U.S.C. § 1341 (mail fraud) and 18 U.S.C. § 1343 (wire fraud).

[26.] *United States of America v. Steven Kurtz and Robert Ferrell*, Indictment No. 0~CR-155E (W.D.N.Y. 2004).

[27.] *Serratia marcescens* is ubiquitous in the environment and is commonly found growing in bathrooms, especially on tile grout. It is also found in dirt and on teeth below the gums. *Bacillus atrophaeus*, while benign, is used to test antibiotics against anthrax, its morphologically similar but deadly bacteriological cousin. Hence, there was no charge possible that would depend to any degree on a claim of dangerousness to public health. The organisms most commonly used for biowarfare and bioterrorism are anthrax, botulinum toxins, brucellosis, cholera, clostridium perfringens toxins, congo-crimean hemorrhagic fever, ebola haemorrhagic fever, melioidosis, plague, Q fever, ricin, rift valley fever, sanitoxin, smallpox, staphylococcal enterotoxin B, trichothecene mycotoxin, tularemia, and Venezuelan equine encephalitis. In contrast to these deadly pathogens, the harmless organisms possessed by Kurtz have never been used as a destructive agent in war or terrorism. Instead, they are used to test the capabilities of anti-biowarfare air purifiers. See http://www.sanuvox.com/PDF%20Brochures/EPA_Homeland_Security_Sanuvox.pdf.

[28.] http://newstandardnews.net/content/?action=show_item&itemid=646.

[29.] *Id.*

[30.] http://www.nytimes.com/2004/06/29/science/29cont.html.

[31.] http://www.caedefensefund.org/letters.html.

[32.] http://www.buffalonews.com/editorial/20040707/3028537.asp.

[33.] http://newstandardnews.net/content/?action=show_item&itemid=646.

[34.] Al Matthews, "SUNY Buffalo art: It's not bio-terror, but is it illegal anyway?" *CNN Headline News*, available at http://www.cnn.com/2004/SHOWBIZ/07/12/buffalo.art.

[35.] Order dated April 21, 2008, *United States of America v. Steven Kurtz*, No. 04-CR-0155A, United States District Court for the Western District of New York, by the Honorable Richard J. Arcara, Chief Judge, 12-page slip-sheet opinion.

[36.] Chief Judge Arcara wrote that he "passes no judgment on whether the indictment could have been drafted in such a way, based on the facts and circumstances as they have been presented here, to allege sufficiently a 'no-sale' theory of fraud." The judge simply found "that the indictment, as currently written, fails to allege such a theory."

[37.] Maureen O'Hagan, "A terrorism case that went awry," *The Seattle Times*, Nov. 22, 2004.

[38.] Betsy Z. Russell, "Feds drop charges in deal that sends Al-Hussayen home," *The Spokesman Review*, July 1, 2004.

[39.] Maureen O'Hagan, "A terrorism case that went awry," *The Seattle Times*, Nov. 22, 2004.

[40.] *Id.*

[41.] As one federal court in Washington observed, "The Patriot Act was passed…with relatively little debate or discussion." *United States v. $6,976,934.65 Plus Interest*, 478 F.Supp.2d 30, 42 (D.D.C., 2007).

[42.] Maureen O'Hagan, "A terrorism case that went awry," *The Seattle Times*, Nov. 22, 2004.

[43.] *Id.*

[44.] See *Brandenburg v. Ohio*, 395 US 444 (1969).

[45.] *United States of America vs. Sami Omar al-Hussayen*, Case No. CR03-048-C-EJL (United States District Court for the District of Idaho), Jury Instructions, June 1, 2004, Instruction No. 48.

[46.] Maureen O'Hagan, "A terrorism case that went awry," *The Seattle Times*, Nov. 22, 2004.

[47.] Betsy Z. Russell, "Al-Hussayen acquitted in terror case," *The Spokesman Review*, June 11, 2004, available at http://www.spokesmanreview.com/local/story.asp?ID=10124&page=all.

[48.] Steve Coll, *Ghost Wars: The secret history of the CIA, Afghanistan, and bin Laden from the Soviet invasion to September 10, 2001* (New York: Penguin, 2004), at 70.

[49.] I participated in the legal team that defended Muntasser and was responsible, in part, for analyzing the extent to which the prosecution indirectly sought to punish constitutionally protected religious and political views.

[50.] Organizations seeking exempt status must file IRS Form 1023 outlining their reasons for requesting such status. When Muntasser signed and submitted the form in 1993, he wrote on Form 1023 that the organization would be devoted to "provid[ing] assistance to victims of natural and man-made disasters…primarily in Bosnia and later in African countries. …[and] develop[ing] a program for orphan sponsorships." See *United States v. Muhamed Mubayyid et al.*, Superseding Indictment (March 8, 2007), Crim. No. 05-40026-FDS (D. Mass. 2007) at 3.

[51.] Exempt organizations include "…any fund, or foundation, organized and operated exclusively for religious [or] charitable [or several other] purposes …" with several exceptions not relevant to Care International's work. 26 U.S.C. § 501(c)(3); see also C.F.R. §1.501(c)(3)-1(c)(1) ("An organization will be regarded as operated exclusively for one or more exempt purposes only if it engages primarily in activities which accomplish one or more of such exempt purposes specified in section 501(c)(3).”). Charitable organizations are defined as having primary missions, such as “relief of the poor and distressed or of the underprivileged; [or] advancement of religion,” among other relevant exempt-status charitable activities. 26 C.F.R. § 1.501(c)(3)-1(d)(2).

[52.] Bench decision on Rule 29 motion for judgment of acquittal and Rule 31 motion for a new trial, *United States v. Mubayyid et al.*, June 3, 2008, Crim. No. 05-40026-FDS (D. Mass. 2007) at 7.

[53.] *Id.* at 3 (“There was substantial evidence at the trial that all three defendants supported and promoted jihad and the mujahideen, that is, religious-based violence and people who engage in it through newsletters, financial donations, lectures and otherwise; although in fairness, there was no evidence that they provided lethal aid or similar support to any fighters.”)

[54.] Testimony of Marcus Owens, trial transcript in *United States v. Mubayyid et al.*, December 17, 2007 (day 22), Crim. No. 05-40026-FDS (D. Mass. 2007) at 92.

[55.] *Id.* at 56.

[56.] Muntasser’s legal team, by the time his post-trial motions were filed, consisted of a number of seasoned criminal and constitutional trial and appellate litigators, including the Boston law firm of Zalkind, Rodriguez, Lunt & Duncan, LLP; Professor Susan Estrich of the University of Southern California Law School; and Kathleen Sullivan, former Dean of the Stanford Law School and by then a partner in the litigation boutique Quinn, Emanuel, Urquhart, Oliver & Hedges, LLP. None of them were able to make much sense of the government’s innovative theory of prosecution. Indeed, the IRS obviously had its own qualms over the clarity of the particular form and its instructions to the user. In the year 2000 the IRS changed the form and attempted to clarify the instructions. This implicit recognition that something was wrong with the form and instructions did not, however, stop the Department of Justice from indicting Muntasser.

[57.] BNA’s *Health Law Reporter*, Vol. 17, No. 10, March 6, 2008, at p. 355.

[58.] Bench decision on Rule 29 motion, transcript at 7.

[59.] *Id.* at 9.

[60.] *United States v. Anzalone*, 766 F.2d 676 (1st Cir., 1985).

[61.] Case Note/Recent Cases, *The Harvard Law Review*, Volume No. 120, page 821 (2007), critiquing *United States v. Rosen*, 445 F.Supp.2d 602 (E.D. Va. 2006).

[62.] Michael Massing, “The Storm over the Israel Lobby,” *The New York Review of Books*, Vol. 53, No. 10, June 8, 2006.

[63.] 18 U.S.C. § 793(e).

[64.] Jeffrey Goldberg, “Real Insiders,” *The New Yorker*, July 4, 2005.

[65.] *Id.*

[66.] *United States of America v. Steven J. Rosen and Keith Weissman*, Case No. 1:05cr225, United States District Court for the Eastern District of Virginia (Alexandria Division), “Memorandum Opinion” on motion to dismiss, dated August 9, 2006.

[67.] “Memorandum Opinion” in Rosen and Weissman case, at 51. The Morison case is reported at 844 F.2d 1057, 1988 U.S. App. LEXIS 4066 (4th Cir. 1988).

[68.] *United States v. Rosen and Weissman* (4th Cir. 2009), decided February 24, 2009. Prosecutors later dropped the prosecution in May 2009.

Conclusion:

[1.] Stephen G. Sozio & Earnest B. Gregory, "Growing trend: prosecution for workers' injuries, deaths," *The National Law Journal*, July 18, 2005.

[2.] David Barstow and Lowell Bergman, "With Little Fanfare, a New Effort to Prosecute Employers That Flout Safety Laws," *The New York Times*, May 2, 2005.

[3.] The Wrongful Death Accountability Act, introduced by Senator Jon Corzine (D. NJ), would have established 10-year sentences for violations. See S.1272, 108th Cong. (2003).

[4.] A bookdealer using this email service would obtain an address ending in "@interloc. com." Interloc was merged into Alibris, a corporation that eventually became involved in the business of dealing in used and rare books.

[5.] *Konop v. Hawaiian Airlines, Inc.*, 302 F.3d 868 (9th Cir. 2002).

[6.] *United States v. Councilman*, 245 F. Supp. 2d 319 (D. Mass. 2003).

[7.] *Id.* In his written opinion, Judge Ponsor noted with irony that in *Konop* the federal government had supported defining the Wiretap Act to exclude from coverage any temporarily stored electronic communications. Because the prosecution's interests in the *Councilman* case, where the government was the accuser rather than the potential accused, would benefit from a more inclusive and expansive interpretation, the Department of Justice "now argues that at least a portion of that [*Konop*] decision should be ignored."

[8.] *United States v. Councilman*, 373 F.3d 197, 218 (1st Cir. 2004) (Lipez, *dissenting*). A different issue is presented when a statute or regulation gives specialized meaning to a word, in which case the dictionary or common meaning goes out the window. See, for example, the Leichter prosecution, discussed in Chapter Three. However, *Councilman* was not such a case.

[9.] Pauline Jelinek, Associated Press, "Defense Official Resigns Over Remarks," *The Washington Post*, February 2, 2007, available at http://www.washingtonpost.com/wp-dyn/content/article/2007/02/02/AR2007020200940.html.

[10.] Anthony Sebok & Spencer Weber Waller, "The Deputy Assistant Secretary of Defense Suggests A Boycott of Law Firms that Represent Guantanamo Detainees," *Findlaw.com*, January 16, 2007, available at http://writ.lp.findlaw.com/commentary/20070116_waller.html (explaining why Stimson's comments may have indicated official policy views); David Yas, Editorial, "The castigating of Cully is proud moment for lawyers,"*Massachusetts Lawyers Weekly*, January 22, 2007, available at http://www. masslawyersweekly.com/cully.cfm; Lisa Wangsness, "Law school deans sign letter condemning boycott: Pentagon official provoked outcry," *The Boston Globe*, January 16, 2007, available at http://www.boston.com/news/local/articles/2007/01/16/law_school_deans_sign_letter_condemning_boycott/. Note that the Pentagon was quick to repudiate Stimson's remarks when pressure came to bear. See *id.*; "The Best Defense," Blog Post, Washington Wire Blog, *The Wall Street Journal Online*, January 12, 2007, available at http://blogs.wsj.com/washwire/2007/01/12/the-best-defense/.

[11.] Pauline Jelinek, Associated Press, "Defense Official Resigns Over Remarks," *The Washington Post*, February 2, 2007.

[12.] "No Bill of Attainder or ex post facto Law shall be passed." Article I, Section 9, Clause 3. States are prohibited from enacting such laws by Article I, Section 10, Clause 1.

[13.] *Black's Law Dictionary*, 8th ed. (West Group, 1999), at p. 620.

[14.] *Sorich v. United States*, U.S. Supreme Court Docket No. 08-410 (February 23, 2009).

[15.] 18 U.S.C. § 1346.

[16.] *McNally v. United States*, 483 U.S. 350 (1987).

[17.] *Scheidler v. National Organization for Women, Inc.*, 547 U.S. 9 (2006).

INDEX